More Praise for
INDESTRUCTIBLE

"It's a massive understatement to say that Pappy Gunn was an American original. In this new book, journalist Bruning looks at the improbable life of the one-of-a-kind Arkansas daredevil pilot who took matters into his own hands when his wife and children were captured by the Japanese in the Philippines."

—*Men's Journal*, **Best Books of 2016**

"This is a beautifully told story of a family separated by war, and of an extraordinary father, driven to avenge his family, who by sheer force of character changed the nature of warfare. A superbly told tale of love, honor, courage, and devotion."

—**Alex Kershaw, author of** *Avenue of Spies*

"Bruning's gripping account of 'Pappy' Gunn's mission to save his family might seem to some like over-the-top fiction, but Gunn's rage really did drive changes to tactics and modifications to aircraft that changed the course of the Pacific War.... Every lover of bigger-than-life-but-still-true tales of wartime heroism will want to read this vividly written history."
        —*Booklist* **(starred review)**

"This is a compelling story with strong characters and a wealth of fascinating incidents, set against some of the fiercest action of the war."
        —*Kirkus Reviews*

"From the opening pages, Bruning grabs you by the collar and pulls you into the story, not letting go as he masterfully guides you through a part of World War II that is largely unknown. This is the work of a skilled wordsmith who knows how to tell a story."

—**Gregory A. Freeman, author of** *The Forgotten 500*

"Paul Irvin Gunn's time in World War II is the stuff of legends—and its fast-paced, page-turning telling in Bruning's book does the man's Herculean feats justice.... A heart-wrenching love story [with a] heroic conclusion...*Indestructible* offers a glimpse of the Pacific theater like you've never before seen." —*Men's Journal*

"Set against the sprawling and violent Pacific War, *Indestructible* is the incredible story of one man's courage, tenacity, and dogged fight to rescue his family caught behind enemy lines. The book left me with chills."

—**James M. Scott, author of** *Target Tokyo: Jimmy Doolittle and the Raid that Avenged Pearl Harbor*

"[A] story of honor, faith, endurance, and love. *Indestructible* is a worthwhile read for anyone interested not only in the history of the war in the Pacific but also of determination in the face of daunting odds." —*Yakima Herald*

"Here is a true story with something for everyone. Love, war, treachery, adventure, and above all an intimate portrait of the made-for-Hollywood life of a man who broke all the rules and remade them to his liking. Finally, we have a book that does justice to the legend of Colonel Paul 'Pappy' Gunn, a giant among heroes of World War II. John Bruning shows us a big-hearted man determined to save his family—and a brilliant scientist-pilot who was determined to win the war along the way."

—**Adam Makos, author of** *A Higher Call and* Devotion

"Fast-paced, sweeping, and often haunting." —*The Oregonian*

INDESTRUCTIBLE

One Man's Rescue Mission
That Changed the Course of WWII

JOHN R. BRUNING

hachette
BOOKS

NEW YORK   BOSTON

Hachette Books
Hachette Book Group
1290 Avenue of the Americas, New York, NY 10104
hachettebookgroup.com
twitter.com/hachettebooks

Originally published as a hardcover and ebook from Hachette Books.

First trade paperback edition: May 2017

Hachette Books is a division of Hachette Book Group, Inc. The Hachette
Books name and logo are trademarks of Hachette Book Group, Inc.

The publisher is not responsible for websites (or their content)
that are not owned by the publisher.

The Hachette Speakers Bureau provides a wide range of authors for
speaking events. To find out more, go to www.hachettespeakersbureau.com
or call (866) 376-6591.

Photo insert credits: (page 1) Nat Gunn Collection; Nat Gunn Collection;
Nat Gunn Collection; (page 2) Nat Gunn Collection; Nat Gunn Collection;
MacArthur Memorial, Bartsch Collection; (page 3) Nat Gunn Collection;
John R. Bruning Collection; Nat Gunn Collection; (page 4) National
Archives, RG-80G; National Archives, RG-80G; National Archives,
RG-80G; (page 5) National Archives, RG-342; Nat Gunn collection;
National Archives, RG-342; (page 6) Air Force Historical Research Agency,
George Kenney Collection; National Archives, RG-342; National Archives,
RG-342; (page 7) National Archives, RG-342; National Archives, RG-342;
(page 8) Nat Gunn Collection; Nat Gunn Collection; Nat Gunn Collection.

LCCN: 2016021715
ISBN: 978-0-316-33941-4 (pbk.)

Printed in the United States of America

LSC-C

Printing 6, 2021

This book is dedicated to my daughter, Renee Bruning. Survivor of brain surgery at age fourteen, four-point student and the bravest person I know. For Renee's sixteenth birthday, she asked me to write a book on a subject I always wanted to tackle. Indestructible *became that gift. Thank you, Renee, for giving me the courage and reason to try. You are the match that lit this fire.*

Author's Note

The dialogue in this book is based on interviews, letters, diaries, memoirs, contemporary newspaper articles, magazine features, film footage, and official reports of the people involved. Whenever possible, I used contemporary sources. While reconstructing the exact words used in a particular conversation some seven decades after it took place is nearly impossible, I've worked hard to accurately reflect the nature of the conversation and the words used that the participants themselves recalled or wrote about at the time.

I'll die before I'm sixty with my boots on and the throttle firewalled.
—P.I. "Pappy" Gunn

Contents

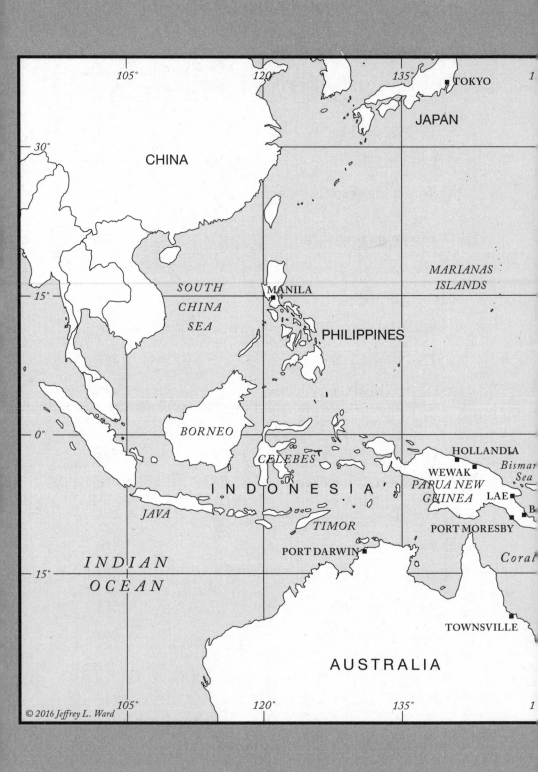

© 2016 Jeffrey L. Ward

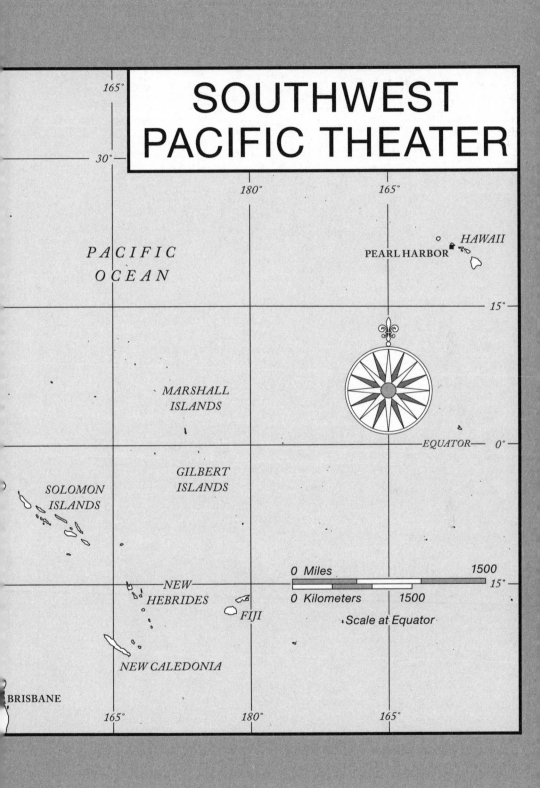

SOUTHWEST PACIFIC THEATER

165°

30°

180°

165°

*PACIFIC
OCEAN*

HAWAII

PEARL HARBOR

15°

*MARSHALL
ISLANDS*

EQUATOR — 0°

*GILBERT
ISLANDS*

*SOLOMON
ISLANDS*

| 0 Miles | | 1500 |
| 0 Kilometers | 1500 | |

15°

NEW
HEBRIDES

FIJI

Scale at Equator

NEW CALEDONIA

BRISBANE

165°

180°

165°

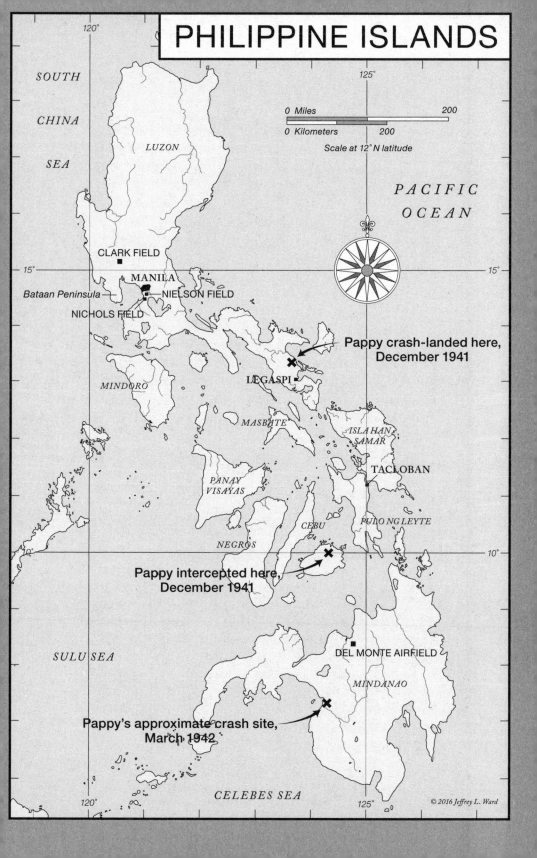

PHILIPPINE ISLANDS

SOUTH

CHINA

SEA

LUZON

PACIFIC

OCEAN

CLARK FIELD ■

MANILA

Bataan Peninsula — NIELSON FIELD

NICHOLS FIELD

**Pappy crash-landed here,
December 1941**

MINDORO

LEGASPI ■

MASBATE

*ISLA HAN
SAMAR*

*PANAY
VISAYAS*

TACLOBAN ■

CEBU

PULO NG LEYTE

NEGROS

**Pappy intercepted here,
December 1941**

DEL MONTE AIRFIELD ■

SULU SEA

MINDANAO

**Pappy's approximate crash site,
March 1942**

CELEBES SEA

0 Miles 200

0 Kilometers 200

Scale at 12° N latitude

© 2016 Jeffrey L. Ward

Preface

March 3, 1943
Thirty miles off the Northern New Guinea Coast

The sharks fed, and men screamed. Those who could fought back, kicking and punching in desperation as the great whites and hammerheads reared up from the depths, their jaws snapping off limbs or tearing men in half. The dead lay floating around the living, blood so thick on the whitecapped swells that those who bore witness to the scene swore the Bismarck Sea turned red that day.

A lucky few found refuge in battered lifeboats, or had scrabbled atop hunks of debris left over from a dozen shipwrecks. Others floated in life belts, treading water among the corpses and wreckage. Thousands had already died. The wounded cried for help they knew would not come.

A sound rose in the distance. At first, it was weak, a mere buzzing barely heard over the chaos on the waves.

The broken men fearfully turned their eyes skyward. The Americans had returned. A few readied waterlogged bolt action rifles or light machine guns they'd carried over the sides of their sinking ships. Such weapons offered a pitiful defense to the juggernaut fast approaching, but they were all they had left. Their air force had been vanquished. Their navy had either been destroyed or driven off. Now, these men bobbed in the Bismarck Sea and knew there would be no miracle to save them.

The sounds of onrushing engines grew deafening, but the straining men could see no aircraft. In the distance, a few appeared thousands of feet above them. Those made no difference to the men in the water, and they were not the ones whose engines filled their ears. The real threat remained unseen.

The water churned around them as if pummeled by rain from a tropical storm. Lifeboats were torn apart, the debris raked by the bullets from scores of heavy machine guns. Their thunderous reports reached the survivors' ears a moment later. Dark, predatory shadows sped over them. The American bombers came in so low and so fast they couldn't be seen until they were practically overhead.

They were new weapons, engineered for a new type of air warfare that had caught the men in the water completely by surprise. There had been no effective defense against them, and their ships were transformed into bullet-riddled conflagrations in mere minutes. In retrospect, the lucky ones had died aboard ship.

The growling engines receded, but only for a moment. They would return for another pass.

Nine thousand feet above the death and misery in the water, the middle-aged pilot, a father of four and a devoted husband who had engineered their fate, watched the scene below through eyes once full of mirth and now devoid of mercy.

All the while, the sharks continued to feed.

INDESTRUCTIBLE

Part One

Philippine Odyssey

1

The Last Normal Day

December 1941
Manila, Philippines

In a handmade four poster bed, beneath a white, homespun quilt, Paul Irvin "P.I." Gunn lay beside his wife of twenty years. Polly's almond-colored hair, always meticulously braided, adorned her pillow. They slept close, paired as lovers whose fire for each other never ebbed. Other couples came and went. These two had thrived despite everything a hard and dangerous life threw at them.

On P.I.'s nightstand rested a standard U.S. Navy BUSHIPS Hamilton wristwatch, a legacy of a career now four years in his rearview mirror, but still worn every day. Slim, solidly built, and scuffed from countless adventures, the timepiece matched P.I.'s own physical traits perfectly. Over the years, both man and watch survived everything from raging ocean storms to plane crashes and combat missions over Nicaragua in underpowered biplanes. The watch had become part of the man long ago. The tiny second hand spun out another minute until the watch showed precisely four thirty.

In the bed, P.I.'s gray-blue eyes shot open. He flung back the quilt and sat up like an uncoiling spring. For him, there was no slow transition between sleep and consciousness. Like the flip of a light switch, he went from dormant to full power every morning at exactly

0430. He never needed an alarm clock; his own internal one was better than anything even the Swiss could produce.

His bare feet found the polished hardwood floor, which the family's servants buffed with coconut husks they strapped to their feet. That weekly process was a source of fascination for P.I. and Polly's two young boys.

"Hit the deck!" P.I. called out, his voice booming through the house. A moment later, he padded into the bathroom to put in his teeth. Long ago, while pioneering the use of float planes on Navy warships, he'd landed his aircraft beside a cruiser and taxied up alongside it. A crane swung out over the side and hooked his aircraft with a cable. As the crew winched the craft aboard, a huge swell slammed broadside into the vessel, which caused it to list sharply, before rolling back on an even keel. The sudden movement flung P.I.'s plane like a pendulum—directly into the cruiser's side. The force of the impact threw P.I. face-first into the instrument panel so hard it permanently damaged his teeth. Later, he had a dentist pull them all and make him a set of dentures.

His morning routine was short and to the point. He turned the shower on, waiting impatiently for the hot water to come. He had stuff to do and patience never suited him. The water warmed and he stepped inside. He showered quickly—no lingering there to enjoy the water on his middle-aged muscles. Showers were functional necessities, not indulgences. He finished and pulled a towel off the nearby rack.

Long ago, back when he wore leather and silk to work every morning, he learned to shave at night. It was an old pilot trick, passed from one generation to the next in the era of the open cockpit biplane. Silk scarves helped protect a pilot's neck from chafing against leather collars, but the wind would whip raw freshly shaved skin. Those who dared the early fabric and wood flying machines were uncomfortable enough in basket seats and freezing environs, so they took to scraping their stubble before bedtime in order to give their flesh time to toughen back up.

Though his open cockpit days were long past, P.I. was nothing if not a creature of habit.

He finished drying off and grabbed his clothes. Despite the tropical heat, P.I. always favored long-sleeved khaki button-down shirts for work. Part of this was a sense of professionalism. Mostly, though, it was a way of hiding an indiscretion from his past life.

He slipped into the shirt, the left sleeve concealing a pair of tattoos. One on his forearm depicted an American eagle clutching the U.S. Navy shield. The Statue of Liberty adorned his left shoulder, an embodiment of P.I.'s youthful sense of American exceptionalism.

He once caught his youngest child, Nathan, staring at his tattoos. P.I. quickly covered them up as he told his boy, "Nath, if I ever spot anything like these on you, I'll whup the hell outta ya."

They were the result of a sailor's shore leave somewhere in the Caribbean during the 1920s, when P.I. had served aboard the light cruiser USS *Omaha*. He was an enlisted man back then, and tattoos were part of the culture.

Now, in this new life, he was upper management. He would never be a stuffy, buttoned-up, chained-to-a-desk office type, but he had gone from earning a few hundred a month as a senior chief petty officer in the Navy to bringing home over a thousand a month in the Philippines. Now, instead of working alongside weathered grease monkeys, his professional circle included some of the wealthiest people in the world. People who looked askance at something as lowbrow as a tattoo.

There was more to Pappy's past that could not be covered up with a shirt. His was a complex and sometimes tortured past. He had once been defined by his family's socioeconomic station in their tiny town back home in Arkansas. In his teens, he recklessly tried to break free of those Southern small-town judgments and create a new life for himself. He was successful—at least until the law intervened.

Since then, he abandoned his birthplace and had seen the world.

Along the way, he invented and reinvented himself many times, layer added atop layer, until he had become a mix of often contradictory elements. No one person ever saw every layer, but Polly came closer than anyone else.

P.I. buttoned his sleeve cuffs and reached for his tie. Solid black, the same one he had worn in the Navy. He finished off with a pair of brown oxfords, another nod to his days at sea. Naval aviators wore brown shoes. Everyone else in the fleet wore black. Through his twenty years, the tension between the black shoes and the brown shoes never abated. If anything, those final years were frequently colored with open hostility between the two factions as the battleship admirals fought to retain their sense of maritime supremacy in the face of air power's revolutionary bombs and torpedoes.

All that rancor between the upstart pilots and the myopic, hidebound fleet types now lay in P.I.'s past. But that pioneering spirit he and his fellow aviators cultivated, that sense of openness to new ideas and innovation, had long since become a defining feature of P.I.'s character. He had no time for those who lacked the vision to see how technology could transform the future.

He bent down and laced up his oxfords while calling out, "Merced! Let's get some coffee going!" Merced was the family's hired cook. Coming to Manila in 1939, P.I. was a little overwhelmed at first by the finishes of polite American society there. Americans were expected to have Filipino servants and butlers and chauffeurs, and they could be hired so cheaply that even enlisted soldiers living off post around Fort McKinley could afford at least one.

His family went from struggling to making it month to month to being waited on hand and foot. Polly, an accomplished and devoted chef in her own right, arrived in the Philippines to find her primary place in the household usurped. When she tried to help prepare the family's meals, the cook pushed back and rebuffed her efforts. So she fired him after checking with P.I. Merced joined the staff a short time later and had no issues with Polly's involvement in the kitchen.

P.I. reached for his watch and strapped it on. The Philippines was the Promised Land for his family. The four children were being educated in first-rate private schools. Polly's load around the household was eased, and now she passed her days with the children or volunteering at the local Red Cross with the wives of other upper middle class families.

Meanwhile, there were layers to P.I.'s new life in the Far East. At first glance, he was a pioneer again in his second career. How many could say that? No wonder he loved the Philippines. Here was opportunity, growth, a wide-open realm full of potential needing only a fulcrum like Paul Gunn to seize the moment and achieve something truly great and lasting. Yet, there was more to his presence in the Philippines than his entrepreneurial spirit. Much more.

He ran a comb through his chestnut hair—a bit thinner than it had been when he had landed a biplane on America's first aircraft carrier, the USS *Langley*—but time had not robbed it of its luster. Hard work and passion kept him young, and P.I. didn't look anywhere close to his forty-one years. He evaded the dreaded midlife paunch, and crow's feet had yet to land on his face.

He turned to regard the bed and its rumpled covers. The quilt they used as a bedspread had been sewn by Polly's mom and her friends back in Florida, spending hours on the back porch of the family's Pensacola house, creating quilts for every member of the family. Polly and P.I. received several, and the four kids each slept under their own Pensacola quilts. When the sewing cabal tired of bed coverings, they crocheted tablecloths and place settings. Polly hoarded the most delicate and precious of those in a cedar chest kept in the dining room, where they were used only for the most formal occasions.

The bed was empty now. Polly was accustomed to this predawn routine. As soon as P.I. hit the shower she'd be up, bundled in a robe, and off to go rouse the children and make sure breakfast reached the table.

There were two constants in P.I.'s life at home. The first would always be Polly and the love they shared. The spark between them first flared two decades before at a church picnic in Pensacola and burned bright through every storm life flung their way.

The second was that four-poster spool bed. Polly's father had lovingly crafted it from maple and gifted it to them on their wedding day. It was a beautiful work of art. He made the spools on each post with a lathe, carefully carving the ornate, threadlike pattern into all four with remarkable precision.

The transient nature of a life in the Navy did not lend itself to such a large, heavy family heirloom, but Polly resolutely ensured that their spool post bed hopscotched across the country with them from base to base as P.I.'s career thrived. From Florida, it had made its way to San Diego, then to Honolulu, finally arriving on a Manila dock two years before with the rest of the family's belongings. Home for P.I. was where Polly was. And where Polly was, their bed would always be.

P.I. swept downstairs and into the kitchen, where Merced was busy carving a grapefruit into decorative pieces. Food was an artistic medium for him, something that P.I. never really understood even after months of eating his intricately sliced carrots and mangos and other treats. Making pretty food seemed a waste of time to him. After all, it was just going to be eaten anyway, right? For Merced, presentation was as important as taste.

He pulled a tin of sardines out of the fridge; a luxury item they had gone years without during his Navy career. Peeling the foil back, he extracted one and walked into the laundry room where Amos, the bright orange tabby cat P.I. had adopted from a departing U.S. Army captain, waited patiently by his dish.

"Honestly, P.I., why do you feed him sardines?" Polly had asked more than once.

The answer was always the same: "That's what the captain fed him. So that's what we'll feed him."

He fussed over Amos, scratched his head and that spot behind his ears the cat loved. A moment later, Dingo, the family's well-traveled Aussie shepherd, climbed out of his laundry room nest to get in on the attention.

Once he greeted Dingo, P.I. stormed into the dining room charged with energy, a contrast to his two sleepy-eyed sons, Paul and Nathan, who sat with Polly at the table. P.I.'s chair was always at the head, and he dropped into it as he wished his boys good morning. Even seated, he looked like a man in motion.

Merced piled the table with pretty food, delicately cut and arranged on white china. Fruit, pancakes, oatmeal, eggs—whatever each member of the family wanted lay within easy reach.

This morning, the table was two members short. Daughters Connie and Julie were up at Baguio, the Philippine summer capital, cheering on their high school's basketball squad. They departed Friday night and would not be back until dinner time Sunday night.

This overnight excursion was a big step for P.I. His teenage daughters took after their mother; they were stunners. Connie in particular had not only inherited her mom's physical beauty, but she radiated the same energetic charm that made Polly so irresistible to men and women alike.

As a father, P.I. had watched with dismay as boys grew enamored with his daughters. Wherever they went, boys were smitten by their charm and looks. When the girls came out to the airfield to see him, the other pilots would virtually mob them, jostling each other as they made offers to take them flying. That was until P.I. laid down the law with his aviator brethren. After that, they were models of politeness. Then he told Connie that there was only one pilot he trusted her with and would allow to take her into the air. Nath and the rest of the family thought that was a remarkably enlightened approach to this, the eternal struggle of fathering pretty daughters. Perhaps not so much enlightened as cunning. P.I. knew the pilot was gay.

He filled his plate, and everyone began to eat. P.I. and Polly made this aspect of the morning ritual an inviolable rule: The family always ate breakfast together before going their separate ways for the day. This meant they got up at 0430 almost every morning, though often the kids would be able to go back to sleep for a little while before heading off to school.

At the table, they would talk through the logistics of getting the kids to school, what work P.I. had to do and where he would be, Polly's plans, or any of the other ordinary daily details that keep a family humming smoothly.

At night, dinner together was the other inviolable family rule. Where the breakfast conversation was all business and logistics, the banter at night ranged from politics to silliness, games and laughter. Special moments were shared, and individual victories celebrated. Back in the '30s, when P.I.'s Navy pay finally broke the two-hundred-dollar-a-month mark, he brought the check home and passed it around at the dinner table. Each child held it and looked at the seemingly astronomical numbers with near reverence until finally it came around to Polly. She grew emotional as she held it, thinking of all the years they had scraped by on enlisted pay and her husband's odd jobs.

"Oh, P.I.," she had said in a soft voice, "I am so proud of you."

Those were the moments remembered always, and the dinner table provided many of those. The breakfast table, not so much.

On this Sunday, P.I. had business to attend. He told the boys and Polly he would be heading over to the airfield but would be home for dinner. Polly planned to take the kids to Mass that morning, a Sunday staple that P.I. avoided. Though they met at a church picnic, P.I. was not a religious man. It was the biggest single difference between husband and wife, one that could have torn other couples apart. Instead, they accommodated each other. P.I. agreed to let Polly raise the children Catholic. Polly agreed to never ask P.I. to convert. Matter settled. It never became an issue between them.

Church and flying. The dual Sunday experience of the Gunn family. P.I. usually worked seven days a week. Always had, and he figured he always would.

In later years, the family would try to recall where P.I. went and what he did that fateful Sunday. Julie thought he'd gone fishing off Alabat Island, a spot about fifty miles east of Manila in Lamon Bay. Polly recalled he had gone with an American businessman to his mining operation on an island off the coast of Luzon. Whatever P.I. said his plans were at the breakfast table has been lost to history. But they most certainly did not involve fishing.

P.I. was usually unfailingly honest with his family—sometimes to a fault. But when it came to the risks of his job, or matters of national security, he put a wall up. That day was a double whammy: He knew he would be facing danger for the sake of national security, so he had crafted a cover story. He didn't like doing that, but in his Navy life he tried to shield Polly from the daily hazards he faced as a pioneering aviator. He made jokes of those dangers and recounted stories of flying mishaps in such a way that he made cocktail crowds howl with laughter. Dig a little deeper, though, and those stories masked a dark reality: Too many of his fellow naval aviators had been killed flying fragile, fabric-covered biplanes.

As a loyal American and veteran, P.I. took both national security and secrecy very seriously. To him, that was the one thing that could trump family, for the safety of his country ensured that his family could thrive. Little did he know that morning that his loyalty to his country and the loyalty to his family would be tested to the breaking point in the weeks ahead, forcing him to make the most difficult decision of his life.

He finished up, tossed his napkin down and swept Polly up in his arms. A lingering kiss, two hugs with the boys, and he was out the door. Today's mission could wait no longer.

2

The Mysterious Traveler

Paul Irvin Gunn slid behind the wheel of the family sedan, a stately four door Buick Roadmaster parked in the driveway. It was verdi green, with a luggage rack bolted on the trunk lid. He'd bought it new in 1939 right off a dealer's lot in Manila, and it had been the family's first factory-fresh ride. It was P.I.'s, too. His very first car had predated World War I, cobbled together from two salvaged wrecks he'd found in his childhood hometown of Quitman, Arkansas. He'd tinkered with it until his jalopy had been the fastest rig in the county, perfect for the moonlit rides he undertook when the Arkansas police were after him and his circle of less-than-respectable associates.

He was seventeen, a criminal of necessity and willing to do anything to keep his mother from bankruptcy. That was a lifetime ago, a layer that he had buried and redeemed with his military service. He even went by a different name back then. The kids in town dubbed him "Bill," because he wore the same long-billed cap for years. It was the only one he'd owned as a child. He became P.I. in the Navy after some enlisted guys tried to call him by his initials— P.I.G. He settled that quickly enough with his fists, and the enlisted bullies never called him Pig again. After that, people just called him P.I.

The 5.2-liter Fireball Straight-8 rumbled to life, sounding smooth and powerful once it warmed up. The engine reflected its owner's care. P.I. maintained it with the sort of joy only a born mechanic could find under the hood.

He threw the Buick in gear as Paul unlatched the front gate. Dingo hovered protectively nearby while Nath waved good-bye. P.I. guided the Roadmaster out onto the street.

The neighborhood still slept, and P.I's car was the only one in sight. For two years, these Sunday morning rides had always been this way, even when the houses around the Gunns' had been filled with the families of officers assigned to nearby Nichols Field and Fort McKinley. This was the tropics; few people went to work on a Sunday, let alone this early.

Now most of the houses stood empty. P.I. passed a long row of them, the Roadmaster still in first gear. Six months before, the military had ordered dependents home as relations between Japan and the United States had deteriorated. Nath and Paul had once never lacked for playmates. Now, they were about the only kids their age left in the neighborhood.

P.I. regarded the passing houses, each one walled off and gated like his, and wished his own family had returned to Pensacola. They would have been safe there until this latest crisis blew over. Polly always refused to go, and the kids unanimously supported her. P.I. kept trying to change their minds, but Polly stood her ground at the many dinner table discussions. Where P.I. was, the family would be, and they would not budge. He gave up after realizing he could not win this battle.

The kids and Polly hadn't gone home, and through the fall the signs of the crisis flared around them. Manila conducted nocturnal blackout drills, testing to make sure the citizens knew how to keep any stray shaft of light from escaping their houses that could help guide Japanese bombers to the capital city.

In church on Sundays, at dinner parties and gatherings, the Americans in Manila fretted over every international development.

Most pinned their faith on Gen. Douglas MacArthur and his army of American and Filipino troops. Still, for some of the six thousand Americans living in the islands in 1941, it felt as if their homes rested at the end of a very long limb. P.I. knew enough about the military in the Philippines to know faith in the local armed forces was probably misplaced. The limb was narrow, and the only hope should the Japanese attack would be a swift response by the U.S. Navy's Pacific fleet.

The Roadmaster reached Highway 54. Across from it stretched Nichols Field, the U.S. Army Air Force's main base for the defense of Manila. Rows of brand new Curtiss P-40 Warhawk fighters—single-engine, sharp-nosed, and spindly-legged—sat parked on the ramp next to the main runway.

He had flown everything from lumbering parasol-winged flying boats to gnat-like biplane fighters during his Navy career, but he'd never been in the cockpit of something as advanced as these P-40s. Back when he earned his wings in 1926 after eight years as an enlisted mechanic, the Navy sent him to one of the first torpedo squadrons in the fleet. There, he helped develop anti-ship-attack tactics in underpowered fabric-covered planes called Martin T3Ms. Those Warhawks on the flight line could reach 350 miles an hour. P.I.'s first combat ride could do 110—without the torpedo. With one of those massive weapons slung under the fuselage, the T3Ms could barely stay above stall speed. It made for hairy takeoffs on the old USS *Langley*, the Navy's first carrier, which had been converted from a collier. With its postage stamp–sized flight deck so narrow the T3M's wingspan nearly matched its width, and its lack of catapults and safety systems, flying from the *Langley* claimed a lot of P.I.'s friends through horrific accidents. Those were the gestational years of carrier operations. Much was learned and refined for the future carriers then on the drawing boards, but those lessons were hard-won with the blood and bones of P.I.'s comrades.

It astonished him how far aviation had come in only a decade and a half. The technology in those P-40s could hardly have been dreamed of in 1930. With retractable landing gear, all-metal construction, an enclosed cockpit, and speeds never seen before in the fleet aircraft he had flown, those Warhawks represented the pinnacle of American aviation development.

From lumbering torpedo bombers, P.I. moved on to float planes, experimental designs, and finally fighters. He joined the legendary *Flying Chiefs*, the Navy's most elite squadron where almost every pilot was an enlisted man. These were the men who started from nothing and had earned their place among the Navy's best through determination, relentless hard work, and skill. The Chiefs made it their personal mission to show the other squadrons—all staffed with officer-pilots—that they were unmatchable in the air. Year after year, they proved they were the best in fleet gunnery and dogfight competitions.

With the Flying Chiefs, he spent several years flying off the USS *Lexington*'s pitching flight deck in countless exercises throughout the Pacific. They had executed simulated sneak attacks on San Francisco and the Panama Canal, and had even covered a mock-amphibious assault on Midway Atoll. In between, several Hollywood blockbusters of the age were filmed aboard the Lady Lex. In 1937, he took part in the search for Amelia Earhart before coming home to Hawaii to finish his Navy career as a patrol bomber pilot.

He was one of the hottest pilots in the Navy's hottest squadron. Given the latest planes and best equipment, the Chiefs were the darlings of interwar naval aviation. Yet, even the most advanced aircraft they had flown in the late 1930s were still fixed-gear biplane fighters that looked like sportier versions of what had gone against the Red Baron and his ilk in 1918.

He studied the P-40s for a moment longer. They were sleek killers in repose, waiting for the moment to unleash their full fury on the enemy. The sight of them made him want to feel a sense of security.

Their arrival that fall signaled that Washington took the defense of Manila seriously, and that meant his family would be better protected. Yet, P.I. knew many of the pilots assigned to those new aircraft. They were raw, barely trained reservists pulled into the Army Air Force after the fall of France in the summer of 1940. Most had never even been in a P-40 before reaching the Philippines.

There had been some flight training in November, but that was curtailed at the beginning of December. The fighter squadrons were on twenty-four-hour alert with the pilots ready to take off within an hour. Earlier in the weekend, that was changed to fifteen minutes' notice. That was well and good should the Japanese launch an attack, but P.I. knew these young, green pilots needed air time in their new planes. Instead, they were cooped up in their ready rooms, dozing or playing cards.

The training situation was so dire that when one squadron was ordered from Nichols Field to a new airstrip farther north, an epic disaster ensued. Given ancient Seversky P-35 fighters built while these pilots were still in junior high school, half the squadron crashed while making the move.

Almost as bad as the lack of training was the colonial culture ingrained in the Americans. For two years, P.I. had been troubled by the party atmosphere pervading all branches of the service. To him, they seemed to be whistling past the graveyard, working minimal hours during the hot tropical days, playing polo and storming the Manila bars in the afternoons and evenings. Meanwhile, Japan was busily taking over China and much of Southeast Asia.

To be sure, P.I. had spent much of his youth pub-crawling through the worst ports of call in the Atlantic Fleet, but these days were different. He kept waiting for the military to get serious. From everything he witnessed, the four-hour workdays and parties had continued for much of the American military, even as MacArthur received more men and planes from the States.

MacArthur knew the importance of the Philippines. The United States had acquired it in the aftermath of the Spanish-American War. The Filipinos revolted against American rule, and from 1899 to 1902 a merciless guerrilla campaign raged throughout the islands. The U.S. Army quelled the uprising through a combination of public works programs and wholesale slaughter of hostile villages. After winning the war, the Philippines became a critical American colonial possession. It served as a springboard for trade into China and other parts of the Far East. It became a hub of economic activity, including mining. The Philippines drew entrepreneurial Americans through the first decades of the twentieth century, and slowly their efforts were transforming the islands into a modern society.

At the same time, when the Philippines fell into America's lap after the war with Spain, the nation struggled to figure out how to defend it. The Spanish had found the archipelago so remote as to be impossible to protect. After the Japanese defeated Russia in a bloody conflict in 1905, the U.S. military faced the same problem. With supply lines stretching seven thousand miles across the Pacific to West Coast ports, there would be little time to reinforce the Philippines should the Japanese decide to attack. Tokyo lay only eighteen hundred miles away from Manila.

Should war with Japan actually happen, the Japanese would hold all the cards in the Western Pacific. At least, at first. Washington belatedly tried to solve this problem by sending more troops, planes, and munitions to the Philippines as tension escalated between the two countries. It felt like too little, too late, though. If war began, at best the forces defending his family were only partially ready to fight.

The sun broke over the eastern mountains, casting long shadows across Nichols Field. The P-40s sat still, silhouetted in the morning light, loaded with fuel and ammunition as their pilots waited nearby for the word to scramble should Japanese planes be detected over Luzon.

Scuttlebutt among the aviators was that the Japanese had begun flying night reconnaissance missions over Luzon from their bases on Formosa Island. The P-40s at Iba Field up the northwest Luzon coast had tried to intercept them, but it had been a fiasco. The air control teams on the ground couldn't even talk to the pilots in the air. They had to have a pilot sit in the cockpit of a stationary P-40 on the airfield, relaying intercept directions from the controllers to the planes in the air. That jury-rigged system quickly broke down, and the Iba-based P-40s had found nothing in the darkness.

P.I. drove north, skirting the edge of Nichols, until he came to Fort McKinley. The influx of reinforcing troops arriving that fall had overwhelmed the Army's ability to house them. The parade ground became a veritable tent city as units fresh off the boat from San Francisco lacked barracks of their own. New construction would address the situation, but it would take months to complete. In the meantime, the men lived in the dirt and mud.

The situation was a total cluster. Too much too late without the infrastructure to support the new troops and gear. Meanwhile, P.I. kept hearing of critical shortages of ammunition, tanks, vehicles, and other supplies. Two weeks before, Connie and Julie had been at Fort McKinley for a charity drive sponsored by a Manila women's group. After the event, both of them had been invited to stay and have lunch with Maj. Gen. Jonathan Wainwright, MacArthur's senior field officer. A hard-drinking former cavalryman and World War I veteran, he didn't mince words at the table that day. He spoke openly of the Army's deficiencies, including the many problems within the Far East Air Force (FEAF). The girls came home that night and repeated everything the general said during the family dinner, confirming most of what P.I. had already picked up around the airport over the past year.

Just to the northeast of Fort McKinley, Nielson Field came into view. Built in 1937, it was one of the only airports in the Philippines to be paved. Nielson's two wide, long concrete runways could handle just about every aircraft type in the Philippines, including the recently arrived Boeing B-17 Flying Fortress four-engine bombers that President Franklin D. Roosevelt believed would act as a deterrent to Japanese aggression.

P.I. turned off the highway and crossed the main runway. At times, when things weren't busy here, he would load up the kids in the Roadmaster and speed down the runway, the Straight-8 thundering. The kids loved those joyrides, the Buick doing the quarter mile as they cheered and laughed.

Those mirthful moments at Nielson gave way to the Army Air Force's arrival at what had once been a civilian-only field. While no combat aircraft were stationed at Nielson yet, a steady stream of military traffic had come and gone each day ever since wooden buildings had been thrown up to house FEAF headquarters and the air intercept center for the northern Philippines. That latter building was full of telephones connected to outlying stations staffed by Filipinos whose job was to report any aircraft overhead. That information was then marked on a huge horizontal relief map of Luzon that dominated the air intercept center's plotting room. It was a primitive system, but it was the only fully functioning way to know if the Japanese were launching an air attack.

P.I. parked beside the Philippine Air Lines hangar. Spacious enough to house four aircraft, maintenance facilities, and desks, the hangar was built late in 1940 just after P.I.'s boss, millionaire Andrés Soriano, incorporated the airline. As he walked inside, the PAL employees there greeted him warmly.

This airline was his project, his pioneering effort out here in the Western Pacific, and he embraced the venture with all of his capacious heart and talent.

P.I. Gunn had arrived in the Philippines in 1939 to work as Andrés Soriano's personal pilot. Soriano owned a host of businesses around Luzon—everything from San Miguel beer to gold mines around Baguio and Paracale. For a year, he flew Soriano all over the islands in a red Beech Staggerwing biplane until P.I. had convinced his boss that serious money lay in the airline business. Only two small airlines had operated in the Philippines through the 1930s, and one had gone under recently. Air travel seemed tailor-made for the area, a way to knit the islands together in a manner never before possible.

Soriano loved the idea of flying between the southernmost island of Mindanao and Manila in just a few short hours, compared with the days it sometimes took by sea. If the right mix of aircraft, investors, and people could be pulled together, a national airline in the Philippines could be a huge success.

Soriano found the right investors, and he found the right man to make it work in Paul Gunn. In quick succession, he made P.I. the company's chief pilot and operations manager. P.I. ran the airline's day-to-day business, flew passengers, scouted new potential routes, and helped establish new airports through the Philippines.

They started small—one run to the summer capital of Baguio in March 1941 became the inaugural flight of Philippine Air Lines. Now, PAL possessed two twin-engine, modern Beech 18 airliners and the older fabric-covered Staggerwing. Things were going so well that he talked Soriano into buying several more planes. Those were somewhere in the Pacific aboard a freighter bound for Manila.

At the operations desk, P.I. checked the day's weather report. It didn't look good. The sky over Manila was supposed to be okay throughout the day, but a near monsoon had engulfed most of southeastern Luzon. Torrential rain had turned the hillsides along the coast down there into rivers of mud, and the dirt airstrip at Paracale, a tiny beachside mining community 120 miles southeast of Manila, was sure to be a bog. This was going to seriously complicate his morning; he was supposed to fly a charter run to Paracale with one passenger. The passenger was an important person in the islands, and he made it clear to P.I. that the flight was of crucial importance to the defense of the Philippines.

He reread the weather report and glanced around the hangar, thinking the situation over. The two Beech 18s sat nearby, wing tips almost touching. Polly's favorite color was a deep, saturated red, and in her honor P.I. had picked it for the fleet's signature paint job. The Beech 18s were redder than the Red Baron's World War I Fokker triplane, jazzed up with white bird stripes running from the nose down either side of the fuselage. The company had painted their civilian registration numbers on their starboard wings in bold white letters.

They were beautiful and capable aircraft, but neither would take to the air on this Sunday morning. Instead, the Staggerwing sat outside, fueled, cleaned, and ready to go.

He knew the passenger well. He wouldn't exaggerate the importance of a Sunday morning flight to a tiny coastal village, but was it wise to take a mid-1930s biplane into the middle of a storm? Granted, the Staggerwing was a rugged plane, capable of landing on the short jungle strips that dotted the islands. It could go where the Beech 18s could not, which made the old bird a valuable asset for Philippine Air Lines.

Originally, it had served as the 1930s art deco version of a Learjet—a luxuriously apportioned executive runabout that was part practical and part status symbol for Soriano and his wealthy business associates. Since becoming part of the Philippine Air Lines fleet, the pilots used it for charter flights to smaller strips around Luzon. Once a week, P.I. flew it to Paracale to pick up a load of gold extracted from the mines there. The Staggerwing could carry a lockbox with 125 pounds of gold per flight, making it the richest thing in the air.

If the weather report was accurate, taking the Staggerwing into a tropical storm would be pushing the envelope, even for P.I., who usually flew in weather nobody else would dare to risk. He was comfortable in the air even in zero visibility. With seventeen thousand flying hours under his belt, he had experienced everything from Atlantic thunderheads to Caribbean hurricanes, giving him the skill and confidence to fly in almost anything. He never held the other Philippine Air Lines pilots to his standards, though. Instead, he let each man decide his limits, and when the weather looked dicey, he let them choose to fly or cancel the flight. He would take to the air if his passenger wanted to risk it. He would soon find out just how important the flight really was, or how gutsy his passenger felt.

Since its inception, the airline had been less a business and more like a family. The first flight attendant married one of the first pilots, and the mechanics and ticket agents routinely met after work at the Gunn house for drinks or dinner. P.I. earned their loyalty by being paternal and protective. Several times, he had walked into the terminal to find a passenger yelling at or mistreating his ticket agent. That always set P.I. off—nobody disrespected his employees. P.I. would storm over to the unruly passenger and grab him under the arm and squeeze. He called this the "horse bite."

With a Cheshire cat grin on his face, P.I. would say to the shocked passenger, "Listen, we do not tolerate knuckleheads around here." The paradoxical combination of the physical pain and P.I.'s demeanor would intimidate the passenger, who intuited that P.I.'s voice may have been calm, but underneath the tranquil façade lay a man who had no issues with violence if pushed to it.

There would be no such problems with today's passenger. The man, slender, impeccably dressed and groomed, was chatting amicably with the ticket agent. He turned and welcomed P.I. like the friend he was.

At fifty-three, Joseph Stevenot was a legend in the Philippines. During the Great War, he served in the islands as one of the first

American aviators. In 1919, he flew the first plane into Cebu Island. He established the first flight school in the Philippines and helped train the first class of Filipino pilots while part of the National Guard. Later, he worked as the Curtiss Aeroplane Company's technology representative in the Philippines, setting up a civilian flight school under the firm's direction.

That was only half his day. Originally, he came to the islands as an electrical expert, working on various power projects as a civilian. Later, he ventured into communications and became an expert on telephone, telegraph, and radio-telephone technology. In the late 1920s, he helped consolidate the numerous phone companies in the Philippines under one corporate entity, Philippine Long Distance Telephone and Telegraph. As its vice president for operations, he set up the first transpacific cable line to the United States. He built phone lines all over the islands even as he branched out into other enterprises, including a mine operation company. He had even been one of the principal partners that established the Philippine Air Taxi Company (PATCO) in the early 1930s.

Stevenot was a gregarious bon vivant with a passion for fishing and excellent booze. He was a philanthropist and a community organizer who played the key role in establishing the Boy Scouts of the Philippines. He made friends easily and had connections all over the world.

He was also a man with pull. Lots of pull. Earlier in the year, he traveled to Washington D.C., where he urged Secretary of War Henry L. Stimson to devote more resources to the defense of the Philippines and to unify the command structure in the islands. That was the second time in two years he lobbied on behalf of his adopted home with members of the D.C. power elite.

Stevenot wore many hats in public, but there was one side of him that few knew about that fall. After he visited Stimson, the War Department put Gen. Douglas MacArthur in overall command of the Filamerican army. MacArthur, in turn, brought Stevenot back to active duty as a major. His exact role at MacArthur's headquarters remains a mystery, but that fall he was overseeing a variety of special communication projects, including at least one considered top secret.

P.I. had told Polly that he was taking Joseph Stevenot to his mining operation on Lahuy Island off the coast of southeast Luzon. His daughter Julie later wrote that he had taken Stevenot fishing at Alabat Island in Lamon Bay. Years later, when asked by reporters, P.I. told them he had been in Surabaya, Java, scouting new routes for Philippine Air Lines. He took national security and its secrets so seriously that he never revealed the true nature of his activities on December 7.

Of course P.I. was nowhere near the Dutch East Indies that Sunday morning, and nobody was going fishing in the weather pounding southern Luzon. There was also no pressing business reason to fly through a monsoon to visit Stevenot's gold mine on a Sunday when nobody would be at work.

A brand-new technology had just reached the Philippines, one that could mean the difference between defeat or victory for MacArthur's air force. Stevenot was racing the clock to help make it operational even as more Japanese reconnaissance aircraft violated Filipino air space. That was the real reason P.I. traveled to Nielson Field that Sunday.

P.I. and Joseph Stevenot shook hands and talked over the weather. Both sensed time was running out for the Philippines. It was not a moment to play it safe when war could break out at any moment.

They would fly.

Together, they walked out to the tarmac where the company's Beech Staggerwing waited, its red paint gleaming in the morning sun.

3

Into the Storm

P.I. climbed through the Staggerwing's fuselage door and settled into the pilot's seat. The interior, while cramped, exuded sumptuous comfort. Beech Aircraft designed it with the discerning executive in mind. A ribbed, three-person bench seat that looked like a miniature overstuffed leather sofa occupied the back of the cabin. The pilot's bucket seat was on the left, with a second seat on sliding rails beside and a bit offset behind it. The cream-colored upholstery complemented the honey-brown armrests. The padded side panels resembled a typical luxury sedan's, complete with hand cranks for the windows.

The Staggerwing did not have a true dual control system, but it could be flown from Stevenot's passenger seat if necessary. The control wheel was affixed at an angle to a metal arm that could be swiveled in a 100-degree arc from one side of the cabin to the other, depending on who wanted to do the flying. Tucked under the wooden instrument panel was a second set of rudder pedals as well.

P.I. went through the Staggerwing's preflight checklist, flipping switches and setting the throttle for start-up. He worked quietly with meticulous concentration. Twenty years of flying during the Golden Age of Flight had taught him to be thorough. The saying went, *There are no old, bold pilots.* In his youthful days as a naval aviator, he had done plenty of bold things. He once helped his squadron earn the prestigious fleet aerial gunnery competition, only to get grounded for a month after celebrating the win by taking a plane on an "unauthorized flight over a foreign nation," which was noted in his official Navy file. He flew relief operations in the Caribbean and bombing missions over Nicaragua. He tested new designs and flew aircraft so dangerous others were not allowed behind their controls.

On one memorable mission, he landed his seaplane in the South Atlantic after running low on fuel—and taxied onto a whale's back. That episode became the stuff of legends throughout the small and tight-knit community of pre-WWII naval aviators.

The men who flew those wooden planes did so by the seats of their pants. They explored, they pushed boundaries, they improvised when what they had on hand did not work. Shortly after P.I. had learned to fly, a Navy crew attempted to fly from San Francisco to Hawaii in a biplane flying boat. They suffered mechanical failure along the way, which forced them down at sea. Given up for lost, the crew miraculously reached the islands almost two weeks later. Without a functioning radio or engines, the crew rigged makeshift sails and let the wind carry them the final 450 miles to their destination.

Such men shaped naval aviation, creating a maritime force that would someday dominate its adversaries. Those early days, though, were a constant balancing act between the peril of pushing the envelope and finding a way back safely to the ground. P.I. sometimes took risks that would have killed lesser pilots, but he had never pushed beyond the edge of his own abilities. That was what had kept him alive when so many of his brother naval airmen had died in crashes.

The starter motor whined, and the Wright R-975 Whirlwind engine sputtered to life. When Soriano ordered this Beech, he wanted power. Beech offered several different options, and Soriano picked the R-975, since it delivered 450 horsepower. That provided enough muscle to get the rakish biplane over two hundred miles an hour in level flight.

P.I. listened to the engine like a conductor listening to his orchestra. His ear was so tuned to the Wright's sounds that he could pick out every individual piston firing, every subtle clack of the push rods and lifters. It was his symphony, though to anyone else the Whirlwind sounded rough and uneven, blatting along at idle as if on the verge of quitting. A bit of throttle smoothed out the engine.

P.I. smiled at that; his mechanics always did an exemplary job of prepping PAL's aircraft for flight. He trained his other pilots to always communicate with their ground crew after every flight to talk through any quirks or issues. In the Navy, he had seen pilots who never did that; they simply climbed out of the cockpit and left, ignoring the ground crew completely. He was on the receiving end of that in his early years as an aviation mechanic, and he was resentful of such treatment. Besides, without talking through the plane's performance, there was no way to know if anything needed to be fixed. The Navy had the pilots fill out forms that were supposed to detail such things, but the aviators hated paperwork as much as anyone else, and stuff always seemed to fall between the cracks. That disconnect led to needless mishaps in the air.

At Philippine Air Lines, P.I. insisted that the air and ground crews function as an integrated team. Not only did that ensure the birds were in top condition, but it kept morale high among the mechanics, since the pilots treated them with respect.

The system worked. PAL had not suffered any significant in-flight mechanical issues despite the beatings the aircraft took on the half-finished jungle airstrips.

The Whirlwind warmed up quickly, and its reassuring purr filled the cabin. That sound always gave him a thrill. Even after all his flying years, he still loved this moment, poised on the threshold of breaking earth's bonds to find freedom in the air again.

He taxied the Staggerwing to the runway and lined up. The throttle jutted out of the instrument panel topped with a wooden knob. P.I. actuated the brakes and pulled the throttle toward him. The engine went from a purr to a growl and then to a roar as he opened the throttle all the way. He twisted a switch on the panel to check the magneto and the distributor. They were functioning fine. The run-up was the last preflight check. No sense in tearing down the runway, only to discover too late that some malfunction inhibited full power. Men died that way.

Satisfied, P.I. eased off the throttle and prepared for takeoff. He checked the runway for other aircraft even though he knew few if any would be flying today. Better to follow routine and be safe than make a careless mistake. All clear; he released the brakes. The Staggerwing lurched forward, gaining speed easily. Light and quick, it skated along the concrete until the tail lifted. P.I. gave it a little right rudder to compensate for the propeller's torque and eased back on the wheel. The Beech's stubby nose rose and the wheels broke free of the runway.

They climbed out over Manila and leveled off at three thousand feet. Unless flying over mountainous terrain, P.I. preferred to fly low. When asked by his student pilots why he did that, he told them to imagine a clear coffeepot boiling on a burner. "When you look at it, you see how the coffee boils at the top but the bottom is calm? That's the way the sky is. Stay low and the air is smoother."

The six-year-old Staggerwing was a tough bird, but it was still only a steel tube and wood frame covered with doped fabric. It wouldn't hold up in the violent air inside a storm front. With heavy rain and stout winds reported at Paracale, he would stay under the weather front while keeping a close eye on the ridges and peaks around the town.

P.I. pointed the nose southeast, setting the throttle to cruising speed. Instinctively, he eased it onto the "step." Nose slightly down, tail slightly high, he felt through the control wheel the negative pressure pushing down on the top wing in this angle of attack. A slight

adjustment, and the Staggerwing accelerated, as if some extra invisible force was pulling it along. A careful observer would have noted a
subtle change in the sound of the slipstream rushing by the cabin—
but only a careful one.

Depending on the pilot, the step was either something natural-
born aviators could find or an aerial version of an old wives' tale.
The debate has raged for as long as humans have taken to the sky.
To those who swore by it, "getting on the step" meant finding the
aircraft's sweet spot—the best power setting and angle in the air to
maximize speed and fuel efficiency. If done right, a pilot could feel
the aircraft catching the slipstream, like a surfer catching a wave just
right. There'd be a rush and the plane would speed up, as if shooting
the curl of an air current.

To get on the step took equal parts intuition, feel, and a technical understanding of the plane's performance. Everything affected
where the step could be found and maintained, from number of passengers to cargo weight and the fuel being burned to, some thought,
the amount of paint and wax on the wings. The step was a moving
target through the course of any flight, and a pilot had to adjust constantly to stay on it. In 1941, there was no autopilot that could do
it for them. It was an arcane skill, one that required artistry at the
controls.

Later generations of pilots, used to hydraulic or electronic controls, modern autopilots, and the computerization of flight derided
the step as a myth. For some, their remoteness from that physical
connection between pilot, aircraft, and sky had been broken by all
the new technologies that made flying less an art and more a technical expertise.

Those who flew with P.I. Gunn swore he could get on the step
and stay there almost as soon as his wheels left the ground. He flew
faster and burned less fuel than any other pilot in the Philippines.
Others who flew with him would find out how many gallons of gas

he had left in his tanks after landing, and they would marvel over the fact while their tanks were all but bone-dry. After two decades of flying, P.I. did it so intuitively that he sometimes didn't understand how pilots of lesser experience or ability had so much trouble finding that elusive aerial groove. It was a difficult thing to teach, and a pilot had to have an elevated natural skill set and awareness to pull it off effectively.

For the Staggerwing, the step meant an extra five miles an hour and a few gallons saved on the run to Paracale. Not much, but it added up, and PAL was still a start-up company searching for any way to trim costs.

They flew on to the southeast, passing over a quilt of rice fields and straw hut villages interspersed with dense swaths of jungle. Ahead, the sky's palette changed from blue to gray to black, as towering charcoal-colored clouds appeared on the horizon to stretch thousands of feet above the tiny Staggerwing.

P.I. held a steady course, and soon the Staggerwing slid under the storm front. Rain and wind lashed its fabric-covered wings. The biplane had no windshield wipers, and the downpour kept obscuring their forward view. Unfazed, P.I. kept careful watch over his instruments to maintain the aircraft's level and hold the course. As they flew deeper into the storm, the air became rougher, and staying on the step became impossible as sudden downdrafts and turbulence tossed the Staggerwing around.

Normally, he was all business in the cockpit. The jovial, outgoing man known on the ground by friends and colleagues alike would turn into the consummate professional in the air. He brooked no horseplay, and more than once disciplined his sons for goofing off in the air when the family went with him on a flight. In weather like this he went further, drawing heavily on an unusual ability to both intensely focus and multitask at the same time. It was a paradoxical skill that the best pilots possess.

P.I. could process every instrument's display with just a scan across the cluster of dials and gauges. He knew exactly what each reading meant in relation to the other, instinctively reacting to their information with whatever control or power inputs they required. He did this all while maintaining an uncanny awareness of everything outside and around the aircraft.

He observed pilots who fixated on one thing—say an instrument cluster—to the detriment of other aspects of their awareness. Pilots who did that flew into mountains or made other crucial mistakes. Some who overfocused on the outside environment could find their senses tricked while flying through fog or a cloud bank. Forgetting to check their instruments, they sometimes ended up inverted, or in a dive, and did not even realize it until seconds before hitting the ground.

P.I. scanned the instrument panel, a rolling process adhered to with a meticulous rhythm—airspeed, altimeter, vertical speed indicator, turn and bank indicator, fuel gauge—then raised his head and scanned the sky. Head down, his eyes checked the panel, making sure everything was in the green. A tweak on the trim settings, a slight adjustment to the throttle or the prop's pitch to keep the plane on the step, and the rhythm started anew.

Young pilots quickly got overwhelmed by the sheer volume of input and the processing required. They called it an overflowing bucket. Once that happened, they got behind the aircraft and the situation, and things rarely went well after that. The masters like P.I. not only had larger buckets, they thought ahead of the aircraft like a race car driver stays a split second ahead of his ride. For P.I., the concentration required to do this, especially in bad flying conditions, was total. No chatter. No fidgeting, no distractions in the cabin. The maestro conducting his symphony.

Through the rain-streaked windscreen, P.I. and Stevenot made out the mountain range that formed Luzon's north-south spine. The jungle-covered peaks and valleys dense with vegetation passed below them in the storm's twilight-like darkness.

They reached Paracale Bay about an hour later. The town was little more than a ramshackle collection of tin-roofed huts clustered along the beach beside the mouth of a nearby river. A few bancas—outrigger canoes—and fishing boats were tied up to the stilts that elevated the huts above the water level. The Staggerwing buzzed low over the village, and P.I. checked the palm trees to get a sense of the wind's speed and direction. This was another old pilot trick that helped confirm what they felt from within the plane. Such sensations could be deceptive, and visual cues from the ground were far more accurate. P.I. could see sharp gusts flaying the palm fronds to and fro, their trunks rocking from the force. This would not be an easy landing.

Across the river, the town thinned out. A few huts and shacks dotted the edge of the beach, and a few more were nestled in the jungle. Beyond them, the ground opened up to reveal heavy equipment, along with larger buildings, cranes, and vehicles. That was one of the gold mines, built where the terrain curved northward into a peninsula that formed the dividing line between Paracale and Malaguit Bays. The airfield had been hacked out of the jungle on the peninsula's northern tip. Unpaved, it was short and rugged, stretching east to west along a few hundred meters of the beach. No drainage, no secondary runways, no ramps, just a stripe of somewhat level dirt and grass bulldozed between beach and jungle. He had made this trip hundreds of times; he knew the runway and the best way to get on it. He couldn't control the elements, though, and a sudden gust at the wrong time could pitch him right into the trees or drive him into the sand.

P.I. flew out over Paracale Bay, the surf white with foam as the storm waves pounded the beach. He dropped the landing gear and turned onto the final approach. The wind was blowing crossways to the narrow strip, and P.I. fought it all the way to the ground with liberal use of his rudder until the Beech seemed almost to be crab-scuttling sideways and down onto the runway.

Exactly what happened next is unclear. The runway was in poor shape due to the storm, and the Staggerwing's landing gear was either damaged on touchdown or one of its tires blew while P.I. was taxiing. Whatever the case, the aircraft could not be flown until the undercarriage could be fixed.

P.I. did not want to be marooned at the hardscrabble mining town for the rest of that Sunday, December 7, 1941. He planned to be back in time to greet his daughters after their school trip to Baguio. Now he worried that their reunion would have to wait until the Staggerwing could be repaired. In the meantime, Stevenot, storm or not, had work to do. He bid P.I. farewell and headed off to begin his mission.

Stevenot's telephone company had constructed the phone lines to the air observer stations on Luzon. Those lines ran to the plotting center at Nielson Field, where Signal Corps and Army Air Force personnel stood by to answer them, then pass the information on to be plotted on the giant relief map of Luzon that dominated the center's main room. Those observer stations represented the only comprehensive air-warning system in the Philippines, and it was a poor one at best. Half-trained Filipinos with binoculars were not going to be able to accurately describe incoming flights of Japanese aircraft—few even knew what Japanese aircraft looked like. The Army Air Force's latest intelligence reports suggested the Japanese flew a mishmash assortment of old German and Italian biplanes and first-generation monoplane bombers that were built under license. The Americans in the Philippines had no clue the Japanese possessed first-rate, modern aircraft that were far more capable than most of the American ones that had reached Manila that fall.

Even if the observers knew what the Japanese were flying, there was almost no effective way to judge their altitude and speed, so what warnings they could give would never provide the information needed to carry out a successful interception.

Only radar, a top secret and revolutionary technology in 1941, could do that. For those associated with it, radar's invisible sweeping eye seemed like something straight out of a Buck Rogers movie.

The British had used radar the year before during the air battles over their home isles. It had given the Royal Air Force's Fighter Command a decisive advantage over the German Luftwaffe. Britain's radar electronically tracked incoming German raids, and the information their systems provided allowed ground controllers to select which available fighter squadrons would go after them. Then the fighters were scrambled to altitudes and bearings that allowed them the highest chance of a successful interception.

A radar network in the Philippines could make all the difference between destroying incoming Japanese raiders or getting hammered by an aerial surprise attack. Washington knew that, but the Army's Signal Corps possessed only a few radar sets and even fewer trained operators. Electronic warfare struggled in its infancy in the United States that fall, but what sets the Army had were being sent to the Pacific as fast as possible. By October, about a dozen of them had trickled into Manila.

They came in two main flavors: the SCR-270 mobile radar system and the SCR-271, which was designed to be placed in a fixed, permanent facility like the ones the British had defending their homeland.

In November, a small advanced party from one of the Army Signal Corps' freshly arrived radar control units—called an air warning company—reached Paracale to scout a location for a new radar site. It would cover Manila's southeast and eastern flank in case the Japanese attacked from aircraft carriers in the Philippine Sea. Since the Japanese had naval bases to the east and northeast, the chances of them launching attacks from their flattops from this direction seemed to the Americans a significant threat to the islands.

On November 29, a few officers and a handful of enlisted men loaded an SCR-270 and an SCR-271 aboard a freighter in Manila Bay that set sail on December 1. Running south down Luzon's western coast with most of the men sleeping out on the deck, the voyage went fine until the freighter steamed right into a monsoon. Waves crashed over, knocking the Signal Corps troops off their feet and sending them skidding across the deck. One of their sergeants, Everett Rosen, was forced to tie his men to parts of the ship, lest they wash overboard.

The swells grew deeper as the storm raged around them, and several times vehicles lashed on deck nearly broke loose. The Filipino crew worked feverishly alongside the Americans to keep them in place.

Four days later, on Friday, December 5, the ship reached Paracale Bay. There were no docks there, nor shoreside cranes to assist with offloading the gear, so all the vehicles and cargo had to be lowered onto barges that were then towed by small boats to the beach at the edge of town. This included tractors, a fifty-foot-long trailer, twenty-ton trucks, and jeeps, as well as the massive crates housing the precious radar gear.

The permanent set was taken to a mining company's warehouse and stored for future use. It would take months to build the fixed radar site; for now the men had orders to get the mobile one up and running immediately.

The advanced party had picked out a mountaintop south of town, accessed by a narrow dirt road built by a mining company. The storms had turned the road into a river of mud, and the incline proved so steep that even the four-wheel-drive jeeps could barely negotiate it. Working day and night that Saturday, they dragged the mobile set, its massive trailer, and the companion trucks up to the top of the mountain. Despite the wind, rain, and muck, they assembled the sixty-foot-tall antennae system and wired it into the command trailer. They soon discovered that part of the antennae array had been damaged in transit. In the dead of night that weekend, as the storm continued to blast Paracale, Sergeant Rosen strapped a gas tank on his back and climbed the array as it swayed in gale-force winds to solder the damaged parts.

The set was functional, but it had to be fully operational so the radar team would be able to report back to Nielson Field. That was where Stevenot came in. He had to find a way to tie the radar into the secure phone lines running to Nielson. While there was a phone line that ran to the town of Paracale, there was nothing to the south, so the handful of Americans laboring on the mountaintop could communicate with the plotting center only via radio. With the mountainous terrain between Nielson and the coast, radio contact was touch and go. They needed better coms.

The situation at Paracale was not unusual that December 7. Of all the radar sets in the Philippines that weekend, only Iba Field's was working properly. It had been the one tracking the Japanese reconnaissance flights over Philippine territory earlier that week. Another had been emplaced on a ridge north of Clark Field, but it was malfunctioning.

The electronic eyes the Americans so desperately needed had yet to gain their sight.

After leaving Stevenot, P.I. caught a ride into town, then called the PAL office in Manila and explained the situation. They had no other aircraft that could get into Paracale, which meant the Staggerwing's replacement parts would have to come overland. At first glance, that didn't seem troubling, but the road from Paracale westward was half finished and washed out in places. Even in better conditions, the road was primitive at best, with patches of quicksand that trapped unsuspecting travelers. It would likely take a few days to get the parts out to the plane, P.I. learned.

One of the mining companies had built a small club for its employees. The commander of the radar men, Lt. Jack Rogers, had bunked down there when he arrived earlier that weekend, while the rest of his men were billeted in a dirt-floor warehouse. In all likelihood, a frustrated P.I. settled in at the club for the night, hoping the parts would be delivered more quickly than estimated.

Before heading over to the club, P.I. ensured the Staggerwing was tied down and taken care of. It rode out the storm at the edge of the little strip. Planes were just tools to P.I., so he never became too attached to anything mechanical. Where some pilots tended to feminize their planes, P.I. Gunn never did. Still, there were memories aboard that Beech—his first flights with Andrés Soriano when he arrived in the Philippines were in this beautiful burgundy aircraft. He flew his family to Cebu and Baguio in it, the kids scrunched together in the backseat, a single lap belt stretched across their slender figures, while Polly rode beside him in the other bucket seat. At times, Paul or Nath would come along and peer over their dad's shoulder to see what he was doing. They had learned never to bother P.I. when he sat at the controls. Several times, they observed passengers attempt to move up to the cockpit in one of the Beech 18s and talk to their dad. That invariably angered him, and he would order the passenger to sit back down. So Paul and Nath would stand behind P.I., watching silently as he flew the airplane. Sometimes, if the flight was an easy one, P.I. would look over his shoulder and explain to the boys what he was doing. He always initiated, though, so the boys never interrupted P.I.'s rhythm at the controls.

Flying was his life, and he embraced it with a calm seriousness that he wanted his boys to learn. He expected both to become pilots, and he gave the boys stick time in other aircraft. Thanks to P.I., both had flown planes long before they ever slid behind the wheel of the family sedan.

He loved to teach his art to others. He was released early from the

Navy in 1937 to teach at K-T Flying Service in Honolulu. There is some speculation that this was done to help foster aviation in America's Pacific territories, ensuring an unofficial Navy presence in the region.

Since coming to the Philippines, he found ways to keep instructing others. For the past two years, he trained most of the Filipino pilots now working for PAL, not to mention the mechanics as well.

He also secretly worked with the nascent Philippine Army Air Corps, teaching its young crop of fighter pilots how to fly the ancient hand-me-down aircraft given to them by the United States. He knew almost all the Filipino aviators in uniform, and at least one would later remember P.I. Gunn held a commission in the PAAC as a lieutenant colonel. He was not only the father of Philippine Air Lines; he also helped create the Philippine Air Force. Few men in 1941 had as much influence as P.I. did on the development of aviation in the islands.

As rewarding as teaching Filipinos was for him, nothing would trump the joy of seeing his boys solo for the first time and ride the clouds like their old man. Flying would be the Gunn family business, and he relished the thought of mentoring his boys along until they could become a part of it. Perhaps in a few years, his boys would even fly the Staggerwing, too.

A new storm blowing in from the north ensured that dream would never happen.

4

The Voice of Manila

The next morning, the world changed forever.

P.I. Gunn awoke early in Paracale hoping that the Staggerwing's parts would arrive later that day. As he waited at the club, somebody turned on the radio for the NBC network's early-morning news report. With Manila eighteen hours ahead of Hawaii, and twenty hours ahead of San Francisco, it was still Sunday morning, December 7, 1941, in the United States.

Don Bell, known for years as the Voice of Manila, usually announced the 0600 news brief, the first of many he did throughout a typical weekday. He was an American, a veteran Marine of the China station who did not like the Japanese. As a broadcaster based in Shanghai, he reported scathingly on the Imperial Japanese Army's depredations in China after their 1937 invasion. The war there forced him to flee to Manila, where NBC's flagship station in the Far East, KZRH, hired him as a newscaster. He quickly became the most respected reporter in the islands, a man whose understated and calm demeanor brought world events to hundreds of thousands every day.

At 0600 on Monday, December 8, Don Bell came over the airwaves, his normally unflappable voice filled with alarm. "Early this morning a large number of strange planes attacked Pearl Harbor. We haven't heard yet as to where they came from, but reliable sources think they came from Japan. Just how much damage they did at Pearl Harbor we don't know. All reports are very vague..."

Word spread fast through the islands, and while the people of the Philippines had lived under the threat of war for months, its actual arrival left most in a state of shock.

The news realized P.I.'s worst nightmares. It meant the Japanese had gone after the Pacific fleet, just as the Lexington's air group had in the many war games P.I. had taken part in during the 1930s. He knew there was only one reason to go bomb the American warships at anchor there. With the fleet out of the way, the Imperial Japanese Navy could launch offensives and amphibious invasions anywhere they wanted in Southeast Asia.

The Philippines would be next. P.I. had no doubt of that. The family's house on Villamor Court was less than a mile from Nichols Field. If the Japanese planned to invade, Nichols would be one of their primary targets.

How many times had P.I. flown over his neighborhood? Hundreds at least since arriving in '39. Looking down at Villamor Court, he always noted that the neighborhood looked like a series of military buildings and barracks from the air. Unless the Japanese had conducted some sort of ground reconnaissance and knew the true nature of the neighborhood, P.I. was certain they'd consider Villamor Court part of the Nichols Field base complex.

That meant Polly and the kids were about to find themselves in the middle of the shooting and bombing. Stuck at Paracale, 120 miles away, there was nothing he could do for them. Stateside, those miles would have meant a two-, maybe three-hour car ride. Here, without the Staggerwing, the distance seemed almost insurmountable. Yet, he couldn't sit on his hands and wait for the parts to show up with his family in harm's way. Besides, if the Japanese attacked Nielson Field, the parts might not even be left to send to Paracale.

In his mind's eye, he saw how it could go down. Incoming waves of bombers would strike at Nichols, releasing their ordnance on the runways while fighters wheeled and strafed. He saw them growling overhead, machine-gunning Villamor Court. Gone would be the days of weekend getaway flights, of Mass in the beautiful Manila churches and company gatherings at their house. Servants and drivers and cooks, the trappings of colonial living, would be a thing of the past. All they knew and loved about their adopted home would be uprooted, living on only in their memories.

How could his family be protected from that? The house would not stop bullets or bomb splinters. If the family tried to take refuge in it during an air raid, it could become their tomb. He needed to get home and find a way to keep them safe.

Other, more dreadful thoughts followed those images. P.I. frequently took his family to the movies. The newsreels shown before the features were often filled with scenes of Japan's war against China. He'd seen the air attacks on the USS *Panay* captured on film by reporters fleeing Nanking as the Japanese reached the Nationalist capital in late 1937. He also watched Japanese bombers carry out bombing raids against Chinese cities. The American newsreels cut aerial footage shot by the Japanese together with film shot by Western reporters on the ground.

To the untrained eye, all looked like chaos. Bombers releasing their deadly payloads over a checkerboard landscape, followed by scenes of Chinese civilians running pell-mell for bomb shelters. Some carried suitcases, some fled with babies in their arms. The footage had no ambient sound, but it didn't take much imagination to hear the terrified cries of those Chinese.

P.I.'s professional judgment and experience let him see more into those images than the average American. He wasn't blinded by the prevailing racism that dismissed the Japanese as a half-baked military power with obsolete aircraft bought or copied from foreign manufacturers. When he saw those newsreels, P.I. realized the

Japanese possessed a first-rate air force with deadly capabilities. The aerial shots depicted tight formations of modern bombers accurately hitting their targets from thousands of feet in the air. That showed the Japanese possessed the technology to produce decent bombsights—no small achievement, as the United States struggled for years to develop one. Those scenes also showcased the pilots and their considerable skills. Those tight formations were not easy to maintain, especially in combat with antiaircraft fire peppering the sky.

Worst of all, those scenes also showed the Japanese had no moral issues with carpet-bombing innocent civilians.

At 0800 Don Bell's voice returned to the airwaves and reported Japanese planes had bombed Camp John Hay, just outside of Baguio, in the mountains of northern Luzon 130 miles from Manila. The war, only a few hours old, had already reached the Philippines—in the exact spot his girls had spent their first weekend away from home.

If he wasn't frantic to get home before, this made him so now. The long-distance phone lines were overwhelmed by the traffic the war's outbreak had caused. P.I. couldn't get through to Polly. He had no idea if his girls were safe. For that matter, he had no idea if the rest of the family was safe.

In the mid-1930s, the Navy sent P.I. to Coronado, California, and the family lived for several years in San Diego. One day he and Polly took the kids into town for the day where P.I. needed to run an errand on the fourth floor of the Spreckels Building. He parked on the curb next to the stately edifice and left the family in the car with the engine running. He would be in and out, he assured them.

He never made it to the fourth floor. While he was in the elevator, an earthquake struck the city. In the car, Polly and the kids watched in terror as streetlights swayed around them and people poured out of the nearby buildings.

The elevator jammed between floors, trapping P.I. at the moment he knew his family needed his calm and comforting presence. With the building evacuated, he was left inside for over an hour and a half. Outside, his family grew almost frantic with worry. Everyone but P.I. had come out of the place. How could they not fear the worst? When he finally extricated himself and returned to the car, he found his loved ones deeply shaken.

It was the one time he wasn't there when they needed him most. He didn't want to ever experience those feelings again.

Now, the situation was far more serious than a mere California temblor. The Japanese Army could be coming ashore somewhere on Luzon that very minute. It was the same army that had raped tens of thousands of women in Nanking in December 1937, whose soldiers played death games with crying civilians as they pleaded for their lives. Stories of babies bayonetted, fathers forced to watch as their daughters, wives, and mothers were gang-raped then murdered by the Japanese, flowed out of China with the thousands of expats fleeing from the debauchery. Many—including Don Bell—tried to rebuild their lives in Manila after their escape. P.I. and Polly had met some of those refugees—they were a mix of Russians, Spaniards, Americans, British, Italians, Dutch, Germans, and Chinese. At gatherings, they would sometimes tell stories of the Imperial Army that made the Mongols look tame.

Connie was seventeen. She'd grown into a beautiful young woman, complete with her mother's eyes and flowing hair. She was refined, a capable young woman just coming into her own. Julie at fifteen was slender, spirited, and brave. She captivated boys with a sort of stormy charisma that would confound as well as attract. She was beautiful, feisty, and independent, but at the same time, she was naïve and as vulnerable as Connie without P.I. to protect her.

Polly, elegant and charming, moved with grace and radiated an X factor that drew everyone to her. Her looks had owned middle age.

Her face was smooth, her skin fair and free from worry lines and wrinkles. She looked considerably younger than her forty years. She was the most beautiful woman P.I. had ever known. She was kind and warm, the type of person who others confided in, knowing their trust would not be broken.

Like most Americans, Polly lived a sheltered life compared to the nihilistic hell rushing upon them now. She was tested at times when P.I. went to sea for months at a stretch, but she never faced death and carnage nor the horrors of an army like Japan's.

How strong was she? P.I. wasn't really sure. He devoted himself throughout their marriage to protecting her from anything unpleasant. If somebody started to tell a dirty joke in front of Polly, P.I. would invariably step in and ask him to stop. The few times his request was ignored, he laid the man out with a swift and sudden jab to his jaw. When it came to Polly and her sensibilities, P.I. was uncompromising. It quickly got around Manila that only a fool would offend Mrs. Gunn.

Rumors of more attacks whispered their way around Paracale. Paratroops, fifth columnists, turncoat Filipinos aiding the enemy— those were the rumors floating around that morning as shock gave way to rising fear. The American mining engineers began to panic. Their families were out there with them, even more defenseless than those in Manila that day. Not an antiaircraft gun nor a single combat battalion had been ranged anywhere near the town. Should the Japanese appear in the bay, they would be at their mercy. Nobody wanted to see the nature of that mercy.

Joseph Stevenot chose to stay at Paracale, at least for the next week or so. Getting the communications system working atop the mountain was more critical than ever now. He had family in Manila, but his duty was out there on the southeast coast, so he would trust in MacArthur's forces to keep his loved ones safe.

P.I.'s duty lay at home. He had to find a way back to his family.

Waiting for the Staggerwing's parts would be nothing but a slow death to him. With the clothes he'd flown in the day before and little else, he bolted from the mining operation, determined to bribe, cajole, hitchhike, or threaten his way back to Manila. Whatever it took, he would be with Polly and the kids before sundown.

5

The Day of Fiestas

Monday, December 8, 1941

Manila was in a celebratory mood. December 8 marked the Feast of the Immaculate Conception, and the predominantly Catholic city was trimmed with blue-and-white banners. Flags bearing the image of the Virgin Mary fluttered from windows and lampposts. Manilans woke up that morning eagerly anticipating the daylong fiestas hosted all over town. Shortly after dawn, dressed in their finest, they flowed from homes to churches to worship at the start of the day. Celebrations, feasts, and parties would come after.

Polly fit right into this aspect of life in the Philippines. Raised in the church in hometown Pensacola, she was also educated in private Catholic schools. She loved going to Mass in Manila. The Spanish who had brought Christianity to the Philippines in the sixteenth century maintained its grandeur by constructing beautiful houses of worship, some of which had weathered countless calamities over the years. Some had been rebuilt many times in the wake of fires or earthquakes, their rich legacy preserved by the faithful parishioners. Polly never worshipped at such stunning, historic places before coming to the Philippines. The Manila Cathedral, the Basilica of San Sebastian, and Quiapo Church of the Black Nazarene inspired awe.

That Monday morning, she herded the kids into the Buick

46

Roadmaster, which a couple of PAL employees had brought back to the house the evening before. The boys wore their Sunday best; the girls fresh back from their Baguio trip wore the school skirts and good shoes P.I. had bought for them. They arrived home on the evening of December 7, avoiding the first bombing raid in the Philippines by about twelve hours.

Paul and Nath went to a Catholic school in town, which was closed for the holiday. Connie and Julie attended the secular American School, though, and rode along, a little jealous of their brothers.

Their chauffeur had taken the day off, so Polly drove them into town, navigating the hectic streets with a quiet mix of panic and determination. P.I. taught her to drive a few years ago in San Diego, where most drove sedately and usually obeyed the traffic laws.

The streets of Manila couldn't have been more different. Horse-drawn carriages, called kalesas, competed for space on the streets with trucks, taxis, and sedans whose drivers practiced a sort of automotive Darwinism: survival of the fastest. They whipped in and out of lanes, cut people off, and when there was an accident, they would scream at each other while ignoring the snarl they'd created. Once, Polly had almost hit a kalesa driver who stopped in the middle of the road, then dismounted to whip his exhausted horse as it collapsed on its side in the street.

When they reached the Redemptorist Church in Baclaran, Americans, Filipinos, German, Italian, and Spanish parishioners mingled outside the tall, sandy-brown archways leading into the chapel. There were even a few Japanese in the crowd—mainly shopkeepers who had converted after emigrating to this diverse and energetic city. They greeted each other warmly, chatting while walking inside.

The church was one of the most modern in Manila. Though recently constructed, it had such character, with its vaulted ceilings, rows of candles in iron holders, and the polished wooden pews, that it brought Polly a profound sense of comfort. This was her refuge;

Mass was never a chore but a joy she loved to share with her children. P.I. came to the Philippines to exercise his pioneering spirit. Polly found spiritual acceptance. Her entire life, she'd been part of a minority religion in the South, and more than once she was targeted for it. She learned to keep her faith to herself, but even that did not shield her from snide remarks or attacks. Then she fell in love with P.I. Gunn, and he became her shield.

Soon after she and P.I. married in 1923, they traveled to his hometown—Quitman, Arkansas—to spend time with his family. One morning, P.I.'s six-year-old niece came into Polly's room as Polly was doing her hair before church. The little girl stared at her through wide eyes until Polly asked what was wrong.

The girl pointed at Polly's long braids piled atop her head and asked, "Is that how you hide your horns?"

"What, honey?" Polly asked, trying to keep the surprise out of her voice.

The girl explained that the town Methodist preacher had said all Catholics were agents of the devil. You could tell who they were, since they all had horns.

Polly smiled and asked her to come closer. The girl hesitated, torn between what the preacher taught her and Polly's sweet demeanor. At last, she stepped forward. Polly took her hand and touched it to her head.

"There. See? No horns."

Polly and P.I. went to church with the rest of the family. The preacher, a fire-and-brimstone type, had been well prepared for the arrival of a Catholic in their little corner of the Ozarks. He spent most of the sermon railing against them and those who leave the true church to marry them.

As a kid, P.I. listened to this sort of nonsense every Sunday and never bought into its bigotry. It seemed harmless back then, though. Now, here he was back in the same church, a worldly twenty-three-year-old listening to the same hate-filled rant. This time, the preacher directed it all at him and his new bride.

This was too much. P.I. stood up, announced that he would not tolerate any slights to his wife or her religion. Then taking her hand, he led Polly out the door. They returned to the family farm, packed their things, and left.

He'd chosen his wife and her religious beliefs over his family. That loyalty to her so soon after they'd exchanged their vows set the tone for their entire marriage. Occasionally, P.I. would go to Mass with the rest of the family, but he never knelt in prayer, and he never truly believed. He protected her right to believe what she wanted with ruthless devotion. Between P.I. ensuring her freedom to believe what she wanted and the acceptance she found in Manila, Polly was happier in Manila than in any other time in her life.

Mass finished up before school started, but Polly needed to rush to get the girls to class on time. A quick hug to them both and they slid out of the Buick. Nath and Paul happily watched them go, reveling in the fact that in a few minutes they'd be playing back at home while their sisters languished in class.

Polly pulled away from the school and turned onto an empty street. The sight of it struck Polly as odd. No morning traffic, no kalesas clopping along. There weren't even many people walking on the sidewalks, or window shopping. Manila went from a boisterous city to a veritable ghost town in only a couple of hours. Only at the banks were there any crowds, and there things looked tense. People clustered around the doors, peering anxiously inside.

When they reached the house, Polly put the unusual scene out of her mind as she led the boys inside. She busied herself with her household to-do list while the boys ran upstairs to change. With the day off, they decided to head down after lunch to the black sand beach a few blocks away to see if the fleet had returned yet. Sometimes, they also caught Filipino jockeys exercising their horses along the water's edge before the races at the local track.

In the meantime, they played in the backyard. As the neighborhood population dwindled, the boys became more resourceful, conceiving games and adventures together as their friends returned to the States. Before all the military dependents went home, they were quite social, running in a pack, and serenading a redheaded girl they had a crush on, singing "Red Sails in the Sunset" to her while sitting on the wall outside her home.

Now, though, they were the last children their age in the neighborhood. They set up their collection of toy soldiers and metal tanks, each adorned with an American star. Some of their classmates included the sons of Spanish families who supported Gen. Francisco Franco's Nationalists during the Civil War. Playing war over at their houses led to a jolt for Nath; their toy soldiers wore German uniforms and their tanks sported swastikas. It made the boys uncomfortable at first, but they didn't let it get in their way of friendships.

As the battle took shape in the backyard, their pet monkey Chi-Chi came out of the little house P.I. had set up for him in a nearby tree. A line ran between two trees, and he would run back and forth on that wire, capering as the kids laughed at his antics.

P.I. had ensured that each child had his or her own pet. The girls didn't care for the monkey—the first time they saw him, Chi-Chi grabbed his penis and started playing with it. A masturbating monkey repelled them, though the boys thought it hysterical. So the monkey became theirs. Amos the cat gravitated to the girls, as did a family of ducks. Their dog, Dingo, protected the menagerie and the children. At the moment, he took point for Daisy and Donald as they waddled around under one of Chi-Chi's trees, their ducklings in tow behind them.

Amos made an appearance. He and Chi-Chi belonged to the same

Army captain and were lifelong pals as a result. The lanky orange cat scaled one of the trees and tight-rope-walked across the wire to give his monkey friend a morning bath. Chi-Chi suffered through the cat's tongue stroking the fur on the top of his head, making chittering noises as he got cleaned.

"Let's take Chi-Chi for his walk," Paul said as they looked up from their war to watch the two animals balancing on the wire.

Moments later, the boys happily walked Chi-Chi on a leash through the vacant streets, where he occasionally darted off to snatch a sunbathing lizard and bite its head off. He would sit on his haunches and chew loudly with a look of triumph on his simian face. The first time this happened, the boys had been so unnerved they ran home and told P.I., who replied laconically, "Oh yeah, he sure loves those things."

They finished their circuit and returned to the yard. The back door opened and Polly stood there, her face expressionless. It was a rare moment when Polly wasn't smiling. She wore a floral print dress she made herself on the sewing machine P.I. had given to her, her hair pinned in place with colorful clips she had found when they lived on Ford Island in Pearl Harbor.

"Boys," she said, her voice shaky, "come in for lunch please." At the dining room table, a plate of sandwiches waited for them.

Polly stood by the radio on a sideboard. It was a portable Motorola they'd bought in Hawaii, one of two they owned. Polly switched it on. The tubes hummed as they warmed up. A moment later, Don Bell's voice burst through a crackle of static. At first the boys were confused, with something about the Japanese attacking Pearl Harbor, then news that hit close to home.

"We have further word that the first civilian casualty during the attack on Hawaii was Bob Tyce, killed at Honolulu's John Rodgers Airport at the start of the attack."

The boys froze, eyes locked on their mom's. Polly sat down, her face turned slightly away from the children. She looked ready to cry.

"Bob Tyce was a partner in K-T Flying Service at Honolulu Airport. He was struck by a strafing Jap plane as he left his office. He fell back into the arms of his wife, who is a nurse, and died shortly after..."

"Oh my God...Mom? Is he talking about Bob Tyce? Our Bob Tyce?" asked Paul.

Polly, her chin on her chest, could only nod. The radio confirmed what she had prayed would not be true. Moments before, she'd received a phone call from Dan Stickle, the head of maintenance for PAL. He told her that the Japanese attacked Pearl Harbor earlier in the day and Bob was dead.

"Mr. Tyce...is dead?" Nath asked incredulously. What was happening? Dan Stickle, Bob Tyce, and P.I. worked together at K-T Flying Service for nearly two years. Their families had good times together. Bob's wife was a wonderful woman with an effervescent personality.

They listened to the radio in silence, Don Bell's voice relating the latest news from Pearl Harbor. Polly sat and silently cried through the entire broadcast, thinking of the battleships tied up beside Ford Island. When they lived there, they watched the huge battlewagons come and go in what was virtually their backyard. They got to know the sailors, and came to love the ships. She and the kids used to run outside when the Lexington's air group made mock attacks on the harbor during the fleet wargames in the 1930s. They would stand by the water's edge, cheering wildly as they tried to figure out which of the diving, wheeling planes was P.I.'s.

They thought it was all grand sport. Now, the Japanese used the same strategy the Navy practiced on itself for years. This was no sport or spectacle. The news juxtaposed on the memories they were lost in seemed so jarring and unreal. Don Bell continued to describe how those ships they knew so well were in flames and many of those sailors dead or wounded.

Where was P.I.? She needed him now, she needed him to tell her what to do. But all the PAL office had said was that he was on his way home. She tried to focus, but she couldn't escape Don Bell's words.

Incredibly, he spoke of a Japanese air attack against Davao Harbor on the Southern Philippine island of Mindanao. He described the bombing of Camp John Hay, Baguio, where the girls had just visited.

Fiestas all over Manila, and the Japanese were attacking? The sudden reality of war on the day's lightheartedness seemed beyond cruel.

"What are we going to do, Mom?" Nath asked.

Polly stared at her boys as they looked to her. She couldn't process the answer.

War. The Philippines were already being bombed. It was sure to get worse.

Her mind screamed, *P.I.! Where are you?*

"Mom?" Paul said, his voice quiet and unsure. They'd never seen her like this.

She forced herself to think. Composure, she had to regain her composure. Her babies were scared and they needed her.

Connie and Julie. They were still at school. That needed to be addressed immediately.

Polly called the school and, miraculously, the connection was made. She asked the principal to put her girls in a kalesa and send them home.

She dropped the receiver on the cradle, spun around, and said to the boys, "First, we need everyone together, here at the house."

Nath and Paul nodded.

"Then we wait for your father to get home. He'll know what to do."

He always did.

When they arrived, Julie was quiet and brooding, perhaps trying not to betray the fear she felt. Connie mirrored her mother's habit of trying to be positive. She gave Nath a hug. Connie was like a second mother to him, and they shared a bond unlike any other between the siblings. She stayed close to him throughout the rest of that day, her voice calming even though the news on the radio went from bad to worse.

Polly swept the girls into her arms, and calmly told them what happened to Bob Tyce. While the shock of the Pearl Harbor attack and being yanked from school had been a profound one, now the events of the day became personal. Together, they cried, Polly crushing them close as the girls thought of Mrs. Tyce and felt abiding grief for her loss. To see her husband die in such a way... Polly struggled to find words.

"I know. I know," Polly finally said. "They've been our friends for years."

When they broke the embrace, Merced brought the girls food. They ate quietly while listening to the bread-box-sized radio.

In the early afternoon, the family spotted planes over Manila. They circled high in the distance in stately formations. The kids climbed atop the roof to watch them, muted gray dots flecking the azure sky, and prayed they were friendlies.

At length, a damaged P-40 limped over Nichols Field. It orbited the strip at about eight thousand feet before finally making its landing. Two more followed. Around three o'clock, a full squadron returned. Eighteen sharp-nosed P-40s, their liquid-cooled Allison engines growling protectively, appeared in the pattern, passed over the house and touched down on the main runway.

They saw and heard no more aircraft that day.

On the radio, Don Bell recited a list of growing bad news. The Japanese seemed to be simultaneously attacking everywhere in the Pacific, from Pearl Harbor to Malaya. Tiny Wake Island and Guam had both been hit. More attacks followed throughout Southeast Asia. The family settled in the living room to listen to the latest developments, their vigil beside the radio broken only when some PAL employees showed up to get the Roadmaster and bring it back to Nielson Field so P.I. would have it available whenever he returned to the airport.

Sometime that afternoon, Bell went off the air. He received a tip that the Japanese had bombed Clark Field, the main B-17 heavy bomber base in the Philippines. Leaving others to cover for him, he drove the fifty or so miles to Clark. When he returned to his microphone that early evening, his voice was imbued with a somber, darker quality that hinted at what he could not say: A catastrophe was unfolding around them.

Sunset arrived as Merced slow-cooked a roast. It filled the house with the homey smell of a dinner lovingly prepared. Instead of being a comfort, though, it added to the sense of unreality in their little enclave. For beyond the walls of their Villamor Court compound, the city they loved was panicking as darkness fell.

The shock of the Pearl Harbor attack had worn off through the day, and the once-empty streets grew clogged with refugees streaming out of the city. Downtown, constables stacked sandbags in front of businesses. There were no basement bomb shelters or subways in the city—they would have just flooded out with the shallow water table. The sandbagged walls were the only alternative to protect the people.

Jittery Filipino soldiers stood on street corners, ancient rifles at the ready, their ears full of dreadful rumors of Japanese paratroops and spies in their midst. They fired at shadows, and when one man opened up, dozens more fired in reflexive fear until it sounded like a gun battle raging in the streets of the capital.

Meanwhile, outside of town, red flares arched overhead. Who fired them nobody knew. What they signaled could not be determined.

Each one added to the fear gripping the city and fueled rumors of fifth columnists working to pave the way for a Japanese invasion.

Between American bases, anonymous gunmen lay poised in ambush. They shot up Army Air Force general Louis Brereton's staff car several times while he traveled between headquarters, forcing him to constantly change his routes.

A run on the banks drained most of their available cash. Manila ran on credit—everyone had accounts at the local grocery stores, hotels, and other businesses. By dusk, the Manila Hotel had switched into cash-only mode. The local markets followed suit. Those who didn't withdraw cash out of their bank accounts found themselves unable to buy necessities.

Polly stressed over that. P.I. was always the one who handled their finances. With him somewhere in the provinces, she knew there was no way he could have pulled cash out of their accounts. They had some emergency money stashed at the house, but it would not be enough, especially if the crisis triggered inflation on survival items.

If things got bad, how would they eat? Could they get out of the country in one of PAL's aircraft? What about the Japanese air force? What about the family pets and all their belongings?

If they fled, they'd have to leave the four-poster spool bed. Polly had hauled that all over the country and across the Pacific. Leaving it behind filled her with a sense of dread and brought into focus the seriousness of their predicament. It was a symbol to the family. Abandoning it now would mean the situation was beyond salvation. They would be fleeing for their lives.

She fought that pessimism with the hope that MacArthur's forces could keep the Japanese away from Manila. The radio had been filled with news of the army and its readiness to fight. Maybe P.I.'s concerns were misplaced. Maybe they would smash any Japanese attempt to bomb Manila, or land troops on Luzon.

After twenty years of marriage, Polly had learned never to doubt

P.I.'s insight on such matters. He hadn't much confidence in the Army. But it was all she had at the moment. It was all anyone had that dreadful night.

After all, she had the children to consider. She tried her best to maintain a sense of normalcy. She forced herself to smile. Connie mirrored her mom. Julie continued to brood and worried for her dad. The boys, the shock of Bob Tyce's death wearing off, naïvely saw everything new as exciting and adventurous. Things were happening. Big things, and the Japanese were sure to pay if they ever came to Manila.

As chaos swirled around them, the house became a bastion in the storm. Don Bell's voice served as the keyhole through which they saw the world beyond, and each dispatch brought more dread. The radio remained on, but after dark Polly moved everyone into the back den as they continued to listen, sitting in chairs and a sofa, bare feet resting on the tile floor.

Not only had the Japanese attacked seemingly everywhere at once, they were winning everywhere at once, too. More and more news leaked out of Pearl Harbor, and while the details were sketchy, the Navy had been dealt a devastating blow.

Merced finished the roast, but Polly refused to let the family eat until P.I. got home. They snacked and waited as the clock dragged its hands.

Two hours after dusk, Dingo dashed out of the house and into the yard. His barks filled the night. Somebody was at the front gate.

6

Terror in the Night

P.I. Gunn, covered in filth and reeking like a barnyard, honked the Buick's horn once as he reached the front gate. With his tie askew and his short hair unkempt, he looked bone weary. Inside, he fairly boiled with anger. P.I. had a temper, and right now he was using all the remaining self-control to keep it in check.

As he waited for the boys, he took a long drag on the Camel cigarette tucked between two fingers on his right hand. When he exhaled, the smoke boiled up over his right eye and clouded his vision a bit. He'd been smoking all day, and the smoke had turned his right eye red with irritation.

Nath and Paul appeared, Dingo in their wake. They unlocked the gate and pulled it clear. P.I. goosed the gas pedal and the Roadmaster slid into the yard. As the rear bumper cleared the entryway, the boys bolted the gate back into place.

"Dad!"

He barely saw them. He stomped up the stairs, brimming with rage.

"Dad, did you hear about Bob—"

"I heard—" he said sharply, the anger seeping into his voice.

"Dad?"

He ignored the boys and swore under his breath. The boys

stopped. Polly hated foul language, and their dad never used it around her. To the boys, that meant things must really be bad.

"Brereton couldn't even get through to MacArthur," P.I. growled. The boys glanced at each other, both without a clue as to what that meant. They'd heard Brereton's name before. He was the general in charge of MacArthur's air force.

"Goddamned idiots," he swore as he stormed through the front door and nearly collided with Polly in the front hall. She ignored his language and threw her arms around him.

"Oh, P.I."

He hugged her close as Nath and Paul stood nearby, astonished at the emotions on display.

"You see? You see what's happened? You should have left, Polly. You should've listened to me," he said with despair, his forehead against hers, their lips inches apart.

She said nothing but just held on to him as the boys stared from the doorway.

"See what happens now when you wouldn't go?" he said again. He sounded like he was cursing himself for giving in to her.

She cupped his cheeks and looked him in the eyes. "That's in the past. We can't dwell on it. You can't. We need you."

He didn't reply at first; he just held her.

"All our friends—" Polly said. P.I. had only been out of the Navy four years, but he had served with many of the old salts manning the battleships at Pearl Harbor. Their families had socialized. Their kids had played together.

Two minds, long in sync, returned to their home in Hawaii. Ford Island first, later a little rental house in Honolulu.

"The Japs bombed the whole area."

"Ford Island, too?" Polly asked.

"Yes."

"Bob—"

"I know. I know."

"What do we do?"

P.I. said, "Well, let's see what happens. They've got to get the fighter pilots sober."

Polly looked up. "What?"

"There's been a lot of drinking going on this afternoon. A whole lot of it."

"Dad?"

Connie and Julie had come out of the den. They were watching their parents, fear in their eyes as they saw how disheveled their dad was.

"How did you get home?" one of the girls asked.

"By boat, bus, train, and car. No other choice. The Staggerwing's part didn't arrive, and even if it had, the Air Corps grounded all civilian flights."

"Well, you're home now. That's all that matters," Polly said. "Dinner's ready."

P.I. added, "I got here as soon as I could. Made it to the train station, had to check in at the PAL office to see what was happening, then get over to Nielson for the car."

"Let's sit down and eat. You must be starving," Polly said.

The family assembled in the dining room as Merced's roast was served by a young Filipino girl. P.I. went to wash his hands. A change of clothes and shower would have to wait. Whatever had happened to him on the trip from Paracale had left him in foul shape.

When he returned to the dining room, his anger began to recede. He switched from venting mode to planning mode as they ate.

"They're going to get the fighters tonight," he announced. The family knew that meant Nichols Field.

"Why do you say that, Dad?" Julie asked.

"'Cause, Miss Priss," P.I. began, using his nickname for her, "they already got the bombers. Now, the moon is just right. Almost full. They'll be able to see even with the city blacked out."

He thought it over. "I expect they'll be here around two this morning. The moon'll be perfectly positioned for them then. Right at their backs as they come in from the bay."

As if thinking aloud, he added, "Right over our house."

Merced came into the dining room and asked if he could leave for the night. P.I. asked him where he lived. When the cook mentioned a small barrio between Villamor Court and downtown Manila, he said, "You need to get away from there. You'll be in the line of fire, too."

Merced thanked him and hurried off into the night while the family finished dinner.

At the dinner table, P.I. didn't talk much about the trip from Paracale. He was more interested in what happened in Manila after he returned. He couldn't come straight home from the train station. To do so would have abrogated his responsibilities to all his employees. Torn, he followed his sense of duty and went to make sure the PAL aircraft were safe. Or at least, as safe as they could be for the time being. When he reached Nielson, he told his staff to pull the Beech 18s out of the main hangar and disperse them round the airport to protect them against air attack.

Far East Air Force HQ was only a short way from PAL's operation, so he drove over to see what was going on. Since he was prior service and so well known in aviation circles in the Philippines, the Army Air Force staffers talked freely with him.

They told him of the attack on Clark Field, home of the Nineteenth Bomb Group, and its fleet of B-17 heavy bombers. Those aerial weapons, upon which President Roosevelt had pinned so much hope, had been caught on the ground by the lunchtime Japanese attack. The field was devastated, and most of the big bombers reduced to burned wrecks. The few that had survived were down at an alternate strip carved out of a Del Monte pineapple plantation on Mindanao.

The Japanese virtually destroyed MacArthur's offensive air arm before it could even get in the fight. Already, the finger pointing had started as to who was responsible for the disaster.

Dispirited, P.I. returned to the PAL hangar to call the U.S. Navy base at Cavite. Though out of the service since 1938, he remained in the Ready Reserve, which meant he could be recalled to active duty in a crisis. He told the family that when he called, there was so much chaos at Cavite that he couldn't get anyone in authority to tell him his status.

He shook his head in frustration. "Lots of drinking going on." The aviators had taken a shellacking. They'd seen horrific things on the ground at Clark; had watched friends die or suffer grievous wounds. They turned to the only solace they knew, and by late afternoon some had begun to drink.

They finished dinner and looked to P.I. for orders. He told them to gather up some quilts and blankets from their rooms and lay some of them out in the corner of the garden. If the Japanese did come, they would go out there and use the thick walls for cover. They would protect the family from machine gun runs and bomb splinters. They should be safe—unless a bomb landed right in the yard.

In the meantime, they would make a family nest in the den, covering the windows with some of the blankets to make it blackout proof. The rest of the house they would leave to the darkness.

As the kids went upstairs to get the Pensacola quilts, P.I. told Polly that one of them would need to be up at all times through the night. Polly insisted on taking the first shift. She could see how exhausted P.I. was, and she still had no idea how he managed to get back given the conditions and the panic.

P.I. would have none of it. He would take first shift. Polly needed to sleep.

The kids reappeared, their arms full of bedding. P.I. and Polly covered the windows as everyone else curled up on the floor or furniture. Gradually, each member of the family fell into fitful sleep while P.I. kept watch over them.

He shut the lights off and listened to the sounds outside. Distant gunshots rang out. Occasionally, he heard the sound of a car or truck pass by Villamor Court. As he listened, he began to plan.

First, he had to move his family away from Nichols Field. In the morning, he needed to find them a place in town. They would need protection from air raids, but digging a bomb shelter was out of the question. Stick a shovel in the ground anywhere in Manila and you'd strike water in two or three feet. No. He would have to find some other way to protect them.

The Beech 18s needed protection, too. They would be useful in the days ahead, and the only way he could get his family out of the Philippines should it become necessary. They must be preserved at all costs. The fact that they were his escape outlet probably never left his mind that first day of the war, and it was part of the reason he had gone to Nielson to ensure their safety before he went home.

Despite the fact that he had moved them to strategic locations on the airfield, his planes were still exposed at Nielson, which was sure to be on the Japanese target list. After destroying much of Clark Field, they would systematically start hitting the remaining air bases. He was sure of that. PAL would have to move someplace the Japanese would not suspect.

PATCO—the old and now defunct Philippine Air Taxi Company—never, ever, operated out of Nielson. Its planes used Grace Park, sometimes called Manila North by the old-timers. The strip stretched alongside Highway 54 and abutted a Chinese cemetery. That could work; it had been abandoned for years and all but forgotten. He resolved to check it out in the morning.

He glanced at his BUSHIPS watch. Almost 0200. They would be coming soon. Outside, the moon hung high in the western sky, suffusing Manila in its silvery glow.

What did the British call nights like this during the Blitz?

A bomber's moon.

The minutes ticked by. P.I. listened and watched, searching for any sign that the Japanese were near.

At two thirty, exhaustion started to get the better of him. Eyes leaden, his brain crying for a respite, he knew he would have to wake Polly soon and get some sleep.

He decided to give it another thirty minutes, then rouse her.

At three, Manila had gone silent. The random shots fired by spooked sentries stopped, at least for the moment. The city slept fitfully.

P.I. finally rose and went to wake Polly. As she slid from under a quilt and got to her feet, P.I. heard something. He paused to listen. In the distance, he could just make out the bass cadence of aircraft engines. A lot of them.

Motors were the audio version of fingerprints for aircraft. Experienced pilots could tell the type of plane flying overhead without ever looking up. They were that tuned to every engine's nuances. The P-40s and their Allisons sounded light and snarling. The B-17s emitted a low, steady drone in the bass clef. The Philippine Air Corps pilots he trained flew old fabric-covered P-26 Peashooters. They sounded choppy and awkward.

P.I. strained to detect what these were. Perhaps some of the surviving B-17s were flying up from Mindanao to refuel and arm for a strike against the Japanese on Formosa. As the engines grew closer and louder, P.I. knew these were unknown to his ear. That meant only one thing: The Japanese were coming.

It was 0309, December 9, 1941. For the first time, Manilans would find themselves under falling bombs.

7

Silver Screen Scenes

The kids woke groggily as their parents pulled them to their feet. P.I. used his chief petty officer's voice to inject urgency in them as Polly reassured and helped them gather their quilts. The engines grew louder now, like an approaching wave ready to break over the beach.

They rushed into the backyard, Dingo keeping pace. Up in his monkey house, Chi-Chi started to caterwaul. They made it and everyone took their positions.

"Lie facedown, keep close," P.I. ordered.

The girls flopped onto the ground, Polly next to them. The boys followed on the other side as Dingo snuggled between them. P.I. squeezed next to Polly and Julie.

"Stay on your bellies," P.I. said, "and keep your mouths open."

"Why open?" one of the girls asked.

"To keep your eardrums from bursting from the shock wave of a bomb," P.I. answered.

They lay huddled together in the corner of the garden, protected by the junction of two sections of the outside wall. Eight feet tall and several feet thick, the masonry work would protect them from bomb blasts and strafing.

The Japanese came in from the west, over Manila Bay. Citizens throughout the blacked-out city shuddered at their approach. Sirens wailed, and searchlights speared the moonlit sky.

The dog, unnerved by the sounds, sprang to his feet. P.I.'s harsh words froze him in place, "Dingo, lie down!"

Nath reached for him reassuringly and the big animal did as he was told. The boys tried their best to comfort him as the cacophony swelled.

Something bright flashed overhead. Nath instinctively tried to turn around and see what it was, but P.I. gently lay his hand on him. "Nath, quit it. Lie down and roll over."

He did as he was told, but not before he caught a glimpse of red streaks arcing skyward with an almost graceful beauty. The sight stirred his adventurous imagination; it all felt so exciting.

The bombers reached Manila. Ancient, World War I–era American antiaircraft guns thumped to life. *Carrrump! Carrrump!* The ground began to quiver beneath them. Dingo burrowed his head into Paul. Chi-Chi started to scream. Donald and Daisy Duck came out of their nest to investigate the family's pile of quilts. Now they, too, began to squawk.

Under the bass drum sounds of the AA guns came the sharp cracks of rifles. Machine guns unleashed long torrents of bullets. Every third one was a bright red tracer—what Nath had seen—and soon they webbed the sky.

Nath and Paul couldn't stand it any longer. They turned over and stared up into the night. At this point, P.I. could not resist himself and rolled over as well.

The silvery moonlight had given way to a crimson glow, crisscrossed with waving searchlights, looking like probing fingers ready to point a target out for the gunners beneath their beams. To the north and east, steady streams of flares burned away the darkness over Fort McKinley and Nichols Field. The Japanese agents launching them were working late on this night.

"There they are!" Nath said excitedly. Above them, a formation of three Japanese bombers appeared.

"By God!" he exclaimed as he spotted the twin-ruddered, twin-engine planes. "They're coming in en echelon. Look at that!"

He'd never seen bombers like these. They looked a bit like the Beech 18s, but with longer, more elegant wings and sleeker noses. Their white bellies seemed to glow in the tracer-laced night sky.

The formation looked incredibly tight for a night attack. P.I. knew that took skill and discipline. He was looking at something none of the USAAF pilots in the Philippines could have done.

"En echelon," he said almost to himself, "I'll have to remember that."

P.I.'s professional judgment did not fail him. The Japanese overhead belonged to the Imperial Navy's First Kōkūtai, whose pilots once terror-bombed Chungking and participated in scores of raids in China the year before. Experienced, battle-hardened and led by an exceptionally capable squadron commander in Lt. Yoshiro Kaneko, the Japanese bombers followed the trail of flares and found Nichols Field.

The antiaircraft gunners poured it on. P.I. said, "Hey! They're finally waking up and fighting back."

In a moment of supreme irony, the Manila air raid siren suddenly blasted the all-clear signal. A few seconds later, the planes overhead opened their bomb bay doors. Incendiaries poured forth, and the family heard the spine-chilling wail of falling explosives for the first time.

The sound seized Polly's senses. She rolled over to look at the unfolding battle above them, and found a strange beauty in the sight. Then the shrieking bombs filled her with terror so intense she began to shake. Unused to the sound, she thought it was people screaming. She prayed, hard for her family and for those trapped in what she later called "the grip of the mailed fist."

Nevertheless, she dug deep and forced herself to not cry out or show fear. She willed herself to not do anything that could make this worse for her children. She had to be strong for them, and not give in to what she felt.

Beside P.I., Julie and Connie cried with fear. Tears streamed and Julie hugged her father tightly as the first bomb exploded with a tremendous roar. The skyline over Nichols bloomed orange-red. The ground shook violently, and the blast wave rustled the trees a moment later.

Chi-Chi howled from his little treetop house.

More explosions followed and seconds later a huge geyser of flame plumed above Nichols.

Just to the north, Don Bell stood atop the NBC building near the Pasig River, reporting on the attack, microphone in hand. He and fellow broadcaster Bert Silan tag-teamed a blow-by-blow account of the bombing even though the two men could not confirm they were still transmitting. One of the first bombs had landed close to the RCA radio transmitter tower, and they weren't sure if it had been knocked off-line. They kept talking, speculating over how the flames rising over Nichols might have been caused by a direct hit on an ammo or a fuel dump. In reality, from nine thousand feet the Japanese bombardiers scored a double bull's-eye on two decrepit Douglas B-18 Bolo bombers fueled and armed for a mission they would never execute. Their ruptured gas tanks and bombs detonated and created the conflagration that could be seen for miles that night.

The first trio of bombers vanished into the eastern sky, then turned north for their field on Formosa. The shooting slackened, but only for a moment. The raid was not yet over.

Another wave of three fork-tailed bombers passed overhead. This time, they seemed so low to Julie that later she would recall seeing the silhouettes of their pilots. Nath could see their big red rising-sun insignia stark against their milk-colored wings. Their engines filled the air with a deafening, cyclic thunder as they swung north and dropped a pattern of bombs on Fort McKinley. Even with all the lead being thrown at them, not one of the planes took a serious hit.

P.I. remembered all of the tents set up on the parade ground on his morning commute to Nielson Field. If the men living in them had not reached shelter, there could be heavy casualties. The former military man in him wanted to jump in the Buick and race north to investigate and help. The father and husband in him overruled that urge. He felt Polly and Julie quaking against him and held them with all the reassurance his strong arms mustered.

The antiaircraft gunners gave it their best effort. They blazed away at the night raiders, their explosive shells raining red-hot shrapnel down on the city and its surroundings. Every Filipino soldier, and many American ones too, stood with rifles, machine guns, and even pistols and threw lead into the sky. They were inexperienced, untrained, and unable to hit anything.

As if providing a professional commentary of his own for the family, P.I. watched the tracers and judged, "Well, they're way off the mark."

He was right. The Japanese did not lose any planes that night.

The inferno at Nichols blazed on, turning darkness to an eerie day on their eastern horizon. Polly looked on at the scene as a third wave of bombers began their attack and couldn't help but think about the suffering of those trapped under the bombs. It all seemed so strange, almost unreal to her. For years, she had read about such bombing raids and seen them in the newsreels. Guernica in the Spanish Civil War, countless towns and cities in China. The destruction of Rotterdam and the London Blitz. Now, those silver screen scenes became her family's stark reality. The fury of total war had arrived on the Gunn family's doorstep.

P.I. looked out at the soaring flames and said grimly, "Those flights were on the button." Searching for anything positive to say, he added, "Well, maybe this will get the knuckleheads at Nichols on their toes."

He knew they would have to do better than this if the

Philippines had any chance. The Japanese were pros. The Americans and Filipinos—well, he had seen them fly and drill for two years. The learning curve would be steep. And painful. Not many would survive.

The attack lasted twenty minutes.

The flares stopped. The antiaircraft gunners were persuaded to cease fire. The sentries and machine gunners still got spooked periodically, and their gunshots echoed across the city.

The family lay together, emotionally wrung out. Chi-Chi finally stopped screeching, but he could not be coaxed out of his tree house. When P.I. grew convinced the Japanese would not come back that night, he climbed out of the family's nest and stared out over the wall toward Nichols.

"What are you going to do, Dad?" one of the girls asked.

He looked at his family, studying their faces. Polly, her beauty undiminished by exhaustion and fear, looked soft eyed but resolute. The boys, their excitement drained, appeared moments from falling asleep. The girls, still fearful and uncertain, peered up at him for reassurance.

He never really understood the girls, or girls in general, though he never admitted that out loud. He knew how to be tough on the boys, mold them into men. The girls? He had no clue. He deferred to Polly on them and almost never disciplined Julie or Connie. Instead, he spoiled them and doted at times in ways that would leave Polly shaking her head. Back in San Diego and Hawaii, he sometimes took the girls shoe shopping. They loved this, because P.I. remembered the sting of owning only one pair of beat-up, hand-me-down shoes as a kid that he wore only to school and church. The rest of the time, his family was so poor that he went barefoot to preserve the pair he had for as long as possible. He never wanted the girls to feel that humiliation, so he ignored Polly's careful budgeting and splurged for his daughters. They always came home with beautiful, expensive shoes—two pairs each.

"You'll be safe here for now. But we're going to move in the morning," he said. "Pack up everything, I'll find us a place in town away from the bases."

He glanced back over to Nichols. "I'm going to go see what kind of damage they did." McKinley was close enough to Nielson that the airport could have been hit too. That meant the Beech 18s may have been damaged or destroyed. He needed to know the score; those planes could mean his family's salvation.

Polly rose to her feet and put her arms around her husband. "You're running toward trouble."

He kissed her. "That's the way I'm built."

She kissed him back. The kids were uncomfortable with the display of affection.

"I wouldn't trade you for a dozen others," she said at last. Then added, "Come back when you can. We'll manage."

P.I. walked toward the Buick, then paused. Turning he said, "Boys, mind your mother, okay?"

They nodded earnestly. Then Nath whispered to Paul, "Why doesn't he ever tell the girls to mind Mom?"

Paul whispered back, "Because they always do anyway."

P.I. was gone a few hours, returning just after sunrise. As he came through the door, the anger at the Army Air Force was gone. The defeat was so vast and overwhelming, anger seemed wasted effort at that point.

The family gathered around him as he told them the news. The bright red airliners had escaped harm. "I'm going to move them to Grace Park," he said. "We'll hide them in the Chinese cemetery there."

That surprised the family. P.I. explained that the Japanese were a superstitious lot, so he figured they would never bomb a cemetery with so many Buddhist shrines. Just in case, he would make sure to camouflage the 18s and build protective revetments for them.

"How bad is it at Nichols?" Polly asked, still thinking about the suffering of the boys there.

P.I. told them, "Well, we have some P-40s left, but not enough to put up a real fight for long. The bombers are mostly gone. Unless we get support, it'll come down to a ground war. If the Navy got hit as bad as it sounds, we're in real trouble. We're kind of on our own."

"What do we do?" Nath asked.

"Sit tight for now. Get packed and we'll move before Wednesday."

He saw the fear on their faces and tried to reassure them. "Hey, we still have a hell of an army."

Given what General Wainwright had told the girls a few weeks before, the words felt like slender reeds to all of them.

8

Running Toward Trouble

Tuesday, December 9, 1941

The Buick roared up Highway 54, P.I. behind the wheel fighting exhaustion. He hadn't slept since Paracale, probably, but there was no time for rest now as he raced the clock to beat the Japanese back to Nielson. Their main daylight raids had reached Luzon at lunchtime the day before. If that held today, he had only a few hours to secure the Beech 18s. His legs throbbed and began to swell, a symptom of lack of sleep and stress as he worked long stretches. He ignored the pain by making a mental list of all that needed to be done.

The list seemed daunting in the face of the wrecking ball swinging at him. The Japanese demolished his family's tranquil life the day before with their curtain raiser at Clark Field. A prologue. That was all it was. P.I. held no illusions: The full weight of Japan's military would soon be levied against Luzon.

When that happened, he must be prepared, or... He would not contemplate the consequences.

He sped along beside Nichols Field. Hangar number four still burned from the early morning's attack. The Japanese had walked a string of bombs right through it, killing and wounding over a dozen men. At least the P-40s still there had escaped destruction. At sunset the evening before, most of them had been transferred to

Clark Field. The Army Air Force knew the Japanese would hit the fighter base, and reasoned the P-40s would be safer in the wreckage of Clark since it would probably not get hit again anytime soon.

At the edge of Nichols Field, he saw the skeletal remains of a fuel truck smoldering in a field. A number of American and Filipino guards hovered nearby. A Japanese agent had driven the truck into the field the night before and set it afire before fleeing. Pan Am's radio navigational system for its transpacific clipper service stood less than fifty feet from the truck, and the Japanese bombers had hammered it to broken sticks. Blackened craters scarred the ground around the wrecked building.

The spy accomplished his mission.

P.I. sped past the scene of perfidy. The rumors of fifth columnists—the military called them Sakdalistas—left the sentries even more jittery and paranoid. They shot at their own shadows and tried to light up passersby and speeding vehicles. On the plus side, most of them couldn't hit a barn from fifty feet, so there had yet to be a friendly fire tragedy around Nielson. But sooner or later, all the panic fire would take a toll.

Just how many spies and fifth columnists operated in the Philippines will never be known. The Japanese records—if there were any—did not survive the war. Certainly there were some conducting attacks and surveillance, but much of what was reported in those early days of the war was hysteria and rumor. The reaction far outweighed the actual physical damage the spies inflicted on the defenders. It made everyone paranoid, jumpy and quick to open fire, which made approaching any security checkpoint a dicey game that December.

Fortunately, P.I. negotiated the sentries without incident and parked the Roadmaster. Hurriedly, he walked past the partly constructed barracks and buildings stretching around the FEAF headquarters complex. Somebody had cheekily started calling that area

"Clagettville" after their former commander, Brig. Gen. Henry B. Clagett. The general had not been amused.

The chaos of the day before was gone, replaced now by intense focus. The Army Air Force personnel looked grim and overworked. Red-rimmed eyes greeted P.I. as he walked out to the PAL hangar to meet with his staff. The military was struggling to awake to wartime realities as a capable foe prepared to strike again.

Signs of this struggle could be seen everywhere. At Nielson, the FEAF staff fought to get food and basic supplies to their fighter units, which were dispersed at different fields. Most had gone a day or more without any rations, and some of the men were sleeping in the jungle without even the bare necessities. Others lacked their ground echelon and found themselves forced to service and fuel their own planes. Without facilities, this meant hand-pumping gas into the tanks from fifty-five-gallon drums. After a long day's flying, it only wore the men out even more.

The radar system at Iba had been knocked out, and the fighter squadron there almost totally destroyed. FEAF HQ ordered the base evacuated, and now the personnel from Iba were somewhere on the primitive road network moving south.

None of the other radar sets was fully operational, which meant the ground observers now served as the only warning line of Japan's next strike. Stevenot and the radar crew at Paracale struggled mightily to get the 270 working, but they lacked the equipment and supplies to lay the phone lines needed for effective communication with Nielson.

The ground observers, spooked by the events of the previous day, deluged the plotting center with false contacts. They mistook cloud formations or flocks of high-flying birds for planes—or panicked and imagined things. This happened all over the Philippines, and reports of paratroops, phantom invasion fleets, and nonexistent air raids made it impossible to deduce the real situation and threats. In

the midst of this misinformation, the Army ordered all civilian sec-
retaries and clerks evacuated from Nielson Field. Since they handled
much of the message traffic, the loss of this manpower made things
even more unmanageable.

The morning air patrols turned into a disaster as well. A P-40
squadron taking off from Clark Field lost two planes on the
dust-choked and bomb-cratered runway. In a supreme tragedy, one
of those Curtiss pilots lost his way in the dust and careened right
into a B-17. He died instantly in the conflagration as both aircraft
burned up. The night before, Interceptor Command scrambled a
flight of P-40s from Del Carmen Field. Not only did they not find
the Japanese bombers, but two P-40s collided on the runway, killing
one pilot.

Without even seeing the enemy, much less engaging it, FEAF
lost five more precious aircraft.

As he reached the PAL hangar, P.I. took note of all the hasty defensive preparations around the field. Somebody painted the windows in
the FEAF buildings black so they could continue to work at night
without sacrificing light discipline. Soldiers dug slit trenches around
the FEAF area, but whoever had chosen their location placed them
too close to the buildings to make them safe to use during an attack.

The day before, when Iba's radar spotted the incoming raid that
had attacked Clark, Interceptor Command thought the Japanese
could be Nielson bound. Most of the headquarters staff evacuated the buildings—but instead of diving for the slit trenches, they
sprinted pell-mell to the drainage ditches on either side of Highway
54. Now, details sweated in the morning sun as they dug new slit
trenches a safer distance from the cluster of headquarters buildings.

Meanwhile, other troops emplaced 37mm antiaircraft guns
around the airport's perimeter. These rapid-fire guns would provide
good defense against low and medium altitude bombing raids, but
they could not reach targets above ten thousand feet.

Yesterday's raid on Clark had come in at twenty thousand.

To P.I., these were all things that should have been done weeks ago, not the day after blood had been spilled. At least the Army Air Force was finally getting serious, but it looked like too little too late. He couldn't waste time on what they were finally doing. The day before, after he returned from Paracale, he tried to give the Air Force officers he knew some advice, but they blew him off. Somebody even said to him, "We don't need any help from an ex-Navy pilot."

The Army Air Force had plenty on its plate, and he faced a host of problems of his own he needed to tackle today before the Japanese returned. It would take considerable effort and organization to make the move to Grace Park. He also needed to find a place for the family to stay, at least for a few days until he could rent an apartment in Manila.

Where would the family be safest? He considered that, running through a list of potential targets around the city and mentally comparing their locations to the houses of friends in town. He made a few phone calls and came up with a temporary spot. One of Andrés Soriano's employees lived deep in the heart of Manila's residential quarter, far removed from the airfields, oil storage tanks, and docks that were sure to be on the Japanese target list. He agreed to house the family for a few days. It would be a tight fit; the family would have to sleep on the living room floor, but they would be far safer than they were now.

Later that morning, P.I. went out to survey Grace Park. The strip had been abandoned for so long that the cemetery now surrounded it. The old runway served as one of the roads through the rows of headstones and shrines. Some of those shrines would have to go to clear enough space for the wingspan of the Beech 18s. Plus, they would have to bulldoze revetments somewhere away from the runway to keep the planes protected on the ground. Still, this could be the perfect spot to operate and keep the airliners safe.

P.I. and his PAL team acquired a bulldozer. Without seeking permission from city authorities or the cemetery's owners, they knocked down all the shrines and memorials that ran along either side of the runway, then bulldozed the revetments for the Beech 18s within the cemetery. These were protective U-shaped enclosures made with high dirt walls, then camouflaged with netting to make them almost invisible from above.

By late afternoon, the aircraft were in place. The other PAL pilots, among them Americans Harold Slingsby and Louis Connelly, joined P.I. at Grace Park along with the ground echelon. The mechanics hauled truckloads of gear over to the new field. They stashed spare parts, oil, fuel, tools, and other equipment throughout the cemetery until they created a fully independent operation again. If the Japanese bombed Nielson like they bombed Clark, Philippine Air Lines would not be put out of business.

While back at Nielson after lunch, P.I. called Cavite again and tried to find anyone in the Navy who could tell him his status. He assumed they would recall him to active duty, but so far there had been no official word on that. At some point, he even drove all the way around the Bay to the Navy facility there and tried to reenlist. Either way, the war's outbreak left the Navy so disorganized he couldn't get a straight answer out of anyone. He remained a civilian, at least for the moment.

P.I. Gunn cared about two things: his family and his country. Above all, he was a patriot and a warrior. His life to 1938 was spent in service to his nation. It was his purpose, his life's work. Nath would later say that if someone waved the flag at his father, he would charge ahead without question. To him, protecting the nation he loved meant protecting the family he needed. By rejoining the military, he felt his family would be safer. The Navy might even be able to get them out of the Philippines via ship or submarine.

The Japanese did not return on the ninth. The P-40s patrolled through empty skies as MacArthur's forces scurried to catch up with wartime realities. News reports announced the call up of all Filipino reservists. The army was mobilizing; farmers, peasants, and city dwellers alike reported to their nearest training depot. There were plenty of men, just a dearth of weapons, supplies, and training opportunities for them.

Meanwhile, a bureaucratic battle broke out over whose job it was to pick up the dead bodies left in the wake of the December 8 bombing raid at Clark Field. Scores of corpses lay in the hot sun that day, and dozens more lay in the skeletal confines of wrecked and damaged aircraft. The B-17 crews had tried to use their ground-bound planes as antiaircraft positions, manning their turret guns to shoot at strafing Japanese fighters. They died at their positions and were left there as the Medical Corps and the Quartermaster Corps argued over whose job it was to go get them.

There were precious few spare parts for the P-40s, and none at all for the surviving B-17s, so the order went out for the mechanics to salvage every possible piece of equipment from the wrecks. They did so for days, stripping the planes while the bodies of their comrades rotted and swelled within them. It would take a week for the bureaucratic war to end and the bodies to be laid to rest.

Back at home, Polly and the children packed small suitcases and prepared to move into town on P.I.'s direction. Polly paid the servants and sent them home with Amos the cat and Chi-Chi the monkey. Others took the ducks. In the scramble to get moved out of the house, the kids did not have time to say good-bye to their beloved pets.

Only Dingo remained with them, but only for a few more hours. He was adopted by the PAL staff at Grace Park, where he had the run of the secret airfield for the next few weeks.

Polly and the children left the Villamor Court house sometime later that day. The kids would never return or see it again. The house and neighborhood were later totally destroyed toward the end of December.

They reached their temporary home before dark, and the family bunked down on the living room floor of a tiny one-bedroom apartment. It would do for now.

P.I. stayed at Grace Park, working through the night to get PAL up and running there. By dawn, the aircraft were well protected and hidden. With all civilian air traffic officially grounded, there would be no runs to Baguio or Legazpi anytime soon for Philippine Air Lines, but P.I. knew the aircraft would be of great value in the coming storm. The Army or Navy might need to contract with PAL to shuttle VIPs around or carry supplies. The buildup in the Philippines that fall had focused on combat power, not logistical support. FEAF had bombers and fighters, but no air transport squadrons. That would surely be a major deficiency in the fighting ahead, a deficiency the bright red Beech 18s might be able to help solve.

Though the Americans didn't know it at the time, bad weather over Formosa had given them a day's grace. The Japanese planned a whole series of air attacks for December 9, only to have their airfields socked in by heavy ground fog again. When it failed to lift, as it had on the eighth, their squadrons stood down. The fog gave P.I. the time he needed to save his precious aircraft.

Dawn broke on Wednesday, December 10, and the Japanese stood beside their waiting planes under a clear blue sky. They climbed into their waiting planes. Engines coughed to life amid clouds of exhaust. as the crews climbed aboard to warm up their birds. One by one, they lined up on their runways and sped into the air, Manila bound.

9

The Noose

December 10, 1941

In the predawn gloom as Polly tried to sleep with her children curled around her on the living room floor, the Japanese invasion of the Philippines began. To the far north, a pair of invasion task forces closed on Aparri and Vigan, two small towns on the tip of Luzon. Lieutenant Grant Mahony, a young Oregonian on his first combat mission, spotted the amphibious force off Vigan while on a solo reconnaissance patrol shortly before sunrise. Dodging in and out of cloud cover, he took note of the number and types of ships below him, then lit out for home at full speed.

As he returned to Nichols Field with this vital information, a Filipino antiaircraft crew opened fire on his P-40. Jumpy, ready to shoot at anything in the sky, these green soldiers could not distinguish between friend and foe—a fact that would nearly kill P. I. Gunn a few days later. One of Mahony's fellow pilots saw the error and he charged the gun crew while brandishing a pistol and shouting for them to stop firing.

He was too late. Normally, the antiaircraft gun crews couldn't hit anything. But luck abandoned the twenty-three-year-old pilot that night, and Mahony's P-40 was shot to pieces. He bailed out and landed unhurt not far from the Filipinos who had shot him down.

His pilot friend rushed to his aid, bundled him up, and got him to the operations center at Nichols, where he reported the invasion fleet to FEAF headquarters.

The day had not even begun, and already the Americans were down one more precious P-40. That left fifty-two available to face a Japanese air fleet of more than three hundred.

A new sighting report quickly followed Mahony's. A Navy flying boat spotted one of the task forces and bombed it from high altitude before escaping southward. More flying boats waded in and launched torpedoes at the Japanese ships.

FEAF quickly put together a strike force of its own. The Army bomber pilots were about to launch a strike against Formosa with the few remaining Flying Forts. Now Brereton ordered a maximum effort against the invasion forces. The B-17s would go in with two squadrons of P-40s as escort. While they bombed from twelve thousand feet, a squadron of overage Seversky P-35 fighters would strafe the laden troop transports. A follow-up attack with another squadron of B-17s would complete the first response to this threat. For some of the Americans that morning, this attack would be the first time they had ever fired their machine guns.

On Formosa, the Japanese also planned a maximum effort to support the two amphibious landings. Short-range Army bombers trundled aloft and turned south to bomb the areas around the invasion beaches. Meanwhile, about one hundred and fifty Imperial Navy aircraft winged their way to targets around Manila Bay.

P.I. and his family had no idea the titanic forces about to clash over their home. The kids and Polly got up to make breakfast and await word from P.I. on whether he found them a new place to live. So far as they could tell, the morning in Manila was tense but relatively quiet. A few sentries fired randomly to break the morning stillness. Overhead, small flights of P-40s buzzed back and forth around Manila Bay and its environs, protecting the city from surprise attack.

The distant thrum of their engines reassured those who recognized them as friendly.

For the civilians in the city, there was no sign of what was about to hit them.

Exactly where P.I. was on the 10th remains a mystery. In all likelihood, he remained at Grace Park, working to improve PAL's new home. But one postwar account of what followed places a PAL Beech 18 at the Philippine Air Force training base at Zablan, a place P.I. frequently visited before the war when he instructed Filipino aviation cadets. If P.I. was the pilot who flew the Beech there that day, he ended up in the middle of the Philippine Air Force's first air battle.

Just before noon, the Japanese reached the Manila area. Again, their timing could not have been better. At Del Carmen, the P-35s had just returned from their strafing runs on the Japanese invasion force. Half the squadron suffered mechanical failure and aborted the mission. Mechanics worked furiously on those birds as other men refueled the remaining planes.

Overhead, the weather gave the men on the ground a short reprieve. The Japanese bombers targeting Del Carmen discovered a thick cloud layer obscured their bombing runs. Rather than dropping blindly through the scud, the squadron commander chose to strike their secondary target. They turned and headed for the docks and shipping in Manila Bay while some of their escorting Zeroes dropped down to strafe the field.

That short reprieve ended for the Americans when the Zeroes dropped out of the clouds and caught everyone by surprise. In slashing passes, they raked the P-35s, setting half of them ablaze and leaving most of the others damaged. With so few fighters left, this in itself was a small catastrophe for the Americans.

It was just a prologue to a day of disasters.

At Clark Field, where most of the remaining P-40s sat waiting to scramble, news of the attack on Del Carmen sparked a full-scale intercept. The pilots sprinted to their waiting fighters, some forgetting their sidearms, flight gear, and even their parachutes. By this point, there were more fighter pilots than fighter planes, and arguments broke out as multiple flyers sought to get into the same P-40. In short order, they sorted things out, and soon the bulk of FEAF's remaining fighters lifted from Clark with orders to intercept bombers reported to be heading from Del Carmen to the Philippine capital.

At that moment, three separate formations of Japanese bombers converged on Manila, just as the American fighter patrol over the city ran low on fuel. The pilots throttled back and descended for Nichols Fields to land and refuel. Their replacements began to take off, and the men coming in could see those P-40s lining up on the runway as they made their approach. Right then, the Nichols tower radioed a warning to them. The pilots checked their tails and saw the mass formations coming in above and behind them, the bombers in stately V's while their Zero escorts buzzed around them.

Some of the patrolling P-40s had only ten or fifteen minutes of fuel left. They could have dived out of harm's way and landed at alternate airstrips. Instead, the Americans chose to fight. They turned and poured the coals to their engines. The biggest American air battle since the days of World War I's Western Front had just begun.

In Manila, the air raid siren wailed to life. People fled the streets as constables and soldiers drew their weapons and aimed skyward from corners or intersections. Even cops with .38 revolvers prepared to blaze away at the intruders. Never mind that the Japanese bombers flew at twenty thousand feet that day; the cops opened fire as soon as they came into view.

In the residential district, the Gunn family watched the mass of planes converge. They were little more than dots at first, too far away to figure out who was who. But the Gunns cheered and prayed and watched anyway without thought of seeking shelter.

The morning patrol climbed valiantly after the bombers. As they struggled to gain altitude, the Zero escorts fell out of the sky upon them. A sprawling dogfight erupted and the American formations broke apart. The Japanese pilots held all the advantages—altitude, speed, and significantly more maneuverable planes. They shot up the Americans and drove them away from the bombers. The P-40 pilots, most of whom were in their first air combat battle, stood no chance. Overmatched and outnumbered, they managed to fire a few snap-shots as the Japanese fighters flashed by them.

The Americas fought for their lives, trading altitude for speed. Soon the battle spread across Manila Bay, with the planes duking it out down to city's rooftops. P-40s roared over the spellbound citizens, Zeroes on their tails, their wing cannons spewing flame as the Japanese pilots took their shots.

One by one, the P-40s ran out of fuel. A few ditched in Manila Bay. Others crash landed in nearby fields. A few managed to shake their pursuers and set down at Nichols, where one pilot jumped out of his P-40 while Zeroes strafed the field. Finding no slit trench or safe haven to hunker down in, he sprinted through the melee and dove beneath a building, where he used his steel helmet to start digging a foxhole. A moment later, another man joined him.

As the morning patrol was driven to ground, the Clark Field P-40s waded into the fray. Once again the Zeroes jumped them long before they reached the bombers. These Japanese pilots from the Tainan and Third Air Groups could be considered among the best-trained military aviators of World War II. They'd flown hundreds of hours in their Zero fighters and emerged from the China campaign as blooded veterans. The green Americans were easy prey, and the P-40s began to burn. They fell out of the sky trailing long black tongues of smoke, an occasional parachute blossoming in their wake.

Some of the American pilots suffered catastrophic mechanical failure at the worst possible moment. Just as pilot Ed Dyess was about to join the fray, he test fired his six .50-caliber machine guns. They refused to work. Despite every procedure, he couldn't get them functional. Frustrated and furious, he broke for home, out of the fight claiming so many of his brother aviators.

As the Zeroes and P-40s skirmished, three formations of twenty-seven bombers each began their attack runs. The First Kokutai's G3M Nell's—the same unit that had bombed Nichols the night before last—walked their bombs through Cavite Naval Yard. Their bombardiers proved even more skillful in daylight than they had in their earlier nocturnal attack. Their bombs blew apart the docks and maintenance facilities. Direct hits destroyed the submarine *Sealion* and another vessel. The base power plant exploded in flames. Warehouses, barracks, and the hospital took direct hits. The Japanese smothered the base with bombs, sparking dozens of fires that raged out of control and spread so quickly that dozens were trapped by the inferno. The Asiatic Fleet's entire supply of torpedoes went up in a tremendous serious of blasts that shook the city and could be felt as far away as Nielson Airport.

All the while, the base's paltry defense of nine three-inch anti-aircraft guns fired gamely at the bombers. But their weapons lacked range and the black puffs of their exploding shells erupted thousands of feet beneath the bellies of the Japanese Nells.

In a single, expertly executed attack, the Japanese destroyed the most important American naval base in southeast Asia. Their bombers did not suffer a scratch.

While Cavite burned, twenty-seven more bombers blasted the Manila docks and dropped their ordnance on the many ships in the bay. One cargo vessel took a direct hit and began belching smoke. The docks burned brightly as Manilans quailed under the onslaught.

The third bomber group, also twenty-seven strong, reached

Nichols Field while Zeroes raked the runway with cannon and machine-gun fire. As a long train of bombs fell on the base, two recklessly brave P-40 pilots tried to get aloft. A bomb exploded in front of one, and the pilot struck the crater. His fighter ground looped, spinning around before erupting in flames. The other pilot barely made it into the air before Japanese fire killed him.

Grant Mahony, the pilot who'd discovered the Japanese invasion force that morning, had just taken off from Nichols to replace the standing patrol. He and his flight of P-40s found themselves swamped by Zeroes less than two thousand feet over the field. The Japanese shot up or shot down the entire flight. Only Mahony and two other pilots successfully landed their planes. One of Mahony's comrades fled across Manila Bay trailing a Zero. He was shot down by the Cavite antiaircraft gunners. He bailed out and ended up in the water, alive but furious to have been downed by his own side.

In a matter of minutes, the Japanese blasted Nichols Field with more than three hundred and fifty bombs. They fell among the hangars and barracks and burned the post exchange. They pockmarked the runway with craters and set the fuel storage tanks afire. Around the field, B-18 bombers and P-40s caught on the ground burned furiously. The main American fighter base was all but destroyed.

In the middle of the chaotic scene, a single plane, hugging the treetops, sped over Grace Park and then Fort McKinley from west to east. Looking like a high-winged, stubby barrel, the plane turned for Nichols Field.

Filipino and American soldiers rose from the drainage ditches alongside Highway 54 and poured small-arms fire at the aircraft. Machine guns joined the fusillade, and bullets began to hit home. The pilot rocked his wings, flashed his landing lights, but nobody on the ground saw the American stars on his fuselage and wings. A man bailed out; his parachute blossomed. The troops on the ground showed no mercy. They poured fire into the helpless American dangling beneath his silk canopy. The aircraft was not a Zero, or a P-40, but a slow, ungainly Curtiss O-52 "Owl" designed to spot artillery fire for the Army.

To the south and west of Nichols Field, a formation of Zeroes descended on the Philippine Army Air Corps base at Zablan while local village church bells tolled a warning. They found the field full of grounded aircraft. One of P.I.'s Filipino friends, Captain Jesus "Jess" Villamor, saw the Zeroes sweeping down on the helpless planes and ran to his own ancient, hand-me-down P-26 Peashooter. He sprinted for the low-winged, early 1930s fighter as the Japanese machine gunned anything that moved. Columns of dirt kicked up around Villamor as bullets tore into ground. A gray Zero sped overhead. The Filipino pilot dove behind a truck as more Zeroes came in from every compass point. Frantic ground crews raced to the six alert fighters, prepping them for takeoff as other pilots followed Villamor out into the maelstrom in a desperate bid to get airborne.

Bombers parked along the strip began to explode in flames as the Japanese found their targets. The Philippine Air Line Beech 18 attracted at least one Zero pilot's attention. A burst of gunfire studded its aluminum skin with bullets. If P. I. Gunn was at Zablan that day, it was the first time he came under direct fire. Ironic that it happened while he wore civilian clothes after a twenty-year career in the Navy.

Two of Villamor's Peashooters blew up nearby as his ground crew pulled the chocks from his plane's spatted wheels. His stubby, open cockpit fighter rushed forward onto the runway, three other Boeings trailing behind him. Somehow, Villamor's P-26 bounded aloft—and into the middle of the strafing Japanese planes.

Taught to fly by both Bill Bradford, one of the old PATCO pilots, and P.I., Villamor was a natural pilot, the best in the Philippine Air Corps. A Zero swung behind him, guns blazing. The P-26 hugged the ground, Villamor dodging trees and even flying under high-tension power lines to escape. He shook one attacker off that way, but another turned for him. He stood little chance—the Zero was a hundred and fifty miles an hour faster than his decrepit monoplane. They were also bettered armed, with two cannon and two machine guns. Villamor's P-26 possessed only a pair of .30-caliber light machine guns.

As the Zero pressed in for the kill, Villamor suddenly executed a half loop and reversed course, coming at the Japanese pilot in a head-on pass. Villamor's bullets found their mark, and miraculously the plane's fuel tanks detonated. Debris rained down into Marikina Valley.

When he returned to Zablan, the Japanese were gone. Smoke coiled over the field, and the runway was a mess. Wrecked training planes, bombers, and fighters burned and smoldered all around the field. The PAL Beech 18, though damaged, was still flyable. Much of the Philippine Air Corps' meager fighting power lay in ruins after that one attack.

Villamor survived the day to become the first Philippine national hero of World War II. In the months to come, he and P.I. were fated to cross paths and embark on a reckless adventure behind Japanese lines.

In Manila, the citizens who dared emerge from cover watched the stately parade of Japanese bombers slowly disappear to the north as fires raged to the east, south, and west, filling the sky with smoke. Cavite lay in ruins, burned to the ground by the firestorm that would rage for days after the attack. Few buildings stood unscathed at Nichols, and the fighter squadron at Del Carmen was strafed nearly out of existence. Flames smothered the Manila docks—fire crews spent hours battling the blazes to get them under control—and enough damage was done to the shipping in the Bay that any merchant ship that could flee promptly did so in the ensuing days.

The Japanese lost a handful of Zeroes and a couple of bombers.

When the Americans took stock that evening, they found only twenty-two P-40s left out of almost a hundred available two mornings before. The Japanese destroyed four-fifths of the American interceptors in two aerial engagements and three days of war. Six more P-40s could be repaired along with a couple of P-35s, but the days of trying to defend Manila against incoming bombers were over. General Brereton ordered that the remaining P-40s avoid aerial combat. They would be used from this point forward as reconnaissance aircraft and to attack Japanese shipping.

It was an unmitigated disaster, the worst in the history of the United States Air Force. Yet, in the days that followed, reporter Clark Lee and others penned stories of great victories off Vigan and Aparri. Their columns circulated throughout the Philippines and the United States, and headlines trumpeted the complete destruction of the Japanese invasion fleet.

While Villamor became the first Filipino war hero, Lt. Colin Kelly became America's first great air hero. A B-17 pilot assigned to bomb the Japanese that day, Kelly's crew reported they'd bombed and sunk the Imperial Navy's battleship *Haruna*. After turning for home, Kelly's B-17 ran into a flight of Zeroes and was badly shot up. With several crewmen dead or wounded and the plane mortally damaged, Kelly stayed at the controls and ordered everyone else to bail out. He held the bomber on course as the last man jumped from the crippled Fort. A moment later, it exploded and killed Kelly instantly.

The destruction of a Japanese battleship, along with Kelly's selflessness, made front-page news across the United States. Schools were later named in his honor, and for days his exploits were told and retold over the radio.

Radio Manila followed suit. MacArthur had been very unhappy with Don Bell's riveting—and uncensored—account of the night raid, and soon after he took steps to control the media better. The news broadcasts filled the airwaves with stories of heroism, ships destroyed, and rugged air battles in defense of the capital. But nowhere did the news outlets report FEAF's true state.

The propaganda only went so far in convincing the citizens of Manila that all was well. Further reports talked of the Japanese getting ashore at both Vigan and Aparri If the fleet was wiped out like MacArthur's communiqué's claimed, how did they get ashore?

In any case, that meant enemy troops lurked in the jungle only a hundred and sixty miles from the capital. In the days that followed, the radio reports spoke of desperate holding actions fought by the Filamerican Army as the Japanese advanced southward. The news always put the best spin on the situation, but those who cared to read between the lines sensed the military was not telling the truth. Tension rose and the city became even more unsettled as nobody knew what was really going on. They just knew the full story was not being told. In the absence of truth, rumors flourished even more. Scary tales began to circulate of respected Japanese shopkeepers suddenly appearing in their small Filipino villages dressed as officers in the Imperial Army. Fifth columnists working with them took over these barrios and hamlets, spreading fear like a contaminant. In response, the military and civilian law enforcement went door-to-door, detaining all Japanese in Manila and sending them to a temporary holding camp at one of the city's stadiums. Several thousand ultimately ended up in custody.

Seeing their neighbors hauled away did nothing to ease the uncertainty of the situation. Fires raged in the ruins of the military bases around the city long into the night. Whispered stories of 20,000 paratroopers landing east of Clark Field circulated, as did rumors of summary executions of captured spies. That night at Nielson, a Filipino was caught waving a flashlight in the darkness toward a field from which a flare had just been fired. Captured by infuriated Filipino troops, the man at first claimed only to be looking for a wayward animal. According to Allison Ind, one of FEAF's intelligence officers, the man was dragged off and killed.

Would the Japanese reach Manila? Were MacArthur's troops making a stand or driving them back? What would happen if they did break through and pour into the capital? The last capital the Imperial Army had captured was Nanking in late 1937. Everyone knew how that turned out. The Japanese had murdered three hundred thousand Chinese civilians in acts of such depraved violence that they were unrivaled in modern history. The Pearl of the Orient now lay within that army's grasp. In the darkness that evening of December 10, 1941, fear and doubt dominated the mood in Manila as its citizens braced to meet their fate.

10

The Middle-Aged Recruit

December 11, 1941
Early Morning

The disaster of December 10 convinced P.I. that Manila was not safe for his family. With less than two dozen P-40s still flyable, FEAF could not defend the city. The paltry number of antiaircraft guns available to the Army couldn't even reach the bombers. Should the Japanese decide to terror-bomb the capital, as they had in China, thousands would perish.

P.I. sat down and talked the situation over with Dan Stickle, his maintenance chief. Friends for almost eight years, they first met in San Diego shortly after Dan joined the Navy as an eighteen-year-old straight out of high school. P.I. recognized great potential in the Iowan and took him under his wing. He later pulled some strings to get Dan a slot at an engine overhaul school at Pearl Harbor when their unit moved to Hawaii. That yearlong school initiated a long series of engineering courses for Dan that fed his passion for the nuts and bolts of aviation. When he left the Navy in 1939, P.I. hired him full time at K-T Flying Service. And in 1940, he joined P.I. at Philippine Air Lines with the official title of superintendent of maintenance. At twenty-four, it was the opportunity of a lifetime.

Dan considered P.I. more than just his employer. P.I. was a friend and mentor, a man he saw as driven, intelligent, and serious. After years of being at his side, including in some very remote and dangerous areas of the Philippines, he also described him in 1958 as a "man-killer." P.I. would do whatever it took to protect himself and those he loved.

Now, the two men faced the biggest challenge of their lives. The Japanese were on the island, pushing south. Where would Dan's wife, Marie, and the Gunn family be the safest? They talked over alternatives, long-term and temporary. None of them looked good. Staying in the city posed plenty of risks. Getting their loved ones to an outlying province might be borrowing trouble as well, what with all the reports of fifth columnists, spies, and Japanese paratroops landing all over the place. Even trying to fly the families out of the Philippines would be extremely dangerous. At least one Japanese aircraft carrier lurked somewhere around the Southern Islands, its planes bombing targets around Davao. To fly south meant that they would run a gauntlet of Zeroes at the start of their escape, plus roll the dice in Mindanao and hope they would not be attacked there as they flew in to refuel. From there, they could head to the Dutch East Indies and Australia.

That would be their absolute last resort. They decided that if it looked as if Luzon would be overrun, they would have no other choice. Better the risks of a flight through Japanese-controlled airspace than certain death or capture on the ground.

In the meantime, Dan learned the Red Cross recently set up an evacuation center in a province south of Manila. If the situation deteriorated in Manila, sending the families there made sense until they could get them out.

As they talked over options, sometime before 0800 word reached the PAL office that General Brereton wanted to see P.I. and his other pilots. He and Dan put their discussion on temporary hold to go see the general. Together with Harold Slingsby and Louis

Connelly, they drove over to Nielson Field and reported in at FEAF Headquarters.

There, they were summarily told that all civilian aircraft were to be taken over at once by Far East Air Force. The planes would be organized into a ferry and transport service for MacArthur.

That included PAL's two bright red Beech 18s. Elsewhere, teams of Army Air Force personnel went off in search of anything with wings that could fly. That meant the Staggerwing would be returned from Paracale and pressed into military service, too.

So much for their last escape option.

The civilian pilots were given a choice. PAL's American aviators could volunteer and serve as ferry crews, in which case they would be commissioned as officers in the Army Air Force, or they could stay in the city as civilians and fend for themselves, though their employer would have no aircraft and no ability to function. PAL's Filipino pilots were cut out completely; FEAF did not want them. Their flying days were over, at least for the duration of the war.

They had no time to think it over. The Army Air Force planned to use the Beech 18s before lunch.

All three Americans volunteered. Dan Stickle also ended up in uniform again, this time as a maintenance officer. He, Slingsby, and Connelly received commissions as first lieutenants. P.I. became a captain. Two months after his forty-second birthday, P.I. would wear his nation's uniform for a second time.

Except there were no uniforms to wear. They would need to go for days, perhaps weeks, without official gear, which meant if P.I. or any of his PAL aviators fell into enemy hands, the Japanese would consider them spies and treat them as such. Treated with a bullet, or a bayonet.

They received their first mission that morning and undertook it less than an hour and a half after being sworn into the Army Air Force. With the Nineteenth Bomb Group's main base at Clark Field indefensible with so few P-40s remaining, the outfit's B-17s would have to operate out of the Del Monte pineapple plantation on a permanent basis. Few facilities existed there, and the primitive base lacked ground personnel. FEAF ordered P.I. to take the two Beech 18s to Clark Field, pick up a full load of mechanic and other vital maintainers, and bring them to Del Monte.

The Japanese could be back at any moment, which lent even more urgency to the mission. It also meant P.I. did not have the time to repaint PAL's bright red airliners. Besides, where would they find the paint? They could be caught on the ground at Clark, or in the air as the next raid arrived, its escorting Zero pilots eager for more aerial kills. A Beech 18 would be easy meat. Being airliners, they were not fitted with any military equipment—no armor plating, no defensive guns, and no self-sealing fuel tanks designed to absorb bullet strikes without exploding. In fact, when P.I. took delivery of the two 18s, he modified them in the PAL hangar with additional wing tanks to extend their range. Both planes were little more than flying fuel cells with eight seats.

At least he, Slingsby, and Connelly would have control of the aircraft. Better that than being kicked to the curb, stripped of their planes and left to whatever fate awaited everyone else in Manila. Once dismissed at FEAF HQ, they departed Nielson for their cemetery hideaway and went straight for the aircraft to preflight them for the mission.

P.I. didn't deliberate long on who would fly the second aircraft. Slingsby was the most experienced pilot he had. He spent years flying in California, working as an aerial photographer, a charter pilot for the San Francisco elite, and as a relief pilot running supplies to trapped civilians during flood season around Sacramento. His dad had started one of the first airlines in the state.

Connelly was thirty-two and only received his commercial air transport license in 1939. Prior to that, he made his living as an aerial surveyor and photographer in Texas before taking a job as the assistant station manager for Braniff Airways at Stinson Field in San Antonio. His range of experiences made him a versatile employee, but for this run P.I. needed his best pilot.

Slingsby took the other Beech. Together, they walked out to the waiting planes. They were graceful, elegant aircraft, more functional looking than the rakish Staggerwing. Capable of carrying six passengers, a flight attendant, and two pilots, they could carry more people than anything else in the Philippines outside of the AAF's heavy bombers. At least one of the PAL Beech 18s included a tiny bathroom accessed through a hatch-like door in the back of the cabin. The toilet looked like a stainless steel soup pot with a flip-top lid. Once, while flying with their father and a few PAL passengers, Nath and Paul took turns dropping Coke bottles into it. When flushed, it simply opened a small hole in the bottom of the fuselage and drained into the sky below. When a bottle fell through the hole, it shrieked as soon as the slipstream caught it. The boys thought that hysterical—until the passengers began to panic at all the odd noises emanating from the back of the aircraft. When P.I. discovered what they were doing, he took them aside and chewed them out. "You could kill somebody on the ground with one of those bottles, boys. Don't ever do that again."

In the cockpit, P.I. went through the preflight routine with practiced speed. The PAL mechanics rotated the props ten times each by hand, an arduous task done to pump out any oil gathered at the bottom of the cylinders. If a pilot started the aircraft before this had been done, he risked hydraulic lock and damage to the engines. P.I. watched the mechanics work, counting the prop revolutions to double-check that all the cylinders were cycled. They were ready for flight. P.I. prepared to start the two radial engines housed in smooth-cowled mounts flared into each wing. He primed the engines, which took seven strokes of the pump, then set both throttles to full open, the fuel mixture to rich, and the props to fine pitch.

He checked the magnetos to make sure they were on before flipping a switch on the instrument panel that read "RH Engine."

First mission in USAAF service. From a Chinese cemetery.

He pushed the starter button. The right engine whined as the two-bladed prop turned over. By the fifth revolution, the engine coughed and gasped. It spewed a plume of thick black smoke out the exhaust stack. A moment later, it began running roughly. These engines were famous for that when cold, and it took several minutes for them to warm up and smooth out. In the meantime, P.I. kept it under a thousand RPMs, lest he overstress it.

He went through the same procedure with the left engine until it belched smoke and stuttered to life. After it warmed up, he eased off the toe brakes on the rudder pedals and let the Beech inch forward down the makeshift taxiway through the cemetery. Taxiing an 18 required considerable skill, as the throttles had to be constantly adjusted. A good Beech pilot rocked his wrist on the throttles, playing them like a virtuoso to make those minute adjustments to keep the aircraft moving in a straight line. He swung onto the runway, went through the final run-up to test the magnetos. Good to go.

He locked the tailwheel in place and opened the throttles, leading with the left one and the right one coming up slightly behind to countertorque. The engines bellowed as the sudden rush of fuel poured into the carburetors. At fifty miles an hour, the tail lifted. As soon as it did, the Beech's nose wanted to drift left. The 18 did not have counterrotating propellers, meaning both sets turned in the same direction, which created gyroscopic procession that pulled the aircraft to the left. Lesser pilots sometimes overcorrected and ground looped their Beech 18s, but Pappy fed in just enough right rudder and right aileron to compensate.

P.I. felt the Beech want to drift left again. With his right hand on the control wheel, he eased his wrist clockwise just a hair more to feed in a bit more aileron. That did the trick.

He sped past the broken memorials and mausoleums of wealthy Chinese merchants until the wheels slipped their earthly bonds. Hardly was air beneath them when P.I. retracted the landing gear. The wheels tucked into their wells beneath the wings and the Beech quickly gained speed. It was 10:05 that morning. P.I. had been a captain for less than an hour and a half.

The run to Clark Field took only a few minutes. P.I. stayed as close to the treetops as he could, the other 18 with him all the way. If they were going to fly through skies controlled by the Japanese, they would do it on the deck to minimize their chances of being seen. P.I. reasoned the lower to the ground, the smaller the shadow they presented for somebody above them to detect.

They reached Clark Field and swung into the pattern. Fires still blazed around the base. Smashed and burned aircraft littered the area, and the main hangar's roof was punctured with multiple bomb hits. They could see through the holes, and the concrete floor inside looked cratered and torn. Earlier in the day, another P-40 crashed right through a B-17 while trying to get aloft. Miraculously, the pilot walked away, though the accident cost FEAF two more aircraft.

The dead still lay where they fell, decomposing among the living.

The 18s touched down on the cratered, dusty runway. P.I. intended to spend as little time on the ground as possible, so it is unlikely that he even left the cockpit. If he did, the look on the faces of those still alive at Clark surely disturbed him. They were dazed, shocked men still traumatized by the December 8 attack. Some shuffled like zombies, going through their assigned tasks relying solely on muscle memories. The place looked and felt like defeat.

Engines running, feet on the brakes, the two 18s waited for the vital personnel to jump aboard before throttling up again and racing for the comparative safety of the sky.

Del Monte lay over five hundred miles to the south. How far could the Japanese fighters fly from Formosa? P.I. didn't know. Nobody had any idea where the Japanese aircraft carrier was, either. He would be flying out of the operational range of one group of Japanese fighters and into another.

The two Beech 18s flew through the afternoon and into the gathering dusk. Once aloft, the aircraft were easy to fly when properly trimmed, though they handled differently in the humid tropical air than they did Stateside. Cruising at just under 150 miles an hour, the flight to Del Monte took around three and a half hours.

They arrived safely in the afternoon, passing over the Del Monte Plantation's country club and golf course before picking out the airfield a few miles away, a gigantic pasture marked with a white sheet in each corner. The ground was hard, absorbent sod covered with grass that a couple of former farm kids in uniform kept cut with a tractor and a towed mower. They wouldn't let any other AAF personnel do the job unless they'd also been raised on a farm. The base sat in a valley ringed by jungle-covered mountains with only the barest of roads to service it.

To one side of the pasture stood an array of tents. These belonged to the Fifth Airbase Squadron, which arrived at Del Monte at the beginning of December to establish this field and turn it into something heavy bombers could use. Col. Ray T. Elsmore commanded the base and oversaw its development. Though he had little equipment, no facilities, spare parts, or even tools, he worked wonders with what his men scrounged from the local area. The place possessed a totally different vibe from Clark Field. Here, the men worked round the clock to build out the base, maintain the B-17s, and keep them camouflaged. Although the Japanese had bombed Davao on December 8, so far they had yet to discover this place. Elsmore's men went to great lengths to ensure that they stayed hidden. The B-17s scattered around the airfield were carefully covered with broad coconut tree leaves that his men had procured some fifteen miles away, then hauled to the strip's dispersal area via a winding mountain road. It took ten truckloads to cover one B-17.

Beneath the coconut camouflage, the few mechanics already at the base worked alongside the flight crews to service and repair their B-17s. Some of the Forts looked like spaghetti strainers, their fuselages and wings torn and riddled with bullet holes. P.I. watched the maintainers patching those holes with whatever aluminum could be scrounged up.

Elsmore's troops dug twelve-by-twelve bomb shelters buttressed with timber and covered with thick layers of earth all around the field. Slit trenches and shallow foxholes abounded, as did .50-caliber antiaircraft machine gun nests. The latter would be useless against all but low-flying strafing Zeroes, but no other weapons reached the area before the war started.

Elsmore's men made a point to meet every incoming aircrew with hot chow and coffee. P.I. and Slingsby were famished—they had been going nonstop since 0830—so the grub was appreciated. The gesture stood in stark contrast to the chaos at Clark Field, where the incoming fighter pilots had to search for food on their own after December 8. Few hot meals had been eaten there since.

Elsmore ran a tight and dedicated organization. Though ill-equipped and lacking personnel to properly maintain the B-17s on hand, his men performed minor miracles every day. Largely thanks to them, sixteen bombers were ready to hit the Japanese come first light on December 12.

While P.I. and Slingsby ate, the ground crews refueled the two Beech 18s from fifty-five-gallon drums. Since the engines consumed about a quart of oil an hour, other men topped off those reservoirs as well. Stockpiles of aviation fuel and oil reached Del Monte just after the war started. Without that shipment, the whole operation would have been for nothing, and Elsmore would have been marooned in the middle of an island best known for headhunters and Muslim uprisings.

P.I. and Slingsby were back in the air before sunset, bound for Grace Park. This time, they navigated over water and through the Central Philippines with part of the trip likely in darkness, though P.I. knew the area so well he didn't require maps. He simply picked a heading and skimmed the wave tops for hours on end. When they reached Cebu, they climbed up over the trees, still staying low as they passed over blacked out towns and cities. Everyone feared the Japanese, not knowing where or when the next air raid would hit.

They reached Luzon, skirted the coast, and came inland over Zablan Field before finally making it back to Grace Park late that evening. After the 18s were set down in the cemetery and tucked away safely in their revetments, P.I. told the PAL ground crew to prep both aircraft for another run tomorrow. To everyone's surprise, the Japanese made no appearance over Luzon that day or evening. It seemed like this was becoming a pattern: one day of maximum effort strikes followed by a quiet day. If the pattern held, the Americans could count on getting hammered on the twelfth, probably around lunchtime.

Unknown to P.I., the FEAF staff had decided that no civilian aircraft should operate north of Batangas Field. Southeast of Manila, it served as the chief fighter and bomber base for the Philippine Army Air Corps. Apparently, FEAF's staff officers planned to base its small transport force at Batangas. Exactly why they made this call is unknown, but it might have been an attempt to minimize the chances of another friendly fire incident like the ones that plagued FEAF since the war's outbreak. The Grace Park strip would be used only long enough until Batangas was ready to take them.

Exhausted after the thousand-mile round trip, P.I. had no energy left to drive out to see his family. Besides, headquarters had already assigned them morning missions, and a myriad of details needed his attention. In such circumstances, P.I. catnapped for twenty or thirty minutes at a time, then returned to work.

This wasn't "volunteering" for ferry duty, as they were told at FEAF HQ. Ferrying meant shuttling an airplane from one base to another to leave it for others to take into combat. Ferry pilots were the ultimate rear-area aviators. Problem was, in the Philippines there was no rear area.

No. Not ferry pilots. Smugglers. They'd be sneaking around, hugging the ground for the foreseeable future carrying whatever needed to be carried just like aerial bootleggers. In such world-upturned circumstances, the serious, meticulous senior manager in P.I. would only get men killed. Playing it safe and by the book was out. That part of P.I. Gunn began to vanish that night.

Beneath the manager cultivated in the Philippines lay the Navy chief he once was. A little deeper down resided the Arkansas outlaw, the kid who could outrun and outsmart the local sheriff to deliver whatever needed delivering, no questions asked.

In the days to come, he would have to do whatever was necessary to stay alive. He would tap his long-dormant inner outlaw, except this time instead of midnight runs between Arkansas counties, he would run the gauntlet of a Japanese-dominated Philippine archipelago.

11

Outlaw Son of a Lawman

Summer 1918
Cleburne County, Arkansas, the Foothills of the Ozark Mountains

The moon shone across the garden and cast shadows through the yard as P.I. Gunn picked his way through the pecan trees toward the family barn. Since he was dressed in overalls and a plain shirt, work shoes, and a long-billed cap he'd worn for years, anyone who saw him would know he was not bound for a social event that night.

He crept past a row of stumps and didn't even give them a glance. To do so would have just aroused fury in him again, and he needed to be on an even keel. Five years ago, his great-uncle John came to visit the farm. A crotchety old goat, he quickly wore out his welcome with P.I. with his never-ending litany of insults toward him and his brother Charley. Nothing they could do was right, and his mom never stood up to him.

One day, the family came home to discover Uncle John had cut down their cherry trees. As they stood in silent shock, he coarsely explained the trees were taking away moisture from the rest of the garden. Never mind that the Gunn family lived on a razor's edge and those trees produced food for them. Cherries were precious treats for them in the summertime.

P.I.'s mom chose to say nothing, concealing her hurt and outrage to spare her uncle's feelings. Charley and their sister, Jewell, followed their mom's cue and held their tongues as well. But not the youngest of the family. P.I., all of twelve at the time, laid into Uncle John with pure fury, shouting at him and calling him a "stupid fool." The outburst ran the codger off. He packed amid a torrent of insults to P.I. personally and the younger generations in general. He never returned.

Good riddance.

P.I. reached the side of the barn, where not so many years back he took to drawing pictures of boats, airplanes, and cars on its sun-baked boards. The harsh winter weather here in the Ozarks long since erased those images, along with the ones he sketched on the nearby fences, but he still liked to sketch at night as he lay in bed after long days of work.

He slipped around the corner, where he found the barn doors standing open, his most treasured possession tucked inside. For the past several years, he worked as the assistant to the only auto mechanic in Quitman. He started as a young teenager, handing his boss wrenches as he peered over his shoulder to learn the mysteries of internal combustion engines. Those days in the shop unlocked his natural mechanical genius. Engines spoke to him in a language few understood in 1918 hillbilly country. Now that a few car dealerships operated in the county seat of Heber Springs, the more prosperous merchants and farmers in Cleburne County began trading their old carriages for the joys of the horseless carriage.

P.I. could never afford one, but he did have free rein over the wrecks dragged off the wagon-rutted dusty roads around the county and delivered to the mechanic's shop. The ones beyond repair collected in what could have been one of the first junkyards in northeastern Arkansas.

After hours, P.I. picked through the wrecks, cannibalizing them to slowly build his own ride. Then he tinkered with it, modifying the engine with some creative ideas he conceived on his own. The result was the fastest jalopy in town. P.I. was a speed demon before the era of rat rods and T-buckets.

Tonight, his new employer counted on that speed and his driving skill.

He fired his car up and quickly pulled out of the barn to head for town. In this period of his life, P.I. was not known by his initials. Nor did anyone call him Paul. His family called him Irvin, while the folks around the county had nicknamed him "Bill," thanks to the trademark hat he wore. His mother hated that and refused to allow nicknames to be used in her presence.

He drove through the darkened Ozark foothills along primitive country lanes until he came to Bee Branch Road. He turned south, the jalopy gliding past stands of pines and rolling farms whose whitewashed houses were dimly illuminated by the moonlight. Fireflies capered in the woods, their yellow-green lights radiating like a thousand tiny lanterns. Cows mooed. Horses neighed. Crickets sang their night songs.

He hated this place. To his marrow, he hated it.

The jalopy rolled down a gentle slope into a swale before the road climbed a long, shallow grade to a crest that P.I. knew all too well. Standing against the velvet sky, he could see the Methodist church steeple rising above the hilltop. The belfry still housed a bell, which the minister rang every Sunday and New Year's Eve. He also rang it before funerals.

Funerals. The bell tolled the day they buried his father on that hill in the cemetery out behind the little whitewashed church. As the car climbed the grade, P.I. could see the outline of the Spanish oak in whose shadow his father had been laid to rest. He could pick out his rough-hewn headstone right at the edge of the cemetery only a few feet from the road.

Every single time he went into town, he passed that reminder of tragedy and loss.

The car pulled even with the headstone. P.I. was seven years old when they gunned down his father and burned the family's store. Quitman prided itself on being the most erudite and education-oriented town in Northern Arkansas, but how erudite could a place be when the biggest social event of the fall was the slaughtering of the hogs?

Truth was, the spirit of the frontier still imbued the place. It was a rough-and-tumble town, and those who got ahead often did so with fists and guns at the ready. Quitman was just a hamlet, really. A few blocks of shops surrounded by a corona of hardscrabble farms and little else. The town coffers could not afford a constabulary, so volunteers served as marshals to keep the peace. Villages all over Arkansas functioned that way at the turn of the century, and there was plenty of hard-drinking riff-raff out there willing to confront those volunteers.

Years later, Jewell Gunn's recollections of Quitman glossed over many bad and tragic moments. Of her father, she only wrote that he had died after a long illness. The rest of the family became keepers of the truth.

Their dad was a jack-of-all-trades type: a cattleman, a farmer, a shopkeeper. A lawman. Every season, he climbed atop his horse and drove his herd to Little Rock to sell them at market. If the price for meat was better in St. Louis, he drove them to Compton, where they were prodded into Missouri Pacific boxcars and shipped north by rail. During harvest season, he and the rest of the family took to their fields, working from dawn 'til dusk to get the crops in. Between those two rushes, he owned a small general store in town.

Somehow, Nathanial Hezakiah Gunn crossed paths with a gang of cold blooded killers. In retaliation to whatever transpired between them, they set the Gunn family store afire and murdered Nathanial in the street.

P.I. was two months shy of his seventh birthday when the knock came at the farmhouse door.

The car reached the crest of the hill. To his right stood the church of his youth. He could almost see the reed organ inside, the three banks of pews arranged so as to segregate the sexes. Men sat on the left, women on the right. Families in the middle. They even entered from their respective sides. In the moonlight, P.I. could see the door his mother used every Sunday along with the other unattached women of the community.

Not long after his dad died, they told him to come to Jesus in that church. The preacher promised to save his soul. Not even ten, he searched for answers. Saved for what? What did that even mean? If his soul was saved, P.I. never felt it. Religion was a Sunday ritual for him out of requirement, not out of piety.

In the years since the preacher's promise, he knew only hardship, trial, and pain. Life had beaten the Holy Spirit out of him long before he grew to be a man.

He passed the church and the road sloped into downtown Quitman. He came to the intersection with the main drag. Across the street and a few blocks beyond was the village park, complete with a bandstand. Aside from hog-slaughtering day, the Fourth of July picnic was the social event of the year in Quitman, a day when everyone gathered in the park to listen to music and drink lemonade the service groups sold from booths. They held games and contests, races for prizes, and crazy tests of manly prowess.

P.I. loved those contests, and one of his best days took place out there, just beyond the bandstand. He and his family went to the picnic late that year after spending all day in their fields. When the crowd in the park spotted P.I., they began chanting, "Bill! Bill! Bill!" while pointing at a greased pole dangling from a scaffold. It swayed a few feet off the ground, tied to the scaffold by a rope. On top of the pole, somebody had nailed a five-dollar note. All day long, the farmers and roller mill workers eyed that money. To the men laboring to grind wheat into flour at the mill, it represented over a week's wages. To the farmers, it was an even larger sum.

Though many tried, nobody was able to climb the pole and bag the cash. Now, in front of most of the townsfolk, P.I. gave it a try. His mother and sister Jewell looked on in utter horror as he scaled the log and got coated with grease. To them, the spectacle seemed distasteful and demeaning. P.I. wouldn't quit; his family needed that money more than he needed his dignity. He slipped and fell time and again, but the crowd only egged him on.

That five dollars was more than he made in a month shining shoes at the local barbershop, the job he worked before the mechanic opened his shop in town. Exhausted and filthy, he launched himself at the pole one more time. Sheer pluck propelled him to the top long enough to snatch the five-dollar bill. He slid down the pole to rousing cheers.

The feat made him the hero of the picnic. To everyone but his mom and sister, anyway. Later that night when they returned to the farm, he gave the money to his mother and asked her to use it for canning material so they could have blackberry jam that winter.

In the moonlight, as P.I. stared across the small downtown at the bandstand, that day seemed like forever ago. Now, if he were to ever achieve escape velocity and get out of this dead-end place, he knew he would have to take chances.

He turned left and motored through downtown Quitman. Past the post office, the barbershop he'd started working at before his eleventh birthday. He made five cents a shine back then, and some Saturdays he came home with a dollar in nickels. He turned almost all the cash over to his mother to help keep the family afloat.

A few blocks later, he passed the Baptist church and turned off into the countryside for the rendezvous. Men waited for him in the darkness, eager to carry out their night's work.

He found them without much trouble, parked, and jumped out to help load the jalopy. A shadowy figure in the Cleburne County underworld known only as Mr. Miller controlled the moonshine stills around Quitman. Cleburne was a dry county, as was White County to the east. Running 'shine had been going on for decades, long before Prohibition practically made it a respectable profession.

P.I. and the other minions loaded boxes of bottled hooch into the back of his car. For this, he made thirty bucks a run. The men in the roller mill down the road earned seventy-five cents a day working from seven in the morning 'til sunset. If he took a job there, he would never be able to set his mother up and get out of town.

This was his last shot to earn the cash he needed. He was almost there, too. This would be his thirteenth midnight run—and his last. He planned to pocket that last thirty bucks, turn over the majority of his roll of cash to his mother, then use the rest as a stake somewhere well beyond the Ozarks.

The last of the boxes loaded, P.I. climbed back into the driver's seat and drove back to the main road. A left turn would take him back into Quitman. A right turn would take him east for Searcy, the White County seat.

Who was waiting for him in Searcy will never be known, but there is evidence he was working for his brother-in-law, Haz Owen. His twenty-year-old sister, Jewell, had recently married Haz and moved in with him in Searcy. On the surface, Haz Owen was a respected businessman and member of the community. He traded and sold mules, owned sale barns around the state, and was a devoted husband to Jewell. Well liked and shrewd, he would eventually control an enormous empire that shipped mules all over the world.

He also secretly owned the Magnolia Hotel, Searcy's most successful underground drinking establishment. And brothel.

The Magnolia received its liquor from the stills up around Quitman. The supplies came in surreptitiously and almost always at night. The hotel itself seemed innocent enough, but for the travelers and men in the know, its back rooms harbored all manner of sins and entertainment. Keeping it going even though there was a Bible college in town that dominated local politics was always challenging for Haz, but Jewell's arrival in Searcy made it doubly so. She joined the local Methodist congregation and quickly rallied the married ladies behind a noisy temperance campaign.

She had no idea she was campaigning against her husband.

Chances were P.I. went to Haz looking for work earlier that year. He had already impressed Mr. Miller and the other 'shiners in the area with his mechanical abilities. They learned to trust the lanky, ambitious boy with the piercing blue eyes and a work ethic second to none. He became their go-to mechanic whenever one of their rum-running rigs broke down.

Now, with the Methodists putting pressure on the sheriff of White County, these midnight runs were getting increasingly dangerous. P.I.'s jalopy could outrun anything in the area. That speed combined with his driving skill made him a perfect addition to Haz Owen's underground business.

P.I. took the work because he needed to know his mother would be okay after he left town. Already he had tried to leave Quitman twice. The first time, he and Charley went to Missouri after hearing a commercial bakery was looking for help. They arrived to discover hundreds of desperate men and boys already lined up, hoping for a chance at one of those jobs. A scuffle started near the Gunn brothers. P.I. stayed on its periphery, but somehow Charley got sucked into the brawl. Soon, he was locked in a furious fight with another man as P.I. watched, ready to move in if Charley needed help. For the time being, his back-country sense of fairness kept him on the sidelines.

At least it did until the man began gut-punching Charley, who bent over in agony and shouted for help. As P.I. rushed to his brother's aid, he saw crimson staining Charley's torn shirt. The other man grappled with Charley, a bloody knife in his hand. Those hadn't been gut-punches—the man was trying to kill his brother.

The sight spawned cold fury. P.I. rushed the man, who tried to stab him, too. P.I. moved too fast and gave him no quarter. Fists flailing, the man recoiled, trying to protect his face. The Arkansas teenager didn't relent. He pummeled the man until he dropped unconscious in the street.

Good jobs were so rare, some men would kill for them. It was a tough lesson for a fifteen-year-old to learn.

After a hospital stay for Charley, they returned to Quitman sobered by their experience beyond the Ozarks. Sobered, but not discouraged. P.I. tried to leave again in the spring of 1917, heading south to Little Rock with a friend named George Hooten. They roomed together on Louisiana Street in one of the capital's rougher neighborhoods, where they worked at an ice cream dairy. After a few months, they both got jobs at an insurance company.

It was a crazy time. The United States declared war on Germany in April. A military draft took effect, and both George and P.I. wanted to join up. P.I. was only sixteen, though, and would need his mother's permission unless he waited until October 1918 and his eighteenth birthday. George was older and able to get into the army, leaving Arkansas that summer to go train as a musician. After his departure, P.I. returned to Quitman and began his night work, counting the days until his birthday.

P.I. turned right and sped into the night, Searcy bound on Rosebud Road. His mother, worry worn and numb from hardship, would never have to fear insolvency again. Not if he could help it.

She and P.I.'s dad married in 1896. For both, it was a second marriage, and they brought six children together into the union. Later, four more would be born, though the youngest did not survive. P.I. arrived in 1900, the baby of the family.

Lights off, P.I. approached the first hamlet between Quitman and Searcy. This was Rosebud, just a few shacks alongside the road with its own orbit of farms. All was still and the road empty. So far so good. He pushed through and kept going; Searcy was now under thirty miles away.

His father had been murdered in August 1907. Only Jewell, Charley, and P.I. were left in the household; the other kids had grown up and were in homes of their own by then. Without any way to support her children, P.I.'s mom rented their farm out and moved everyone into a small house in town later that fall.

One cold and windy night in March 1908, when P.I. was in second grade, the house they leased caught fire. The family awoke to the terror of sweeping flames and smoke filling their bedrooms. They barely made it out alive. All their possessions burned in the fire.

Homeless, broke and bereft of everything but their nightclothes, two uncles stepped in to rescue them. Uncle Charles and Jim virtually ordered P.I.'s mom to come live with them outside of Lonoke, a tiny hamlet southeast of Little Rock. The family made the journey in the year of 1908 only to discover that Uncle Charles was anything but their savior.

Always clad in white suits that made him look like Colonel Sanders, he spoke with an affected genteel Southern accent and looked down on those who earned their living with their hands. He owned a plantation along with various business enterprises with his brother Jim. He lived comfortably for the time, but was by no means as rich as he pretended.

Instead of moving the Gunns into his home, Charles rented them a nearby cotton farm he owned. It did not take long for the family to realize this arrangement effectively made them sharecroppers for Uncle Charles. He treated them harshly and with such disdain that P.I. nursed a lifelong hatred for the man.

They lived in abject poverty. To earn a few extra pennies, P.I. and Charley would pick black walnuts every fall and go into town to sell them to farmers waiting their turn at the local gin with wagonloads of cotton. It was desperate work, and it stained their fingers black for weeks. It also stained their clothing, which stigmatized them as the poorest in their school.

P.I. shoved those thoughts out of his mind and focused on the road ahead. The first dangerous choke point on his route came into sight. If anyone were trying to intercept him, the iron bridge over Cadron Creek would be an excellent spot. He feathered the brakes as his wheels hit the bridge's wooden planks. No sign of trouble. He eased the rig to the other side. From here, he would have to pass through a few more hamlets before the road wound through the foothills northwest of Searcy. Those narrow turns in the hills held potentially more danger.

P.I. would do anything to spare his family the humiliation and privation they faced in Lonoke. He remembered those days as little more than indentured servitude to Uncle Charles. School was a trial. Between the walnut stains on his hands and clothes plus his ancient, hand-me-down, brass-tipped shoes with worn-through soles, he looked like a ragamuffin. The other kids treated him as such. He learned to fight in school yard scraps, holding his own and winning more than he lost. He learned how to take a punch, but he also learned to win. Fists flailing, his spirit unconquerable, he would go down fighting but never show his enemies weakness. He never ran. He never surrendered. He learned to fight not just to defend himself, but to punish his enemies. He found that was the only way they would leave him alone.

They lasted three years on that rented cotton farm, hoeing and planting and picking whenever the kids were not in school. Slopping hogs, milking the one cow, and a myriad of other farm chores forced P.I. and Charley to grow up fast. P.I. vowed to get ahead and fight his way out of this poverty trap. Every slight, every humiliation, every night without enough to eat became fuel in P.I.'s heart to find a way to contribute and save his weary mother.

Charley, though talented and intelligent, suffered from the

experience so thoroughly that it destroyed him. Bitter before he could even vote, he turned to liquor and women as he came of age. While he had bright moments and professional success at times, by his twenties his life took shape as a slow plunge into a sordid abyss.

As P.I. grew older, he saw how scrupulously his mother played by the rules. He also saw how those rules took the family nowhere. Uncle Charley turned them into virtual slaves by those rules. Education was supposed to be the way out, but in those days it cost over a dollar a month to keep each child in school. His mother struggled mightily to scrounge the cash, and the boys ran errands for pennies in town—work that the locals derisively sneered to be so low that "even niggers" wouldn't stoop to it. Eventually, poverty forced P.I. out of school after finishing sixth grade.

They called him hillbilly. White trash. P.I. grew up boiling with rage at the rule book designed to keep folks like the Gunns on the outside of prosperity.

Screw the rules.

He drove through Joy, another tiny cluster of clapboard buildings and frame houses, and sped onward, his cannibalized creation purring with silky smooth perfection. It might not have looked like much, but that engine would not fail him. P.I. tended to it with all his skill until he milked every last horsepower out of its block.

Two good things happened to P.I. during those years in Lonoke. The first took place while he and Charley walked back from town after selling walnuts one fall. It was a hot, humid day and the road was little more than a ribbon of dust. They wallowed through it, sweating the five miles back to the rented farm.

Suddenly, a beautiful new touring car pulled alongside the boys. They had seen such magnificent vehicles and marveled at them in town. Now, like a dream come true, the gent behind the wheel asked them if they wanted a ride.

Eagerly, the boys clambered aboard. Soon they were flying down the road, dust in their eyes and mouths all but forgotten in this moment of sheer exhilaration. When they arrived at the farm, Jewell saw P.I. smiling from ear to ear. It was a notable moment; his sister could not remember seeing P.I. radiate such happiness.

As P.I. stood in the yard, still wearing the duster he'd put on earlier that day, a broad-brimmed hat shielding his face from the sun, the touring car's owner turned around and sped off for the main road—and promptly ran over and killed one of the family's precious hogs. While it did dampen the moment, P.I.'s love for all things mechanical was born from that day.

The following summer, the whole family labored in their cotton fields, hoeing weeds in the summer heat. In the distance, they heard a buzzing sound. Turning their heads from the soil to the sky, they made out a fragile biplane puttering among the scattered clouds. P.I., leaning on his hoe, watched the craft with spellbound amazement. Long after it had flown out of sight, he stayed rooted in place, his eyes locked upward as if praying the airplane would return.

He was small and wiry then, with outsized blue eyes that stood out on his slender face. Quick, alert, a shock of light brown hair always draped over his forehead, he seemed ill suited for a life in the dirt. Uncle Charles may have had a death grip on his family, but the sight of that airplane set his imagination free.

"Someday," he said aloud as he stared skyward, "I'm going to drive one of those things."

From around the rows of cotton plants, the family laughed. P.I. shrugged off the gentle ribbing and talked of nothing else for days. When the family tired of the talk, he retreated to his imagination and sketched his dream on paper late at night. To the rest of the family, it seemed a senseless fantasy, like talking about a vacation to the moon. To P.I., the dream took root and sustained him in the worst moments.

Nobody thought a Gunn would ever drive a car, either. Yet here he was, with a ride of his own, tearing through the foothills in charge of his own destiny at last. The steep banks and wooden bridge over West Hog Thief Creek lay ahead. Another choke point. He skimmed across the bridge and pressed on, getting over East Hog Thief Creek a few minutes later.

Almost there. No sign of trouble. Another twenty minutes and he'd be unloading at the rendezvous point in Searcy. Haz would slip him the cash, and in the morning he would give his mother the better part of four hundred dollars. That was almost ten grand in 2016 currency. The Gunns had never seen that kind of money. His mother would never have to worry again.

Of course, if she knew what he was doing, she'd be furious. God-fearing Methodists did not smuggle liquor. He didn't care; this was his family's salvation, and his ticket out. With his mother set, he could leave Quitman and join the military in October. The draft was in full effect now that America had entered the Great War the previous spring. In some places around Arkansas, the draft triggered riots, and stories of violence circulated through the outlying villages. In some places, there seemed to be more resistance than an eagerness to serve the country, a fact that perplexed P.I.

The pines and Spanish oak that flanked the road to Searcy closed in until it seemed as if he was driving through a narrow, winding canyon whose walls were made of leaves and branches. This was the wild part of the county. Rolling hills, sharp corners, swampy terrain here and there, while farms became sparse.

He rounded a bend, lights off now and navigating only by the light of the moon. Two hulking shapes materialized in the midnight gloom. P.I. slowed down. What was this?

Trucks. They'd been set across the road, and now he could see figures darting around them, rifles in hand.

They were waiting for him with this makeshift roadblock on this narrow, final stretch before Searcy. He stopped a distance from the roadblock and started to make a quick Y-turn to run away. He knew he could outrun them, and in the moonlight there would be no way to make a positive ID.

A sheriff emerged from behind him before he could turn all the way around. Mousetrapped at the last minute, P.I. sat in his jalopy as the police descended on him. The jig was up. Seventeen years old, with only a sixth-grade education, P.I. Gunn found himself escorted to the White County Jail by a posse sent into the night by his aunt's own activism.

In that moment, dreams of flight never seemed more beyond his reach.

12

The Noose

December 12, 1941
Philippines

Friday morning dawned over Manila's empty streets to reveal a city under siege. Throughout the city, civilians flung up air raid shelters practically overnight. Philippine president Manuel Quezon drove through town to check on those inside whenever the Japanese appeared overhead. Constables stood on every corner, quick to use their weapons at passing aircraft, or anyone caught violating the blackout restrictions. Antiaircraft guns now dominated some intersections, emplaced there to protect strategic sites such as the oil and fuel farms, the docks and the major government buildings. Some of those guns were manned by the New Mexico National Guard, and Manila citizens would greet them each morning with hot coffee and sandwiches.

With gas rationing in effect, cars almost vanished from the city's thoroughfares. The kalesas still trotted about, but there were far fewer as their drivers left for the Army or fled into the countryside.

To the south, the B-17s at the Del Monte pineapple plantation took off to strike the Japanese landing ships off Aparri and Vigan. Six got aloft; one suffered catastrophic engine failure during takeoff, losing two of four at the same time its hydraulic system failed. The sudden loss of power on one side caused the plane to ground-loop.

It spun right into another B-17 then broke in half. More precious aircraft lost, and yet another example of what happens when modern aircraft were thrust into primitive operating environments without the logistical support to properly care for them.

Later in the day, MacArthur's PR machine heralded the B-17 attacks as exemplary displays of prowess and devotion. Behind the bold words, the truth was that dropping bombs on moving ships from twenty thousand feet served no purpose other than to kill fish. The attacks did represent the best the American bomber crews could do, but to the Japanese juggernaut they represented annoyances at best.

With airfields seized on Luzon proper, the Japanese transferred their shorter-ranged bombers and fighters to those strips. Most belonged to the Imperial Army Air Force, and while not as capable as the Navy's sleek bombers and Zero fighters, they increased Japan's combat aviation power over Luzon significantly. In addition, the fields now could be used as a refueling stop by the Imperial Navy's aircraft in order to launch raids deep into the Central Philippines.

As Japan's morning strike forces assembled over their air bases for the flight south, Dan and Marie Stickle sped through Manila's residential district in P.I.'s Roadmaster. Pulling up at the family's temporary apartment, Dan conferred with Polly and laid out the situation.

Manila wasn't safe any longer; they needed to get out, and there was no time to waste. Dan stood about as tall as P.I., but with a broader, more muscular build. Though only twenty-four, he could be imposing, forceful, and directive. Polly agreed to go with him. Bundling the kids up, taking only their overnight bags, they raced for the Buick and settled in with Marie. In minutes, Dan pointed the Buick southward for the provinces.

The drive proved surprisingly serene. The Buick bounced down country roads past well-tended rice paddies and through small villages with thatched-roof houses that seemed totally untouched by the war. They saw no signs of panic; no scenes of fleeing refugees. In fact, they encountered few vehicles beyond an occasional farmer's cart pulled by water buffalo.

As he drove, Dan explained the situation. P.I. was somewhere to the south, flying one of the 18s. He wanted the family out of Manila and would catch up to them once he returned. Dan would drive them to the Red Cross evacuation center, head back to Grace Park, and let P.I. know where they were.

Nath and Paul asked Dan about their dog. The big Iowan appeared annoyed by the question, absently answering that Dingo was fine and had the run of the cemetery. Dan was more concerned about their safety; a dog seemed of little consequence except to children whose hearts lay with their pet.

They reached the location of the Red Cross center sometime in the early afternoon. Instead of a bustling facility set up in some appropriate building, there was no sign of it. Dan asked around and discovered the evacuation center had been relocated.

The locals told Dan that the radio reported Japanese troops landing at Legazpi on Southern Luzon. The city was in enemy hands, and now they were marching northward for Manila.

Troops in the north. Troops to the south. Manila in between. Dan didn't need a map to realize that they were directly in the path of the advancing Japanese. Around Manila, Japanese aircraft paraded largely unopposed. They strafed and bombed Clark Field and Iba, sank most of the Navy's PBY patrol planes as they rode the waves in Subic Bay. A massive formation of over fifty bombers swept over the city to bomb the Philippine Air Force's main base at Batangas.

Against orders, P.I.'s friend and former student Jesus "Jess" Villamor led six Peashooters into the sky to intercept the oncoming raid. In a display of steel nerve and raw skill, he dove into the attacking bombers, his two machine guns chattering until they cut one of them out of the formation. It went down in flames, a morale victory in the midst of catastrophe. The incident solidified Villamor as the Philippines' preeminent aerial war hero.

Bombs still fell on Batangas, and everywhere else defeat ruled supreme. At Paracale, the air warning troops finally got their radar working, only to discover most of them didn't really know how to use it. Fully manned, it failed to detect a single B-17 that thundered directly over them on its way to bombing the Japanese invasion force off Legazpi. A P-40 also swept over the bay undetected. Thinking a friendly vessel offshore was Japanese, the pilot raked it with machine gun fire until it blew up, killing much of the crew.

Shortly after, both the air warning unit and Joseph Stevenot were ordered back to Manila. Without any combat troops in the area, they were practically defenseless. The Americans blew up the priceless SCR-271 permanent radar, but tried to get the mobile one back to Manila. The swampy road made that impossible, and the vehicles bogged down en route. Lieutenant Rogers left several men behind to guard the vehicles while he led the rest of the detachment overland on foot to find help. Along the way, the weary men cast away much of the remaining top secret radar gear. Japanese troops later reached the marooned vehicles. The men left behind blew them up, then tried to escape while under fire. Several died; one escaped and joined a guerrilla force.

Stevenot reached Manila safely and rejoined MacArthur's staff, where he went to work under Gen. Charles Willoughby.

P.I.'s whole Sunday venture to Paracale ended in ignominious failure. At least the Staggerwing was repaired and flown out before the Japanese arrived. It would join a growing hodge-podge of civilian aircraft employed by FEAF for all manner of duties in the months ahead.

While all this unfolded around the Philippines, Dan faced a dilemma. P.I. wanted his family out of the capital, but that decision had been overcome by events. They couldn't just sit and wait to be captured by the advancing Japanese. They couldn't go north; the Japanese were there as well.

Dan realized the only option was to return to Manila, but it was so late in the day that if they went straight back, they would not arrive until after sunset. Driving the Buick in blackout conditions did not appeal to him. Instead, he elected to take the family to a country compound not too far away that belonged to one of Andrés Soriano's business associates. They would be safe there for the moment.

They reached the estate before dusk and received a warm welcome. The Gunn family was given the run of the property, and the kids promptly headed out back for the beautifully maintained pool. They spent the rest of the day swimming and relaxing, the war seemingly a million miles away. Meanwhile, the adults conferred and tried to figure out what to do.

The options weren't good, and they could not come up with any better ideas. Despite the danger of air attack, at least in Manila they would be close to P.I. and the aircraft that could get them out of this mess.

They spent the evening in peace, surrounded by opulence and comfort. Andrés Soriano had friends everywhere (and not a few enemies), and his business connections spread like tentacles all over the Philippines. The Gunns learned long ago that his connections opened doors wherever they went in the islands. And on this night, it was most appreciated.

Polly could not have known at the time, but the war affected even the billionaire himself. About the same time his PAL employees joined the FEAF, Soriano volunteered for duty in the Philippine Army and was commissioned as captain. He and P.I. now held the same rank. Things were changing, and this last night of colonial tranquility was at best an echo of what would never be again. Places like this one would soon be home to Japanese officers and administrators whose rule over the Filipinos would look nothing like the benevolent and paternalistic one they had known for the past forty years.

They did not linger on Saturday morning. A quick bite to eat, many thank-yous to their hosts, and they loaded up into the Buick for the drive back into Manila. While the two families made their way home, the Japanese marshalled for a maximum-effort air assault. Though the children probably didn't know it, Dan Stickle sensed it: They were racing the Japanese bombers back to Manila.

When they reached the tiny apartment the two families found P.I. waiting for them. He saw Polly and wrapped his arms around her. The kids flung themselves into his embrace until wife and children were wrapped up by his strong arms. P.I. was disheveled. He smelled terrible and his eyes looked hollowed out. To Nath, he seemed older, like he'd aged years in the last few days. The family hug continued, Don and Marie looking on perhaps a bit awkwardly. Their young marriage did not share the depth of P.I.'s and Polly's.

For P.I., being their protector gave him strength and a sense of power. He was larger than life to them, and he loved the way they looked up to him. He was the family's rock in a storm, the one who shielded them from slings and arrows. Polly—she was the nurturer who gave them their spiritual compass and set the boundaries of their hearts.

At first glance, Polly and P.I. seemed a mismatched couple. She was devout; he was profane. He was adventurous, she seemed content in hearth and home. He went full throttle through his days. She was industrious, but knew how to relax even when P.I. could not find his off switch. Yet, those differences made their marriage work. They each gave what the other lacked, and the emotional tether that bound them ensured their lives of balance. P.I. gave Polly's life zest, adventures, and passion. Polly gave P.I. his center of gravity. In almost twenty years of marriage, they never stopped growing together, even when circumstances forced them to be geographically apart.

For Julie, her dad was infallible. Always right, always quick to guard or knock down obstacles for her, he was heroic to her—and that would last until she had reached adulthood and sought a life of her own. Connie felt the same way; her dad seemed larger than life, always capable and ready to handle any challenge. He ensured her safety and sense of family; he protected her and cared for her in ways that men of his era would never do. They shared a kindred love of shoes, born from the days he owned only one pair and made his monthly nut by polishing other men's loafers.

The soft spot he shared for both his daughters was never far from view.

To Nath and Paul, their dad was manhood personified. A warrior, an explorer, a pioneer. He lived with passion a life never small or constrained. He did what was right for those he loved. He was true to them and they knew him to never be wrong. He taught by example, by discipline, and by lectures spawned from their misdeeds. They idolized him.

They hugged him close, and the tension and uncertainty drained away in his arms. P.I. was there, and everything would be okay. A deeper look at his careworn face may have given them pause.

At length, he broke the family embrace and told them, "I found a place in town for us to live. Our furniture is being moved there now."

No more sleeping on apartment floors. Polly felt a sense of relief. At least for the moment, their situation was resolved. Better news was the fact that their house on Villamor Court had not been looted, and their possessions were safe. If all went well, she would sleep with P.I. in their spool post bed later that night.

Together, the family drove over to the new place. Somehow in all the chaos, P.I. found them the bottom floor of a two-story duplex as far from any military targets in Manila as possible. When they arrived, PAL employees appeared in trucks filled with the family's possessions. While they unloaded furniture and carried it inside, P.I. hugged the family one more time and promised to return later that night.

The family went inside their new home to unpack and try to settle in while P.I. drove back to Grace Park. Around Manila, the Japanese bombers reached their target areas. They rearranged the rubble at Clark Field, strafed and bombed Del Carmen, and pounded both Nieslon and Nichols.

At least this time, the American antiaircraft gunners displayed improved marksmanship by damaging eleven of the fifty-four bombers that attacked Nichols. Still, there was no stopping the Japanese. They hit the field in three waves—while nearby, P.I.'s PAL employees rushed to pack up the last of the Gunn family's household items from Villamor Court.

The first wave came in west to east, right over the neighborhood. Perhaps the heavy antiaircraft fire threw off the bombardiers that day. Perhaps they simply miscalculated. The first string of bombs slammed into Barrio Baclaren a few blocks away, killing and wounding civilians and Army personnel alike. Several American P-40 pilots who lived in the area rushed to aid the wounded and dying. One aviator spotted a woman buried to her shoulders in the rubble of her house. He dug her out—only to discover the bomb had torn her entire lower torso off.

The succeeding two waves dumped hundreds of bombs on the airfield and its environs, cratering the runways, demolishing outlying buildings, and sparking fires all over the complex. The survivors picked themselves up and began gathering their dead comrades. At least one fighter pilot who had seen a friend die beside him in the attack escaped into a bottle later that night.

The bombing stopped, but the raid did not. As the high-level planes turned north for home, the escorting Zeroes dropped down to strafe Nichols and Nielson. Without any P-40s airborne to give them trouble, their cannon and machine guns played havoc among the ruins of both facilities.

For all the damage done, the Japanese did not find the two PAL Beech 18s tucked away on that secret airfield at La Loma Cemetery only a short distance away. The PAL ground crews camouflaged the strip by building portable shacks and huts that they emplaced on the runway. Instead of an airstrip, the area looked like a slum surrounded by a cemetery.

Even as the Japanese savaged the bases around them, P.I. prepared for his mission that day. He rose before dawn and flew a resupply hop in the morning before driving over to the apartment in Manila. Beyond the catnaps, he barely slept. Yet he kept pushing himself and would not give the afternoon run to another pilot. It was simply too dangerous to ask Connelly or Slingsby to do it for him.

He picked NPC-54 for the mission, PAL's first Beech 18. It had been completed at the Wichita, Kansas, factory in August 1939, but Soriano ordered it equipped with more powerful engines and an extra fuel tank in the nose. The nine-cylinder Pratt & Whitney R-985 Wasp Juniors produced about 450 horsepower, much better than the standard 330-horse Jacobs L-6s the 18s usually sported.

P.I. wanted the extra power to carry heavier loads of fuel and passengers. Now, he was glad to have those extra two hundred horses for the additional speed he could coax out of the Beech. The less time in hostile skies the better, and on a day where Japanese planes raided targets all over the Philippines, he needed every possible advantage to survive.

FEAF wanted a flight of staff officers delivered to Del Monte, along with a mixed cargo of vaccines and medical supplies for the men living on the edge of Mindanao's primordial jungles. It is not known if the passengers came to Grace Park, or if P.I. had to pick them up at Clark Field. If he was forced to do the latter, it makes his survival on this day even more miraculous: Clark Field was bombed and strafed throughout the day.

If the Japanese weren't danger enough, several weather fronts moved in between Luzon and Mindanao during the morning. Flying without a copilot, P.I. skirted the Japanese raids, flew under or around the storm clouds, and managed to get down safely at Del Monte. He stayed only long enough to offload the cargo and refuel. Sometime around 1700, he rolled down the grassy pasture at Del Monte and lifted off, bound for Grace Park again.

He would not make it back to the cemetery.

13

American Red Baron

Dusk, December 13, 1941
Central Philippines

The Zeroes found the DuPont Dulux teak red Beech 18 somewhere over northern Cebu.

Alone in the cockpit, P.I. climbed from wave top level to six hundred feet over the south shore of Cebu in order to get over some hills. He flew on at that height, perhaps getting a little careless in his exhaustion.

Overhead, a trio of Mitsubishis from the veteran Third Air Group spotted P.I.'s plane while escorting the first Japanese bombing raid on Cebu City. They dove to the attack, coming down on P.I.'s right rear quarter. Unarmed and without any visibility to the rear, he never saw them coming.

A sudden flash of tracer bullets filled the air around the Beech like Arkansas fireflies. A split second later, the Beech shuddered from bullet impacts in the right wing. The lead Japanese pilot was a capable marksman.

Instinctively, P.I. broke into the onrushing Japanese fighters, the Beech's wings rolling perpendicular to the ground as he tucked the control wheel into his stomach and turned as tight as the twin Beech could manage.

The move surprised the Japanese pilots, who had been used to seeing such easy quarry turn away from them and try to run. The sudden maneuver threw off the lead pilot's two wingmen, one of whom didn't even fire. The three fighters overshot P.I., and he saw one of them zip past his port wing.

Full of fuel in unprotected tanks, without any guns to fight, and without the speed to outrun the quicksilver Zeroes, P.I. knew he only had one chance: He needed to outfly them.

He dove for the jungle-covered hills below, intent on forcing them into a game of low-level chicken with trees and hills, but in seconds the Zeroes jumped him again, the muzzles of their 20mm cannons spitting flame from their wings. More tracers streaked past the fleeing Beech. The airliner trembled as bullets smacked the fuselage, wing, and right engine, sounding like hammer blows on a tin roof.

As they wheeled for another pass, P.I. ducked into a narrow valley, zigzagging to throw off their aim as he skimmed the ground. This wasn't treetop level. This was grasstop level.

The Zeroes couldn't make steep diving passes on the Beech without plummeting into the ground. P.I.'s lawn-mowing altitude meant they simply could not pull up in time after their runs. That forced the Japanese to dive behind him and try to chase him just above the ground. It was a guts game, and the Japanese showed they were all in.

Down the valley they went, the Beech whizzing below trees and around hills as P.I. used the terrain for cover. Every time the Zeroes got in range, the Beech skittered away. P.I. banked and rolled, briefly hugging the slopes of the valley before careening back down across its floor. At least once, he felt the 18 hit branches as he cut his margin with the earth to virtually nothing.

His years as a Navy fighter pilot saved his life that day. Muscle memory from countless mock dogfights triggered that last-second turn into his attackers. "Pull into the line of fire," he was told over and over until it was coded into the DNA of his flying skills. Age and sedate airline duty did not dull his reactions.

Every time they opened fire on him, P.I. turned into them as best he could. Each time, he threw off their aim just enough to give him a few more seconds of life. He never flew straight, constantly turning and jinking to make himself the most difficult possible target as he skimmed along the ground.

The chase ensued for several minutes until the Japanese pilots finally gave up. Either they proved not as daring as the desperate Arkansan, ran low on fuel, or they lost him in all the twists and turns he led them through in the valley. They broke off their pursuit, climbed out over Cebu, and headed for northern Luzon.

P.I. stayed on the deck and ran for home, knowing he wasn't out of the woods yet. As he reached Cebu's northern shore, the right engine began to overheat. He nursed it along, but he could see cannon and machine gun gouges in its cowling. How much longer would it last? He didn't think very long; he needed to get down quickly.

With the sun setting off his left wing, P.I. skimmed the whitecaps of the Visayan Sea, nursing his battered plane along. The right engine was dying; he could tell from the anguished metallic cries it made as he forced it to keep producing power just a little bit longer.

He decided to divert to Zablan Field, the Philippine Army Air Corps base. He reached the Luzon coast as darkness fell. Pushing north, still as low as he dared, he limped toward Zablan and called the tower on his radio.

No response.

He kept calling in the clear with his voice set. Nothing.

In the postsunset gloom, he spotted the field and lined up on the runway, still calling his approach on the radio. Unknown to P.I., the radio was full of Japanese bullets following a Japanese attack on December 10. The Filipinos at Zablan had no idea one of their own was coming in with a crippled bird.

Around the strip, alert machine gunners heard the Beech closing on the strip. P.I. tried to turn on his landing lights as a signal that he was friendly, but they were shot out, too. He was going in dark, facing men who spent the last few days getting strafed and bombed with impunity.

The crews behind those guns spotted the onrushing plane and didn't hesitate. They unleashed their weapons in a torrent of fire, stitching the Beech from nose to tail. The right engine took more hits. It sputtered and coughed, but P.I. somehow kept it going as he turned away from the incoming streams of "friendly" bullets. He escaped into the darkness, but the Beech was mortally wounded.

The smell of avgas filled the cockpit. The Filipino gunners had hit a fuel tank, and it was now leaking out into the cabin. That the bullet which pierced the tank hadn't touched off a fatal explosion was a minor miracle.

P.I. knew he could never make Grace Park now. He eased the nose toward Nichols. It would be a gamble—the field there was pockmarked with scores of bomb craters. Drop a landing gear into one of those holes, and NPC-54 would whipsaw into a ground loop and probably explode.

He didn't want to risk that, and he didn't want to block a runway with his burning wreck. But what to do? He couldn't bail out, not without a parachute. Even if he had one, he could not make it to the door before the Beech fell out of level flight, since it lacked an autopilot.

Pilot and plane were bound together; they would share the same fate. He'd have to ride her in.

A few minutes out from Nichols, he attempted to lower the landing gear. Nothing happened. He tried the manual release. That didn't work either. Three times, he tried to shake the gear loose, rocking the aircraft as hard as he dared. The wheels remained in their wells, tucked inside the engine fairings beneath each battered wing.

P.I. activated the flaps. Nothing happened. He tried again, but the hydraulic system was shot out, too. Without the flaps, the Beech would stall at a much faster speed. A belly landing in the dark was already dicey enough. Now he would have to go in hot as well.

He lined up on the grass meridian between the runways at Nichols. Staying as low as he could, he barely cleared the perimeter fence and slammed into the ground. The Beech slid along, out of control, the right wing tearing off. It careened across the darkened airfield and came to rest without anyone on the ground even detecting it.

P.I. climbed out of the cockpit, surprised that no crash crews were rushing toward him. He looked over the wreckage, stuck a cigarette in his mouth and set off, hiking through the bomb craters toward the battered remains of the base hangars, intent on reporting to somebody.

Later, the PAL mechanics counted 130 bullet holes in the right wing. The fuselage, tail, and left wing had been peppered as well. Somehow, P.I. escaped without a scratch.

Before dawn, P.I. returned to his family. Creeping inside the new duplex so as to not wake anyone, he stepped into the boys' room and paused. Since Connie had been born, there had been many late nights at work for P.I. While flying in the Navy, he always maintained side jobs to send extra money back to his mother. After she had died in the early 1930s, he kept working after duty hours to build the family reserves.

He came home every night, fingers black with engine grease, and visited each child as they slept. Their peace was his comfort, and he would stay with them quietly for several moments before turning for the spool post bed and his waiting wife.

This time, in the predawn darkness, he saw Paul and Nath tucked in their beds. The room was so small that little space was left between them. The whole family would be cramped in this place, but P.I. knew they would not be here for long. Either the Army would win and drive the Japanese out, or he would fly them to safety somewhere far from the war's reach.

Try to, anyway. He had not even received his official orders putting him on active duty with the Army Air Force, and already the Japanese had shot him down. Between the friendly ground fire, the weather, the accidents, and the marauding Japanese, trying to evacuate the family by air would be courting death for all of them.

But what choice do I have?

He stepped into the room and stood beside Paul, gently putting one hand on his eldest son's shoulder. He held it there a moment, then moved to Nath and did the same. The boy stirred and opened his eyes to see his father's reassuring face before sleep reclaimed him.

Filled with dread for their future, silently cursing himself for ever getting his family in this situation, P.I. wearily turned and left the room.

Tonight, he would sleep with his wife. How many nights did they have left? She'd say that was in God's hands, but he would do anything to keep this life intact.

After he showered and scrubbed away the dirt, grime, and sweat, he curled up beside Polly, who stirred awake. He told her what happened. Normally, he preferred to shield her from this sort of news. This time, he didn't want her to hear secondhand through the PAL rumor mill that her husband had escaped death by a whisker.

Their bond transcended every challenge they faced. Where other marriages ruptured, theirs grew closer. True, he could be confounding, and at times he absentmindedly left Polly and the kids waiting in the car for him for hours while he poked his head into the hangar to see how things were going. He would get lost in work, and the world for him distilled down to whatever engineering issue he faced.

Other days counterbalanced such obliviousness. There were the nights out, filled with dancing and laughter. They developed shared hobbies and loved making home movies together. They went to great lengths to shoot film others could never get. When they lived in Hawaii, a volcano had erupted on one of the islands. P.I. took the family up to see it, and Polly sat beside him with the family's home movie camera. As he circled the volcano, he got so excited that he began barking orders to Polly on how best to shoot the scene.

In a lesser marriage, that could have sparked a nasty fight, but Polly never reacted in anger. She knew P.I.'s heart, and she understood his passion sometimes got the best of his civility. So instead of firing back and telling him to stop being an ass, she looked at him and said, "Okay, tell you what. You take the movies. I'll fly the plane."

P.I. froze at the controls, eyes locked on his bride, as the entire family burst out laughing. Soon, he couldn't help but join in.

The best parts were late nights like these. Polly was his first love, and he often said to anyone who would listen that he had never seen anyone as beautiful. There in the dark, huddled together, he saw her as no other man ever would. No makeup, bed hair, lips devoid of color. Her natural, undone self. Pure, shared intimacy. On nights like that, he looked upon her and knew peerless beauty.

In time, sleep overtook them, this middle-aged couple still in love after two decades together. Their union kept a world turned bad at bay, at least for a few moments.

14

Refugee Allies

December 14, 1941

Eva Gurevich peered out the window of her second-story flat and into the scene unfolding in the yard below. Another truck had just arrived with more furniture going into the apartment below hers. The family there scurried this way and that, unloading boxes. The men with the truck eased a piano out of the back.

She was no stranger to refugeedom. As a girl, her family fled the Bolshevik Revolution, crossing through Siberia in a *Doctor Zhivago*–esque odyssey. Her father brought the family to Tientsin, China, where they tried to reestablish their lives among other displaced Russian Jews.

They thrived in China for almost twenty years. Eva grew up, met and married her husband, Boria, had a son together. But as good as life was, China was never truly home.

Then the Japanese invaded China. They captured their city in the summer of 1937, and the Gureviches found themselves in the middle of a war for a second time. They tried to hang on while the Japanese promised to respect the international community in Tientsin, but living under an increasingly cruel military occupation was no place to raise their son.

They fled the chaos for the hopes of a better life in Manila, where Boria found a job with a lumber company while they worked to get their son, Leo, to America. His name was on the immigration quota waiting list. Perhaps someday.

Now, the Gurevich family found itself in the path of another Japanese conquering army. Eva watched, heartbroken, as families were again displaced by soldiers and war. She and Boria took in another family, the Rifkins, whose neighborhood was badly damaged in the Japanese bombing raids. Though cramped in their three-bedroom flat, at least food was plentiful for the moment. They would make do. What else was there? They all knew that this time, there was no place to run.

Eva descended the stairs and knocked on the back door of the apartment below. A moment later, Connie answered it. Eva, petite with graying hair and immaculately dressed, smiled warmly at Connie and asked if her family could help in any way.

Polly came up behind Connie and introduced herself. Eva's warmth and charisma matched Polly's, and as they talked, the two women felt an instant kinship. Julie saw them as mirrors of each other. In short order, Eva, who made her own cosmetics, promised to share her cache of homemade beauty products with the Gunn ladies, who were astonished with the quality of her concoctions. Underneath the cheerfulness lurked the mind of a formidable chemist.

Eva knew what it was like to be displaced from home and hearth. She practically ordered the Gunn family to come to dinner that night. Polly tried to beg off, not wanting to put her new neighbor out, but Eva would have none of it.

The Gunns' piano cemented their friendship. The first-floor apartment proved too small to absorb a house full of furniture, and the instrument turned the living room into an obstacle course. Eva asked her son, Leo, to come down and play something. Before long, the Gunns' new flat was filled with a beautiful melody. Polly was so taken by his talent that she asked if the Gureviches wanted the piano upstairs in their apartment.

Leo Gurevich was a professional pianist. At twenty-one, he'd played most of his life, and it had long since become his abiding passion. When the Gureviches fled Tientsin, they'd had to leave most of their belongings behind, including their piano. Now, thanks to Polly, they would have one in their home again. The men moved it upstairs.

That night, after a huge Russian-style feast shared among three families, Leo sat down at the piano and played a few classical pieces with soulful passion.

He stunned the guests with his talent. Connie and Julie had taken lessons and were passable players. In Honolulu, Polly had made Nath and Paul learn to play as well. But they resisted, hating the instrument and their teacher. When the boys complained their male instructor had been acting inappropriately with them, P.I. put an end to the lessons—and almost an end to the instructor.

Now they saw what their mother once wished for them. Leo's skill captivated the room that night. From the classical pieces, he moved on to some of the latest big band tunes. The bright, airy beat stood in stark contrast to the tension and sadness they all experienced since the war began. He then busted loose with some boogie-woogie. P.I. and Polly were not fans of boogie woogie, but Leo played with such joy that it won everybody over, and they escaped the world around them late into the evening.

The meal and solo concert solidified the friendship between the two families. That relationship would be a vital one in the months to come.

While Polly and the children settled into their new place, P.I. returned to the air over and over. NPC-56, the other PAL Beech, remained undamaged, and he flew it all over the islands in the ensuing days. Occasionally, he was spotted by puzzled members of the Philippine Observer Corps, who reported to MacArthur's HQ the presence of a bright red twin-engine bomber. Where he was at any given moment was often anyone's guess. He flew payroll runs to the

American garrisons on outlying islands. He made sometimes two trips a day down to Del Monte, carrying personnel out with each hop.

With sheer recklessness he evaded Zeroes that now roamed with impunity over the northern islands. Nobody flew on such a razor's edge as P.I. Gunn during these dark December days. On every mission, he raced his unarmed red plane through the cracks in the earth, scuttling through valleys and down into canyons to avoid the roving fighters. He came home with branches stuck in his engine cowling, or dangling from the underside of the 18's fuselage. His PAL secretary later claimed that at least once he returned with strands of seaweed dangling from seams in the aluminum underbelly. When over water, he flew so low that his props sometimes chopped the whitecaps, kicking up saltwater froth that coated the underside of his wings. The PAL ground crews spent hours each night polishing the 18 to keep corrosion at bay.

Japanese bombers struck the Manila area with daunting frequency. All the prewar airfields were hit again and again, until the bombs simply rearranged the rubble. There was no letup, and FEAF's surviving fighters dispersed to makeshift fields elsewhere on Luzon. The Japanese hunted them relentlessly.

Since the Japanese ensured Batangas was no safe haven, the PAL operation stayed at Grace Park and continued to operate as sort of a semiautonomous appendix to overall FEAF operations. Thanks to their careful camouflage, the Japanese never discovered P.I.'s secret base among the dead.

They did discover Del Monte. Soon, bombs began falling there, too. The first raid came from the Japanese aircraft carrier *Ryujo*, which was supporting the landings at Davao and Legazpi.

Fortunately, the B-17s were no longer there when the Japanese attacked. The day Eva and Polly met, three Fortresses sortied from Del Monte to strike at Japanese ships off Legazpi. One returned.

That disaster convinced Generals MacArthur and Brereton to send the surviving heavy bombers south to Darwin, Australia, some fifteen hundred miles from Del Monte. The strips on Mindanao would be used as a staging base for further B-17 raids, but the bombers would no longer be stationed in the Philippines. Hopefully, they could be better maintained in Australia, far out of range of marauding Japanese aircraft.

With the bombers gone, FEAF was reduced to a little more than a dozen fighters, the PAL Beech 18, the surviving aircraft of the Philippine Air Corps, and a growing, if motley, collection of oddball civilian planes. They were scraping the bottom of the barrel already, and the main Japanese amphibious invasion had not yet even begun.

Between flights, P.I. checked out NPC-54, the Beech 18 he'd crashed at Nichols. In ordinary circumstances, the plane would have been sold for scrap. The right wing was virtually shattered. The leading edge was bashed in, the propeller blades bent like fishhooks around the cowling. Bullet holes peppered the fuselage and wings. Here and there, cannon shells gouged typewriter-sized chunks out of the plane's aluminum skin. The control lines were torn up or severed altogether; the hydraulic system was a sieve. The landing gear was damaged, fuel tanks were punctured—the list was long and depressing.

P.I. got to work. Spare parts were virtually nonexistent, so the mechanic and backyard engineer got creative.

The right wing needed to be rebuilt, but there was not much aluminum sheet metal available for such an effort. What was on hand, or culled from wrecks, was already earmarked to keep the P-40s patched and flying.

P.I. and the PAL mechanics went into Manila, found an abandoned house, and tore off its tin roof. They used the material to reconstruct the wing's leading edge and patch the bullet holes. They fixed the fuel tank and worked through the myriad of other issues until the plane was almost serviceable—except for the small fact that the right wing was still severed from the fuselage.

P.I. reattached it with baling wire.

NPC-54 received a new lease on life. It rejoined the fold at La Loma Cemetery, where Slingsby, Connelly, and P.I. took turns flying it.

Every day, P.I. and his pilots risked their lives with these low-level runs through Japanese-owned skies, but FEAF was so obsessed with combat aircraft that little thought or time was given to the transport section at Grace Park. P.I. would receive the assignments for the day from FEAF HQ. He made the runs or assigned them to Slingsby and Connelly as needed. How he carried the missions out was up to him. In between missions, nobody at FEAF seemed to know or care what the PAL gang was up to.

At the same time they were flying these missions, Capt. William Bradford, a former PATCO pilot and engineering officer at Nichols, was given the task to organize the other civilian aircraft into a serviceable fleet of transports. While searching for aircraft, he came across the old Bellanca Skyrocket he once flew for PATCO. It had been abandoned on a remote field somewhere on Luzon. He put it back into service and painted huge American flags on either side of its fuselage in hopes the troops on the ground would not shoot at it. Bradford's men found other planes as well, including at least one other Staggerwing and an ancient Waco biplane.

Later dubbed "the Bamboo Fleet," this hodgepodge of planes and daring pilots soon became the most vital aspect of USAAF aviation in the Philippines. For the moment, though, the fleet was FEAF's bastard stepchild. Bradford and P.I. were left virtually to their own devices, lost in the cracks of all the chaos engulfing the Filamerican forces on Luzon.

During the middle of the month, the repeated defeats triggered an exodus of field grade officers. They started to appear beside P.I.'s Beech 18 with travel orders, sending them south to Mindanao— and out of the line of the Japanese march. The scene, repeated every day at Grace Park and Clark, caused P.I.'s temper to slowly boil. He commented many times on all the colonels he hauled away from the fighting, instead of up to the front lines. He considered them little more than cowards, abandoning their posts even as their skills were needed the most.

How much truth there was in P.I.'s opinion is unclear. Many of the men escaping south received orders out of Luzon because their skill sets were needed to try and reconstitute the air force elsewhere. With Japan in firm control of the seas and skies, there would be no chance of that happening on Luzon. Others who flew these transport missions echoed P.I.'s sentiments, though, and some told tales similar to what wrangled the Arkansan so much.

P.I. tried to set the example for his gang, taking as many flights as he could each day, and always selecting the most difficult or dangerous ones. Several times, he flew to the front lines of Northern Luzon to deliver critical medical supplies, landing on rough strips barely suited for the Beech 18. On other flights, he slipped south to Cebu or Panay, or made runs to where the Navy had dispersed some of its surviving PBY Catalina flying boats.

One time, he flew frozen turkeys down to Colonel Elsmore's men so they could have a Christmas feast. To the Army Air Force maintainers down there living on subsistence-level rations, the turkeys were a godsend. They devoured them so quickly that P.I. later jokingly complained to Elsmore that they didn't even save him a turkey sandwich.

Even as he flew these missions, he looked for ways to get his family out. While surveying new routes for PAL before the war, he'd flown into dozens of tiny dirt and grass strips all over the islands. In some places, where he planned to set up a PAL station, he stockpiled fuel. Now, they gave him options the Japanese did not know about. The American high command didn't, either.

He considered Mindoro. It wasn't a long flight from Manila, and he had plenty of fuel squirreled away on that island. He could take his family, dash down, and leave them there until he had the break in operations that allowed him to fly them farther south. At least they'd be away from Manila.

That was a risky option. Every day, news came of Japanese task forces sighted off islands all over the Central Philippines and Luzon. What if he got them to Mindoro, only to have the Japanese land and take the island? P.I. knew the Filamerican forces on the outlying islands were too small and poorly equipped to hold out for long. They could not drive off the attackers. In that case, he might deliver Polly and the kids right into another Japanese invasion. They would either die trapped in the fighting or fall into Japanese hands.

He couldn't risk that.

He decided to wait a little longer. From everything he heard, the Japanese were still quite far away from Manila. Their advance seemed slow; maybe MacArthur's troops were making a gallant stand and the city could be saved after all.

Meanwhile, the Japanese bombers struck Luzon every day. While their accuracy remained incredibly good, civilian sections of Manila still took damage from stray bombs. During one attack, Carlos Romulo, one of MacArthur's public affairs officers, was caught in the open during one noontime raid. A bomb exploded less than a hundred yards from him, blowing him across a street and knocking him unconscious. He awoke, wounded and groggy, to see a man vanish in a second bomb blast. When Romulo got to his feet, he discovered he was drenched in the man's blood.

Such moments repeated themselves around Manila every day. P.I.'s fear for his family's safety generated another bit of backyard engineering.

When he found a large cylindrical steel tank—a water tank, or an industrial boiler—P.I. tore out its insides and constructed three levels of shelves fashioned from plywood and chicken wire. Then he ordered the PAL employees to deliver it to the new apartment.

Nath happened to be outside when a flatbed truck arrived with the tank strapped on the back. The driver stopped the truck in the street before the duplex, then bailed out to help the others offload it. Using a couple of two-by-six boards, they built a ramp off the back of the bed. They began pulling the straps off the tank.

"Mom, there are some men out here unloading something," Nath said as he rushed inside.

"What on earth—" Polly said, looking out the window. Together, she and Nath went outside to talk to the employees, whom they recognized.

When Polly asked what was going on, one of the men said, "Captain Gunn told us to bring the tank to you. It is an air raid shelter."

Ten feet long about eight feet in diameter, it could easily fit the four Gunns, plus the Gurevich and Rifkin families. P.I.'s backwoods engineering mind conceived an elegant solution to Manila's high water table. He couldn't dig a shelter for his family, so he built one that would at least protect them from shrapnel and perhaps concussion waves.

Polly studied it for a long moment. "Will you bury it in the street?"

"No. Captain Gunn told us to lie it on the street in front of the house. There are racks so you can climb inside."

Polly shook her head. "Okay. Do whatever my husband asked of you."

They turned the tank sideways and rolled it down the makeshift ramp, but it was so heavy that it kept going when it hit the street. It rolled to a stop in front of their neighbor's yard.

"Well, it rolled just like Captain Gunn said it would," the driver cracked.

"Yes, just like he said," Polly echoed through a grin.

Then she froze, replaying what the driver just said. She stepped closer to him and asked, "Why do you keep calling my husband Captain Gunn?"

"He's a captain now."

"In the Navy?" Polly asked incredulously. P.I. retired as a senior chief warrant officer. He never held a commission as an officer.

"No, ma'am. In the Army Air Force."

Nath and his mother shared a look.

The Air Force?

The PAL employees finished setting up the makeshift shelter and wedged it into place, still a house over from its intended destination. They said farewell and left the Gunns to inspect their new home during bombing raids.

That evening, P.I. staggered home. He looked even older and more bone weary than the last time they had seen him. Connie met him in the street, and he shared a short moment with his oldest daughter.

"Dad, why is the shelter next door?" she asked. She and Julie had been off getting certified in first aid so they could work at a Red Cross station.

P.I. smiled through his exhaustion and replied, "Didn't want that eyesore cluttering up the yard."

They chatted together in the evening's twilight, Connie looking at P.I. through her mother's eyes. She looked so much like Polly, and carried herself with such grace and dignity. No wonder why so many boys wanted to be her suitor.

At length, P.I. said to her, "You know, Connie, I made a mistake bringing the family to the Philippines."

"Daddy?" Even at seventeen, she still called him that. His comment caught her off guard. To hear him admit to making a mistake? This was a first.

"This war... it isn't going to be a one-night stand."

Later that night, he reiterated that thought and told the family not to listen to all the talk around town about this being a short war. From what he could see, it was going to take years to fight this one to a finish. In the meantime, he and the other aviators still left on Luzon would do whatever they could to keep Manila out of Japanese hands.

If only General MacArthur felt the same way.

15

Routine in Chaos

Guyenne Sanchez was nothing if not persistent, and it did not take him long to find the Gunn family's new home. Born into the Spanish aristocracy in the Philippines, he was a trim and dapper young man, impeccably dressed and coiffed. The first time he showed up at the house looking to call on Connie, Nath and Paul thought their dad would eat him alive. P.I. preferred rough and rugged men with work-worn hands and straightforward characters. The family's first impression of Guyenne was just the opposite—he came across as a dandy.

Guyenne first met Connie at Nielson Field earlier in 1941 and fell hard for her from the outset. Instead of a direct approach to her heart, he undertook a patient campaign of courtship. First, he won P.I. over. Charming, easy to laugh, and possessing a broad range of knowledge, he held a well-paying job with Andrés Soriano's tobacco interests. P.I. could see at once that he could offer Connie a life of comfort that he only recently was able to share with Polly.

That meant a lot less to P.I. than most would have thought. Money never trumped heart in P.I.'s worldview, and as he got to know Guyenne, he saw beneath the fabulous clothes and polished shoes a man

of great character and values that harkened back to a more genteel age.

The courtship began with P.I.'s blessing. Polly liked Guyenne,
too, and soon the boys were won over as well. Within a few months,
he was accepted as an extended member of the family.

He loved Connie with a deep and abiding passion that she, however, never felt herself toward him. Guyenne pressed on in hopes
Connie's heart might someday open to him. He visited the Villamor
house often, bringing small gifts for the family and frequently staying for dinner. Gradually, the Gunns were drawn into a circle of his
Spanish friends, most of whom were pilots like Guyenne or worked
for one of Soriano's companies.

In the days after the family moved below the Gureviches, Guyenne called on them every day. At times, he arrived just in time
for the latest air attack on the city, and he would scrunch down into
the makeshift bomb shelter in the street with the rest of the Gunns.
Other times, he showed up with his circle of friends, including the
Garriz brothers, Raleigh and Charlie. They were identical twins, in
their early twenties, who tried to put distance between themselves
and their Spanish roots by Americanizing their names. Yet, both
had fought in the Spanish Civil War. They were jovial and easygo-
ing, but underneath their charm beat warrior hearts.

At night, the twins, Guyenne, and the Gureviches would often
be together, doing their best to shut out the war and all the news of
Allied defeats across the globe that Don Bell glumly reported each
day on Radio Manila (NBC's KZRH). They escaped into song and
games and lots of laughter.

It became part of the routine in this twilight hour of America's
rule. The front to the north and south seemed to have stabilized,
at least for the moment. MacArthur's communiqués extolled heroic
stands and brave soldiers, and for the moment they seemed credible.
Life simply continued on with new patterns to account for the war's

effects. Gas rationing, blackouts, daily runs to the bomb shelter. They formed the basis of this new life as the old ways were grafted onto them.

Without their hired staff, Polly began cooking again. That was a simple joy she hadn't experienced since Honolulu. She often cooked alongside Eva, trading kitchen secrets and sharing family recipes. Leo's constant playing on the piano formed the soundtrack of this part of their lives. At times, the happy moments together with old friends and new were punctuated by the realities they faced. One night, the Garriz brothers arrived fuming at a scene that they had encountered in Manila earlier that day. A Filipino antiaircraft crew set up their weapon in an intersection, and as Japanese planes flew over, the Garrizes saw they did not know how to actually fire it.

They rushed over and gave the gun crew a quick lesson, based on their experiences in the Spanish Civil War. The Filipinos looked overwhelmed and out of their element. They were, of course. Until a few weeks before, they lived quiet civilian lives in villages all over Luzon. Now, with little time to train, they were expected to operate and maintain complex weapon systems. It was simply beyond their capacity without more instruction and practice.

The news of the gun crew's lack of training seemed a portent of things to come. The vast majority of MacArthur's troops were Filipinos, and he staked the defense of the islands on their ability to defend them.

What if other units were similarly trained...?

The point was reinforced to the rest of the family by the local constable. He stood watch at the end of their block and seemed nice enough. But every time Japanese aircraft passed overhead, he drew his .38 revolver, took careful aim skyward, and emptied it. The snub-nosed pistol probably had an accurate range of less than a hundred feet, so all he did was waste ammunition. Yet to him, he preserved his honor. Revolver empty, he would bound down the street and duck into the bomb shelter with the rest of the Gunns.

As these anxious days wore on, Polly did something totally out of character. Perhaps thinking of the future and of P.I.'s plan of escape should the family need to get out of Manila, she took Guyenne aside and talked to him about the most precious items in the household.

There were plenty of memories tied up in the things that filled her home. The Singer sewing machine was an extraordinary gift from P.I. one year early in their marriage. She loved to sew and create, and she once mentioned wistfully to him in passing how much more she could do with that particular model, knowing its price was out of their reach.

P.I. went out and bought it anyway for her. In the years that followed, she created entire wardrobes for each member of the family. On the mantel stood a photo of the boys at Pearl Harbor, dressed in immaculate replicas of P.I.'s Navy uniform, down to the chief petty officer stripes on their shoulders that she had lovingly stitched for them with the Singer.

There were the Pensacola quilts, and the wind-up Victrola record player that had been the nexus of so many after dinner gatherings from San Diego to Villamor Court. There was the family's first new car and the piano.

Most of all, there was the spool post bed. Home was where that bed was, and it would always be so in Polly's ordered world. She told Guyenne about it, despite it being such a personal and intimate part of the household. It was a sign of how much trust she vested in the young aristocrat. His persistence might not have unlocked Connie's heart, but he gained access to the family's.

During the days, while P.I. was off scraping the treetops, Connie and Julie continued their recertification as Red Cross aides. The classes went for hours, and they had already been through them once before. But in the hasty move they'd lost their cards, and now they went through the training again while the Japanese bombed Manila's docks, the shipping in the harbor, and the airfields every day.

P.I. came whenever he could, but for a week the family saw little of him. He slept most nights at Grace Park, if he slept. Most often, he catnapped between flights and overseeing the maintenance of the PAL aircraft.

On the night of December 20, 1941, the Japanese landed at Davao City on Mindanao. The assault on the southern Philippines was designed to cut the Filamerican military off from the Dutch East Indies and Australia. The next night, eighty Japanese transports steamed into Luzon's Lingayen Gulf, carrying almost fifty thousand hardened combat troops.

MacArthur meant to defend the beaches and keep the invaders at bay, but the assault waves quickly gained beachheads and drove the untrained Filipino troops off every time they came into contact. The Japanese quickly exploited the situation and pushed south off the sands of Lingayen Gulf. Most of a Philippine infantry division disintegrated trying to stop their advance.

MacArthur faced reality; the Filipino Army was not ready for prime time. They couldn't defend Luzon proper or the rest of the islands. The only thing left to do was try and dig in and wait for help. He activated War Plan Orange 3, a prewar strategy that called for the Filamerican army to retreat into the Bataan Peninsula, the thumb of land pointing down into Manila Bay. MacArthur originally rejected the plan as too defeatist, believing he could defend the entire island on the beaches. The Japanese proved him wrong. Once inside Bataan, the troops were to hold out until the Navy brought help. Of course, the prewar plan assumed there would be a Navy left to rescue the troops.

That the remnants of the Pacific Fleet could get to the Philippines in early 1942 was doubtful, and MacArthur knew it. He had no other option, save destruction. At least while his men held out on Bataan, they could deny the Japanese use of Manila Bay.

P.I. got wind of the change in strategy when he was ordered to fly butchered meat from Mindanao up to a rough-hewn airstrip on Bataan. He carried the food in for the quartermasters, who were scrambling to try and get as much of the supplies around the island as possible into Bataan even as the troops fought a series of rear-guard delaying actions.

P.I. saw the end in sight. With the army fighting a withdrawal into Bataan, it would only be a matter of time before Manila fell. The time had come to get the family out.

On December 23, he stayed just long enough to tell Polly it was time to go. Each member of the family needed to pack a single small bag. He would be back for them as soon as he could.

He returned to Grace Park to work through the final details of their escape. All the while, the situation at the front in north Luzon grew worse by the minute. The quartermasters didn't have the vehicles to save both the troops and the supplies they forward positioned when MacArthur ordered the beaches defended. Even when there was available transport, politics thwarted the supply troops. At Cabanatuan, the Army stocked warehouses with enough rice to sustain the army on Bataan for a year, yet President Manuel Quezon appealed to MacArthur to leave it in place out of fear the local civilians would suffer from its loss. Orders went out to the troops to not take food from Filipino farms or businesses. There were plenty of Japanese merchants on the islands, some of whom had already appeared in Imperial Army uniforms, if rumors were to be believed. Thousands of tons of food sat in their shops from Manila to Baguio, but again MacArthur heeded President Quezon's demands and ordered the Army to leave those stocks alone as well.

Around Manila, the tempo and mood changed overnight. On

the twenty-third, the Army began piling supplies on the docks for shipment over to Corregidor Island and Bataan via the few remaining vessels in the bay. Massive amounts of material, everything from Christmas packages from home to grand pianos, lay dumped nearby on the docks, left behind by civilian cargo ships in their haste to empty their holds and get out from under Japanese bombs. The mess and chaos on the docks, combined with the daily raids, slowed the entire process down and eventually ensured that massive amounts of food and vital supplies were abandoned there or destroyed.

In the confusion, the Philippine Army Air Corps received orders to blow up its own aircraft and report to Bataan to be employed as infantry. Dutifully, they set fire to their beloved, if obsolete, collection of Martin B-10 bombers and stubby Peashooters. Only after flames consumed most of them did somebody countermand the order. Too late. Some of the last planes left to the defenders of the Philippines were needlessly thrown away.

Such self-inflicted wounds would come back to haunt the Allies in the weeks ahead.

To add to the crisis, Luzon's railroad system collapsed at the worst possible moment. The American quartermasters counted on using the trains that ran through Luzon's central plain to carry much of the materiel south toward Bataan. At various stations, they planned to transfer the supplies to trucks and rush them into Bataan's hastily established supply depots.

It didn't work out that way. The Filipino railroad workers, terrorized by machine-gunning Japanese aircraft, panicked and fled. Rail cars and locomotives were abandoned helter-skelter, and a political dispute over who should man them ensured that nobody did. The quartermasters and troops tried desperately to save what they could, but it often came down to saving frontline soldiers or getting food and ammunition out. They got the men; the Japanese frequently got the supplies.

The final blow came in the early morning hours of Christmas Eve, 1941. A Japanese amphibious convoy appeared in Lamon Bay to the east of Manila and northward up the coast from Paracale. In the darkness, about nine thousand Japanese soldiers came ashore against negligible opposition. At dawn, FEAF threw some of its last fighters against the beachhead, and patched-together P-35s and P-40s made a valiant effort to stop the landings. Their strafing inflicted casualties but failed to stop the Japanese. The Japanese pushed inland, fighting their way westward until by noon, they were within twenty miles of Manila's outskirts.

Late that morning, MacArthur called General Brereton to his headquarters to have a face-to-face discussion with him. He told his air general that the U.S. Army Forces in the Far East (USAFFE) was moving its HQ to Corregidor Island, the tadpole-shaped fortress just off the southern tip of Bataan. He intended to continue to direct the campaign from the tunnels bored into the island's rocky hills. President Quezon was departing with MacArthur and his staff later that day.

Word was passed to destroy any supplies or equipment that could not be carried into Bataan. The massive fuel tanks and oil farms around Manila would be burned. Storage facilities, warehouses full of gear, ammunition caches and magazines would soon be set to the torch. In such an environment, MacArthur had no use for an air general without airplanes. He ordered Brereton to escape to Australia with a skeleton staff. When he got to Darwin, MacArthur told him to establish a new headquarters and send all available help north to the Philippines. A convoy of transports led by the U.S. Navy cruiser USS *Pensacola* was sailing across the Pacific with planes, ammunition, troops, and artillery for the Philippines. Orders from Washington diverted the convoy to Australia. MacArthur wanted Brereton to see that its crated aircraft were assembled and thrown into the fight to hold Bataan.

Brereton later wrote he did not want to go. He asked MacArthur to let him stay, continue on with the fight by his side. MacArthur refused. He told Brereton he could do more good for the Philippines organizing things in Australia. The truth was more nuanced; not only was Brereton an air force commander without an air force left, but FEAF's performance in the opening days of the war caused MacArthur to lose confidence in Brereton. Sending him to Australia was his way of getting rid of a senior officer he no longer felt could serve him.

When dismissed, Brereton headed back to FEAF HQ, which had been moved from Nielson Field to underground facilities at Fort McKinley. He drew up a short list of officers he needed to establish a functioning headquarters and gain control over the Army Air Force personnel and equipment in Australia. Then he and his aides calculated how many planes he would need to get everyone out.

When they finished working out the details, they called for Captain P.I. Gunn.

16

Christmas Eve

December 24, 1941
Manila

The bombers came that morning, a broad formation of twin-tailed G3M "Nells" crewed by the aerial sharpshooters of the First Kōkūtai. They paraded over Manila Bay, attacking the two remaining U.S. Navy destroyers still at anchor near Cavite. Continuing on, they pounded the docks and piers with a veritable carpet of bombs. Waterfront buildings collapsed, spilling so much rubble into the streets as to make them impassable. Other bombs cratered the avenues, and at least one exploded next to a streetcar. The blast threw it like a toy into a nearby building, which caved in on top of it.

The raid sparked dozens of fires, left rail lines twisted like crazy straws and buried men, women, and children alive under heaps of debris. The raid also flattened Engineer Island, the neighborhood at the mouth of the Pasig River.

The Gunn family scrambled to their bomb shelter and rode out this worst attack yet from the safety of its steel confines. More than once, they heard falling antiaircraft shrapnel *ting* off its sides as they huddled together on the chicken wire shelves. Before the attack, they had been preparing for Christmas, and the mood in the household had been dismal. The beating their beloved city took from the Japanese that morning punctuated their dark morale with stark terror.

After the all clear sounded, they climbed out of the shelter and returned to the apartment to try to find some semblance of normalcy in this worsening nightmare.

Polly reeled inside, knowing there would be no gifts for the children, no peace of midnight Mass—not even a Christmas tree. Even if they could have gotten one, there was no room in the apartment for it. They waited in stasis, ready to leave as soon as P.I. came for them, while the waterfront burned in the distance.

Where was P.I.? When would he get them out?

At that moment, P.I. was back in Manila, speeding through the city in the green Buick with his mind racing furiously over his latest orders. Moments before, he had landed after a supply run down to Del Monte. The PAL mechanics went right to work on the red Beech, NPC-56, to prep it for another flight.

On the ground, he learned FEAF HQ wanted him for a top-priority mission. Exactly what happened that confused morning and afternoon will never be fully known, but it is likely that when P.I. landed, he learned about the flight to Australia.

Brereton's staff wanted their most experienced pilot to evacuate them to safety. FEAF HQ requested that he report immediately to General Brereton, but it is unlikely that he did so. Instead, Brereton was told P.I. had not come back in yet from the Del Monte run. Somebody, probably Dan Stickle, bought him some time with that lie.

Later, Brereton received word that the PAL aircraft needed forty-eight hours before they were flight worthy again. That might have been true for NPC-54, but it was not for the other Beech 18. Earlier in the month, P.I. took over two other Beech transports that belonged to the Philippine Army Air Corps. They had survived the bombings earlier in the month, and working with his connections in the PAAC, he was able to save them by hiding them at Grace Park. At least one of those 18s was serviced and ready to fly.

So the PAL team was feeding FEAF false information. There was only one reason for this: P.I. needed time.

MacArthur's staff had assured P.I. for days that Manila would be defended. But now, with the Japanese landing seemingly everywhere, the fall of the city seemed imminent.

Meanwhile, the nearest air base in Australia was over eighteen hundred miles from Del Monte. He'd have to refuel along the way at airports in the Dutch East Indies, and he didn't know that area well. How long would he be gone?

His mind played through scenarios, his loyalties torn between family and duty. He searched for ways to get his family out. What if he flew them to Mindoro now? Then raced back and got Brereton's people loaded up?

If he did that, he might end up delivering his family right to the Japanese.

What about leaving them at Del Monte?

Japanese troops were already on the island.

Where else? His mind raced. Panay? Cebu? Same situation. The Japanese were landing everywhere. Who knew which island would be next?

P.I. never disobeyed a direct order in his entire Navy career. Now, two weeks into his Army Air Force career, he faced the decision of his life.

He had to find a way to follow orders *and* save his family.

If MacArthur's troops held their ground, it would be at least a few days before the battle for the capital was joined. That might give him just enough time to get to Australia with Brereton's staff, then turn around and fly back for his family. If they were packed and ready to go, he could get them aboard within minutes and make a second run down to Australia with them. He wouldn't be leaving the family to their fate on whatever island he left them at in his haste. Instead, he would have them close and they would go out together.

Could he chance that? Would Manila hold long enough for that to work? MacArthur's staff officers promised him all week that the capital would be held for as long as possible, even as the majority of the army retreated into Bataan.

He thought it through as he pulled up to the duplex and parked by the makeshift bomb shelter. Even if the Japanese overran Nielson and Nichols, he could still get the Beech into Grace Park.

What if they overran Grace Park? He could land on one of the broader streets in town—Dewey or Quezon. There were stretches of both that were straight enough and long enough for an 18 to use.

It seemed the only option. If he disobeyed the order, grabbed his family now and flew them out, he would be abandoning the commanding general of the Army Air Forces and his staff in the Philippines after America's most powerful general issued a direct order to get them off the island. He would be declared AWOL, probably considered a deserter and subject to the full weight of the military's judicial system. He couldn't do that. Not after a twenty-year Navy career that made him a legend among those men who wore the wings of gold.

The only way this would work was if he flew out and got back as quickly as possible. The forty-eight-hour delay the PAL employees passed to FEAF would actually work against him. He was racing the Japanese Army now.

He hurried into the apartment and found the entire family waiting for him. His appearance shocked them anew. He looked ragged and filthy, his face more lined with worry, his clothes so foul they recoiled at the stench. For days, he flew one mission after another and did not have time to even clean his face, let alone shower. Nor had he shaved, which was another shock to the family, since he prided himself in being clean cut.

"P.I.," Polly said, "take a shower. Get some clothes."

"No time—" he protested.

"No," Polly interrupted, "go take a shower. Now."

He didn't argue. He knew he looked terrible and stank on ice. He bolted for the bedroom, the kids trailing in his wake.

"I have to leave," he said as he rushed into the bathroom.

Polly followed him in as he turned the water on and grabbed his razor. The two talked furtively while he cleaned up.

A moment later, he flew through the bathroom door back into the bedroom. He grabbed a bag and tossed it on the bed.

"I've been ordered to take out some VIPs," he said to the family as he pulled out a couple of pairs of shirts and trousers and stuffed them in the bag.

"I've got to go to Australia," he continued. The kids stared at him, rooted in place.

Dad is leaving?

He stopped and looked at them. "I have no choice. It'll take a day to get down there."

He swung around, pulled some socks out of the dresser, and added them to his bag.

"A day there to service the Beech."

He went back into the bathroom, grabbed his shaving kit and came back out.

"And a day to fly back up."

The kit went into the bag.

"Three days. You got that?"

They all nodded.

"Three days, we'll meet at Grace Park. Bring one bag. We're getting out together."

Everyone nodded at the plan. Relief mingled with their sense of dread at the thought of P.I. thousands of miles from home.

"I'll be back for you."

He zipped the bag up and slung it over a shoulder. He took Polly in his arms and gave her a long kiss. Then he moved toward the front door.

"Three days. Be ready."

He paused. His children looked up at him, fear and uncertainty in their eyes. He stepped to Connie and kissed her lightly on the lips. A hug, a few whispered words, then he moved to Julie and did the same thing.

The gesture surprised the boys. They'd all been kissed by their dad, but he'd never kissed the girls on the lips before. Anything new, anything out of their dad's normal behavior ratcheted up their sense of unease. Everything seemed wrong as they watched their dad say good-bye to his daughters.

P.I. moved to Paul and gave him a kiss on the lips. He never did that before either. Nath stared on, waiting to see how his dad would say good-bye to him.

The youngest Gunn pinned his faith on that right then, even as his father took his head in his hands and kissed him quickly on the lips. He wrapped Nath in a bear hug and whispered in his ear, "You take care of your mother, no matter what. Okay?"

"I will," his son solemnly replied.

Nath was the fighter. He inherited P.I.'s heart, and the old pilot knew it. Paul, he was bookish, whip smart, and always thinking. Nath was a budding man of action. In that moment, P.I. anointed him the family's protector until he returned.

He opened the door as Polly came to his side. They shared a long embrace and a final, impassioned kiss. Then P.I. handed his wife a roll of cash. When and where he acquired it or even how, the family never knew, but the wad contained over thirty-five hundred dollars. "Use this. If anything happens, use this."

Polly took the money.

He hugged her a final time, then slid into the Buick and drove away. The family stood together in the doorway, watching the car vanish beneath a backdrop of smoke clouds and fires raging in the distance.

"Dad kissed me on the lips," Nath finally said.

"That was odd," Paul added.

Polly hugged her babies and tried to set them at ease. "That was just the excitement of the moment. Nothing to worry about."

How hollow those words sounded.

P.I. returned to Grace Park and the waiting Beech 18, where FEAF ordered him to make available two transports. NPC-54 was not fully repaired yet, so he told Harold Slingsby to take one of the PAAC Beech 18s.

At Fort McKinley, FEAF Headquarters had devolved into total chaos. The bombing raid earlier that day had filled the underground passages there with choking dust. Bloated black clouds of smoke hung in the air, fed by the fires along the waterfront and the city proper. Officers burned documents on the floors of their offices. Elsewhere, the operations shop lay deserted, as was the chief of staff's. Brereton and his small circle of aides were huddled in his office, trying to figure out how to best escape from the Philippines.

Brereton, fuming and waiting on word from P.I. Gunn, finally decided he could wait no longer. When he learned that a Navy PBY was about to depart for the Dutch East Indies, he commandeered a couple of seats on it for himself and a few key members of his staff. At four that afternoon, they left Fort McKinley and drove off to find the PBY.

Signs of disintegration were everywhere. Contradictory orders were issued. Some units received no orders at all. Others were told simply to get to Bataan by any means possible. A mad scramble to get out of the city began, while some of the AAF officers left behind by their commanding general drowned their resentment with alcohol at McKinley's Army-Navy club.

P.I.'s commanding officer, Col. Lawrence Churchill, who was in overall charge of FEAF's Air Service Command, likely didn't even know P.I. and Slingsby had been ordered to fly out of the Philippines. Few officers knew of Brereton's departure, and even fewer knew where he was going. When Churchill walked into the FEAF officer's club he found a few familiar faces morosely trying to eat dinner. Totally perplexed by the scene, he asked, "Where the hell is all the staff?"

Gone. The ones around the table were deemed not essential enough to save. They ate like the damned, knowing if help did not arrive, all the defenses on Bataan could not save them from the clutches of the Rising Sun.

Brereton's escape, meanwhile, was fraught with mishaps. The group made its way to Cavite and took a small boat across Manila Bay to the southern tip of Bataan to get to the PBY. They finally reached it after dusk, but when they tried to take off, they struck a fishing boat, badly damaging the patrol plane. The pilot scrubbed the mission.

They returned to Cavite, and drove through the night to another PBY hidden on the northern shore of Laguna de Bay. Brereton and his men drove through checkpoints and columns of panicky troops retreating from the Japanese. At one point, a fleeing Army truck sideswiped their sedan and crumpled one of its fenders. They had to pull over and hack the damaged fender off before they could continue.

A fifty-mile car ride to Los Banos concluded with a furtive overland hike through the light of a fingernail moon, a local Filipino guiding them to the PBY's hiding place. Just before dawn on Christmas Day, Brereton's party finally got airborne, bound for Java.

At Grace Park, the PAL gang did not know what was going on at FEAF HQ. They didn't even know that Brereton left Fort McKinley earlier that afternoon. P.I. still assumed he was under orders to get the general out. For hours, they waited for Brereton, using the extra time to work on the Beech 18s.

When Brereton failed to show up, P.I. decided to fly over to Nielson and see if the general was waiting there for him. The flight only took a few minutes, but it was an unforgettable one.

To the south, the men at Nichols field began demolishing the base. Explosions rocked the area, and huge fireballs rolled skyward as the fuel tanks, ammunition, and oil caches blew up. At the same time, nine P-40s bound for the new strips at Bataan came in to land at Nielson. One pilot crashed into the antiparatroop barricades set up on one of the runways. Another careened into a hangar and exploded. Somehow, the pilot escaped, but as P.I. came in to land, the burning remains of both aircraft filled the area with smoke.

He landed and found a skeleton ground crew still at the strip. When P.I. went to talk to them, they were busy fueling the surviving P-40s. Nobody knew where General Brereton was. Frustrated, P.I. took the Beech back to Grace Park to try and figure out what was going on.

It took all night to sort through the confusion. Ultimately, five officers showed up at Grace Park with orders to fly to Australia. Lt. Col. Lester Maitland, the former commander of Clark Field and current executive officer of Air Service Command, was the highest-ranking of the bunch. With him was Lt. Col. Charles Caldwell, FEAF's personnel officer. Any hope of reestablishing a headquarters in Australia would ride with his skills and knowledge of the available officers and men. Along with these two senior men were three lieutenants, all aides to General Brereton or other top officers.

They climbed aboard P.I.'s NPC-56 while six others filled Slingsby's Philippine Air Corps Beech 18.

Shortly after midnight, they left Grace Park and headed south. The trip was a dicey one from the outset. The latest reports they received included numerous references to Japanese air attacks in northern Borneo and other places in the Dutch East Indies. Because of the confusion and delay, they would be making the most dangerous part of the trip in daylight.

They refueled at Del Monte, then flew southwest to Tarakan, Borneo. They almost ran out of fuel, but they made it to the runway on fumes. The next hop took them due south to Makassar, a field on the southwest corner of Celebes Island. They refueled again, then pressed on for Koepang, Timor. P.I. landed there with less than fifty gallons of gas left in his tanks.

Almost two days after they left Grace Park, P.I. set his bright red Beech 18 down at Batchelor Field outside of Darwin, Australia. He was spent, but he was way behind schedule and burning to get back north. While his aircraft was fueled and prepped he went off in a desperate search for news from the Philippines.

What he discovered left him thunderstruck. MacArthur declared Manila an open city just after P.I. departed Grace Park. MacArthur chose not to defend the capital at all. Instead, he told the Japanese it would not be defended in hopes of saving the city and its people from destruction.

P.I. tried to process the news. MacArthur's staff, Brereton included, must have known all along that this was the plan. They lied to him, and the deception formed the basis of his decision on Christmas Eve.

Rage replaced the shock. How could they do this to him? Did they not know what it meant? He just traded his family for a couple of field grades and their lieutenant lackeys. Two thousand miles from home, the Gunn family protector could do nothing to save his wife and children from the Japanese.

17

The Last Broadcast

December 25, 1941
Manila

The children awoke to a Christmas without stockings, without lovingly cooked delicacies, without gifts—and without their father.

P.I. always picked presents out himself for each member of the family. No matter how busy he was, he delighted in taking the time to find just the right thing, and on Christmas morning, he would sit beside Polly, all smiles as his tokens were unwrapped. In such moments, the family saw him as full of joy and happiness as they ever had. But they also knew that in the back of his mind, he was working through some engineering issue with the 18s or the Staggerwing. Even at his most relaxed, part of P.I.'s brain would always be on work.

The cramped apartment was made even more dismal by the pall of smoke covering the city that morning. Nichols Field burned to the east. The oil refinery had been set afire, and now it gushed great clouds of black smoke. Warehouses, storage facilities, supply dumps, gasoline stores—they were all set aflame to deny them to the Japanese.

Standing out front that morning, the family looked on at the apocalyptic scene with utter bewilderment. What did it mean?

So far, Don Bell and the folks at Radio Manila had not made any announcements that the Japanese were about to enter the city. Filipino troops and American trucks and vehicles raced through the streets, careening around this way and that seemingly without purpose or pattern.

Church was out of the question. It was far too dangerous to venture out. Besides, these holy sites were anything but safe in an air attack. Just a few days before, the monastery and church of Santo Domingo had been pulverized to rubble by falling bombs.

Caught up in the confusion, all they could do was return to their tiny apartment and share time together. Polly, normally able to be cheery and light even in the worst moments, could not even rouse herself to smile. The typical Christmas meal they'd shared these past few years in Manila would be impossible to make. The plentiful fruit, the sweet potatoes, meats, and vegetables were simply not available. Besides, they had not even had time to fully unpack, and much of the kitchenware remained in the boxes stacked around the apartment.

Polly settled on oven-roasted chicken. Through the morning, she worked to prepare it with Connie's and Julie's help. In the distance, explosions rattled the city, shaking their windowpanes.

At noon, the Japanese bombers came. The family scrambled to the bomb shelter as they paraded overhead with complete impunity. Gone were the valiant if futile interceptions by the likes of Jess Villamor. The antiaircraft guns didn't even attempt to bring them down, either.

The city shook to the rolling thunder of the bombing. The Gurevich family joined the Gunns in P.I.'s hillbilly shelter until the all clear finally sounded.

Shaken, they stumbled back to their duplex. As Polly finished dinner, the sound of Leo's piano playing filled the first-floor apartment. Connie could see the family had reached a breaking point.

Even the boys looked terrified. So she took it on herself to step up. She radiated calm, helped her mother as best she good, and checked on Nath and Paul every few minutes. She came into her own that day, shouldering the load as her mother struggled to find strength.

In the afternoon, a motorcycle pulled up out front. It was Guyenne, his white linen suit covered in gray soot from the refinery fire. He came in, his normally cheerful face ashen and anxious. He brought bad news. The military seemed to be pulling out of the city in complete disorder. Ships had been coming and going from the docks for the past twenty-four hours and frantic efforts to load supplies aboard them had devolved into chaos. Now, heaps of food, medical gear, and civilian belongings had been abandoned on the piers. Word got around the city of this unguarded bounty, and thousands of desperately poor Filipinos descended on the waterfront to pick through the rubble and loot everything they could carry. It turned into a frenzy that the few authorities left in the area could never hope to contain.

Outside, in the smoky twilight, the Garriz brothers arrived, also covered in ash and soot. They shared more stories of chaos, confusion, and looting.

Before dinner that evening, Don Bell came over the radio to announce that Manila had been declared an open city. It would no longer be defended, and all military personnel were leaving the capital. The blackout would no longer be in effect, and residents were asked to turn their lights back on after sundown so the Japanese would know the city was no longer a military target.

The news confirmed everything they'd seen and been told that day. As their Spanish friends bid them good evening, promising to check on them in the morning, the reality of what that meant settled on each member of the family.

There would be no way P.I. could come back for them. Not now. Nielson Field could be in Japanese hands at any minute. The December 27 rendezvous would never happen.

They were trapped in a dying, panicked city, its food stores being looted or blown up, the police force impotent, the Filamerican Army abandoning them. The American high commissioner of the Philippines, Francis Sayre, attempted to reassure everyone, stating that the Philippines would still be defended to the last man. But the words seemed like so much rubbish in light of the realities seen in the capital's streets.

That night, the horizon glowed reddish orange from the fires encircling the city. A night before, even a sliver of light escaping from a window was liable to elicit a gunshot from a trigger-happy constable. Now, the Filipino cops prowled the streets, ordering households to tear down their blackout curtains. Few people had heeded the radio's call, and even the zealous efforts of the constabulary couldn't keep the lights on. The citizens simply feared the Japanese would ignore the declaration and use the lights as navigation points for another night raid.

The next morning, Eva and Polly huddled to discuss the situation. Eva's family had endured the Japanese occupation of China; she knew what to expect.

"Don't try to hide anything," she told Polly, "the soldiers will find it. They always do. And if you've hidden anything they might think suspicious, they will kill you."

Polly looked around the apartment. There were photos of P.I. everywhere. He was either in uniform or standing next to an aircraft. The Japanese would want to know all about him, no doubt about it. But what would that mean to the family?

Eva had noticed the photographs as well. "Leave them out. Don't put them away."

Polly looked quizzically at her.

"Tell them your husband died in the bombing of Cavite."

She nodded.

"Be sure the children say exactly the same thing."

Polly gathered the children and repeated this to them. They practiced and rehearsed until there would be no mistake. P.I. Gunn, U.S. Navy, had died December 10, 1941, at Cavite.

At one point, the city received a small morale boost. Working furiously, FEAF mechanics had managed to patch together three P-40s. That morning, haggard pilots climbed into them and took off from Quezon Boulevard. The roadway was so straight and wide it served as a perfect makeshift runway. The sounds of American engines provided a welcome change for once. They stayed low, banked out over Manila Bay, and headed to the new jungle strips on Bataan, among the last aircraft left to the defenders of the Philippines.

The days after Christmas became a tension-filled waiting game for the family. Julie and Connie finished their medical training and spent exactly one day at their assigned Red Cross station. They treated an elderly Filipino lady and a young American soldier, J.C. Baxter, who fell hard for Julie. He'd been left behind to blow up strategic sites around the city and was injured during one of those projects. After he was back on his feet, he became a regular visitor to the duplex.

The Spanish boys came by every day, helping to keep up the family's morale and puzzling through ways they could help. At one point, they came up with the idea to make the Gunns Spanish citizens. If Guyenne married Connie, one of the Garriz boys married Julie, and one of their old Spanish friends married Polly, they'd be safe from the Japanese.

But Polly would have none of that. Nobody knew what the Japanese would do to the American civilians in the city. For that matter, nobody had any idea what would happen to any of the white Europeans living there. But their fate seemed to be foreshadowed by the sudden appearance of one of P.I.'s employees one afternoon.

His name was Otto; he was a German national who had been part of PAL's ground crew. After Hitler declared war on the United

States, the authorities in the Philippines arrested and interned all German nationals alongside the Japanese they also detained. Now, with Manila's fall imminent, the retreating Americans released all their internees.

Embittered by his treatment, Otto asked around to where P.I.'s family could be found. He showed up at the door, waving a pistol at Polly and shouting that she and her family would get to experience prison life themselves in short order. Polly kept her composure as the man wielded the pistol and ranted. Perhaps her fearless calm mollified him, as he eventually left without causing any further trouble. As if the situation wasn't scary enough, having a disgruntled Teutonic mechanic threaten them with a gun left Julie and Connie absolutely terrified.

Meanwhile, the bombings not only continued, they actually grew worse. The Japanese either ignored or did not know about the open city declaration. They pounded targets around the city all week long, inflicting more damage on the already scarred and soot-covered capital. MacArthur's communiqués were filled with the standard lines, like "We are holding on all fronts." They were so ridiculously optimistic that if one read them and nothing else, it would seem as if the Americans were winning the war.

One look in the streets of Manila would disabuse anyone of that fantasy. On the thirtieth, the Manila newspapers began to break ranks from the military's censorship and began publishing articles about what to do if Japanese troops entered the city. Stay indoors, stay calm, do not offer resistance, those articles advised. Yet the radios still gushed with the gallantry of the troops, and how they were holding despite being desperately outnumbered.

On New Year's Eve, the Gureviches and Gunns tried to celebrate together in the upstairs apartment. Guyenne came. So did the Garriz twins and others. They filled the apartment with food and friendship, doing their best to celebrate the night in the face of so much uncertainty and death.

At nine thirty, Don Bell came on Radio Manila, his voice cracked as he read the news. As he wrapped up his broadcast, he told his audience, "Chins up, keep 'em flyin'." The station began playing "Three Cheers for the Red, White, and Blue," but midway into it, the signal suddenly cut off. Static filled the Gureviches' living room.

Radio Manila went off the air.

To the north, a gasoline storage farm was put to the torch. Flames shot skyward, illuminating the city in a hellish orange glow. To Polly, it seemed as if the heavens themselves were ablaze. As it burned, Leo played the piano. The Spanish boys played the accordion, or sang. One of Julie and Connie's schoolmates added her voice.

Together, as the city burned, they sang "God Bless America." Leo sat at the piano, eyes closed, head thrown back, lost in the music and in the moment. They sang with poignancy, the Americans desperately homesick. As midnight approached, Leo began to play "The Star-Spangled Banner." The Russian Jews, whose dreams of coming to the United States had been shattered by its Army's failure to protect them, added their voices to the Gunns'. Guyenne and the other Spaniards joined in. They knew the words by heart. For Polly, it was a moment where she felt more American, and more proud to be an American, than any other time in her life. Tears flowed and the gathering unabashedly became emotional. They knew this would be the last celebration for a long time. The song ended, voices died away until only silence remained. It lingered until somebody broke the spell by checking a watch and starting the countdown. They rang in the New Year as brightly as they could manage. The silence returned, but the party did not break up. Nobody wanted to go to bed and see what the future held for them. Instead, they clung to this moment, and each other, as explosions rumbled through their beloved city and the piers began to burn. The radio played only static now, except for the Tokyo station, but nobody wanted to listen to it. They stayed in the Gurevich apartment, talking in quiet voices, the mood of the party drifting to melancholy. The gathering did not break up until after two.

Four mornings later, Nath stood by a window overlooking the garden. His father had told him to look after his mother, and he intended to do just that. Since New Year's, he had stationed himself every day by the window so he could scan the road and the narrow view of the neighborhood his perch afforded. He rarely moved, and never asked for relief. Instead, he stood watch from his vantage point with patience that belied his youth.

He turned from the window that morning. "Mom," he called, "Mom! Come quick!"

Polly rushed to Nath's side to see what her youngest had seen.

A Japanese soldier, a wicked bayonet fixed to his rifle, stood in their front yard.

"What do we do, Mom?"

The soldier advanced to the door and rapped sharply on it.

"Let him in," Polly said, her voice barely a whisper.

Part Two

The Legend of
Pappy Gunn

18

Early Legends

Did you hear about Pappy Gunn? He took a whole British base hostage so he could get his bird back in the fight. Brereton's gonna court-martial him for that one."

"Brereton's gone. Went to India when things on Java went to hell. Gen. Howard Brett's in charge now."

"That's right. Pappy fixed up a DC-2, or maybe one of those new Lockheeds that came in with the Pensacola's *convoy. Worked nineteen hours straight and collapsed from fatigue. Again."*

"Yeah, I heard he and Slingsby flew it up to a B-17 wreck, landed in the middle of nowhere, and pulled the wing off the damned thing. Slung it under the DC-2 and flew it back. Had about an inch of clearance to the ground with it. Put Slingsby in for a Distinguished Flying Cross for that."

"Hear about Pappy Gunn?"

"He was going back to rescue his family. He and Cecil McFarland, whose wife lived in Cebu. Mac was going to find a way into Cebu from Del Monte. Pappy had it all fixed up ahead of time to meet his wife and kids on Bataan. He ran out of fuel. Crashed in the jungle."

"That man is unkillable."

"Hates the brass as much as the Japs. Doesn't give a damn who he pisses off."

"Told me they betrayed him, tricked him into leaving his family behind. It's eating him up."

"Friend told me that the son of a bitch talked his way into an Aussie fighter squadron. Knocked down a flock of Zeroes over Rabaul, but they got him, too. Spent three weeks in the jungle, eating bugs and berries he figured were safe since the birds were eatin' 'em, too."

"Yeah, I heard that when he stumbled into Gasmata, he was thirty pounds lighter and his hair turned white."

"Tried to dogfight Zeroes in a Wirraway? What's a Wirraway?"

"You know those T-6s they taught us to fly with back in training? Yeah. One of them with guns."

"That guy is indestructible."

"He can fly anything. Told me once he landed on a whale. Just rolled up onto his back. Whale didn't seem to mind too much."

"Accommodatin' whale."

In the darkness, Pappy stood before the Filipino sergeant, backlit by the glare of exploding artillery shells a few miles away. The Japanese were attacking the Bataan boys again.

"You sure you can get them out?" Pappy demanded.

The Filipino nodded solemnly. He and his men were using little fishing boats to move between Bataan and the Manila area, evading Japanese patrols by sailing at night.

Pappy pulled his wedding ring off and handed it to the sergeant. "Give this to Polly. That way, she'll know I sent you."

Then Pappy reached into his pocket, pulled out a roll of cash. Thirty-five hundred dollars' worth of greenbacks and Philippine pesos. He pressed it into the sergeant's waiting hands. "Ten days. Quezon Boulevard."

"Ten days."

The old aviator, face lined with stress and worry, turned and walked for his plane, tucked under the trees at the edge of one of Bataan's jungle airstrips.

"Where's Pappy Gunn these days?"

"Flew four missions into Java, hauling supplies, pulling people out.

Took another flight of P-40s up to Darwin, that one led by Major Pell. Those guys sure did get it."

"There I was in the scramble shack, and I swear to God in walks Pappy Gunn with a goddamned lizard on his shoulder."

"I hear they're going to court-martial his ass. Deserves it, too. Son of a bitch can't be pointing guns at people."

"So he crashes in the jungle, right? Everyone thinks he's dead."

"Well, he turns up on some field on Mindanao, and there's Connelly with a broken B-17 he can't get started. Pappy rolls right up and gets to work—straight outta the jungle. Gets that engine purring and hitches a ride back to Oz."

"I tell ya, I've never seen the guy sleep. He's always under an airplane."

"Only one with a shirt on, too. Long sleeves, huge sweat stains. Why, he looks like he took a shower with his clothes on."

"I hear he flies naked. Gets airborne and strips down to a loincloth."

"Flew with him once. Asked him where his maps were. He pointed to his flight kit, but when I opened it there was nothing but a bottle labeled 'Panther Piss.' He grabbed it, took a swig, and told me not to worry about it. He could smell the way. Turns out, there was a dead cow that he'd smelled and seen on his last run in. He navigated by stench. I swear to God!"

"So MacArthur went out on a B-17, right? But after they got off at Del Monte, the left engines started running rough. You know a Fort can fly on two engines. But you can't lose both on one wing and stay in the air. Nothin' but water and sharks below, that Fort starts dropping out of the sky when number two goes out. Then number one goes, and they're just about finished. Suddenly, there's Pappy Gunn in that Twin Beech of his. Pulls up alongside, waves all kindly like, then slides a wingtip under that Fort's and holds 'em up all the way back to Darwin. The general didn't even get his feet wet."

"Pappy's family? Any word?"

"*Nothing. Heard they were rounding up all the Americans. Putting them in some camp or something. He's going mad over it.*"

Pappy landed on Quezon Boulevard ten days after his meet-up with the Filipino sergeant. The scout would not fail him. If he could get his family out, Pappy knew he would.

Manila had no blackout anymore, now that it was in Japanese hands. Even this late at night, lights burned throughout the city. Pappy idled his engines, waiting anxiously for the rendezvous to be completed.

Nobody came.

Minutes passed, Pappy grew tense. Where were they? He couldn't stay on the ground for much longer.

Headlights.

Was it them?

A Japanese truck.

He swung the tail around and goosed the throttles, racing down Quezon Boulevard back into the velvet sky. Heartsick, frustrated and despairing, he wondered if somewhere below, the sergeant and Polly and Nath and Paul and Julie and Connie had been just a little too late.

19

The Perilous Consequence
of Not in Stock

Early January 1942
Brisbane, Australia

Not in stock, my ass. These knuckleheads are gonna cost us the goddamned war."

P.I. turned to the two mechanics he'd brought along. "You boys ready?"

They held Thompson submachine guns across their chests, looking like a ragged band of mercenaries with their curious mix of Aussie and American uniform parts and civilian clothes.

The mechanics nodded. The old guy from the Philippines seemed to be at least half insane to even think of doing something like this. Yet he got things done when everyone else around here ran in helpless circles.

They were with him, whatever the consequences.

"Good. Follow me."

P.I. stepped to the entryway of a squat, single-story building. Some civilian company's sign hung above it. Probably a wholesale grocery warehouse or something similar. At least it was a grocery warehouse up until a few weeks ago. Now commandeered by the

U.S. military, the army's quartermasters had filled it with supplies. Their prewar mind-set led them to think that was the objective—get stuff on the shelves and keep it there to grow their horde. Units were allotted exactly what the supply manuals said they could have, not what they actually needed. The by-the-book world clashed with the reality of the emergency, and in that conflict everyone who wanted to fight lost. The parts, equipment, and supplies sat on the shelves, guarded by layers of red tape and truculent rear-area types.

P.I. was starting to hate them almost as much as MacArthur's staff. He took one more look at his confederates, then flung open the door and stormed inside, drawing a pair of Colt .45 automatic pistols from twin shoulder holsters as he went.

A smartly dressed U.S. Army Air Force supply clerk, fresh off the boat from San Francisco, looked up to see a furious middle-aged banshee with captain's bars adorning a civilian shirt collar, striding toward him. Face red, guns drawn, the clerk quailed at the sight. He was being robbed? In Australia?

P.I. covered the stunned clerk and told the mechanics to get what they needed. They disappeared into the warehouse proper, pulling gear off the shelves and rooting around in cargo crates in search of items on this run's foraging list.

Swiftly, they hauled their bounty back to a truck. It took several trips, all the while P.I. menaced the clerk with his brace of Model 1911s.

Welcome to Australia. Bring ammo.

In country for only a few weeks, he was done with bullshit and dumbasses in uniform. MacArthur and his staff betrayed him. They lied, tricked him into leaving Polly and the kids behind. If they'd just told him that Manila was going to be declared an open city, he could have taken an hour to fly them to Mindoro, then return to Nielson and carry out whatever mission MacArthur's brass could dream up.

They didn't tell him; yet he still had to work for these same people. Every day forced him to swallow his bitterness and salute the very men who cost him his family. Now, they only got in his way as he tried to get things done. Official channels? Right. Requests got lost or denied. Parts never arrived. Chaos reigned and "no" was the standard answer from the brass.

He owed them nothing—no loyalty, no cloying subservience, no gratitude for his officer's rank. The Army Air Force? Hell, he was a Navy man. So far, all he saw out of the AAF was incompetence and lies. The service was a den of idiots so divorced from reality they were getting young kids killed every day.

What was that compared to a court-martial? If they decided to go after him—fine. They could take his rank; he'd never asked for it. They could try to lock him up, but he would find a way to escape.

All these assholes ever do is bury themselves in bullshit. They got me once, but I'll never play by their rules again.

If he was ever a genteel, wealthy airline manager, the war was turning him into somebody else. Since Manila's surrender, all pretense of civility in P.I. evaporated, replaced by barely contained fury and a short fuse. Get in his way and get a .45 barrel in your nose. If he had to lie, cheat, steal, or shoot his way back to Luzon, he would. Whatever it took, he would get back to Polly and the kids.

They finished picking through the warehouse and headed for the door. P.I. took a last look around, then with a flourish holstered his pistols before pushing outside to the truck. With the vehicle loaded, they piled in and sped off, bound for the prewar civilian airport just outside of town called Archerfield. There, Aussies and Americans worked side by side, trying valiantly to assemble a fleet of dive bombers none of them had ever seen before and knew nothing about. The planes belonged to the Twenty-Seventh Bomb Group and had been crated up in the States prior to Pearl Harbor for shipment to Manila in a convoy escorted by the U.S. Navy heavy cruiser *Pensacola*. The ground echelon and the pilots of the Twenty-Seventh had arrived in the Philippines just before the war started while their aircraft lingered on West Coast docks. Now they found themselves in the middle of a shooting war without planes, weapons, or gear.

With the Japanese in control of the seas and air of the Western Pacific, Washington rerouted the *Pensacola*'s convoy to Brisbane. It arrived on December 22, 1941, with fifty-two A-24 Dauntless dive bombers and eighteen P-40s, along with a bewildering mishmash of B-17 maintainers, Warhawk pilots, a couple of Army artillery regiments, and thousands of tons of random equipment. Everything from bombs to aviation oil, gas masks, folding cots, medical equipment, and .50-caliber ammunition had been sent aboard these ships.

There was no headquarters, or even any American forces to receive them, so like shipwrecked survivors, the men of the *Pensacola* convoy organized into something called the South Pacific Task Force. It was a makeshift mess that put untrained men into duty slots they did not know how to perform. Orders were verbal, confused and contradictory. There was no organization chart, no firm hierarchy of command. Nobody knew who possessed any real authority to do anything.

So almost nothing got done. Meanwhile, the Japanese pressed ever closer to Australia's shores, enforcing a sense of desperation on those combat crews willing and trying to get into the fight. They found themselves drowning in bureaucracy, red tape, and a distinct lack of help from the rear-echelon types who all too frequently did not share their sense of urgency.

P.I. Gunn's truck pulled up alongside the dive bombers, where his mechanics jumped out and called for others to offload it with them. A moment later, Col. John "Big Jim" Davies approached P.I. With command of the few men of the Twenty-Seventh Bomb Group who'd escaped from the Philippines, he was in charge of getting both the P-40s and the dive bombers constructed.

Davies stood six foot four and possessed a broad, muscular build.

Back in the 1920s, he'd been a javelin thrower at Cal Berkeley before making a career out of the Army Air Corps. He spent the Depression careening around the country at treetop level with attack squadrons, loving every minute of it. He was tough and rugged with a can-do attitude and a hatred of red tape that matched P.I.'s.

The situation left him as enraged and frustrated as P.I. He vented often in official reports he ordered typed up and sent to MacArthur's headquarters. He was pissed off and ready to start court-martialing the people standing in the way of getting his aircraft constructed.

P.I. saw the lanky javelin chucker as a kindred spirit—and about the only officer who ranked him that he could respect.

Davies watched P.I. climb out of the truck's cab and went over to talk to him.

"Do I want to know how you got all that stuff?" he asked.

"No."

"Very good," said Davies, then added, "Get more."

P.I. grinned. "Sure thing."

The two men had met at Nielson Field just before the war, where they discovered their similar temperaments. When they ran into each other in Brisbane, the two teamed up. Davies knew P.I.'s vast experience would be useful in the current mess, so he arranged to have him transferred to the Twenty-Seventh. P.I. turned out to be one of the few men with broad engineering and mechanical knowledge under his command in those early weeks of 1942. Almost none of his mechanics had made it out of the Philippines.

Davies flew to Australia on December 18 to round up the Twenty-Seventh Bomb Group's dive bombers, taking along twenty of his most trusted and experienced pilots. The outbound planes did not have enough room for Davies's ground crews. Those men ended up starving in the jungles of Bataan, carrying rifles alongside the increasingly emaciated troops who courageously held the line against repeated Japanese onslaughts.

Those men were the only Army Air Force mechanics in the Pacific who knew anything about these A-24 Dauntless dive bombers.

Without their expertise, Davies relied on the *Pensacola* convoy's personnel. There were aviation mechanics aboard those ships, but they were trained only on the incredible complexities of the Boeing B-17. They pitched in eagerly, working alongside the pilots to assemble the A-24s, but these were totally foreign aircraft to them. The pilots were of little help; few had any mechanical knowledge.

The A-24 was an aberration in the 1942 Army Air Force. Seeing the success of the Stuka and other dive bombers, the brass decided they needed their own. As a stopgap until a new design could be developed, the Army went to Douglas Aircraft and asked for a batch of Navy dive bombers, which were called SBD Dauntlesses. After minor modifications were made, the Army Air Force renamed it the A-24. In a service built for long-range strategic bombing, the two-seat Dauntless was a misfit from the start. There was little institutional knowledge of these aircraft or how best to employ them. Ultimately, only a few squadrons ever used them in combat.

Each dive bomber carried a crew of two: a pilot and a tail gunner. The pilot had a pair of fixed machine guns in the nose, plus a thousand pounds of explosives to drop on the Japanese, while the tail gunners used twin machine guns in a hand-operated, flexible mount in an open cockpit, just like a World War I plane.

When the men at Archerfield began uncrating the disassembled A-24s, they found a complete mess. The rush to get these planes packed and sent to the Pacific meant that the Stateside mechanics tore them down practically right off the flight line. They were haphazardly thrown into the crates with minimal documentation and not enough cushioning material to protect the more delicate parts. It was like dealing with a gigantic metal jigsaw puzzle with thousands of pieces and no box art to illustrate what the finished product was supposed to look like.

They found parts encrusted with mud from airstrips used during the 1941 Louisiana Maneuvers. Other parts were broken in shipment. Critical things like flight instruments reached Australia in useless pieces, which would have been a mild annoyance in the States. In Australia, it was a game-stopper. There were no spares to be found anywhere. There were not even any extra tires for the landing gear, and the ones that shipped out from the States were worn almost smooth.

As they stumbled along, uncrating the parts for each dive bomber, Davies's men made costly mistakes. The worst came when they accidentally destroyed the solenoids for the forward-firing machine guns. They'd been taped inside the shipping crates in small boxes, which nobody noticed. Once the crates were opened and emptied, the men dragged them to burn pits and set them afire with other trash, not knowing that they inadvertently just disarmed all fifty-two A-24s.

Those solenoids were switches that let the pilot fire the guns electrically from a trigger mounted on his control stick. Without them, they couldn't complete the circuit, rendering the guns useless. A search revealed the convoy did not arrive with any extra solenoids, which meant Davies would have to requisition them from Stateside depots. That would take months.

Not that it mattered in the short term. Vital pieces proved to be missing, somehow left behind in the States. This included the electric trigger motors connected to the solenoids. Even if they didn't burn those up, the guns were nonfunctional without those motors, and no replacements existed in Australia that January.

They continued to work anyway, hoping somehow the parts would catch up to them. Then things started to break. Poorly made parts failed when tested. Others broke as the crews tried to install them. In the tail gunner's open cockpit, a half hoop of metal functioned as the mount for the twin .30-caliber guns used to defend the dive bomber's rear. Poorly made by a Douglas Aircraft subcontractor, the ring mounts buckled under the weight of the Browning machine guns. That left the few A-24s assembled without any functional guns.

Then somebody discovered that Army Air Force bombs would not fit on these dive bombers. Douglas had built the Dauntless to Navy specifications, and nobody had told them the Army used different bomb release systems. The Army Air Force took delivery unaware of the issue.

The Twenty-Seventh Bomb Group's long-awaited planes possessed no working guns and could not carry bombs. It was enough to make the Philippine veterans scream with rage. The A-24s were in such bad shape that Colonel Davies finally blew his stack and demanded that those who had packed them up Stateside be prosecuted for "criminal negligence."

The situation wasn't any better across the way at Amberly Field. That was a Royal Australian Air Force base just outside of Brisbane, where the P-40s had been taken for assembly. It took a week to get the first one built, and as the scratch crews worked on the others, they discovered that nobody had bothered to send along any engine coolant. The P-40s' engines used Prestone, like a car's antifreeze in its radiator. Men were dispatched to scour the city for coolant. The search became countrywide, but initially they managed to find only enough for one aircraft. As the P-40s came together, they needed to be test-flown. To do it, the crews had to drain the precious Prestone from one P-40 to the next.

In the middle of all this insanity, P.I. flew into Archerfield in his bright red Beech 18 sometime before New Year's. He was a captain without a command, an airline manager without an airline. But he took one look at this ad hoc effort to create an air force, rolled up his sleeves and joined in. Without any orders, he simply attached himself to Davies's outfit and worked alongside the pilots and ground crews with tireless determination. Davies later made it official and ensured his transfer to his command. P.I. quickly impressed everyone with his mechanical skill and engineering talents. He soon showed other useful traits as well.

P.I. watched some of the young lieutenants as they bravely tried to follow procedures and order the supplies they needed. The officer in charge of the Brisbane base area, Col. Alexander Johnson, ate them alive. He was a martinet, famous for chewing out the Philippine vets for not having proper uniforms, ignoring the fact that they had escaped with only their lives and the clothes on their backs. He had no tolerance for slovenliness, and had a propensity to spout off at anyone he could bully. To one group of young pilots soon bound for combat, he said, "Second lieutenants are expendable."

One of the pilots replied, "Sir, in wartime, everyone is expendable."

Colonel Johnson, safe in Brisbane, thought otherwise.

His "leadership" style engendered considerable tension and set the tone around the city. As Davies's young lieutenants sortied forth to find parts and supplies, they were blocked everywhere. Since American troops and materiel had washed up in Brisbane, the stuff off-loaded from their ships had been haphazardly dumped in temporary depots all over the city. Anywhere a suitable building could be found, it was requisitioned and filled with truckloads of random equipment. There were few, if any, quartermasters in that first convoy, and the mess quickly overwhelmed the men assigned to straighten it out.

Nobody could find anything. Nor did they seem to want to be bothered. Instead, they wanted paperwork that didn't exist from headquarters that hadn't been established. If the chaos in the Philippines was bad, Australia was a complete disaster. Even the port of Brisbane was full of unsorted materiel that sat in crates for weeks while Aussie longshoremen drank tea and adhered to union hours, unmoved by the Americans who tried to spur them to unload the ships.

Davies's green lieutenants, most in uniform for a year or less, couldn't make any headway in such an environment. P.I. would see them come back from foraging missions with little to show for them, frustrated beyond reason. They needed guns. They needed parachutes. They needed uniforms and basic amenities for the men, who had been quartered at two racetracks around town.

P.I., the old-salt Navy chief, stepped into this morass. He'd been a scrounger in the Navy, knew the ins and outs of the supply system. His first foraging trips led to the same results. The clerks simply told him, "Not in stock. Sorry."

They told him to fill out forms in triplicate, send them up the chain of command. That was a joke. What chain of command? South Pacific Task Force had been renamed to United States Forces in Australia. The personnel office occupied all of 220 square feet. There would be no engineering division or supply division officially established until May.

When all else failed, P.I. started stealing what the Twenty-Seventh Bomb Group needed. At first, he simply appropriated what was left around that he could get his hands on while nobody was looking. The stuff they really needed lay in the warehouses, and for that he concluded force was needed. He rounded up a crew and turned military outlaw.

While working on the planes, he met a long-service master sergeant named Jack Evans. Jack had been a B-17 crew chief in Hawaii with the Twenty-Eighth Bomb Squadron prior to the war. He was assigned to the P-40s when he reached Brisbane. The two men quickly became inseparable, and together with a few other enlisted men, they staged robberies throughout Brisbane.

The guns were mostly for show, but P.I. was in no mood to suffer fools. Every moment the bureaucracy and confusion delayed construction of the aircraft meant his chance to rescue his family diminished. He knew the score; the men still fighting in the Philippines could not hold out forever.

He used the guns to cut through red tape and indifference with shows of force. What he could not steal, he made. He found several machine shops around Brisbane and contracted with them to build what had not been shipped from the States. The Mars Machine Tool Company fabricated entirely new ball mounts for the A-24's tail guns to specs that P.I. designed on the spot.

He swiftly encountered yet another issue. As the Aussie craftsmen built what they needed, funds for such projects could not be procured quickly. The purchasing officer was another lowly lieutenant, and he was as bogged down in as much red tape and confusion as anyone else. P.I. couldn't steal what Mars built for him, so he paid out of pocket for the parts. He did this more than once, amassing over $16,000 in receipts. That's almost $250,000 in 2016 dollars.

One way or the other, he was going back to the Philippines.

Three shifts a day, they worked nonstop to get the planes assembled and functional. Finally, they finished the first couple of A-24s. A young lieutenant took one of them for a test flight to ensure that it was fully functional. Being back in the air proved so exhilarating that he forgot common sense when he spotted a beachside resort he recently visited while off duty. He dove down to buzz it, coming in from the water. As he reached the surf, he dug a propeller blade into a swell, lost control, and ended up crashing on the beach.

For all the effort it took to get one plane readied, its destruction by joy ride elicited comments that could not be reprinted.

In the first part of January, more convoys from the West Coast arrived at Brisbane, bringing in more gear and personnel. The reinforcements were desperately needed, but initially the added people only exacerbated the unfolding mess. Officially, the Army Air Force personnel were supposed to live in tents set up for them at the two racetracks, but many of the officers simply walked away from those austere quarters and found hotels in town instead, engendering the wrath of Colonel Johnson, who thought the sight of so many ill-dressed officers in downtown hotels unseemly.

The nighttime parties were wild, and the well-paid American servicemen brought plenty of cash. Some of the Aussies in uniform came to resent the Yanks, whose fat wallets they could not match. Tension grew, and brawls broke out all over the city nearly every night. The conflicts culminated later in the year with the Battle of Brisbane, a wild riot and gun battle involving thousands of men that killed an Australian serviceman and injured hundreds of men on both sides.

Order gradually came out of the chaos. The crews finished constructing the P-40s and the pilots test-flew each one. Enough Prestone was finally combed out of the Australian civilian population to get all the fighters operational. Mixing a batch of newly arrived pilots with veteran P-40 jocks from the Philippines into one outfit called the Seventeenth Provisional Pursuit Squadron, the men and machines were finally ready to go by the middle of January.

They would have to make their way thousands of miles from the southeast coast of Australia all the way across the continent to Darwin. From there, they would have to navigate over water and refuel on islands in the Dutch East Indies before making the jump to the Philippines and Del Monte Plantation on Mindanao.

None of the pilots had the sort of navigational experience to pull that off. But P.I. did. He volunteered to take them back to the Philippines while Davies and the rest of the Twenty-Seventh finished up building the A-24s. He could lead the P-40s to Bataan, find out where his family was, and get them out in the Beech.

At 0830 on January 16, 1942, P.I. took off in the Beech 18 to lead the first half of the Seventeenth Provisional Pursuit Squadron northward. Jack Evans and two other crew chiefs sat in back surrounded by boxes of tools that were likely the fruit of P.I.'s equipment runs. They'd be the only ones available to maintain the P-40s, at least for the foreseeable future.

P.I. left Brisbane as a budding legend among the ground crew and pilots he came to know. They watched this oddball captain work longer hours, solve more problems, and go to more reckless extremes than nearly anyone else to get them in business. Stories of his exploits quickly rose and grew in the retelling until fact and fiction were almost indistinguishable. P.I. himself loved to tell ridiculously overblown yarns from his Navy days, regaling the young pilots with his backwoods storytelling skills.

Some who met him concluded he was a pathological liar. Others wanted him court-martialed for his robberies and rank insubordination. Done with military niceties, he just didn't care whom he offended. If the man was in his way, P.I. would drive through him any way he could. It rubbed a lot of people the wrong way, but it made him a hero to those tilting against bureaucratic windmills.

The fact that he was twice the age of those he worked alongside was not lost on anyone. They didn't call him "Captain." P.I. had never been an officer, and the rank really meant little to him, especially since he didn't have a command or any official position. They didn't call him P.I. though, either. Some began to call him "Pops," or "Gramps." Then somebody tried "Pappy," and the nickname seemed to suit him. It got picked up, spread around the small Army Air Force population in Australia until that was all anyone called him. The nickname became a dividing line in his life, a new name for the person the war had created. Some used it derisively, but the nickname was born from endearment, and it fed his budding legend.

They revered him or despised him, but there was no middle ground with P.I. "Pappy" Gunn. More importantly, he didn't care what anyone thought. He was fighting two wars: one against "knuckleheads" in friendly uniforms, and one against the Japanese.

The first leg of the mission back to the Philippines started terribly. Two P-40s aborted with mechanical issues, and the squadron commander, Maj. Bud Sprague, couldn't find P.I.'s Beech after he took off. He decided to abort, get back to Amberly Field, and regroup.

One by one, the P-40s touched down, leaving P.I. wondering where his charges went.

An hour later, Sprague tried again. This time, they made it 320 miles north to Rockhampton, where Pappy waited for them. The pilots set down to refuel, but one suffered complete electrical failure and the pilot crashed on landing, wiping the aircraft out.

One fewer fighter for the embattled defenders of Bataan. The sight must have made the men there sick. Fortunately, the pilot survived unhurt.

They reached Townsville another 360 miles up the coast later that afternoon. Again, the inexperienced pilots suffered a mishap when one of the Philippine veterans clipped a house on landing and took off part of his wingtip.

They spent the night at the Queens Hotel, grabbing a final bit of the easy life before heading west across the heart of Australia the following morning.

Pappy related to these young fighter jocks, whose humor was his own. Hell, they were him twenty years and seventeen thousand flight hours ago, just with bars on their collars instead of stripes on their sleeves. He liked them, and he would do everything he could for them. He knew the odds and the lack of training stacked the deck against them so thoroughly that most would not survive. The knowledge weighed heavily on him even as he guided them north to Bataan and their rendezvous with the Japanese. They would need more than one understrength squadron to do any real damage, but at least it was something.

The flight the following day was a rugged one. One by one, the P-40s suffered mechanical failures or accidents. Tires blew; parts broke. Pappy followed the railroad lines, using them to navigate into the interior. By the time they stopped for the night, they were down to just six ships flying wing on the Beech 18.

After a night of rest, Pappy led them to Darwin on the far north coast. Batchelor Field would be their springboard into the ferry route through the Dutch East Indies, but Major Sprague wasn't going to leave until he could get as many planes in as possible. In dribs and drabs, the stragglers trickled in until fifteen pilots, three crew chiefs, and Pappy Gunn formed the spearhead of the Army Air Force's reinforcement effort for the Philippines.

On Monday, January 19, 1942, the little force assembled on the flight line to find General Brereton waiting for them. Peering intently at them through his wire spectacles, the general greeted them with a sardonic "I'm so glad to see so many volunteers."

A ripple of tense laughter went through his audience.

Brereton waited for it to drain away then began to talk again. He came to Darwin to deliver bad news, and he didn't have the temperament to be diplomatic about it. The ferry route to the Philippines no longer existed. The Japanese had invaded the Dutch East Indies. They'd taken Tarakan on Borneo and captured key airfields in Celebes.

There was no longer any way to get fighters up to Mindanao.

While the men were still reeling from that news, Brereton unleashed the other blow. He was sending them north to defend the Dutch East Indies.

"We will be heavily outnumbered," he said, noting that they may get some British Hurricanes from Singapore to assist, but right now the situation there looked pretty bleak as well.

Things were so confused at the moment that Brereton could not give them an exact destination. He mentioned Ambon Island; Balikpapan, on the east coast of Borneo; and the Dutch airfield complex at Kendari on Celebes Island. The pilots looked at each other, grim and unsure. Nobody but Pappy had ever heard of those places. They were going to need new maps.

Brereton explained that they now belonged to a new joint Allied organization called American-British-Dutch-Australian Command, or ABDA Command. Yet another layer of dysfunctional higher administration trying to operate with too few resources and now with too many Allies with too many divergent national goals.

Brereton didn't bother to pretend it wasn't going to be a cluster. At the end of his speech, he said he would do the best he could to evacuate them when the time came. The meeting lasted twenty minutes. Then General Brereton bid them good luck, climbed into a bomber, and left. The men retreated to discuss the news and let time take the edge off their shock.

They weren't expected to counterattack; Brereton made it clear there was no chance of victory. They were being sent north as meat shields in fighter planes to buy the Allies a little bit of time. They left Amberly feeling like the vanguard of a new air force for General MacArthur, like the tip of a spear, thrown from Brisbane to the beleaguered men of Bataan. Now they felt like they were simply being sent north to die.

For Pappy, the change of destinations left him aching with guilt and rage. They were too late, and as he walked away from the flight line his mind replayed all the delays and obstruction they faced at Archerfield. If only they could have built the P-40s faster, they could have beaten the Japanese to the punch and slipped into the Philippines before the ferry route was overrun.

Now he had to lead the men into a new campaign, far from his family and where his heart lay.

Yet, as dismal as the situation looked, he refused to give up hope. With the ferry route in Japanese hands, he could not get to the Philippines in the Beech 18. He needed something larger with more fuel and endurance. A B-17, maybe? Perhaps when the chance came, he could get ahold of one. If not, he would think of something else. In the meantime, he needed to get the boys safely north to do what they could for the Dutch.

20

Daniel Boone of the Dutch East Indies

January 23, 1942
Darwin, Australia

The Japanese coveted the oil fields in the Dutch East Indies. They needed those strategic sites to carry on the war in China, and now the war in the Pacific. In fact, their entire offensive from Pearl Harbor to the invasion of the Philippines was designed to ensure the success of the Dutch East Indies campaign by keeping the American fleet at bay.

It had worked better than the Japanese calculated. Now, they stepped up their timetable of invasion and began chipping away at the flanks of the Dutch East Indies with small amphibious landings, well supported by aircraft.

The British, Dutch, Australian, and American warships in the area lacked firepower. They were overage and overused; most should have been consigned to scrap years before. They could not stand against the full might of the Imperial Japanese fleet with its modern carriers, battleships, and fast cruisers. The only hope to defend the most vital islands—Sumatra, Java, and Borneo—was airpower.

The Depression ensured the Dutch didn't have the resources to build a large air force. By 1942, their squadrons in the Far East flew a motley array of second-rate planes, some of which they purchased from the Americans and Germans. The fighter pilots could choose between has-beens so obsolete they stood little chance against the Zero, and never-weres like the Curtiss-Wright CW-22 Demon, a plane so bad that nobody else wanted it.

Yet, airpower gave the Dutch their best chance to save the East Indies. If American bombers and fighters could rush to their aid, they could bomb and sink the Japanese amphibious task forces at sea before they could get troops ashore. They needed P-40s. They needed A-24 dive bombers, which were perfect weapons for the pinpoint accuracy required to hit ships at sea.

The odds were long, but the campaign hung in the balance. The Allied aircrews would have to battle their way through the Zeroes sure to be protecting the amphibious task forces. For the inexperienced Dutch pilots in their obsolete bombers, that would be a death sentence unless the Army Air Force could get P-40s to the East Indies to fly cover for them.

The P-40s would serve a defensive role as well. The Japanese would surely be launching air attacks of their own against Dutch airfields, cities, and ports. Sprague's men would have to do double duty, escorting antiship missions while trying to intercept incoming raids.

As the campaign took shape to the north, Pappy and the other pilots waited at Darwin for the order to deploy north. They used the short lull to train while Pappy worked with the three crew chiefs to patch together a P-40. Every plane was needed for the fight ahead.

They worked through the day in searing heat, vainly fighting off Darwin's vicious mosquitoes and infamous black flies. The flies in particular were an insufferable part of the Darwin experience. These little monsters were everywhere, flying in great dark clouds that engulfed a man so thoroughly they often crawled under his eyelids.

As they sweated away in the stifling conditions, ABDA Command kept changing their ultimate destination as the Japanese stayed one step ahead of the Allies. On Thursday, the twenty-second, orders finally arrived. Kendari was a no-go. So was Balikpapan. Allied reconnaissance discovered two amphibious assault forces steaming for both locations. The Dutch did not have the ground troops to stop them on the beaches, which meant sending the precious P-40s into either place would doom them when the airfields were inevitably overrun.

ABDA Command ordered Sprague's men to Java instead. The defense of the East Indies was coalescing around holding that island. The P-40s were crucial to that defense. Hold on long enough, and the Twenty-Seventh Bomb Group could get into the fight, along with the B-17s and more P-40s. It was the only hope left for the Allies.

The morning of the twenty-third dawned to find the intrepid group of aviators making final preparations for their flight. They would have to cross 540 miles of open water, something none of them except Pappy Gunn had ever done. They lacked any survival gear like Mae West life jackets, shark repellant, and dye markers. There was no air-sea rescue force standing by to save them if they went into the drink. Everyone knew what that meant: Mechanical failure over water was a death sentence.

Their first stop would be a Dutch airfield on Timor. Once they got there, they would island-hop west for Java. This first leg would be the most dangerous—and the longest.

Pappy Gunn led the way, getting aloft sometime before 0900 in NPC-56, PAL's much-traveled Beech 18. Behind him, fourteen P-40s formed up in a long, loose line abreast. They winged their way north, the fighter pilots draining their belly tanks before switching to internal fuel.

Halfway to Timor, one of the P-40s dropped out of formation. The pilot had forgotten to switch from external to internal fuel and his belly tank had run dry. His engine coughed and sputtered, then quit. He fell behind and about a thousand feet below Pappy's Beech before he was finally able to restart his Allison. Everyone breathed a sigh of relief when he regained his spot in the formation.

The flight took a little under three hours. The sea stretched from horizon to horizon, leaving their fifteen planes like a tiny bubble of mechanized humanity in an otherwise empty and uninhabitable stretch of the planet.

In the cockpit, P.I. stared down at the vast expanse below him through a pair of mirrored sunglasses. The midday sun turned the cockpit into a furnace, even with the side window open. The slipstream was warm and did little to cool the aircraft. Like an automobile driver rolling down a long desert highway, he struggled against drowsiness.

He went through his routine, scanning the instruments to ensure that everything was in the green. The Beech purred along, the flight smooth. Pappy peered out over the nose at the water below, the white caps sparkling in the sunlight. The smell of the ocean, the equatorial heat of the wind whistling through the side window took him back to a flight long ago. His mind wandered; for a moment, he indulged the memory.

Nineteen years before, his honeymoon had started with a similar scene. The Gulf of Mexico shined in the springtime sun as Pappy and Polly soared above it in a Navy surplus flying boat he and a friend had rebuilt.

The cockpit was open, with just a tiny glass windscreen to protect their faces from slipstream-induced bug strikes. A pair of wicker seats were mounted side by side in the cabin, and Polly huddled against her new husband while he held the control wheel and guided them west toward New Orleans. The Pensacola paper sent a reporter to their send-off, since it was the first time anyone from the city had gone on honeymoon in their own aircraft.

Photos were snapped and hands were shaken as they donned helmets and goggles for the flight.

That day remained one of Pappy's happiest memories. Polly's slender form pressed close while the slipstream whistled around them. For Polly, such an adventure was impossible before this exuberant Arkansan blew into her life. She existed in a bubble, a sheltered middle-class Catholic girl with a routine no different from countless others. Church on Sundays, school during the week. Her social life revolved around the local parish. Then Pappy showed up at a church picnic one Sunday and everything changed. He liberated her from convention, from a straitjacketed life that bound so many other young women of her generation. Now, as they flew westward, they chartered a course that would surely be full of unique and adventurous moments.

Approaching Biloxi, Mississippi, the flying boat's engine began to run rough. Pappy decided to set it down in Biloxi Bay and tinker with it. He alit on the water, taxied over to dock, and got to work while Polly looked over his shoulder.

When he was satisfied, he told her he wanted to take it for a quick test flight to make sure everything was all right. He left her on the dock, her baggy flight overalls tugged by a coastal breeze.

Over the bay, the engine running flawlessly, Pappy banked over a small island and thought he saw something unusual along its shore. He dropped the nose and went down for a better look. A dead person lay facedown in some weeds. Pappy figured the chance of anyone in the bay actually spotting the corpse to be pretty low. It was well hidden, surrounded by cattails and tall grass and only easily visible from the air. Much as he wanted to continue his honeymoon journey, duty prevailed on him. He returned to the dock, told Polly of his discovery, then set off to find the police station so he could report the body. The local sheriff listened to Pappy's story with barely concealed skepticism. Nevertheless, he knew he needed to check it out.

He took two of his men, found a boat and putted out into the bay to recover it, ordering the newlyweds to wait for him at the dock.

Time passed slowly. The couple fidgeted impatiently, wanting to get on with their honeymoon. The boat vanished around one of the islands. It did not return. They scanned the horizon, hoping to catch sight of the sheriff while they made small talk and felt a little awkward. This was their special day when they would become lovers. At least, that night they would, but the hotel was still hundreds of miles away and they were running out of daylight to get there.

It felt as if Pappy's discovery was squandering their moment. Nobody would have known if he simply ignored the sight, alighted on the bay to pick up Polly, and continued their journey.

Pappy would have known, and that was what mattered. Duty versus family would always be the competing forces in their marriage, and from day one that struggle existed. Reporting the body was the right thing to do. Polly recognized it, and she would never have asked anything else of her man.

When the boat finally hove into sight and pulled up to the dock, the sheriff's mood turned foul. They had searched the island from the boat and found no sign of the corpse. Now they didn't believe Pappy, and the sheriff questioned him some more, sounding more dubious this time. Irritated, Pappy invited the lawman to come with him in the Curtiss and he would show him the corpse.

The sheriff nervously looked over the flying boat. Clearly he had never flown before, but rather than lose face in front of his men, he agreed.

The two men climbed aboard the flying boat. Pappy taxied it out onto the bay and opened the throttles. The Curtiss skipped like a stone over the water until finally bounding aloft. The sheriff could not conceal his terror, which Pappy thoroughly enjoyed. He horsed the flying boat into a sharp series of maneuvers—banking into unnecessarily hard turns while climbing and diving just to give the sheriff a good tossing about in his wicker basket of a seat.

Antics aside, Pappy did locate the corpse again. He flew several tight circles over it to make sure the sheriff not only saw the body, too, but turned green as an Oregon forest from airsickness. The lawman finally had enough. He pointed toward the dock. Pappy nodded and flew him back, making a particularly rough landing to punctuate his displeasure at the sheriff's treatment of him. By the time they clambered out of the flying boat and back onto the dock, the sheriff looked ready to throw up.

He probably never flew again.

By the time they returned to the dock, it was too late in the day to continue on to New Orleans. The sheriff dropped the couple at one of the nicer hotels in Biloxi for the night.

Early the next morning, a sharp rap on their hotel room door roused Pappy and Polly from deep sleep. As they lay in the bed nestled together, trying to gather their wits, the rapping stopped. They started to drift back off to sleep until the rapping restarted, this time louder and more insistent.

Infuriated at being disturbed, Pappy bellowed out from under the covers, "If this goddamned hotel is not on fire, you better start running."

The knocking didn't stop. A moment later, as Pappy was winding up to really lay into whoever was applying their knuckles to his door, he heard the sheriff's voice. "Mr. Gunn, Mr. Gunn, we need to talk."

Trying to control his temper, Pappy climbed out of bed, pulled on his cuffed, faded blue dungarees, and found his undershirt. Polly retreated into the bathroom as Pappy flung the door wide. The sheriff stood looking gravely concerned.

"What is it?" Pappy said with a long sigh.

"You the folks who flew out of Pensacola yesterday?" asked the sheriff.

"Yeah."

"You said you were on your way to New Orleans?"

"Yeah, what about it?" Pappy said impatiently.

"Well, when y'all didn't show up in New Orleans last night, word went out that y'all went missing."

Apparently, the Pensacola paper called the *New Orleans Times-Picayune* and asked their counterparts to photograph the aerial honeymooners as they came in to land on Lake Pontchartrain. When they failed to arrive, the *Times-Picayune* sent a telegram back to Pensacola, sending Polly's family into a panic. All along the Gulf Coast, the telegraph lines burned up with frantic messages to local law enforcement agencies to be on the lookout for the couple and their Curtiss flying boat. Search teams were already out looking for them.

Pappy found his shoes and went with the sheriff to go cancel the red alert and reassure everyone back home that they were safe. After a good laugh over breakfast, Pappy refueled the Curtiss, and he and Polly set off again under the springtime Southern sun.

The memory, played and replayed countless times on countless flights, vanished from his mind's eye. He was back in the Beech again, scanning the instruments and checking to see if all the P-40s were still flying on his wing.

From day one, Polly, we lived large together.

He went through his rhythm, flight instruments, engine gauges, everything in the green, back outside to see the fighters strung out around him. They were so young, those pilots, that they had not yet mastered the art of tight formation flying. He noted that, just as he noted the incredible skill of the Japanese nocturnal raiders who bombed Nichols the first night of the war.

Though the professional in him never shut off, in the back of his mind, Polly lived. The ache for her never left him; it cycled in the background every waking moment, bursting to the forefront when he was not fully occupied.

From his love for her and their children, guilt welled and burned. In his mind, he railed against the brass and their deception. Under it was his own sense of responsibility. How could he have left them? Orders or not? Couldn't he have just made the time to get them to Mindoro before flying out?

If only they told him Manila was to be declared an open city. Of course, he suspected that they didn't tell him intentionally. The airline manager turned captain would surely have taken the time to get his family to safety, and Brereton wanted his men out immediately.

Brereton. That lying son of a bitch.

He replayed those final hours in Manila over and over, seeking ways he could have saved them. Torn between duty to family, and duty to his country, railing against the deception that caused him to make the wrong choice.

No. I made the wrong choice.

No matter what he was told, no general should ever have come before Polly. He would never forgive himself for that. At least, not until he got them back.

The Timorese coast appeared white and green on the distant horizon. Pappy had navigated once again with pinpoint accuracy. He, Major Sprague, and their pilots touched down at Koepang just in time for lunch. In the cockpit of one P-40, a pilot struggled to unstrap himself. Sprague and the others checked on him and found the man burning up with a fever. They got him out and sent him to the local hospital, where doctors diagnosed him with dengue fever.

Pappy looked around the base. There was not much to see. A few Dutch officers and enlisted personnel maintained this little outpost, which consisted of a couple of hangars and buildings and little else. The Dutch failed to stock the base with enough aviation gas for it to function as a refueling point between Darwin and Java. To make this run possible, the U.S. Navy sent a destroyer to Koepang to offload barrels of gas for the P-40s. The pilots, working with the Dutch, were forced to refuel the planes by hand, but it was better than being marooned in the middle of nowhere.

When Major Sprague returned from the hospital, he assembled the squadron to announce a change of plans. He didn't want to leave a single P-40 behind while the pilot recovered from dengue fever. A lone fighter flying in their wake to Java would be no match to the Japanese formations said to be prowling the skies around the islands. Instead, he elected to take half the remaining pilots with him and go on ahead. The rest of the men would stay at Koepang until their stricken comrade recovered enough to fly.

That afternoon, Pappy led Sprague's group 240 miles westward across the Suva Sea to Soemba Island. Though Japanese air patrols were seen in the area, the Americans somehow slipped through their cordon and flew through empty skies that day. They landed at a primitive jungle strip just before sunset where a P-40, flown by one of the Philippine vets, blew a tire and was knocked out of action until it could be replaced. There were none that would fit the P-40 at Soemba, which meant somebody had to get one and bring it back. It felt like they'd never get to Java. Not as a full squadron, anyway. It was all indicative of how slender a shoestring this emergency deployment was for the Americans. Little preparation and logistical support existed for them. They'd have to improvise a way to get the job done.

After dark, Major Sprague took Pappy aside and asked him to go back to Koepang, radio Darwin for a replacement tire, and wait until somebody flew it up to him. By the time it arrived, Sprague hoped their sick pilot would be well enough to travel, and Pappy could lead them to Soemba, replace the tire, and then get everyone to Java at last.

Sprague was asking a lot of Pappy, and he knew it. Pappy would be flying alone through skies dominated by the Japanese. Aside from his pair of Colt .45s and a tommy gun, Pappy did not have any way to defend himself. He already experienced Zeroes firsthand and knew the deadliness of their cannon and machine guns. This time, if they found and crippled his Beech, he would most likely disappear at sea, missing in action forever. Sprague was asking him to do what he didn't want his own pilots doing—and they could fight back with their six .50-caliber machine guns.

Pappy could have asked for a fighter escort back to Koepang. Just two P-40s flying cover for him would have increased his odds of survival enormously. He could have refused to go at all, though that would have meant leaving another P-40 behind. Instead, he agreed to do it. He knew the desperation in the moment. The squadron needed every plane and pilot in Java, and he had the contacts at Darwin to ensure they could get a tire sent posthaste. He promised to double back to Koepang, score the tire, and lead the rest of the squadron back as soon as he could.

He spent the rest of the night in fitful sleep, the sounds of the jungle around him as his mind played over the odds of his survival and how to maximize his chances. It was a long night among young men whose bravery he respected, but whose futures looked almost as grim as his.

The next morning, the twenty-fourth, Sprague and the rest of the P-40 pilots took off and headed west, the rising sun at their backs. Alone, Pappy checked over the Beech a final time before lining up on the runway for his own flight into the sun.

Once aloft, he discovered a storm moving in over the Suva Sea. Pappy decided to stay as low as he could to minimize his shadow on the water while presenting a very difficult target for anyone trying to hit him with a diving attack. He knew how tough that was from his days in VF-2, where he'd seen more than one fighter pilot get fixated on his target and fail to pull out of the dive in time to avoid hitting the water.

The weather closed in—massive clouds pregnant with rain passed overhead and lashed him with sudden downpours. He broke into clear skies, only to encounter another broad storm front.

As he scuttled along, props practically whipping the whitecaps, two light gray dots materialized under those dark and ominous clouds. Pappy studied them intently, hoping he'd see a familiar American shape take form as they closed the distance with him.

An anxious minute passed. The dots seemed too big to be Zeroes. Sure enough, he soon detected four engines on each plane. Yet they didn't look like B-17s. Did the Dutch have anything with four engines? He didn't know and didn't want to risk it. He altered course and started to run. The Beech was no thoroughbred, and the two bogeys turned to give chase. They nosed down into a gentle dive, trading altitude for additional speed.

Pappy eyed them anxiously. They were closing on him, but only very slowly. Perhaps they had a ten- or fifteen-mile-an-hour edge in speed. He'd be more maneuverable, but if those big planes sported Japanese meatballs on their wings, they would no doubt be bristling with guns.

They turned out to be parasol-winged flying boats called Kawanishi H6Ks, armed with four machine guns and a 20mm cannon. Though the Beech possessed a slightly higher maximum speed on paper, Pappy's NPC-56 stayed aloft on war-weary engines that could no longer produce the kind of power needed to get the Beech over two hundred miles an hour.

They still had some altitude to burn before getting to him. They could drop down behind him, just above the water and let their nose gunners spray away at him. If that failed, they could box him in and move up on either flank and let the flying boats' other gunners have a crack at him.

He could see it happening in his mind, playing it out as if he were behind the controls of one of those big flying boats. He'd flown that type of plane during his Navy years. He knew their strengths and weaknesses. That was what he would do to knock down a lone airliner.

He searched for a way out of the tactical trap before he fell into it. In a pinch, he could always outmaneuver the H6Ks. That would be the Beech's lone advantage. If they got into firing range, he could turn and juke and throw the gunners off. Still, he'd be entirely reactive, almost at their mercy, until they either hit him or ran low on fuel and gave up the hunt.

He suspected those huge hulls and wings held far more fuel than the Beech could, which meant they probably wouldn't give up and break for home before his gauges ran into the red.

He glanced up at the storm. Ahead, the solid front gave way to a scattering of swollen squalls with short breaks of clear sky between them. If he couldn't outrun them, maybe he could hide up there and try to slip away for Koepang.

It was his best chance. He pulled the control wheel toward his stomach. The Beech lurched off the wave tops and arrowed for the clouds. The flying boat pilots noticed the maneuver but couldn't react in time to cut him off. Pappy shot into the nearest cloud and vanished into its murky depths.

Inside the cloud, Pappy turned back onto his course for Koepang, watching his instruments with one eye, while making sure he stayed out of sight to the flying boats prowling for him below. This worked until he ran out of cloud and broke out into the open. The two H6Ks spotted him right away and gave chase. Again, he raced for the next squall, coaxing every bit of speed out of the tired Beech.

He made it, but for the rest of the flight, he played cat and mouse through the clouds with those two relentless Japanese crews. Finally, about twenty minutes out of Koepang, he shook them off and managed to sneak away.

Well aware that they could be back at any moment, Pappy wasted no time getting down on the ground at Koepang. After he cut the switches and climbed out of the Beech, he rushed off to tell the Dutch there were Japanese planes in the area. The officer in charge of the base greeted him with a mix of skepticism and apathy that perplexed Pappy. He urged the Dutch to clear the field of all aircraft. Those flying boats probably carried light bombs. Even if they had dumped them while in pursuit of his Beech, they could radio back to their own bases that Koepang held juicy aircraft targets in need of bombing. It could be a matter of minutes, it could be a matter of hours. Either way, Pappy sensed the Japanese were coming.

The Dutch didn't seem to care. Frustrated, he stormed off to try and figure out what to do next. Scattered around the field sat about a dozen Lockheed Hudson patrol bombers from an Australian squadron. Koepang lacked revetments, which meant these vital planes were vulnerable to blast and shrapnel damage. Pappy found the Aussie leadership—they were from Number 2 Squadron, Royal Australian Air Force—and urged them to get their planes off the field as quickly as possible.

Where the Dutch ignored him, the Aussies listened. They decided to get the Hudsons over to a tiny auxiliary field about thirty miles away at Mina River. They could be hidden there in the jungle, and chances that the Japanese even knew the field existed were probably pretty low. Problem was, the strip was nothing more than a narrow landing ground; it lacked any sort of facilities, and the Dutch had failed to stock fuel at it. The Hudsons would need avgas.

Pappy took off in the Beech not long after and guided the Aussies to the strip. After he saw the Hudsons were down safely, he returned to Koepang. Working furiously while the Dutch refueled the Beech, he radioed Darwin and requested the tire Sprague's men needed. Then, he made contact with the USS *Peary*, the USN destroyer that delivered the avgas to Koepang. After two decades in the Navy, he still had a lot of friends in the service, and he arranged to have the destroyer bring fuel to the Hudsons at Mina River. The destroyer lost two of its boats in the surf during the delivery and had to flee the area when word came of an impending Japanese air attack. In their haste to depart, they left a boat and its crew behind. But the Aussie Hudsons received the gas they needed to continue the fight.

Later in the day, Louis Connelly, his former PAL employee, flew the tire up to Koepang, Timor, while en route to Makassar with a delegation of American officers looking to hire shipping to run the blockade to Bataan. Pappy loaded the tire into the Beech, but it was too late to head back to Soemba. Worried that any minute the field would be hit, he parked the Beech as far away from any likely targets as he could, then headed off to check on the Seventeenth Provisional's pilots. The one with dengue fever was even worse than the day before. He was in no shape to fly, but the rest of the pilots needed to get back to Sprague. Pappy decided he'd lead them up to Java in the morning. The hospitalized man would have to fend for himself for a while.

The night passed in tense silence. Pappy and the other Americans were half-expecting to hear the distant rumble of Japanese engines telegraphing an inbound nocturnal raid. By dawn, he was up and prepping the Beech. Could he have been wrong after all? Were the Japanese so preoccupied elsewhere that they didn't have the resources to bomb Timor? Pappy didn't think so. The situation was still very dangerous, and he intended to get out of there fast now that there was plenty of daylight.

Together with seven P-40s, Pappy took off for Soemba. They stayed low to avoid any roaming Japanese patrols and reached their destination without incident. They replaced the tire on the damaged P-40, refueled by hand out of fifty-five-gallon drums of avgas, then continued on to Java.

Major Sprague's united squadron set up shop at Surabaya. It represented the most capable intercept and escort force the Allies possessed in the Dutch East Indies, but that was not saying much given the terrible aircraft the other fighter units had on hand. The Seventeenth's P-40s were welcome sights to the locals, who were under no illusions as to the odds they faced. The Dutch needed hundreds of P-40s and hundreds more bombers. The Americans delivered a little more than a dozen.

Even that small drop in the bucket was an incredible achievement. What had started as a relief effort for Bataan turned into the longest aerial deployment of fighter planes in American history to that point. Aircraft assembled by unqualified men and flown by low-time pilots who had little navigational training had managed to traverse almost four thousand miles without a single fatality. All things considered, it was a remarkable achievement—one that grabbed the attention of a war correspondent named George Weller.

From 1939 to 1941, Weller covered the war in Europe before moving east and ending up in Singapore. He later met and interviewed many of Major Sprague's pilots, both in Java and in Australia. He also met Pappy Gunn and marveled at what others said about him. He later described Pappy as "a leathery-faced American pilot who flies an aging bi-motored Beechcraft and has remained anonymous while accomplishing some of the most incredible scouting flights of the Pacific War...like some Daniel Boone of the Indonesian archipelago."

Java was sure to become a very dangerous place soon, and Pappy knew his Beech had little chance of survival in the middle of a full-scale air war. He needed to get back to Australia right away to help get the next contingent of American aircraft into the fight. As a result, he stayed at Surabaya just long enough to refuel and send a telegram to Darwin that read, "One Beechcraft, one nitwit en-route."

Pappy and the Beech were somewhere between Java and Timor when the Japanese struck Koepang the next day. Without any air warning system, six Zeroes, hugging the treetops, swept over the field with guns blazing and caught the Dutch completely by surprise. They shot down two unarmed Dutch airliners in the pattern, killing everyone aboard (including a female civilian pilot) before turning their attention to the planes on the ground. In short order, their strafing runs destroyed the P-40 left behind for the pilot with dengue fever, and set fire to the hangars and the few other buildings there.

It was the disaster Pappy feared would happen. Fortunately, Number 2 Squadron RAAF and its precious Hudsons avoided detection at Mina River and were saved. Later, when Pappy was recommended for the Distinguished Service Cross, America's second highest award for valor, part of the award's narrative credited him with saving those Aussie aircraft with his quick thinking on the ground at Koepang.

The Japanese raided targets all over the Dutch East Indies that day. Roving bands of Zeroes caught several more unarmed airliners and shot them down. Not far from Soemba, two A6M Zeroes discovered an Australian DC-2 that had just delivered a group of P-40 maintainers to Sprague at Surabaya and was now trying to make it back to Darwin, just like Pappy was. The Zeroes pounced on the helpless aircraft and raked it with cannon fire. The crippled bird plummeted into Soemba Strait, where the crew of four somehow escaped their sinking craft. They spent the next thirty hours in the water, one man unconscious and being held by the copilot, while the aircraft commander gave up his life vest to another member of the crew who did not know how to swim. They fought off repeated shark attacks before making it to Soemba, where Indonesians rescued them and got them back to Australian authorities.

Pappy's worst-case scenario—flying through hostile skies in an unarmed airliner—came true. In one day, Zeroes shot three down in flames, killing almost a dozen people. Yet, for all the destruction their fighters caused that day, the Japanese somehow missed a solitary Beech 18 that hugged the wave tops while its middle-aged pilot grimly ran their gauntlet on his way back to Darwin.

21

Eighth Avenue Rules

January 2, 1942
Manila, Philippines

The knocking came again. Nobody moved. Nath felt rooted in place by the window, staring at his mom and Connie as they looked at the door. The façade dropped. Both mother and daughter looked terrified.

Nath. Your mother's a special person. You gotta take care of her.

Across the yard, Nath could see more Japanese soldiers moving in the street. Some came out of a house up the block. There were dozens of them.

You take care of your mother, no matter what.

Those were the final words his father had spoken to him on Christmas Eve. But how was he to protect his mother from this?

He was eight years old when the bully had knocked him down. Skinned knee leaving a trickle of blood down his shin, he had limped home with Paul's help. To him, the bully was massive, one of those kids with a pituitary gland on fire. He was also a few years older.

The family had moved recently from Ford Island to a little house on Eighth Avenue in Honolulu. The neighborhood kids ran in a gang called the White Rats. Nath and Paul were the new kids, and they had been taking their lumps for it.

Tears streaked Nath's cheeks as they reached the house. P.I. had looked him over and asked, "What happened to you?"

Paul told their father what had happened.

No hugs followed. No words of sympathy. Polly stood watching, but said nothing. She knew this was a moment for the men in her life.

"Okay," P.I. had said. "We'll settle that."

He walked into the kitchen and returned with a broom. Nath had stopped crying, but he still felt the sting on his knee, still felt the warm trickle of blood on his lower leg.

P.I. broke the broom handle in two. He gave the end to Nath and said, "Now, here's what you do. I want you to act like you're playing horsie, okay?"

The boys loved to ride around on sticks, pretending they were horses. They nodded obediently, uncertain why their father wanted them to go play after this.

"Listen, you ride around, playing and havin' fun. You get as close to the kid who knocked you down, and I want you to use that broom handle and hit him in the head."

"Yes, Daddy," Nath said. The boys exchanged glances.

"Go on, go get it done."

They scrambled outside and vanished up Eighth Avenue.

A few minutes later, they came rushing back, Paul in the lead. "Dad! Dad!"

P.I. had been waiting for them. He stepped onto the small, six-by-ten front stoop overlooking their tiny front yard and asked what had happened.

"Nath hit that kid just like you said!" Paul related. "Hit him right in the head. Blood went everywhere!"

"Good," P.I. said. "Now, both of you—inside. Leave the front door open. I'll be calling for you in a minute."

As they did as their father asked, they saw P.I. sit down on the front stoop, legs dangling over the side, Camel tucked between his lips on the right side of his mouth.

He didn't have long to wait. The other boy's father soon appeared, his son in tow with a big bandage wound around his head. Blood was starting to seep through.

Pappy looked him over. As Pappy later told Nath, at that moment he thought, *Nath really did a job on the little bastard.*

The man turned off the sidewalk and walked into the yard, red faced and full of indignation. He was at least a head taller than P.I., barrel-chested and with a pot belly to match. Nath thought he looked like a bully himself.

P.I. said in a low voice, "Can I help you?"

The man pointed to his boy and exclaimed, "Your goddamned son hit mine with a club!"

P.I. looked nonchalant, but he was coiled like a snake ready to strike. The man began to rant at him. When he took a breath, P.I. called for Nath and Paul to come out.

Sheepishly, the kids appeared on the stoop behind their dad. P.I. said to Nath, "Is that the boy who pushed you down?"

"Yes, Daddy."

"Well, Nath, go stand next to him. Let's get a look at you two."

Nath stepped onto the lawn and walked over to the other boy, who was at least a half head taller.

"Well," P.I. said to the other kid's dad, "sure looks to me like your boy is taller."

That didn't sit well with the bully's father. "He hit him with a goddamned club! In the head!"

"Yeah, I told him to do that."

"You what?" the man roared, advancing on P.I.

Like a lightning bolt, P.I. shot off the stoop, pure fury in motion. Fists flying he caught the larger man on the chin, the jaw, and the side of the head. It was over almost before it began. The man dropped to the lawn, unconscious, at his boy's feet.

Stunned, the bully dropped on one knee, calling his dad's name. He didn't move. Then P.I. touched his shoulder and said him, "Look son, next time you decide to pick on somebody smaller than you, I want you to remember something. A boy with a stick in his hand is as big as any other man."

The bully looked on at P.I., eyes brimming with tears.

"Now, son, help your father home."

That day had been a turning point in Nath's life, the day his dad showed him how not to be a victim. If you wanted respect on the street, you had to be tough. You had to be willing to fight for yourself. And when the odds were stacked against you, you never fought fair.

The bully never bothered him again, and the boys of the White Rat gang welcomed Nath and Paul into their ranks as equals.

The Japanese soldier knocked again.

"Nath, please answer the door," Polly said to him gently.

He walked over to it and reached for the knob.

"Remember what we've talked about," Polly told them, "and be respectful."

Nath had heard the stories. He knew what was happening in China.

He turned the knob.

He would do anything to protect his mom and sisters. No rules, no fair play. Whatever it took. Eighth Avenue rules all the way. Eleven years old, he would die for them.

He opened the door, ready for the worst—and came face to face with a meek teenager in a private's uniform.

The Japanese soldier stood maybe five three. His rifle and bayonet were taller than he was, which made him look somehow vulnerable.

His eyes were full of fear, but as he saw Nath standing in the doorway, that fear turned to surprise.

Soldier and son stared at each other, unmoving for a long moment. At last, Nath took a slow step backward out of the doorway and motioned the uniformed boy inside.

The private cautiously moved forward. He stopped when he saw Polly, Julie, Connie, and Paul in the living room, all of them regarding him. Polly politely bowed. Taking her cue, the kids did the same thing. The soldier broke out into a nervous smile. He bowed in return and said something in Japanese.

"Do you speak English?" Polly asked.

The soldier's smile grew broader and he shook his head slightly.

Polly pointed to a chair and asked him if he'd like to sit down. The Japanese shifted his gaze around the room. Five Americans. He'd probably never seen a white person before. The girls were taller than he was; Nath was almost his height. The soldier looked intimidated. He shook his head again and bowed. He would not sit down.

For a moment, nobody knew what to do next. Then the soldier said something and pointed out the window to the house across the street. The Gunns understood; he was one of the Japanese who just moved in there the previous night.

Connie and Julie stayed quiet, letting their mom take the lead in this exchange. Paul, too, did not say anything. After about thirty minutes of awkward attempts to communicate, the soldier headed back for the door. Nath followed and saw him out.

That first encounter with the enemy had gone no way like any of the Gunns thought it would. For days, they had stayed awake, their minds filled with worst-case scenarios and the stories of the Japanese in China. Quietly, they hoped for the best but all felt besieged by fear. An encounter with a teenager in uniform, as nervous and fearful as they were, had never even entered their thoughts. The family relaxed—just a little—and awaited the next development.

They didn't have long to wait. The private returned a few hours later with two Japanese officers, one of whom spoke broken English. Nath admitted them into the apartment, and the scene was repeated. This time, the officers spotted the photos arranged around the room. They regarded them closely, then demanded, "Where is husband?" While pointing to P.I.'s pictures in his Navy uniform.

Polly told them, "My husband is dead."

"Where? When?" they asked.

"You killed him at Cavite during the bombing."

That quieted them for the moment. They began flipping through the family photo albums, marveling at all the places the Gunns visited. The pictures of Ford Island and P.I.'s Navy aircraft especially drew their attention.

They began asking questions. Polly answered everything at first. Then they turned to the kids and peppered them with the same ones.

"Where is your father?"

Inevitably, they gave the exact same answer each time.

"He died when Cavite was bombed."

They found the photo of the boys dressed in their chief petty officer uniforms that Polly had sewn for them. Then they looked over the photos of Paul and Nath in their Boy Scouts attire. They were too young for military service—both in the photos and in the moment—but the Japanese officers still asked about it. Polly had to explain that she had made those uniforms herself.

They began to search the apartment, rummaging through closets, opening drawers, and examining the family's personal possessions. In a bedroom closet, they found a movie screen. It was in an aluminum tube, and when they pulled it out and realized what it was, they asked to see the films the family had made.

Polly and the boys set up the 16mm projector in the living room. The officers and the lone private who originally visited took seats as the first film began to play. In minutes, the scenes flicking on the screen captivated them. They watched the film Polly shot of the volcano erupting in Hawaii sometime in the mid-1930s and asked to see it again. And again. And again.

At last, they moved on and wanted to see the other reels. Some had been taken on Ford Island showing the flying boats there and Battleship Row circa 1935. Other scenes included the carriers *Saratoga* and *Lexington* coming and going from Pearl Harbor. The officers saw this as an incredible intelligence find, despite the fact that the films were shot in the mid-1930s and the configuration of these ships had changed since then.

They politely left that afternoon amid bows and smiles, but over the next several weeks, they kept returning sometimes twice a day. Each time, they would ask the same questions over and over. They'd want to see the movies again. They'd search the house, ask about P.I., grilling the kids as well as Polly. Later, more senior officers showed up along with an interpreter. The questions started all over again. The family never felt threatened, but the constant barrage of repetitive questions grew tiresome and annoying. But Polly and Eva had prepared everyone well, telling them to always remain respectful no matter what they did. Eventually, they confiscated the film, and the Gunns lost their home movies forever.

A captain came over almost as often as the teenaged private. He spoke to Polly and told her to stay in the apartment. Eva and her family, since they were Russian citizens, were free to move about the city, so they did the shopping for the Gunns.

One morning, Polly was listening to the radio with some of the other members of the family when the Japanese-controlled announcer read a bulletin instructing all Allied civilians to report to the University of Santo Tomas. The Japanese had turned the school into a prison that would be used as the internment center for all foreign nationals whose countries were at war with Japan. The announcer wrapped up the bulletin with a veiled but ominous warning that the

Japanese authorities would take harsh action against anyone who did not turn himself in immediately.

The bulletin became a staple of every news broadcast. Polly listened to them all that day, unsure what to do. The Japanese captain next door kept telling her to remain in the apartment, yet the radio bulletins became more strident as the days wore on. She finally called the Japanese consulate in Manila to find out what she should do. The consulate official she spoke to said she and the kids had to report to Santo Tomas, but if an officer in the Imperial Army had ordered her to stay put, she needed to obey that order.

It seemed like either way, she and the kids could be punished. The situation made her feel increasingly unsettled. Unsure what to do, she spent many hours talking over options with Eva, but stayed put.

One day, in early February, the private appeared on their front step again. He was alone this time, which had rarely happened since the first day he'd knocked on their door. The Gunns let him in. He looked unhappy and afraid again. He stood surrounded by the family and produced a bottle of Coca-Cola. He forced a smile, then pantomimed pouring the Coke. Polly went and got glasses and gave one to each member of the family. The soldier put the bottle to his mouth and pulled the cap off with his teeth. Nath had never seen anyone do that before; he was impressed.

With the cap still between his lips, he poured a little bit of Coke into each glass. After he palmed the cap away, he held the bottle up and toasted the Gunns. They followed, glasses raised, and together the boy-soldier enemy and the family of a fierce warrior shared a final drink. It was a moment of humanity, tinged with tension and sadness. His captain later explained the boy was being sent to Bataan, where not only the Filamerican Army was disease wracked and starving, but the Japanese troops were as well.

The officers left the next day; only the captain remained behind. Polly, afraid that if he left, too, they would be punished for not turning themselves in at Santo Tomas, decided she needed to act. She sat her children down and laid out her plan. She would go to Santo Tomas alone, explain the situation to the authorities there and register the family. Then she would either return to wait out what the captain's next orders would be, or she would gather up the children and take them back to Santo Tomas.

That evening, she packed a small suitcase for the children; each held a few changes of clothes, some toothpaste, soap, and some food. She told them, if anything happened to her and she didn't come home after a day, Leo would take them to Santo Tomas and drop them at the gate.

The next morning, Polly stood before the spool post bed one final time, memories of the many places it had been playing through her mind. It was the one constant in their marriage, their one heirloom. She shuddered at what might happen to it.

Then she went to hug her babies. Nath had never felt such fear before—he couldn't even remember a time when his mother was not close by watching over him and Paul. She stepped out into the front yard and departed for Santo Tomas.

They waited all day in tense anticipation. The hours dragged. Julie and Connie made lunch, then dinner for everyone as Eva and her family stayed close. Night fell and the city, which had been alive with the sound of Japanese military convoys, seemed muted and quiet. Nath took shifts at the window periodically, waiting and watching for his mom to come back up the street. But Polly never returned.

22

Pappy and Miss EMF

January 26, 1942
Darwin, Australia

Pappy Gunn stood on the flight line at Batchelor Field, calculating all the carnage he could wreak with his new ride, number 40-2072.

New was a relative term, of course. This Boeing and its four-engine cowlings were streaked and stained with oil and grime. Puddles of fluid—oil? hydraulic?—pooled in the big plane's shadow. One man took a look at it and quipped that she was "pieced together from holes." That wasn't inaccurate. Cinder block–sized cannon holes, shrapnel strikes, and bullet tears had gouged the plane's aluminum skin on earlier combat missions, Japanese fire had wounded three men aboard her. Their blood still spattered the fuselage in places, though ground crews in the Philippines had done their best to scrub it clean. That was a task nobody wanted to remember.

Her engines had crossed the Pacific, flown hundreds, if not thousands, of hours with minimal maintenance. Now they wheezed and puked smoke, drank oil, and sometimes worked.

She was Pappy's now, and he didn't see its holes, its overtaxed motors, leaks, and patchwork skin. He saw range. Firepower. Bomb load. Guns. Yes. Lots of guns and bombs.

Pappy Gunn had just scored a B-17.

The Boeing B-17 Flying Fortress (or "Fort"), the raison d'etre of the prewar Air Force and ultimate expression of American airpower. It was the plane designed to destroy economies, shorten wars, and demolish enemy fleets. When trouble brewed in the Pacific, FDR hadn't asked where the carriers were, he asked where the B-17s were. They were considered America's most damaging instrument of power projection in the prewar arsenal.

Yeah. She'll do.

On the twenty-sixth, when Pappy returned to Darwin in the PAL Beech, Colonel Johnson placed him in charge of Air Transport Command, a unit that he just created by appropriating all the castaway aircraft lying around Australia that were so ancient or damaged that they couldn't be used in combat.

Then he handed them over to Pappy. A handful of pilots came along with this command of misfit planes. Captain Pappy Gunn now had a purpose and a unit to run. Granted, his command totaled fourteen officers and nineteen enlisted men, but Harold Slingsby was among them. So was Cecil McFarland, one of FEAF's staff officers, whom Pappy had met in the Philippines at the outset of the war. The downside was he had to work with some Australian group captain who'd been put in overall charge of transport operations on the continent.

"Allies" greatly annoyed Pappy. He found them to be obstacles to getting anything done, and they were most useful only in absorbing the full weight of his wrath.

Thanks to the martinet in Brisbane, whose supply depots he had been robbing, Pappy Gunn took ownership of every broken-down piece of junk that limped back to Australia. This included the three ancient Douglas B-18 Bolos the Twenty-Seventh Bomb Group guys had used to flee the Philippines, the PAL Beech 18, two Philippine Air Corps Beechcraft, three B-24A Liberator four-engine bombers, and six Lockheed Lodestars that Pappy had ordered for

PAL just before the war. The Army Air Force had commandeered those planes off the Pensacola convoy, and they represented the only new aircraft available in Australia to move things from point A to point B.

Then there was Miss EMF.

For Pappy, it was love at first sight, but for anyone else with half a brain and common sense, the sight of this damaged, scarred, and filthy beast serving as a ride into combat would have sent them scurrying off to something more safe.

Pappy climbed inside and sat in Miss EMF's cockpit. He'd never been inside a B-17 before. This was a C model, of which Boeing's plant in Seattle had produced only a few. Most Cs ended up being crashed by Royal Air Force pilots in England as Lend-Lease offerings, but a few came west across the Pacific. Miss EMF was one of those that made the long flight from Hamilton Field, California, to Manila in October 1941.

She lacked power turrets. In later models of the B-17, two gunners manned .50-caliber machine guns mounted in open windows in the fuselage. Those were called the waist guns. Miss EMF had awkward-looking, birdcage-like blisters in her sides, making it look like the fuselage had broken out with boils. Later models included a ball turret in the belly sporting two machine guns. Usually the smallest gunner on the crew would be stuffed into that thing and would spend his missions beneath his craft, spinning in circles looking out for fighter attacks from below.

That was high-tech compared to what Seattle did with Miss EMF. No turret in the belly, just a long, coffin-shaped appendix hung beneath her. The unfortunate enlisted man who got that job had to lie down in it, facing backward, and spend hours at a time on his belly, peering down along the underside of Miss EMF's tail over the barrel of his machine gun. They called it the "bathtub."

Miss EMF was first shot to pieces during a raid on the Japanese at

Davao on Christmas Day. Ten Zeroes intercepted her and her flight mate, and riddled both planes with cannon and machine gun fire. The attacks wounded three men inside Miss EMF, and after she limped back to Australia the ground crews counted over a hundred holes in her fuselage and wings. The Nineteenth Bomb Group—desperate as it was for planes—took one look at all the damage and cast her away as unfit for combat. This at a time when they went to heroic lengths to get any B-17 back in the fight. Miss EMF was unwanted even by the most needy.

Since then, she had found employment on transport runs around Australia, suffering so many mechanical failures that some cheeky ground crewman had painted "Miss EMF" on her nose. It stood for "Every Mornin' Fixin'."

Pappy didn't care. He could fix anything. That Curtiss flying boat he'd flown on his honeymoon? The Navy had declared it beyond repair. He and his best friend at the time, Pat Barnes, had painstakingly rebuilt it themselves, appropriating parts on midnight runs around Pensacola.

He hadn't known how to fly then, but he'd coveted the chance to get into the air. Once they'd fixed the Curtiss, Pat taught him to fly on the weekends and during their off duty hours. Two years later, he had gone from being a naval aviation mechanic to being accepted into the prestigious enlisted pilot program. He'd learned to fix what he would fly, then learned to fly from civilian pilots at the Pensacola airport before the Navy made him an aviator.

That had set the stage for a career filled with flying and fixing scores of different aircraft. He'd piloted fighters, bombers, float planes, and long-range patrol craft of all shapes and sizes. His career had straddled the Golden Age of Flight and the dawn of the modern monoplane. Biplanes, carrier-based torpedo bombers, sea-planes, flying boats—he'd made a career out of learning each one's quirks and traits. He'd flown them off pitching flat-tops, catapulted off the decks of cruisers and battleships. He'd set them down in storm-tossed seas and primitive muddy airstrips. In between, he'd spent much of his daily life among the clouds.

Yet, in all those years, he had never, not once, piloted a four-engine bomber.

How hard could that be? It was just an extra pair of throttle controls, right?

He looked over the massive black instrument panel. It resembled something out of a Buck Rogers serial, with dials and gauges and switches everywhere. No wonder it took Stateside pilots dozens of hours of transition training to become competent with this complex war machine.

Pappy took a minute to figure out how to start it up. Then he took off for Brisbane. That was the sum total of his transition training.

He was the air transport commander for the USAAF in Australia now, but he had no intention of hauling staff wienies around anymore if he could help it. Nor was he going to sit behind a desk and lead from the ground. As far as he was concerned, the command meant only one thing: The Army Air Force had just given him his own personal strategic bomber. He intended to make good use of it.

23

Voiding the Warranty

Getting stuck in Australia was the only sure way Pappy's family would remain in the Philippines. With a B-17's range, he could bypass all the ferry route's refueling stops through the Dutch East Indies and fly straight to Mindanao from Darwin. He planned to seize any opportunity to do it. First, he needed to get more fighters up to Major Sprague's beleagured force in Java. Pappy met up with two dozen grass-green fighter pilots and their freshly assembled P-40s just outside of Brisbane on the afternoon of January 29. They were young and cocky, eager for combat, which they saw as a chance to prove themselves. None had ever seen a Zero or felt the terror the Japanese plane inspired with its performance and maneuverability. In fact, the few stories they'd heard about the Mitsubishi Zeroes were discounted by some of the pilots as pure, fantastic rumor.

They were fresh off a convoy from California, which had also delivered another fifty-five crated P-40s. Their recent arrival ensured they did not have a chance to train, and few of these new pilots talked with any of the old hands from the Philippines to pick up combat tips.

It took all afternoon and most of the evening to refuel the new

P-40s from hand-pumped fifty-five-gallon drums. By the time they finished, it was nearly midnight. The pilots retired to a small hotel in town that had become a magnet to the local Australian women. The place was overrun with excited though weary pilots and their dates, drinking and celebrating. Most ended up dragging their beds outside and sleeping communally under mosquito netting on the hotel's veranda to beat the heat.

The next morning, Pappy and one of his command's B-24s led the two dozen fighters deep into the Australian outback. It didn't take long for their inexperience to show once they got in the air. They formed up on the wheezy old B-17 in a giant flock-of-geese V formation. But it was a ragged V, which even one of the P-40 pilots called "disorganized." Sharp formation flying is the sign of an excellent pilot—anyone who has ever watched the Blue Angels can see that. These young bucks were full of spirit, but they simply hadn't had time to develop the skills.

Just after lunch, they reached the airfield at Cloncurry and got on the ground after a whole lot of confusion in the pattern. One pilot's plane suffered hydraulic failure and its gear didn't fully extend. He crashed and burned on the field but somehow walked away as the precious .50-caliber ammo in the plane's wings detonated in the flames.

The thermometer read well over a hundred degrees, and they labored to prep and fuel the remaining fighters for the next jump in the ferry route. The process took forever—there were no gas pumps to pull up to and fill up. Again, they had to manhandle the dreaded fifty-five-gallon drums to each aircraft and muscle the gas into each tank.

They finished too late to continue, so everyone crashed at the local hotel again. On the morning of the thirty-first, Pappy and Miss EMF led the neophytes aloft alone this time. The B-24 departed for other duties.

Pappy flew without a copilot or navigator. In fact, he probably didn't have a crew at all at this stage, unusual for a giant plane like a B-17 which normally took ten men to fly. Around him, the young bucks spread out into another ragged V. Storm fronts and squalls filled the sky around them, and Pappy detoured around the worst of them.

After another refueling stop where one of the P-40s lost its brakes and crashed into a fence, they continued on for Darwin. Though they didn't know it, they were racing against another massive monsoon.

They got to Darwin first, but just barely. A solid wall of black clouds filled the horizon, and the men could see sheets of rain slanting down out of it. Ahead of the main storm were smaller ones, which Jim Morehead (one of the P-40 pilots) later called "roll clouds."

This was weather that even a veteran pilot quailed before. While serving with the Flying Chiefs off the carrier *Lexington*, Pappy had been out with the squadron at night doing practice landings on their flat top. When they finished up, they headed for San Diego. In the dark, Pappy ran into fog so thick that he became disoriented. His fighter stalled and spun out. It was only at the last second he was able to right his ship and pull it out above the wave tops.

He'd learned to trust his instruments, not what his body was telling him in such moments. The sensations that bouncing around in a turbulent cloud can inflict on the human body are disorienting and deceptive. The violence inside those storms can flip a plane over on its back and the pilot may not even be able to tell—unless he was faithfully scanning his instruments.

Young pilots have a hard time trusting gauges over their bodies. The weather bearing down on Darwin that night could end up causing casualties.

Pappy didn't waste any time. He bored in for Batchelor Field in one final sprint to the runway. As they got into the pattern, he had no choice but to drop down into the roll clouds, giving the fighter pilots a gut-check moment as they tried furiously to stay in formation and not collide. One angry young buck thought this crazy, and later confided in his diary he had wanted to shoot Pappy down.

Instead, Pappy led them down through the scud and growing darkness without a single casualty or crash landing. Just in time, too. As they taxied to the parking ramp at Batchelor, the main storm blew in over them. Fruit-sized raindrops pelted their aircraft and soaked them to the bone the minute they climbed out of their cockpits. Wind lashed the area and over the next twenty-four hours, the storm dumped six inches of water on Darwin.

The fighter pilots would stay at Darwin, sleeping on the floor of the Batchelor Field O Club until the storm blew over.

In the meantime, Pappy Gunn went rogue.

It probably started with a priority mission that took him away from Darwin and the next ferry leg to Timor for the fighter pilots. A contingent of British staff officers from Gen. Archibald Wavell's headquarters who had come down to consult with ABDA command in Java needed a ride back to besieged Singapore. Pappy flew straight on to Java through the worst of the storm, without a copilot or navigator. He did round up a scratch crew of enlisted men, either at Darwin or on Java once he arrived. It made sense. Singapore was 2,100 miles from Batchelor Field, and most of that chunk of sky was now owned by the Japanese air forces.

He made it to Singapore and dropped off the British staff officers. At that point, Miss EMF had been in the air almost constantly since the twenty-ninth. Pappy had flown from Brisbane to the southern tip of Malaya with minimal maintenance in a worn out and battered B-17 whose Wright Cyclone R-1820 engines demanded constant inspections and work.

He didn't stay long in Singapore, turning Miss EMF east for Ambon Island. Exactly why he crossed the entire length of the Dutch East Indies at the exact moment the Japanese were busily invading the major islands has been lost to history. He may have been ordered to help with the evacuation of Allied aviation personnel and civilians on Ambon, which had been ongoing since January 16. Since that was already largely completed by the end of January, it seems Pappy probably possessed an ulterior motive: Sneak back to the Philippines to rescue his family.

With a B-17, he could have refueled at Ambon and flown on to Del Monte Plantation. His old friend Bill Bradford was still running the PAL Beech Staggerwing to Bataan and the Visayan Islands along with the Bellanca and other light craft in what became known as the Bamboo Fleet.

Pappy may have been planning to get back and find his family, leaving the bomber at Del Monte for something small that he could fly into and out of a small landing area near Manila.

He reached Ambon on February 3, 1942, just as the Japanese splashed ashore from nearby amphibious ships. Pappy spotted the enemy ships, saw the troops, and thirsted for some revenge. Miss EMF carried no bombs, so he went off in search of some. It isn't known if Pappy landed at Ambon or not. If he did, he was probably the last Allied pilot to use the airfield. The Dutch and Australian troops defending the area surrendered later that day—and were massacred by the Japanese who had been angered that one of their ships had been sunk by an offshore mine.

Pappy turned up a few hours later with Miss EMF at Koepang, Timor. As he arrived, the jittery Dutch gunners opened fire on his B-17, knocking out his right outboard engine.

By this point, Pappy had been flying almost nonstop for five days. The B-17 did not have hydraulic boost controls—the ailerons and elevators moved by cable and muscle power alone. Without a copilot to spell him, his middle-aged body failed him. His face and legs swelled up, and when he landed at Timor he was so physically debilitated that he may not have even been able to walk until the circulation returned to his legs.

It was probably there on the ground at Koepang, his B-17's engine still smoking from the friendly fire hits, that another piece of the Pappy Gunn legend was formed. Again, exactly what happened will never be known for sure.

The story went that Pappy taxied over to the burned-out hangars at Koepang, only to find the Dutch mechanics there preparing to quit for the day. It was only 1600, and Pappy wanted bombs, gas, and his engine repaired, but the Dutch told him they'd do it in the morning.

Not good enough.

He started arguing with the Dutch, whom he didn't like anyway because (1) they shot his engine out, and (2) he really hated the way they treated the Javanese. He also found them aloof, stuffy, and hide-bound by rules. All that, on top of their being "racist sons of bitches," prompted Pappy to start calling them, "those goddamned Squareheads."

A Dutch Air Force commodore appeared and demanded to know what Pappy thought he was doing. Pappy explained what he needed and the reason for the urgency. The commodore told him his men would not be working overtime.

Yeah. Not.

Pappy limped back to Miss EMF, climbed inside the fuselage, and emerged with a tommy gun. He swung it around toward the locals and unloaded a burst right above the Dutch officer's head.

He stared malevolently at the commodore and snarled, "Have a seat on that barrel over there. You're relieved of command."

The commodore did as he was told. His mechanics got to work on Miss EMF's damaged engine.

Pappy didn't trust these "Allies." Rather than pitching in to help as he would usually do, he stood watch over the mechanics, the tommy gun's barrel swinging between their former commander and themselves.

Several hours into this odd standoff, a senior American officer appeared. In several retellings by a USAF colonel and a brigadier general, the officer was none other than General Brereton himself, but that seems unlikely, as Brereton was probably on Java that day.

Whoever it was found Pappy, haggard, face swollen, hair askew, and stewing in cold fury.

"What's going on, Pappy?" he asked.

The Arkansan told him, and then asked that the commodore be reported for slowing down the war effort.

The American considered this for a moment, and decided to use that request to defuse the standoff. He agreed to report the commodore, but in return Pappy had to surrender his tommy gun.

Pappy liked that tommy gun. He didn't really want to give it up. After all, his crew of thieves had scored a lot of supplies with help from that weapon. In the end, he agreed. He handed the American general his weapon. The Dutch commodore was freed, but the mechanics finished work on Miss EMF and got the engine running. By then, it was too late to go bomb the task force off Ambon.

As Pappy was preparing to leave, the American officer pulled him aside and sprung his trap. If he had to report the commodore, Pappy would be reported as well for taking Allies hostage. That was a court-martial offense.

Whatever.

He'd been doing all sorts of things that could have gotten him court-martialed. Much more painful was the direct order he was given to return to Java. This aborted his clandestine mission to get back to the Philippines. Dispirited, angry at the Dutch, and frustrated that he couldn't attack the Japanese ships at Ambon, he climbed back into Miss EMF and pointed her west, carrying him away from his family.

Whether the incident actually happened or not is anyone's guess. In one version, the officer and mechanics were British, not Dutch. If that was the case, it might have occurred in Singapore. Or, it could be one more wild yarn that emerged from Pappy's one-man war that February. Whatever the case, it makes for a great story, if not great history.

When he landed at Java, he learned that Allied reconnaissance planes recently discovered a Japanese task force steaming south through the Makassar Strait. A scratch force of Dutch, British, and American warships had been sent north to intercept the Japanese fleet out of fear they were coming to land on Java itself.

The whole ABDA Command defense of the Dutch East Indies revolved around holding Singapore and Java. Singapore looked like a lost cause by February 4, but the Dutch were determined to defend Java to the last plane and ship.

Pappy knew that if the Japanese reached the island and pushed troops ashore, the Dutch lacked the men and fighting spirit to hold them off for long. That meant anyone who couldn't get a ride out would be captured or killed. Major Sprague's men included.

The situation seemed critical at the time, and a few weeks later Pappy's worst-case scenario unfolded at Java. This time, the alert proved a false alarm. The Japanese task force was actually bound for the port of Makassar on the southwest tip of the Celebes.

That morning, the Allied warships sent to intercept the Japanese force came under severe air attack. Without fighter cover, they were highly vulnerable to the skilled and veteran Japanese bomber pilots. The enemy bombers severely damaged one Dutch and two American cruisers, one of which was so badly handled it was knocked out of the campaign. The task force turned around without even reaching the Japanese amphibious group.

At Surabaya, Pappy ordered Miss EMF loaded with bombs. No more flying around getting shot at—he was going to take the offensive this time. The ships were about 550 miles from Java, making this a long and dangerous flight. Over such distance, Miss EMF could carry about four thousand pounds of bombs.

With his scratch crew of gunners, one of whom Pappy designated Miss EMF's bombardier, the old Navy vet took off and headed into battle. His navigation skills led them to the Japanese task force. Zeroes flying cover attacked the B-17 while Pappy's makeshift bombardier tried his hand at their first target.

The high-altitude run scored no hits. This was a type of bombing Pappy never practiced in the Navy. He knew the ins and outs of dive and torpedo bombing, but Miss EMF could do neither. A dive bombing attack required a seventy-degree descent, something that would have torn the wings off their big Boeing. Nor did it have a bomb bay designed to carry a torpedo. Level bombing would have to do.

After the first run failed, he wheeled the bomber around through increasingly heavy antiaircraft fire. The ships below carried a mix of heavy guns and 25mm cannons in triple mounts. The Japanese sailors filled the sky with explosive shells, but Miss EMF seemed charmed and rode through the storm as the bombardier released on another ship.

Second run, no hits.

Pappy dropped the nose and bored through the hornet's nest again. Fighters slashed past Miss EMF, her gunners furiously trying to drive them off with desperate bursts from their .50-calibers.

No hits. Angry and frustrated, Pappy refused to give up. With a few bombs still in their racks, he dove lower and lower to make each successive pass. His inexperienced bombardier stood no chance of hitting a moving ship from twenty thousand feet—that became very clear. At ten thousand, he missed again, so Pappy kept dropping lower.

They made seven attacks through curtains of flak with Zeroes on their heels. The final one Pappy made right off the wave tops as if he were going to launch a torpedo. Instead, they tried to pitch their remaining bomb into the side of a Japanese ship. It must have been a terrifying sight for the unlucky gunner lying on his stomach in Miss EMF's bathtub, his chin practically on the white caps. The bomb missed, but Pappy felt far more comfortable down low than parading around a mile over the task force. It was just like those days with VT-3 during his first year out of flight school.

They didn't hit anything, but at least they'd gotten into the war and took a few swings at the Japanese. For Pappy, that proved a most welcome change from always being on the receiving end.

It also gave him some ideas. They percolated in the back of his mind as he returned to Java, refueled, and made his way back to Brisbane over the next few days. Miss EMF needed a lot of work. Flying the length of the Dutch East Indies with minimal maintenance, suffering battle damage, and abusing the already worn-out Wright Cyclones had surely voided the company warranty on this two-hundred-thousand-dollar bomber. If a Boeing or Wright tech rep had found out what Pappy had done, they would have lost their minds. No Flying Fortress should have ever been pushed so hard with so little maintenance. The engines alone required full oil replacement every hundred hours or so, along with daily inspections and more thorough ones every twenty-five flight hours—and that was for noncombat flying. Add in the accumulated battle damage, and it was time to give Miss EMF some TLC.

At Brisbane, Pappy was so exhausted he couldn't continue. Lee Coats, a B-17 pilot from the Nineteenth Bomb Group, took Miss EMF south to Melbourne and an Allied overhaul facility there.

In the meantime, Colonel Johnson had monkeyed with Pappy's unit. He made Air Transport Command the overall umbrella organization for a new group of squadrons that would be assigned the ragtag mix of planes given to Pappy a few weeks before. A full colonel would be in command of ATC now, and Captain Gunn was given the freshly formed Twenty-First Air Transport Squadron.

In reality, little changed at first, except to add another layer of bureaucracy to Pappy's daily life. The truth was, he didn't care about commands and titles. He didn't care about promotions or medals. He wanted his family back and the Japanese defeated. In that order.

With Miss EMF, he had flown over twenty thousand miles. In one six-day stretch, he'd flown her single-handedly for 120 out of 150 hours. But all that effort didn't get him back to Luzon.

He had heard nothing of his family since December. He didn't know what was happening to American civilians in Manila, and he didn't know if Polly and the kids had been able to escape to Bataan. Had Dan Stickle been able to do something for them? Nobody had heard from Dan since FEAF HQ bugged out on Christmas Eve.

He didn't know, and in the unknown, his worst fears played out in his capacious and imaginative mind. In such moments, having the incredible imagination he possessed had to have been sheer torture. It may have been part of the reason he worked himself to collapse. With work, he could occupy at least part of his mind and keep the demon fears at bay.

P.I. and Polly Gunn on their wedding day in the early 1920s. They met at a church picnic, and the instant attraction they felt drew them into an epic, lifelong love affair that led to adventures around the world.

P.I. and Polly prepare to depart for their honeymoon in P.I.'s flying boat on their wedding day. The flight to New Orleans became their first of many adventures they shared as a married couple, and one of the family's favorite stories to retell.

A family portrait taken during the final years of P.I.'s Navy career. The family moved frequently during P.I.'s time in the service, eventually making the journey first to San Diego, then later out to Hawaii where they lived initially on Ford Island before later finding a house in Honolulu.

Gunn posing with one of K-T Flying Service's aircraft at the Honolulu Airport shortly before he received the job offer to be the founding manager of Philippine Air Lines.

NPC-54, the first Philippine Air Lines Beech 18. Pappy was shot up and crash-landed this aircraft at Nichols Field during the first week of the Pacific War. It was later rebuilt—one wing was reattached with baling wire—and flown out to the Dutch East Indies, where it was destroyed in a Japanese bombing raid.

NPC-56, the legendary Philippine Air Lines Beech 18 that saw so much service in the first months of the Pacific War. Pappy had all the company's planes painted Polly's favorite shade of red.

An interior shot of a Philippine Air Lines Beech 18, showing the comfortable, if cramped, conditions in the main passenger cabin.

Mechanics and maintainers of the 3rd Attack Group pose in front of an A-20 Havoc the men were assembling in the field. The 3rd overcame its primitive facilities and a critical shortage of tools and spare parts with ingenuity and innovation.

Pappy's Folly was the first B-25 Pappy and Jack Fox began to modify. Early efforts to cram .50-caliber machine guns in its nose led to serious weight and balance problems, but through trial and error Pappy and Jack Fox worked out the kinks. They named the craft as a poke in the eye to all the many naysayers who thought their entire idea to be foolhardy, or even a criminal destruction of vital government property.

The basic rules of Santo Tomas Internment Camp on display along the main gate. Failure to abide by them could lead to severe punishment and beatings.

Japanese guards address a group of female internees at Santo Tomas. Originally, the camp was run and administered by Japanese civilians with a minimal military presence. As the war situation worsened for the Japanese, the camp increasingly fell into the dreaded Imperial Army's brutal control.

The makeshift shower and cleaning areas built by the internees at Santo Tomas left little privacy. The Gunn boys feared these areas, as frequent thefts of vital necessities often took place here.

Miss Mary Lynn, a veteran of scores of combat missions, was modified to the specs created by Pappy and Jack Fox. It served not in the 5th Air Force, but in the Solomon Islands with the 13th Air Force's 42nd Bomb Group, a testament to how quickly the strafe concept spread through the Pacific Theater.

Pappy in the cockpit of an early B-25, most likely one that had originally been bound for Dutch service. Jack Evans, his crew chief, served alongside Pappy wherever he went after they first met in the chaotic Dutch East Indies campaign. Jack later died in a Stateside training accident while piloting a North American T-6 Texan.

The wrecked carcasses of Bell P-39 Airacobra fighters stacked up at the 5th Air Force's boneyard at Eagle Farm. Pappy helped organize, rebuild, and get hundreds of fighters and bombers dumped there back into fighting shape during the fall of 1942. It became the first of many special assignments General Kenney gave him.

Men of the 3rd Attack Group pose with Pappy in front of a B-25. Left to right: John "Jock" Henebry is at far left, while Pappy is second from the right with Doc Gilmore beside his right shoulder.

A 5th Air Force B-25 skip-bombs a Japanese warship off the coast of New Britain. Following the Battle of the Bismarck Sea, no Japanese ship was safe when in range of Kenney's 5th Air Force.

The Air Apaches of the 345th Bomb Group destroying a Japanese frigate with masthead bombing and strafing tactics in the South China Sea during the final stages of the Pacific War. The tactics and aircraft modifications Pappy and his circle of friends developed in late 1942 proved so devastatingly effective that the Japanese never figured out a way to counter them successfully.

Strafing B-25 Mitchells of the 345th Bomb Group bring carnage and chaos to the Japanese Army Air Force units caught on the ground at Wewak in the summer of 1943. Pappy's strafers, when paired with parafragmentation bombs, became the ultimate weapon against such targets and played a vital role in seizing control of the air from the Japanese in the Southwest Pacific.

March 1945, the ruins of Manila as seen from a U.S. Army liaison aircraft.

Colonel Paul Irving Gunn, USAAF in one of his only formal portraits in full uniform.

After three long years, the family was finally reunited in Brisbane in March 1945. Pappy was so weak from his wounds he could barely stand, while Polly and the kids were still suffering from the effects of prolonged starvation and their brutal treatment in Santo Tomas Internment Camp.

Pappy and Polly Stateside after being reunited in Australia, posing with the head of North American Aviation, James "Dutch" Kindelberger. On this visit, Dutch made it clear he owed a huge debt of gratitude to Pappy. Prior to the field modifications of the B-25, Dutch told the Gunns that he feared the Mitchell would be phased out of production in favor of the B-26 Marauder and A-26 Invader.

24

Where the Weak Are Prey

February 1942
Manila

Morning came; Polly did not. The kids sat together in the living room, practically trembling with fear and worry. Losing their father had been hard enough, but they had grown used to his absence for stretches during his Navy career. Polly had been the constant in their lives. Always there, always with them, tending to them, considering their every need. Until the weekend before the war broke out, the girls had never spent more than a night away from their mother.

Now, they had to face the ugly possibility that they might not see her again.

The uncertainty bored holes in them as they waited and prayed for her return. Finally, Leo came downstairs with Eva, who gently reminded them of their mother's plan.

It was time to go to Santo Tomas. Paul and Nath picked up their canvas bags. The girls had wicker suitcases. There was a flurry of activity as they prepared to depart.

The living room, cramped as it was, had been a place of comfort. These were their possessions; each one had a story. The Victrola sat on a table, its stack of records nearby. How many times had the kids wound it for their parents so they could dance to Bing Crosby and

Tommy Dorsey? How many times had they watched their parents in the Villamor Court living room, swaying together and laughing as P.I. led his wife in a rhumba? P.I. liked to end a song with a flourish, and often he would dip Polly as the final tinny notes played through the Victrola's antique horn.

The rows of photographs arrayed on the mantel and tabletops told the family's story. Wedding pictures, scenes of the honeymoon flight. Connie as a baby; the first family portraits when Nath arrived to complete their little clan. P.I. full of vitality in his uniform, jauntily posed before an aircraft. Polly, eyes shining, smiling with a happiness they all longed for.

The apartment had never been home. But these things were.

"Ready?" asked Leo in Russian-accented English.

Connie was naturally in charge now. She nodded and the children filed out of the apartment. They wondered if they would ever see it again.

Eva had called a kalesa for them, and they found it waiting on the street outside the duplex, its brightly colored carriage seeming out of place on this dark and fearful morning. The children climbed in back and Leo squeezed in with them. There was hardly room for all of them, so they clutched their luggage on their laps.

Eva waved good-bye, her face tense with worry as the kalesa's pony clip-clopped down the street. It would be a long drive to Santo Tomas at its speed.

The kids had not seen their city since the Japanese captured it. Now, they peered out of the carriage feeling numb with despair. Instead of Filipino constables guarding intersections, Japanese soldiers now took their place. Their rifles with foot-long bayonets looked far more menacing in the hands of these troops compared to the teenage private they'd first encountered. The sight of them standing watch over intersections they once passed through without a thought left them chilled.

It wasn't just the children who felt that way. Here and there, Filipinos moved on the sidewalks. Gone was the prewar bustle and brightness of the Pearl of the Orient Seas. In its place was the somber, cautious movement of a conquered people unsure of what to expect from their new masters. Eyes averted, they shuffled about their business with grim faces. The entire city seemed under a pall.

It took two hours to reach Santo Tomas. The Catholic university, the oldest college in American territory, had been founded in 1611 and opened eight years later. Its three-story main building remained one of the most beautiful architectural icons in the Philippines. Over the centuries, it weathered countless floods and earthquakes, storms, and conquering armies, and all the while its clergy educated the citizens of Manila.

The campus possessed a majestic quality, thanks to that main hall and its ornate façade, with that central clock tower and its arched windows. The classrooms were constructed with tall, heavy windows to help cool the place from the midday heat. Those rows of windows added to the building's luster at night, when interior lights streamed through them and suffused the entire hall with a beautiful orange glow.

Around the main hall stood a few more modern buildings, erected as the campus grew over the centuries. The rectangular, three-story education building stood across a small green, flanked by palm trees. Its outdoor breezeways between classrooms on the second floor gave it a distinctive colonial look. On the other side of campus was the seminary and chapel, both of which were off-limits to the prisoners. A gymnasium plus two large sporting fields split by a small copse of trees dominated the rear third of the campus. On that far side of those fields, a wrought iron fence ran along the east–west boundary of the campus, connecting with the older stone walls that ran north–south. Altogether, the university formed a square in the heart of Manila, about 450 meters on a side. Since it was so centrally located, the students commuted to class every day from their homes around the city. There were no dormitories or overnight facilities for anyone aside from the Jesuit priests in the seminary.

Not that it mattered; school was canceled now, and there would be no spring term 1942. Instead, the campus housed some thirty-five hundred civilian prisoners, who filled the classrooms and labs with bedding and personal items to overflowing. Around the buildings, the internees built makeshift showers and wash basins for laundry. The ad hoc additions dampened the grandeur of the campus. Now it looked like a cross between a Hooverville and a refugee camp thrown up in the middle of an architectural treasure.

As the kalesa drove up toward the wrought iron and masonry front gates, the Gunns could see throngs of Filipinos crowded around the entrance. Others lined the ten-foot-high north–south stone walls, throwing packages over to the people inside the campus.

The kalesa stopped. The driver could go no farther into the crowd. The children said good-bye to Leo and stepped down into the street. People were everywhere, shouting and shoving. Nath held his bag tight to his chest, a trill of terror playing through him as they pushed into this sea of strange faces.

At the gates themselves, Japanese guards stood, rifles up, bayonets catching the morning sun. They looked angry and overwhelmed, which made them aggressive. They shoved people away, shouted and gestured as people crowded around them.

Connie in the lead, her face set with determination, led the others through the chaos. They lined up at the main entrance, people jostling and pushing around them as they searched for their mother. She had promised to meet them at the gate if she couldn't get out. They finally spotted her, wearing the same white blouse, khaki slacks, and brown oxford lace-ups she had worn the day before when she set out for the camp. Nath saw her smiling at him, and in that moment his fear vanished. Warm and loving, she beamed at her babies, seemingly oblivious to the madhouse around them. Nath stared at his mom's smile and knew no matter what, as long as they were together, they would be okay.

Connie still in the lead, they pushed their way toward her, the throng around them forgotten. Their family embrace broke the tension, and they lingered in it for a long moment like stones in a stream as the current of people flowed around them.

Once inside the gates, Polly left to complete their processing paperwork, then returned and led them to the main building. The classrooms were now dormitories, and the place was already overcrowded. The camp had opened the month before; they were latecomers and would have to settle for what was available. The night before, she learned that right after the camp's formation, the prisoners established their own internal leadership, the internee committee, that dealt with the day-to-day logistics they all faced. She went to talk with them to explain her situation. The committee was not impressed. There was no allowance in the organization of the camp to keep brothers and sisters together with their mom. Everyone was segregated by gender.

Polly broke the bad news as gently as she could. The girls would be with her in a room full of women, but the closest she could get the boys to her was a room six doors down the hall on the third floor.

Nath and Paul looked at Polly, unsure of what that meant at first. Then it dawned on them: They would not be able to live with the rest of the family. The news shocked them. How could they look after their mom and the girls when separated?

The entire camp had been set up that way, strictly segregated by gender, living communally. Nath and Paul would be down the hall from their mother in a room full of some forty men.

They were led to their new quarters, a former classroom now crammed with beds only a few feet apart. The mattresses were cheap and thin; there was no privacy. The boys sat down on their beds and slid their canvas bags beneath them. They weren't even next to each other, which made the boys feel even more isolated. Paul's assigned bed stood next to a wall; Nath's was in the middle of the room.

The men around them, dressed in shorts and sandals, seemed uninterested in their arrival. Nobody greeted them, and few even looked their way. The mood in the room was morose and even a little hostile. Paul said hello to one of the men near his bed. The man ignored him. Nath watched and felt a sense of complete disorientation. The boys had spent their lives around their dad's Navy friends. As wild as they could be, they always looked after the Gunn kids. They'd taken it on faith that adults would always be that way. But here they were, about the only kids in a room with dozens of beds, and the men here made them feel like complete interlopers.

They were Americans, too. Why would they behave this way?

They decided to go explore and get out of the room. Together, the boys wandered the hall, peering into the bathrooms. Each floor had two of them, and they always seemed crowded. They soon discovered the doors had been taken off the stalls, so there was absolutely no privacy. The moment they tried to use one, the other men in line grumbled at them, "Hey, don't take all day, kid."

They found the showers—or what passed for them. In one bathroom, four heads had been rigged up over a drain in the floor. Men would crowd in, ten to twelve at a time to take turns under the heads.

That night, Nath hesitated as he made it to the front of the shower line. All these men around him and none of them were being kind. If they noticed him, it was to chew him out for something he'd done wrong. Now, he couldn't bring himself to get naked in front of them.

The men had no sympathy. "Hey, kid! Hurry up. Hurry up!"

At last, he took the plunge, stripping down and getting under the water. He'd only just gotten wet when one of the adults ordered him out. He scrambled off to get dressed and brush his teeth with Paul.

That night, in a room full of snoring strangers, Nath lay on his bed, squeezing his eyes closed as he tried to imagine himself any-where else but there. The sounds were all foreign to him, and in the middle of the room, separated from Paul yet surrounded by others a foot on either side of him, he felt claustrophobic.

He passed a long, hard night. In the morning, as the men cleared out to go eat breakfast or report to their work assignments, Paul motioned Nath over to his bunk. "Look at this," he said to his little brother.

He unzipped his canvas bag. Everything but the clothing had been stolen out of it. The food, the bar of soap his mom had packed, tooth-paste, brush, socks—all gone. Nath went back over to his bed and grabbed his bag.

Same thing. Everything but his change of clothes had been looted by the men in the room.

Adults stealing from children? This was so far out of the realm of their experience that the boys didn't really even know how to pro-cess it. They ended up doing what any kid would—they told their mother.

Polly was furious. Each makeshift dormitory was overseen by an inmate room monitor. They were supposed to resolve disputes and ensure that everyone got along while following the rules the Jap-anese imposed on them. Polly marched straight over to Paul and Nath's room monitor and reported the theft as the boys looked on.

"Lady, we're not gonna take care of these kids," the man snapped. "If they can't keep track of their stuff, that's their fault. Not ours."

Authority had always meant protection to the boys. Now they were being victimized by it. Standing there watching their mom get lectured by the one person who most controlled their daily existence left them deeply shaken. The room monitor would not keep them safe, and he made it clear that whatever the men in the room got away with would be their fault for not being better prepared for it.

Nath had no idea how to react to this new reality. They'd been taught by church and parent to believe in the fundamental goodness of people. Now, they'd seen for the first time the dark side of human nature. Disillusioned and confused, Nath reached back in his mind for the lessons P.I. had instilled in him, but they seemed to have no relevance in this new world. He had no idea who had taken their belongings, and even if he had, how was he to take on an adult? The Eighth Avenue rules seemed inapplicable; they certainly couldn't fight the whole room.

Paul turned to Nath and said, "Feels like we're rabbits in a den of wildcats."

Polly confronted the internee committee with righteous anger and related what the other prisoners had done to her sons. The members of the committee did not show her much sympathy. The situation for boys without fathers was a bad one. Fortunately, an American school administrator named Bertram Godfrey Leake recognized the problem. Leake watched the men prey on the weak and young boys without fathers and knew the situation needed to change. He managed to secure one floor of the education building for preteen and teenage boys who were simply too young to be packed into rooms full of aggressive and selfish men.

The committee gave Polly the option to move the boys over there. Polly faced a terrible choice for any mother. She could keep the boys close, but the men in the room would no doubt continue to exploit them. Or she could put them in another building on campus a lot farther away.

She knew the right thing to do, as difficult as it was to admit. They would be safer away from her. Heart heavy, she went to meet Bertram Leake and later that day, the boys carried what was left of their personal belongings over to the second floor of the Education Hall.

The boys found Leake to be an adult they understood. He was forthright and concerned about their well-being. He explained to the boys that there were plenty of adults they would need to watch out for during the days when they were out in the main prisoner population. They'd be safe in the Education Hall, but any adult could be a predator. They should be on their guard, and unlike life on the outside, they did not necessarily have to follow every adult's direction. It was every man—and boy—for himself.

The new space turned out to be much better suited for them. The boys made friends quickly, and found some interesting characters in their midst. One British boy in the room was obsessed with Napoleon. He talked about him nonstop and sometimes mimicked him. The other kids called him Nappy, and his erratic behavior made it seem like he was right on the edge of a nervous breakdown. Some of the other kids they recognized from school, or from their social circle in Manila.

Gradually the number of boys swelled so that Leake's operation spread to three rooms. One of the Gureviches' closest friends arrived not long after the Gunn brothers. Abraham Zelekofsky was Nath's age, a child piano prodigy with thin arms and a ghostlike complexion. He'd never done anything but play the piano and learn musical theory. He was slender and his body was undeveloped. In the *Lord of the Flies* world behind the wall at Santo Tomas, such a talented child was nothing but a target.

That he didn't have a father to protect him made things worse for the boy. Like other Russian refugees, his family fled the Revolution to settle in China. In the late 1930s, his dad secured British papers and passports for them so they could escape to Manila. Those get-out-of-the-Asian-mainland documents now came back to haunt them. Though Russian and officially neutral, the Japanese saw only the paperwork and threw the family behind bars. However, they deemed Abraham's father's job in Manila to be vital to the city's function and did not intern him. Instead, they gave him a waiver to remain outside the walls.

When he came to the building, Abraham's mom was relieved to see a friendly face and asked Nath to watch out for her boy, even though he would be two doors down in a room for younger boys. Nath took the mission seriously and said he would do his best to protect him.

The days passed; the family gradually grew accustomed to the camp routine. In the mornings, the boys would line up for breakfast with their mom's meal chit and bring their food over to the main building to eat as a family. Then the internee committee assigned Connie to the camp hospital, so she rarely ate breakfast with them after that. They tried to eat lunch and dinner together whenever they could, but Paul ended up working as part of the kitchen staff. Soon he could not make all the family meals, either. Polly did her best to hold them all together in the midst of fighting so many forces that pulled them apart. The kids reciprocated, doing their best to take care of their mom.

Though always spirited and capable, Polly never operated without an umbrella of support. As a child, she lived with her father's protection always present. She went straight from his house to the one she and P.I. established after their marriage. While he was gone for long periods at sea and she learned to function without him, she always knew that if an emergency happened, she could contact the Navy and he would return home. She always ran the household smoothly in his absence, but the big family decisions were either made by P.I. or figured out together.

She lacked that safety net now, and the stark realization of how truly alone she was shook Polly to her foundations. There was no average day at Santo Tomas; every day required survival-level decisions that she needed to make on behalf of herself and her children. There was no umbrella of protection over her, or waiting in the wings should she find herself out of her depth. Now, totally out of her depth, she was the umbrella for her children. How to protect them in a prison, when so few aspects of life were under her direct control, posed an almost insurmountable challenge. It wore her down psychologically, while the physical demands of camp life took their toll as well.

With their mother not always there for them, the boys realized they needed to fend for themselves. They learned not to trust adults unless they first proved trustworthy. Too many either wanted to use the children to do extra work or chores around the camp, or sought to exploit them in other ways. At first, the threat of sexual assault weighed on the family's mind. As the lack of food sapped everyone's strength, that became less of a concern.

Other things became far more dangerous to the boys, including snitches. One woman spent her days sitting in a chair, watching everything that went on around her. She reported every infraction of the rules from public displays of affection to smuggling contraband. Every rumor overheard and misdeed she witnessed she passed on to the Japanese in return for extra food. She survived by betraying her fellow inmates.

She was not alone. For extra food and perks, others became informers, too. Some helped the Japanese ferret out the men in the camp who had concealed their military identities. Julie's friend J.C. Baxter was one of those who had shed his uniform once the Japanese reached Manila, hoping to ride out the war in the internment camp instead of a POW compound. Gradually, the Japanese hunted these men down. Once discovered, the soldiers took them to nearby Fort Santiago, which had become the headquarters of the Japanese secret police, or Kempeitai, and tortured them for information. If they survived, they were dumped into the POW compounds springing up around Luzon.

One morning, Nath and Paul were walking to the showers when they spotted Dan Stickle. Last time they'd seen Dan, he was a lieutenant in the Army Air Force. To stay with his wife, Marie, he'd disposed of his uniform, concealed his military background from the Japanese occupation authorities, and turned both himself and Marie in at Santo Tomas's front gate.

He'd been a close family friend for years. Seeing him lifted the boys' spirits. Here was an adult they could trust, who would look after them. But Dan walked by without so much as a nod or eye contact. When they told Polly of the incident, she whispered to them that there were ears everywhere. Dan was risking his life to be in the camp with Marie, so they needed to play along and protect him. That was another switch for the boys, a reminder that their world had been turned upside down. Instead of Dan Stickle, the man who tried to get them to safety out of Manila, looking out for them, the boys would have to be his silent protector, guarding his deadly secret.

The daily drudge of survival among their fellow inmates was occasionally punctuated by the intrusion of Japanese troops. In 1942, the camp was administered by Japanese civilian authorities with just a small cadre of soldiers to guard the inmates. They manned the lookout positions along the walls. They carried out inspections in the living spaces, searching for contraband items, the most coveted of which was cash. Each inmate was allowed to bring in only a thousand pesos, and they could not have more sent in to them from the outside. They could use that money to purchase food from the Filipino-run kiosks at the front gate, but once the cash was gone, the inmates were totally dependent on the food provided from the kitchens. Even at the beginning, there was never enough of that.

The inspections inspired terror in the family. The soldiers could be brutal if they found anything they didn't like, and Polly was hiding considerable contraband. She'd begun to keep a journal of the family's experience, and such writing was strictly prohibited. She hid her pages inside her clothes and never let anyone but the kids see that she had them.

Polly also held on to the wad of cash that P.I. had given her on

Christmas Eve before he left for Australia. He told them the war would not be a short one, and she took that to heart. The cash was their lifeline. It could supplement their meager camp rations with fruit and vegetables purchased at the kiosks by the front gate. The cash ensured they could pay for essentials that other inmates simply couldn't afford. Yet to be caught with it could have resulted in the severest punishment.

To protect the money, Polly put her sewing skills to work, unstitched her mattress and concealed the cash within it. She'd made sure that it was secreted away well enough that when the soldiers came and patted their bedding down, they would detect no incriminating lumps or hear the crackle of cash as their hands squeezed the mattress. While the troops searched, the inmates had to stand at attention outside their rooms in ranks three to four deep, waiting tensely to see if anything would be found. The soldiers were known to be brutal, even to their own.

One morning, Paul and Nath awoke to see the camp's military units drilling in a nearby open stretch of the campus. One of the young privates kept screwing up, which prompted the boys to break out in laughter. The man lacked any soldier skills in his DNA; he was clumsy and always a beat behind the rest of the formation. Finally, one of the noncommissioned officers had enough. He walked over to the private, screaming at him through the next drill. When he screwed up again, the NCO rained blows and kicks down onto the luckless man. Stunned by the sight of such brutality, the boys whispered of it later for days. If they could inflict such harm on their own men, how would they react to a prisoner who did something seriously wrong?

They did not have to wait long to find out.

On February 14, 1942, three men escaped from Santo Tomas after the evening roll call. They slipped away over the fence late that night and were not missed until morning. The Japanese in Manila caught them within hours and returned them to the camp.

That morning, the three men were tied to stakes outside the main hall. Word went round that the Japanese wanted the entire inmate population to assemble outside with them. Slowly, the inmates streamed out into the open, the morning sun hot on their skin. Nath had been at the Education Hall when the order came round, and he walked outside into the crowd wondering what was going on. Somewhere, his mother, Paul, Julie, and Connie must have been in the crowd too, but with over three thousand people standing in that open area, he had little hope of finding them.

Then he saw the three bound and staked prisoners, helpless, bare from the waist up and blindfolded. Several Japanese soldiers stood nearby, and when an officer gave the word, they whipped the three men with sand-filled rubber hoses. The crowd stared on in complete shock. The soldiers viciously swung with all the force they could muster. The blows split skin. Blood dripped onto the grass beneath them, and the sounds of bones cracking echoed across the campus. The three men wailed in agony. Their screams brought no succor; there would be no mercy.

The inmates watching recoiled. Some turned away. Others fled. Nobody forgot the sight, or the message the Japanese made with it. To escape was foolish, and the consequences depraved.

The Japanese later took the escapees out of Santo Tomas, lined them up in front of open graves and shot them at close range by pistol fire. They fell into the graves, still alive. Filipino workers were forced to bury them, even as they groaned and cried.

Nobody tried to escape from Santo Tomas after that day.

Nath walked away from that scene changed forever. His childhood days were over. He understood that now beyond any doubt. Running on the beach, watching the fleet come and go as their pet monkey capered on his leash. Serenading redheaded girls. Playing soldier in the safety of their backyard. That was not his life anymore, and in that moment he recognized it was gone for good.

Survival mattered. He couldn't be soft; he couldn't rely on others. Those American men in uniform he spent his entire life around would not be back anytime soon to rescue them. Now, the ones in uniform were to be hated, feared, and avoided. He knew that they would not survive if the family played by the old prewar rules. The game had changed, and Nath realized he would have to grow hard and change, too. He would need a new playbook. He would need to be stealthy, cold-blooded, and bold. Otherwise, he and his loved ones would simply become victims of this hellish place.

Nathan Gunn walked toward the education building, the sight of those tortured men lingering in his mind. *Whatever it takes*, he silently vowed. *Whatever it takes.*

25

Wainwright to MacArthur: Where Is Captain Gunn?

March 20, 1942
Darwin, Australia

Singapore had fallen. Sumatra, Bali, Timor—all in Japanese hands. Those fresh-faced pilots Pappy brought to Darwin? The few who made it back did so with grim faces, aged beyond their years, a lifetime of gruesome memories closeted deep within them. Most never escaped—including Major Sprague, who was killed in action. For all the carnage, the P-40 pilots scored only a handful of kills against the Japanese.

In the Philippines, Gen. Jonathan Wainwright still held out on Corregidor and Bataan, but MacArthur had escaped to Australia under orders from FDR. The end was near on Luzon, and the other islands would surely fall once the army there laid down its arms.

The men on Bataan clung desperately to their last defensive lines, their uniforms rotting off their bodies. Wracked by diseases, down to quarter rations, they'd been forced to kill and eat their cavalry horses just to stay alive a few more days.

Wainwright was hunkered down in MacArthur's old headquarters on Corregidor, pleading for supplies, support—anything for his men. Ridiculous amounts of money had been thrown at ship captains to brave the Japanese blockade, but once the Dutch East Indies fell, few wanted to risk their ships with a run into Manila Bay.

Not that there were many of those left anymore. Scores of ships tried to flee Singapore in the days before it fell, only to be destroyed on the high seas by Japanese warships or patrolling planes. Few survived those tragic encounters.

As the Indies collapsed, another mass exodus unfolded. The Japanese swept the seas south of Java with aircraft carriers, cruisers, and destroyers. Their planes ranged and scouted ahead, blowing anything they encountered out of the water. Thousands perished in the holocaust between Java and Australia in those last frantic days before the Japanese ruled supreme.

Gone were many of the ships Pappy had known in his youth. Countless times in the 1920s, he had landed on the stubby flight deck of America's first carrier, the USS *Langley*. Proud of his service aboard that old "Covered Wagon" of naval aviation, he'd used to speak of her with great fondness.

The Japanese sank her south of Java while she was trying to get a deck load of P-40s to the embattled Americans there. Most of her crew died in the disaster.

The cruiser *Houston* was sunk somewhere off Java; nobody knew where. She went missing with an Australian cruiser while trying to escape through the Sunda Strait. Pappy spent part of his naval aviation career serving as a scout pilot in floatplanes based on cruisers. He felt the loss of her as keenly as anything else. Those sailors were men of his breed; the old-timers aboard her were men with whom he passed some of the greatest moments of his youth.

Now there was nothing left of the Asiatic Fleet, those glorious ships Pappy's boys would watch from the seawall down the street from the house on Villamor Court as they steamed proudly back to Sangley Point after weeklong maneuvers—gone. Some just vanished at sea without so much as an SOS. Others dashed off frantic contact reports before going forever silent.

So many ships. So many old Navy pals lost aboard those ships. The devastation left Pappy grief-stricken, angry, and even more determined to do something—anything—to stop the carnage.

Now, Australia itself was under attack. Aircraft from the same Japanese carrier task force that devastated Pearl Harbor plastered Darwin in mid-February, leaving the port devastated. Batchelor Field's hangars were little more than broken sticks, and the town was virtually deserted.

When the carriers went looking for other targets, the land-based bombers came. Now, only a handful of P-40 pilots remained with battered, patched-together planes to challenge the Japanese. They took off, dodging bomb craters to give battle against the rising odds, the last line of defense before Oz itself came under the Rising Sun.

They were coming. Nobody doubted that. It wasn't a matter of trying to save the Philippines anymore. Now, the American and Aussie brass argued over whether to defend the northern shore, or give it up and withdraw everything south.

Pappy endured these chaotic, pain-wracked days by throwing himself into work. Laboring until he dropped, he flew, fixed, and helped form the nascent transport service in Australia. When these binges ended and he collapsed, sometimes sleep would not come despite the exhaustion. His mind flashed anger, guilt, and frustration. He would awake a tormented man and throw himself back into a cockpit, bound for wherever.

Wrong as the decision was, he was still bound by that sense of duty, even if the people running the show at headquarters were his enemies, too. There was a job to do here; he was needed in this crisis. He couldn't just steal a B-17 and fly to Del Monte on Mindanao, then find some way up to Luzon. They would declare him a deserter and arrest him. His access to aircraft would be sealed off, and he might end up in prison, his family still in Japanese hands. Even if he escaped, there would be no way to return to the islands. FEAF and the RAAF had appropriated every civilian airliner left in Australia. As much as he hated the Army brass, he needed their planes. He needed to temper himself, if just enough to not give them an excuse to lock him away.

If he could blend his duty into a rescue operation, he might just be able to get them out. Problem was, time was against him. The Japanese were sure to conquer the Philippines in a matter of weeks, maybe even earlier than that. If he didn't figure out a military reason to get back up there soon, he never would. With Miss EMF unavailable, the chances of such a mission seemed increasingly remote.

The chance finally came in mid-March, shortly after MacArthur reached Australia. General Wainwright sent him a desperate appeal for quinine, an antimalaria medicine. Thousands of his men on Bataan lay fever-wracked in overcrowded field hospitals, suffering from malaria. If only somebody could get through with a supply of quinine, those men could get back in the fight. The defenders might be able to hold out a little longer until more help arrived.

Wainwright asked for three million tablets. Since virtually no ship captain wanted to run the blockade, and a submarine mission would take too long, the resupply effort would have to be undertaken by the Army Air Force. Pills were light and easy to store aboard aircraft; it would not be a challenge to carry that sort of cargo. The challenge would be getting the aircraft to where Wainwright needed it. A B-17 could make the jump from Darwin to Del Monte on Mindanao Island, but there was no way to land one on Bataan. The fields there were all short, primitive fighter strips hacked out of the jungle. While a few planes from the Bamboo Fleet still remained active in the Philippines, they flew sporadically and under constant threat. Trying to offload the quinine at Del Monte, then smuggling up to Bataan in the wheezing planes of the Bamboo Fleet looked like the only workable way to get Wainwright his supplies. That was a slender reed at best, however, as it would have taken many trips and lots of risk by the few remaining pilots in the islands.

The situation gave Pappy an idea. He volunteered for the mission and offered to do it not in a B-17, but in NPC-56. He knew he could get the venerable Beech in and out of Bataan from Mindanao and deliver the quinine in one flight. That would spare the extra step of having to round up whatever planes the Bamboo Fleet could get working for the mission. Plus, in Pappy's mind, he knew he could use the Beech to go find a way back to his family. This was the nuanced balance between duty and his own personal agenda he needed.

Only one problem: The only plane that had the fuel to get from Darwin to Del Monte in the Southern Philippines was the B-17. The Beech needed refueling stops along the way, just like P-40s did. With the ferry route long in Japanese hands, there looked to be no way to get the PAL airliner back to the islands.

Pappy thought it through and ran some numbers. If he lightened the aircraft and increased its fuel capacity, he figured he could just make it to Del Monte. The old bird—still lacking guns and armor—could be refueled there on Mindanao for the final run to Bataan. Once back on Luzon, he could use his contacts on the ground to find his family and get them back. The Beech would be their lifeline to Australia.

Pappy set to work stripping everything he could off NPC-56 to save weight. Whatever could be pulled out, torn out, or hacked out, he removed. Every ounce counted. The passenger seats went. The toilet his boys dropped Coke bottles through went. Extra radio gear, survival equipment—pitched out. Pappy spent days at the task, then figured out a way to cram five ninety-five-gallon fuel drums into the passenger area. Four hundred and seventy-five gallons of extra gasoline packed in there behind him. He'd be a flying lighter should a bullet pierce the fuselage.

Whether it was ever repainted from its prewar bright red is not known. Likely by this time, somebody had sprayed a coat of olive drab over its sleek wings and fuselage. At least that gave him a little extra chance to slip through the Japanese cordon undetected.

The extra 2,850 pounds seriously overloaded the Beech. With the internal tanks full, the rated payload of the 18 was only 254 pounds. He'd only been able to take so much stuff out of the aircraft and it was still eighteen hundred pounds overloaded. Most pilots wouldn't even try to get airborne under those conditions. The two Pratt & Whitneys just didn't have the horses to do it.

Carrying the extra fuel wasn't enough. He needed to find a way to get the gas in the passenger cabin into the internal tanks. As he modified the aircraft, he constructed a Rube Goldberg system where he could use a rubber hose and hand pump affixed to one of the drums to get the gas into the main internal system.

He couldn't pilot the plane and pump gas, not when he would be flying right on the wave tops to avoid detection. Perhaps at altitude, he could trim the plane, step out of the cockpit and pump, returning periodically to make sure the aircraft remained in level flight. Doing so would increase his chance of detection, so that wouldn't work. He concluded that he would need a copilot, at least to get to Del Monte.

Not just a copilot, but a coconspirator. Getting the quinine to Bataan was important, but it was just an official ticket back to the Philippines. This medical mission of mercy would be his cover for another rescue attempt. Whoever crewed the plane with him would have to be okay with that.

He found his co-conspirator in Maj. Cecil McFarland, whose wife and unborn son were left behind in Cebu City. He had served as the oil and fuel officer for FEAF at the start of the war. In the dark days after the Japanese landed on Luzon, he heroically tried to rescue as much fuel as he could from the approaching Imperial Army. At one point, he even found a row of tanker cars on a rail line north of

Manila—and he'd tried to separate them from boxcars full of artillery ammunition as Japanese planes strafed and bombed the area.

McFarland possessed plenty of Oklahoma-born courage. In February, Colonel Johnson put him in charge of one of the new squadrons in Air Transport Command. He and Pappy got to know each other and discovered they'd both left behind family. The two began to plot together and work through how they could get everyone out.

The first leg between Darwin and Mindanao would be the trickiest. Pappy would fly while McFarland pumped gas through the makeshift system in the main cabin. They decided to fly at night to minimize detection and try to get into Del Monte just after dawn. From there, Pappy intended to take McFarland to Cebu then continue to Bataan, deliver the quinine, and pull his own family out.

That was the reason he selected the Beech for this mission. Miss EMF couldn't set down on Quezon Boulevard, or any of the small dirt strips on Bataan. This mission required something small and agile enough to get in and out of tight spaces, but large enough to hold the entire family. NPC-56 was the only thing available that could do it.

At least, he thought he could do it. With McFarland on board, the bird was two thousand pounds over its factory-rated max load.

At 1800 on March 20, 1942, Pappy and McFarland finished their final preparations and climbed into the modified Beech. With the quinine loaded aboard and all the gas drums topped off, they taxied to the end of the runway at Batchelor Field. Pappy tested the magnetos, ran each engine up as usual. Like all the other Philippine refugees that spring, NPC-56 continued to fly with only minimal maintenance. The engines were so worn out and unreliable that no civilian airline company ever would have let that plane off the ground. It didn't need a mere overhaul anymore. It was in such bad shape that an overhaul would be just a Band-Aid. NPC-56 needed new engines and a myriad of fresh parts.

They sounded rough and abused to Pappy's mechanic's ear. He'd done everything he could for them with what he had on hand. Now, he just had to trust they'd hold up and get them off the ground. Still, they worried him.

Should he abort? Spend some extra time to find new engines or a better aircraft?

He listened to the engines tell their story to him, options running through his head.

There were no new motors for the Beech in Australia. Nor was there a different aircraft option. This was old territory in his mind, and he cast those thoughts aside quickly. He stared out at the runway ahead. This stunt could get him killed. Overloaded, full of fuel, if they couldn't get the Beech into the air, they surely would die in a ball of fire at the end of the runway.

If he died, his family would be thrown to the hands of fate. Their salvation depended on him; he couldn't afford to take wild risks.

He glanced across the instrument panel. Everything was in the green. He could turn around now and come up with a better plan.

What better plan? He was out of options. This was it. And if he didn't try, he knew the guilt would devour him so thoroughly that he might as well be dead.

He eased the throttles forward. Nothing hard or abusive. The runway was long and wide; they had plenty of room to take off.

The overloaded Beech waddled forward, gaining speed with such sluggishness that a less desperate pilot would have probably cut the throttles before the point of no return and taxied back to the ramp. Considering the stakes riding on this mission, Pappy pushed the throttles toward max power.

Halfway down the runway now, the Beech continued to struggle, so Pappy fed in more throttle until both were wide open and the engines howled. The airspeed indicator passed sixty. The tail didn't come up. The ribbon of concrete on their nose was fast running out.

They passed the point of no return. No chance to cut the throttles and ease the plane to a stop now; there just wasn't the runway left for that. They would get aloft, or they would die in a fiery crash when they hit the edge of the strip. With all the extra fuel aboard, there would be no way to survive a wreck.

The tail lifted. The Beech tried to veer left, pulled along by the engine torque, but Pappy corrected with the rudder with swift precision. The airspeed indicator crept past a hundred. Heavily, almost reluctantly, the wheels broke contact with the concrete. Pappy pulled the control column back, just a bit. The nose came up and the Beech lumbered aloft. The minute it left the ground, Pappy retracted the landing gear to reduce drag. The airspeed indicator jumped, and the plane climbed a little more quickly.

They made it aloft. Now, they just needed to navigate through fifteen hundred miles of Japanese-held territory. Fifteen hundred miles, over twelve hours of airtime. The fuel tanks behind them precluded smoking. When he couldn't light up a Camel, Pappy would often stick a half-chewed cigar nub in his mouth. But no nicotine for half a day? He'd be ready to kill somebody by the time they got to Del Monte.

They flew on northward, the sun setting off their port wing. McFarland pumped gas; Pappy navigated and kept the Beech on the deck. As darkness fell, they made detours around the small islands east of Timor.

They broke into the Banda Sea and flew straight into a typhoon. The weather turned so foul it caused Pappy to climb off the wave tops. Turbulence threw them around and hampered McFarland's midflight refueling efforts. Soon, they were trapped in a world of blacks and grays, their windscreen lashed by rain and wind, the aircraft pummeled by sudden downdrafts that forced Pappy to stay on the manual controls without respite hour after hour. Like Miss EMF, the Beech didn't have hydraulic boosts for its ailerons or elevators. Fighting the forces of nature demanded muscle power, and lots of it. The physical endurance that required was nothing short of staggering, the equivalent of curling weights in absolute darkness for ten hours straight, where one mistake could potentially be fatal.

All the while, he scanned the instruments and tried to calculate how much the howling wind was pushing them off course. He wanted to come into Mindanao up Moro Gulf, then cut overland near Cotabato City, one of the key nav points along the island's west coast. Doing that now while trapped in the storm seemed a remote possibility. They couldn't see the stars; they couldn't navigate by features below them. Pappy could only keep watch on the compass and ensure the nose remained pointed in the right direction. The rest he left to feel and fate.

Around 0400, the Beech's left engine began to sputter. Pappy nursed it along and fed in more power for the remaining fan to compensate. He couldn't push it too far; he knew the engines were on their last legs.

It didn't do any good. The left engine gradually failed until at last it gave out altogether. Through the storm, Pappy saw its prop windmilling uselessly and changed its pitch until the blades were flush with the slipstream—a process known as feathering. That way, the blades didn't create drag.

A Beech could fly on only one engine—provided it was in good shape and could produce power. The pilot needed to trim the aircraft and compensate with the controls, but it could be done by a skilled pilot. In a storm, with worn-out engines, overloaded—that was a different story.

They began a slow descent, Pappy trading altitude for airspeed, trying to stretch things as long as he could. At six hundred feet, he dropped out of the bottom of the typhoon to see dawn breaking over distant mountains to the east.

One look around and Pappy knew they were over the Moro Gulf.

He could see the tip of the Zamboanga Peninsula ahead and off to the left. Somewhere to the right beneath the rising sun would be Cotabato. Pappy's nocturnal navigation was almost perfect once again.

As they began to cut across for the gulf's eastern shore, a shape materialized on the water ahead of them. Through the rain-streaked windscreen, the two Americans realized it was a ship. Few Allied vessels remained in the area, so they assumed it to be Japanese.

They turned to avoid it, limping for the coast, the fuel drums in the passenger cabin now empty. Pappy could keep it aloft on one engine for a bit longer, but they were in no shape for a fight.

Aboard the ship, probably the seaplane carrier *Mizuho*, Japanese sailors spotted the lone American plane with one engine out, and the vessel's scout pilots wanted a crack at an easy kill.

Four stubby, two seat biplanes shot off *Mizuho*'s catapult rails, banking for Pappy and Cecil McFarland.

Pappy could not fight. He could not maneuver much on one engine. He could not run away. The Americans had one chance: Hide in the clouds and creep away.

As the float planes bored in toward them, Pappy pushed the throttle to the stop and limped for cover.

26

The Indomitable Luck of Pappy Gunn

March 21, 1942
Over Moro Gulf, Mindanao

The Beechcraft reached the cloud layer with seconds to spare. The stubby little single pontoon float biplanes bored in after it, but the scud reduced visibility to only a few yards. They blundered around as Pappy eyed his instruments and coaxed NPC-56 toward Cotabato. The right engine maintained power, but its abused and worn pistons growled and popped in protest.

Safe for the moment, Pappy knew they couldn't stay in the murk forever. Low on fuel, airborne now for twelve hours, they needed to get on the ground. Del Monte lay a few hundred miles to the northeast—within their grasp, but barely.

Pappy dropped out of the cloud layer to get a visual on the coastline and orient himself. The Beech burst out into the gray morning at six hundred feet—and right into the path of one of the float planes searching for them. The two planes careened toward each other as the Japanese pilot opened fire with his two cowl-mounted light machine guns. Red tracers lit the sky around NPC-56. Bullets struck home. The Beech shuddered, but Pappy kept control. He ducked the nose down, but another torrent of lead cut through the wing and fuselage. He could feel the Beech grow even more sluggish. It was wounded—badly wounded.

In a flash, the biplane sped past the crippled Beech. The right engine began to lose power even as the float plane began to turn for another pass.

They weren't going to make it to Mindanao.

Just off the 18's nose lay an island partially shrouded in the morning's rainy gloom. It was only a short distance away, but even that looked like a reach. He tried for it anyway; the only other option was to crash in the gulf and swim for it.

The Beech stumbled downward, Pappy fighting the controls all the way, while Cecil began to mumble a prayer beside him. The island loomed before them as Pappy coaxed just a bit more flight time out of their dying bird. They hurtled over the surf breaking on the island's beach, props throwing spray in their wake. In its final seconds, NPC-56 carried them bare feet above the sand until finally, its battered engine could give no more. Pappy pulled the nose up just as the bottom of the fuselage smacked into the beach, bending the props back like bloomed flowers. It skipped into the air in one last death gasp, then slammed back down into a farmer's field of taro plants. They skidded along, completely out of control, Pappy and Cecil helpless observers as the Beech careened for a grove of coconut trees at the edge of the farm.

They plunged into the grove. The right wing collided with a tree and tore off, but still the aircraft kept going. A second later, the left wing struck another tree and peeled off the fuselage. Wingless, the body of the Beech finally came to rest deep within the coconut grove. Overhead, the float plane buzzed around, its crew uncertain of the Beechcraft's fate.

McFarland looked over at Pappy, cigar butt still clamped between his teeth. Both men were bruised and would be sore for days, but somehow they'd escaped serious injury. It was a miracle their aircraft had not exploded.

Silently, Pappy reached down and grabbed his flight bag.

"You know it was my prayer that saved us," McFarland said, turning to Pappy.

"How do you mean?" Pappy asked as he fumbled around in search of something inside his bag.

"Well, you kept saying 'Oh shit! Oh shit! Oh shit!' while I was promising the Lord that I would mend my ways if he got us out of this mess."

Pappy pulled out a bottle of bourbon from his flight bag as McFarland kept chattering. He cut him off by handing him the booze. "Here," he said, "you first."

McFarland popped the cork off and took a long swig from the bottle.

"Hey, don't drink all of it!"

They heard something outside in the coconut grove. Pappy went rigid. Lightning-quick, he drew his pair of Colt .45s and peered out of the windscreen into the treescape.

He turned back to McFarland. "Somebody's coming. Play dead, Mac, until we know who they are."

"Okay."

A moment later, somebody reached the side of the fuselage. Pappy and McFarland lay motionless in their seats, Pappy's Colts in his lap, hands atop them.

If this was a Japanese patrol outside, they would have to fight. Pappy and Cecil knew what fate the Japanese meted out to downed aircrew. Stories circulating in Australia recounted bayonetings, torture, and even death games. At best, they could look forward to life in a prison camp.

Pappy refused to go out that way. If this was to be his last stand, so be it. He'd try to catch them off guard and take as many as he could with him. He held the .45s tight and prepared for a shoot-out. Whoever was outside began moving along the side of the fuselage, toward Pappy's side window. He heard the footsteps crunching on the leaves. Closer. Closer.

Only a few feet away now.

No prayer, that would be hypocritical.

Something scraped against the side of the fuselage, just behind Pappy's side window.

Polly...

"Hello, sir," came a voice in accented English.

Pappy opened his eyes and found himself staring at a young Filipino farmer. The tension broke, replaced by relief.

"Hello, yourself," Pappy replied with affected casualness.

Leaving a .45 in his lap, he grabbed the bourbon and offered it to the Filipino. The man politely declined, so Pappy took a swig.

"Hot damn, that hits the spot."

He passed the bottle back to McFarland, then holstered his .45s. A moment later, they were outside the wreckage talking to the Filipino.

"Seen any Japs around here?"

The Filipino shook his head. "No, sir. We see only their ships as they go by."

As they talked, a car drove up and the plantation's owner climbed out. He walked across his ruined taro field, inspecting the wreckage as he went.

Pappy started to introduce himself, but the owner cut him off. "I know who you are, Mr. Gunn. You are Philippine Air Lines. I have flown with you from Cotabato to Manila many times."

Recognition dawned on Pappy's face. "Oh yes! I recognize you now." Leave it to Pappy Gunn to crash-land on a business associate's plantation.

Pappy looked around at the remains of NPC-56. It was officially the last flight of Philippine Air Lines. His post-Navy career had been wrapped up in getting the business going. He'd been a pioneer out in the Western Pacific. Now it was all over. At least until after the war.

The loss of his midlife's work hit him hard. Sadly, he said to the plantation owner, "The airline is no more." He pointed to the fuselage wedged among the coconut trees and added, "That was my last plane."

The momentary exultation at surviving the crash soon gave way to profound despair. How would he get to Polly now? With the Beech gone, there would be no way to get into Manila, unless he could round up Soriano's old Staggerwing. Who knew if that was even still flying? Besides, assuming he was able to get them off Luzon, no amount of modifications would get the Staggerwing to Australia. That was beyond even his engineering ability.

He was stuck. He might be able to find and rescue Polly and the kids—or they could be waiting on Bataan for him. That looked like the easy part now. Once at Del Monte, though, the few PBYs and B-17s still flying south to Australia were filled with high-priority personnel. It was almost impossible to get a seat on one of those planes without serious pull from a senior officer.

They wouldn't be safe at Del Monte. Not for long, anyway. He hadn't gone to these lengths just to dump them in harm's way all over again. He would need to think this all through very carefully. In the meantime, they checked the fuselage wreckage and found the quinine cargo intact. The need for it on Bataan was probably greater than ever, so they could not just abandon it. They would have to get it across the mountains to Del Monte and hope the Bamboo Fleet could carry it the rest of the way to Wainwright's men.

They talked the situation over with the plantation owner. He agreed to help them in any way he could. First, he laid out the situation on the island for them.

The Japanese had landed at Davao in December, which was on the south coast. After taking the port, they seemed content to stay there and use it as a staging base for further operations in the Dutch East Indies. On March 2, 1942, a small force of Japanese landed on the Zamboanga Peninsula to establish a seaplane base. The Filamerican forces in the area retreated at first contact, then dispersed to conduct guerrilla attacks against the Japanese.

At least for the time being, the rest of the island remained in Filamerican hands. If they could get across the bay undetected by the Japanese ships and aircraft in the area, they stood a good chance of reaching Del Monte safely.

The plantation owner aided them in the first step of their journey. He gave them a boat and crew, who helped load the quinine aboard and smuggled them to the Cotabato coast. There, they found their way first to the city, then up north to Del Monte. A Filipino infantry division defended the city of Cotabato, and it is quite possible they stumbled into their lines and found a ride to Del Monte through them.

When they reached the American base, they found it totally transformed. No longer were aircraft parked out in the open; Colonel Elsmore's industrious bunch had bored deep tunnels into the nearby mountains that were large enough to hide five or more P-40s. After the Japanese had discovered the main airfield, the Americans furiously built many auxiliary strips all around the area that they masterfully camouflaged then stocked with aviation fuel and oil.

From these fields, the Americans played a shell game with the Japanese bombers, moving the dwindling number of P-40s and transports around to avoid their destruction on the ground. The remains of Bill Bradford's Bamboo Fleet still flew in and out of the area, but the aircraft left to his pilots were in such terrible shape that it was a wonder they could still fly.

Jess Villamor remained in the area as well, running between

Bataan and the Southern Islands in an ancient biplane trainer that could barely touch ninety miles an hour in level flight. He was part of a brave and doomed group of aviators doing everything they could to keep the men on Bataan from dying of starvation or disease.

Pappy and McFarland arrived on this scene and reported to Elsmore. Both still wanted to get north, but Elsmore radioed back to Australia that the two lost airmen had turned up. FEAF HQ sent back word that Pappy was to get to Brisbane as quickly as possible.

McFarland would be left behind.

Philippine president Manuel Quezon reached Mindanao about this time with a small entourage. With the collapse of his nation's defenses imminent, he was heading to Australia. A B-17 flew into Del Monte to pick them up, and Pappy hitched a ride back aboard it.

Pappy reached Darwin safely, then caught another ride to Amberly Field. He wanted to get a flight of bombers up to Del Monte and do some damage to the Japanese, but the B-17 groups had been savaged by the fighting for Java. The dive bombers the Twenty-Seventh had assembled didn't have the range to get up there, and nothing else was available. Still he wanted to find Colonel Davies and pitch the idea to him.

In the meantime, Wainwright still needed the quinine, and FEAF wanted Pappy to try again with one of the Lodestars. He'd be going up again in a small, unarmed craft that would need to be modified to handle extra fuel to pull off the flight.

He might just get one more chance to rescue his family after all.

If Pappy was eager to get down, get a Lodestar, and prep it for the flight, Wainwright grew equally impatient. In the days to come, he sent repeated radio messages to General MacArthur asking, "Where is Captain Gunn?"

Captain Gunn reached Brisbane toward the end of March. When he touched down at Archerfield, a novel sight greeted him. Lined up on the ramp stood over a dozen beautifully clean twin-engine bombers the likes of which he'd never seen before. Caged-glass nose, big cowlings housing powerful radial engines and a twin tail, just like the Beech 18. Forward of that double tail, each bomber sported a clear Plexiglas defensive turret bristling with a pair of .50-caliber machine guns. More guns poked from its nose and fuselage sides, and under its belly lurked another turret, this one retractable.

They were camouflaged green and brown and looked like deadly raptors in repose, waiting for men to give them life and set them loose in the sky.

Pappy climbed out of his ride and wandered among them, marveling at their design and construction. Incredible. After months of dealing with worn out castoffs and machines that couldn't fight, here at last was real help from the Stateside factories.

Davies and his band of Philippine and Java vets would finally get aircraft worthy of their courage and daring. They'd need more men, no doubt there. The Twenty-Seventh's dive bombers carried only two, a pilot and gunner. These new crates looked to hold five or six at least. Somebody would need to teach the boys how to use the bombsights in these things. The A-24s carried what looked like a telescope sticking through its armored windscreen. While in a seventy-degree dive, the pilot would peer through it and line up on his target.

These new planes were level bombers, just like the bigger B-17s. They probably used the same Norden Bomb sight mounted in the Forts. Maybe the bombardiers from the Nineteenth Bomb Group could help with that and teach the Twenty-Seventh the workings of that very complex system.

Whatever. Davies could figure it all out. He wanted to go talk to him about getting those planes up to Del Monte to help Elsmore out. Maybe somebody at higher headquarters would listen to Davies.

As he walked the flight line, Pappy ran into a sergeant and began to chat him up. The new planes, built by North American Aviation, were called B-25 Billy Mitchells—named after the legendary Army

Air Corps general who proved the power of the bomber by sinking several battleships during exercises in the 1920s. Mitchell had been a loose cannon, fearless in his effort to promote aviation and pull the military's hidebound, intellectually strangled generals and admirals out of the nineteenth century. He had made enemies throughout the establishment. Inevitably, he'd been court-martialed and run out of the Army.

Pappy came of age as an aviator at a time when Billy Mitchell was the biggest single advocate for military air power. He'd been the pioneer, the man who championed the vision of how the airplane would dominate wars to come.

Few listened. But Pappy and the small group of military pilots certainly did. They drank every word in and believed the gospel like no others. After his court-martial, Mitchell became a tragic hero to them. Of course, almost all he had prophesied came true in the opening months of the Second World War.

Davies and his crew of supply-depot-robbing Philippine refugees would ride into battle in a plane named after a renegade genius. Pappy almost certainly loved that serendipitous connection.

As he talked to the sergeant, the man dropped a bomb on him. These American planes did not belong to the Americans in Australia.

"What the hell do you mean?" Pappy demanded.

"They're for the Dutch, Captain."

Thunderstruck, all Pappy could do at first was stare at the sergeant as his mind processed that insanity.

"The goddamned Squareheads?" he finally managed.

"Yes, sir."

How could the brass do this to their own boys after all they'd suffered through? The thought of it roused Pappy to full fury.

It got worse. The sergeant mentioned they'd been sitting there on the flight line for days, unclaimed. The surviving Dutch aircrew who had escaped from Java were still trying to get organized into a squadron-sized force and had yet to take delivery of them. Few of the Dutch pilots had ever seen a B-25, let alone flown one. Their crews gunned ancient Martin 139 bombers built a decade before; Pappy knew there was no way they would be ready for something this hot without a lot of training.

Pappy reviled the Dutch, considered them to be borderline cowards. That was unfair—the Dutch air force in the Indies fought heroically almost to extinction. It didn't matter; Pappy's personal experience with them had permanently colored his opinion of their willingness to fight.

He concluded that these magnificent planes would be wasted on the Dutch. They'd fuss around, maybe start training, but they wouldn't take them into action anytime soon.

Pappy stalked off, anger burning holes within him.

God, what Davies's men could do with these planes—they could finally start fighting back with something that could really hurt the Japanese.

The Army Air Force lacked everything in Australia. They were told not to expect much more; America was committed to beating the Nazis first, and the Pacific would get the leftovers. They accepted that with disgruntled resignation. Now, even the leftovers were going to somebody else. What was Washington thinking?

27

The Canberra Commandos and the Numerous Troubles That Ensued

Early April 1942
Australia

The Dutch were the bastard stepchildren of the Allied cause in the Pacific that spring. In the early days of ABDA Command, many Dutch officers treated the Americans officiously or with aloofness. After navigating all the dangers required just to get to Java, the Americans found this treatment insulting. The relationship between the Allies only deteriorated from there, as the Americans promptly ran roughshod over convention and order, which caused the disciplined Dutch no end of pique.

In battle, the Dutch fought fiercely at times, especially their navy. But their air force engendered a lot of criticism by the Americans for its perceived lack of aggressiveness. Some American officers later alleged that Dutch bombers would sortie against an incoming Japanese amphibious task force, only to jettison their bombs and return to base to report fictionalized heroics.

Gen. Enis Whitehead, who would rise through the ranks to

become one of MacArthur's top air officers, did not mince words about the Dutch. In a 1945 interview, he called them a "shame to the white race." He added, "No one ever heard of a Dutchman with any guts."

The characterization was deeply unfair, but it was shared by Pappy and many of the Americans in Australia who fought in the Dutch East Indies Campaign. With the final defeat on Java came further recriminations and contempt from both sides.

Altogether, about nine hundred Dutch servicemen escaped to Australia. Their supreme commander fled to Ceylon, where he set up a new headquarters while putting Maj. Gen. L.H. van Oyen in charge of the refugees in Australia.

ABDA Command dissolved at the end of the Dutch East Indies Campaign in early March. That left the relationship between the Dutch in Australia, MacArthur, and the Australians all very unsettled and complicated. MacArthur seemed to share much of the prevailing sentiment about the Dutch, and when Washington tried to get him to integrate their air units with American ground personnel, MacArthur would not have it. He objected repeatedly until the subject was dropped.

The Dutch in Australia ended up falling between the headquarters cracks. They held their allegiance to the remains of their own chain of command, but their headquarters now lay on the far side of the Indian Ocean without an infrastructure—without even a country, since their homeland surrendered to the Germans in the spring of 1940. This left the Dutch colonial authorities running the show in the Far East. With their colony in Japanese hands, now they were warriors without a home.

The Dutch aircrew ended up as tenants on RAAF bases without any training planes, few instructors, no logistical system to get parts, ammunition, uniforms, or even shoes. In effect, they became wards of the Australian government.

They did have combat planes, and that gave them leverage in this otherwise totally unequal relationship. Before the collapse of Java, the Dutch had paid cash for virtually an entire new air force worth of American combat planes. They were being shipped across the Pacific by the hundred: B-25s and P-40s, light attack bombers and transports. The last delivery was scheduled to arrive in December 1942. By then, the Dutch would have over 450 new planes—more than MacArthur had in April 1942. That put the Dutch air force in the unique position of having more planes than pilots left to fly them.

As the first aircraft deliveries reached Brisbane, the Dutch formed a single bomber squadron at a base outside of Canberra. Called Number 18 Squadron, these few pilots and crew were augmented with Australian personnel and fell under RAAF command. To the Americans, the Dutch lacked any sense of urgency, preferring to hang out in the local bars to standing up a combat-capable squadron. The derision grew so bad that some of the Americans started calling the Dutch "Canberra Commandos."

The Dutch had their own point of view. The survivors in Australia endured a meat grinder that cost them their homes, their families, and most of their brothers-in-arms. They wanted to fight, but they were stuck in the twilight zone between commands, orphans without a home nation not under the Rising Sun or the Nazi jackboot. The American chain of command was still in a chaotic formative stage, while the Aussies were reeling from the loss of so many of its young men both at Singapore and in North Africa fighting the Germans. The Dutch were the appendix attached to this body of defeat and misery. They possessed no pull, no authority, and they remained at the mercy of their disorganized hosts. Little wonder that they did not get right back into the fight.

The B-25s Pappy saw on the flight line at Brisbane arrived in early March as part of the first batch of aircraft the Dutch purchased.

General Brett wanted them transferred immediately to the USAAF so they could be sent into battle immediately. At a conference on March 20, he and General van Oyen worked out an agreement that would get the planes to the Americans in return for replacements to be delivered later in the spring. That would give the Dutch more time to reorganize and allow the USAAF units to join the fighting in New Guinea.

It didn't work out that way. General van Oyen apparently either had difficulty getting his higher headquarters in Ceylon to approve the deal, or there was some sort of a communication delay. Whatever happened, the aircraft did not get transferred, the Dutch air force knew nothing about the deal, and the B-25s ended up sitting in Australia unused and trapped in administrative limbo.

At the end of March, Pappy Gunn unwittingly dove headfirst into this international morass.

Shortly after he saw the B-25s, he flew into Charters Towers, just outside of Townsville in northeastern Australia, in search of his friend Big Jim Davies. Davies was hard to miss these days. Besides being one of the tallest officers around, he roamed around wearing RAAF flying boots and Australian Army desert-issue shorts, and he would sometimes be seen with an albino parrot on his shoulder. Colonel Johnson would have lost his mind had he seen Davies, but since his outfit had been thrown out of Java, Davies and his men were consigned to the remote base west of Townsville.

At Charters Towers, Pappy climbed out of his bird and walked across the flight line clad in a crushed leather flight jacket, his officer's cap raked to one side. The cap was in bad shape after months of sitting on Pappy's head through all manner of adventures, and by now it looked like somebody had sat on it. He leaned forward as he walked, like he was leaning into a typhoon. It was a gait that others remarked on in later years. His face, leathery and burned bronze by countless hours working in the sun, was furrowed and lined from dehydration and stress. A few months ago, he had the face of a man half his age. Now, he looked wizened and aged beyond his years.

He found Davies and learned that the Twenty-Seventh Bomb Group was no more. The survivors who once took A-24s into battle on Java were folded into the freshly arrived Grim Reapers of the Third Attack Group. Davies now commanded the amalgamation.

Once again, he was a leader of aviators who possessed virtually no aircraft. A few A-24s remained, enough to outfit one squadron. The other two squadrons in the Third were grounded until somebody got them more planes.

Pappy was that somebody. He told Davies what he'd seen in Brisbane. They both believed the Dutch wouldn't use those aircraft anytime soon. Neither man knew anything about the deal cut between General Brett and General van Oyen, but even if they had, patience was not their strong suit. Those new planes needed to get into battle, and the Third could get them there within a matter of days.

Together, they conspired to go get the B-25s and bring them back to Charters Towers.

Exactly what happened next has been largely obscured by decades of bar tales, exaggerations, and purposefully vague official documents. In one of the final entries of the Twenty-Seventh Bomb Group's war diary the unit historian wrote, "Numerous troubles ensued" when they went to get the B-25s from the Dutch. Of the troubles that ensued, here is what is known.

Davies later said in an official interview that he had been ordered to pick the planes up. That might have been the case, as General Brett might have told his most aggressive and red tape–hating group commander to end the standoff in Brisbane and simply take the planes. No record of that order, if it was issued, exists.

Davies and Pappy went over to Townsville to meet with Col. William Eubank, the former commander of the Nineteenth Bomb Group. He was at FEAF Advanced Echelon Headquarters, but was about to punch out of the theater to go join Brereton in India as the operations officer for the Tenth Air Force. His imminent departure might have made him more receptive to the plot these two rascals hatched.

They wanted Colonel Eubank to issue them an order authorizing the Third to take immediate possession of the aircraft. Eubank is said to have been reluctant at first, but the two men won him over as they talked about how quickly they could get the planes into combat.

Authorization in hand, they returned to Charters Towers, rounded up a posse of pilots and enlisted men, and jumped aboard an ancient Douglas DC-2 mail plane the following day. They hopscotched southward from base to base as the mail plane carried out its assigned route until they finally reached Brisbane late on April 1, 1942.

The next day, Davies showed the authorization to the Dutch there at Brisbane. They knew nothing about any of this and shared no enthusiasm for giving their planes away to this band of ill-dressed Americans. They stonewalled and tried to buy time while they checked this out through their own channels. Pappy and Davies persisted until the Dutch agreed to let the Americans go check out their B-25s. One way or the other, the Third would be getting B-25s; it made sense to the Dutch to let them familiarize themselves with the bomber.

Big mistake. The Americans climbed into the B-25s, went over the controls, and went for short test flights. The men, used to egg-beatering around the countryside in ponderous A-24s, found the Mitchells to be "balls of fire." They were fast, maneuverable, capable of carrying well over twice the bomb load of the A-24; it was love at first flight for all of them.

The next day, the Americans walked out to the flight line, popped the crew hatches open on the B-25s, and settled into their cockpits. To those at the field, it looked like a repeat of the test hops from the day before. Except this time, when the Americans took off, they did not return.

Instead, they flew to Charters Towers, lair of the Grim Reapers.

As Pappy landed with his "stolen" B-25 and taxied to the ramp, a middle-aged civilian, short of stature with brown hair and inquisitive eyes, watched him. Pappy shut down the engines, then he and Jack Evans emerged from the bottom of the bomber. Evans was one of the lucky few ground crewmen to escape from Java aboard one of the last B-17s out during the frantic evacuation earlier in the month. The Fort was so crowded with desperate Americans that he volunteered to remain behind, apparently the only one. The crew made sure such a brave man would not be lost; they pulled him aboard and brought him back to Australia. He and Pappy linked up again, and from the moment they hit the tarmac at Charters Towers that spring afternoon, the two became inseparable.

The civilian recognized the B-25 as one of the planes delivered to the Dutch and wondered what it was doing up here at Charters Towers. Just two men flying it seemed strange, especially since one was a master sergeant. Where was the plane's copilot?

He approached Pappy and coldly demanded, "Captain, where did you get your B-25 time?"

Pappy stopped and gaped down at the man.

Who the hell is this guy?

The civilian pressed him, "Did someone check you out in that plane down at Archerfield in Brisbane?"

That pissed Pappy off. Why was some civilian pestering him with stupid questions? "Who needs checking out?" he blasted back. "Besides, the fucking thing has a throttle and stick in it, doesn't it? That's all I need."

The retort rocked the civilian on his heels. He tried to rally, "Well, I guess all it needs is a throttle and a stick."

It sounded lame even to the civilian as the words fell out of his mouth. To Pappy, it meant he was done with this runt.

"Right now, all I need is to take a piss, so outta my way. We can talk later."

Pappy brushed past him, bound for the nearest latrine. Then a funny thing happened. Pappy possessed such magnetism, even when annoyed, that people tended to get sucked into his orbit. The civilian followed Pappy to the latrine, introducing himself as Jack Fox, the tech rep North American Aviation had sent out with the first load of Dutch B-25s. That was why he recognized the plane.

Pappy reached the latrine and said, "I couldn't find the god-damned relief tube in that hot son of a bitch and I almost blew a gasket."

Fox stood there, dumbfounded. Nobody talked like this old pilot, especially not him. Before he could say anything else, Pappy belted him again.

Unzipping, he turned his head and regarded Jack Fox and quipped, "Well, ask me anything you want and I'll tell ya the truth, 'cause a man with his dick in his hand can't lie to ya."

Fox recovered enough to ask him where he'd picked up that B-25.

"From the goddamned Squareheads. Where else?"

"Squareheads?"

"Squareheads—Dutch."

Pappy went on to tell him how he walked out to the flight line at Archerfield, climbed into the B-25, looked over the controls, and left. As he regaled the tech rep with the caper, not knowing that Fox had come out to troubleshoot the Mitchells for the Dutch, Pappy joked about how dumbfounded the "Squarehead" air force types must have been when they saw their plane leave.

Fox had every right to be furious. He considered those B-25s to be his babies, his life's work. He'd come out to Australia to see that they performed as advertised for their buyers, the Dutch air force. Now, some middle-aged captain had just admitted to stealing one.

It was all so outrageous that Jack Fox couldn't help but burst out laughing. Any thoughts of censure or reporting Pappy's caper to the authorities at headquarters vanished. The profane part of Pappy may have left him slack-jawed at first, but beneath that the two soon discovered they shared a kinship love of engineering and all things aviation. The two men quickly became fast friends. Their partnership would prove to be game changing in the months ahead—and devastating to the Japanese.

In the meantime, Jack Fox must have been more than a little shocked to see not just one of his B-25s out on the flight line later that day, but *all* of them. Something in the sight flared a part of him long since suborned in his managerial career at North American. He looked on at the sight and felt it rising in him. He was always a can-do type of man, somebody who could puzzle through a problem and not be wed to convention. Now, he was surrounded by a group gone rogue, and all he wanted to do was be a rebel with them.

North American sent him to Australia to help get the B-25 in combat. The Third Attack had his planes; now it was time to help them get into the war.

Except the Dutch had pulled most of the bombsights out of the aircraft. The few that were installed apparently were older, less accurate ones than the secret Norden bombsights they were supposed to have. The Dutch also cached the spare parts for the B-25s at a warehouse in Brisbane. For the Third to become operational, they needed the spare parts and the bombsights.

The Mitchells reached Australia via a new ferry route that stretched from the United States down to South America, across the Atlantic and Africa east to the Land Down Under. Half of their bomb bays were taken up with gigantic additional fuel tanks that extended their range. The Third wanted that extra gas, but some of the B-25s they absconded with didn't have them installed anymore. So the Third flew back down to Brisbane to get those tanks and quite possibly the bombsights at the same time.

Pappy thought they were warehoused either at Melbourne or Brisbane under Dutch control. They set about trying to find out exactly where their erstwhile Allies stashed all this stuff. When Pappy found out, he walked in and handed the clerk a requisition for the bombsights. The Dutch, furious over the disappearance of their B-25 squadron, refused to give the Americans anything else. Pappy convinced them to be more generous by drawing his .45s and threatening to shoot the senior Dutch officer present.

After that, the Dutch helped load the bombsights into Pappy's B-25.

At this point, administrative havoc had broken out over what the Third Attack was doing. The Dutch leadership in Australia strenuously protested to FEAF HQ, which may have issued a sort of all-points bulletin to detain the aircraft and get them back into Dutch hands.

At Brisbane, the men installed the long-range fuel tanks and were ready to go. But before they could get back into the air and vanish down their Charters Towers mouse hole, a major showed up and tried to take custody of the aircraft.

An argument ensued between the major on one side, Davies and Pappy on the other. The major had oral orders, probably issued in a hasty telephone call. Davies produced Colonel Eubanks's authorization order and said, "Major...a signed order supersedes an oral one."

Pappy threatened to court-martial the major if he didn't let them go. He also added that the planes would be hitting Japanese targets in a few days.

The major finally relented, saying, "I guess a written order does supersede an oral one."

The Third got their B-25s in the air before anyone could change their minds. They arrived back at Charters Towers, and the ground crews immediately went to work prepping them for their first combat missions. New Guinea was the new hot spot, and they would soon be sent north to fly and fight over a primordial jungle region so remote few Americans knew it even existed.

With the fall of the Dutch East Indies, the Japanese moved to isolate Australia by advancing along the northern New Guinea coastline with the intent of capturing the main Allied base on the island at Port Moresby. To support those operations, the Japanese captured Rabaul on the northeast side of New Britain to use as a harbor, staging base, and airfield complex against Port Moresby. They also took Gasmata, another airfield on New Britain.

While FEAF HQ barraged the Third with demands to surrender the B-25s, the attack pilots flew six of them to Port Moresby, refueled and bombed Gasmata. They reported destroying thirty Japanese planes on the ground without the loss of a single (Dutch) B-25.

The Third figured that FEAF couldn't take bombers away from men willing to fight. The Dutch remained upset about the entire affair, but they received new bombers in May. Number 18 Squadron went into action in January 1943, flying exceptionally courageous missions against the Japanese in the Dutch East Indies. In two years of heavy combat, the unit lost 102 men killed in action.

On the afternoon of April 7, 1942, Davies returned to Charters Towers at the head of the formation that had bombed Gasmata the day before. A spontaneous celebration broke out upon their arrival—the Third Attack was in business, and finally the Americans possessed a weapon that could pummel the Japanese.

The celebration didn't last long, at least not for the conspirators. Orders arrived that evening demanding that Davies and Pappy report to FEAF Headquarters in Melbourne. Immediately. Something big was in the wind. As they piled into an airplane, they all silently hoped it would not be their arrests and courts-martial.

28

Killing von Gronau

Pappy, Jim Davies, and a Philippine veteran from Twenty-Seventh Bomb Group named Jim McAfee strolled into FEAF Headquarters that night looking like a band of cutthroats. Non-reg pants, boots copped from the Aussies, Pappy's hat looking like it had been run over by a jeep. They were dusty, foul smelling, and sleep deprived. But they were also vacillating between excitement and fear. Were they about to get their comeuppance for the purloined Mitchells? Or were the rumors on point for a change, and the Third was about to be given a new assignment?

They were hustled into a conference room with B-17 pilot Frank Bostrom, the man who flew MacArthur out of Mindanao. Next to him stood a balding, fifty-something general named Ralph Royce. Born in Michigan, Royce was a ring knocker—West Point grad—class of 1914. He served on the Western Front in observation planes during the First World War, going from a second lieutenant to lieutenant colonel in four years.

General Royce reached Australia in January, where he became chief of the air staff for U.S. Forces in Australia. For the past three months he had quietly ridden a desk in Melbourne. Not anymore.

General Brett asked him to volunteer for a new and difficult mission. He realized it was more an order, less an opportunity to volunteer. He would be going into the field, and from all appearances he was not thrilled with the idea.

Royce told the unlikely trio that General Wainwright was calling for help. He wanted bombers to fly up to Del Monte and surprise the Japanese ships on blockade duty, causing as much havoc with them as possible while some resupply ships could slip north and get to Bataan. The Robenson Commission, which MacArthur had tasked with finding merchant captains willing to run the blockade, actually coaxed a few ships to the Visayan Islands. The Japanese had sunk several en route, but three had reached Mindanao and Cebu. From there, the crews had refused to steam the rest of the way to Bataan. The plan was to carry the cargo north in smaller, interisland vessels. Two five-hundred-tonners were already loaded and ready to go at Cebu.

A show of force was needed to break the blockade long enough so these vessels could get to Bataan and disgorge thousands of tons of food and supplies for the desperate men on their last reserves of strength.

Cebu was the choke point. Enough food reached that island to sustain the Bataan garrison for six months, plus the troops in the other islands for a full year. But getting it past the blockade ships proved virtually impossible. Most of the steamers that tried were caught, captured, or sunk by the Japanese. Only about a thousand tons of supplies reached their destination.

With bombers paving the way, this could be the chance to give Bataan's defenders a new lease on life. They were down below quarter rations now, and the men were so emaciated and sick that they could hardly function, let alone fight. Without the supplies, their collapse was only a matter of days.

To General Brett, and probably Royce, too, the mission seemed like a fool's errand. Too little, too late without the infrastructure in place or the planes to do the job right. Brett kept objecting to the plan, but MacArthur would not budge. The Army Air Force would help those men, whatever the cost.

When the idea was first hatched in March, barely any flyable B-17s existed in Australia. Perhaps a few could be scraped together, but what could they do against the might of the Imperial Japanese Navy? The Forts, while crewed by exceptionally brave men who readily rode into battle with the odds stacked against them, did not distinguish themselves as ship killers. A tally conducted in the spring concluded that only a handful had been sunk during hundreds of high-altitude, level-bombing attacks. The real score was even lower, as surviving Japanese records showed after the war. The B-17 made a great platform for destroying industries and neighborhoods when used en masse, but bombing a ship from five miles above it pretty much did nothing but kill fish.

MacArthur faced an ugly quandary: urgently wanting to help Wainwright but without the weapons and means to do so.

Then the Third Attack Group dropped both in MacArthur's lap. The B-25s could make it to Del Monte. They could range through the Philippines to hit shipping while operating from some of the secret, more primitive strips around the islands. Pappy Gunn, more than anyone else in Australia at the time, knew the islands. He knew the auxiliary strips—he even supervised the construction of some of them before the war for PAL.

The Third would take their B-25s up to the Philippines with Davies leading them. Bostrom had scraped together three B-17s, all that could be patched up for the attack. Royce would be in overall command. They were to prep the planes and leave as soon as possible. The situation was critical.

Meanwhile, Wainwright continued to press MacArthur on Pappy's estimated arrival with the Lodestar full of quinine. What happened to the original shipment Pappy got to Mindanao is unknown. Perhaps some of it stayed at Del Monte, or it was lost en route to Bataan. Whatever the case, the men defending the peninsula continued to be ravaged by malaria outbreaks.

MacArthur's HQ either did not know Pappy was now part of the Royce mission or chose not to be straight with Wainwright, who received word that Pappy would be departing within forty-eight hours.

Bostrom returned to his squadron to get the B-17s ready to go. Davies led his crew back to Charters Towers, where they met with Jack Fox and bombarded the surprised tech rep with questions on the B-25's fuel system. To get to Del Monte, they needed the long-range bomb bay tanks. Those would be removed once they arrived at Mindanao, allowing for a full bomb load to be carried.

Pappy threw himself into the task of getting the B-25s ready for this mission. He kept one foot in the cockpit and one hand in the toolbox the entire time. Evans rarely left his side, and the Third Attack's ground crews, some of whom witnessed Pappy in action building the Twenty-Seventh's dive bombers earlier in the year, worked furiously right alongside him. The work required trips down to Brisbane, where the men loaded up their bombers with spare parts, rations, cigarettes, hooch, medicine, and anything else they could carry that might be useful to the starving men of Bataan.

Pappy would be going back in style, not in an unarmed transport with little chance to survive against even the weakest aerial opposition.

Just as the men finished their frenzied preparations, the Japanese unleashed a massive offensive against the men on Bataan. Debilitated by months of jungle living and little food, the front lines collapsed. On April 9, 1942, Bataan's surviving defenders laid down their arms in surrender.

The Third was too late.

The news resounded like a hammer blow at MacArthur's headquarters. MacArthur had ordered them to stand to the last man, or go out in one glorious counterattack. What nonsense—the men could barely walk, and such pronouncements showed just how divorced from the situation MacArthur's headquarters had become.

Over seventy thousand Filipinos and Americans fell into Japanese hands that black day. Wainwright quickly radioed MacArthur to tell him the he did not authorize the surrender. In fact, General King, in command on Bataan, went ahead and made the decision in hopes of preventing a massacre of his broken troops.

Now, only Corregidor Island was left in American hands in the northern Philippines. Surely the "Rock," as the Americans called the island, could not hold for long. The catastrophic news reached Pappy as he worked round the clock to finish prepping the B-25s. The news left him devastated. With the loss of Bataan, his last realistic chance to find and rescue his family had evaporated.

After everything that had happened over the past two weeks, he thought somehow he could use his new B-25 to rescue them. In the back of his mind, he knew it was a dim hope at best. Without anyone to contact on the ground, without knowing exactly where Polly and the kids were, and without a place to land the medium bomber, that small window of hope slammed closed.

Maybe his plans to rescue his family were little more than Hail Marys all along, and he had been in denial. As he labored in the Australian heat, reality finally gripped him.

He could not escape the guilt with an act of redemption now. He would somehow have to live with it and keep functioning.

He smothered his grief with work, refusing sleep until he dropped again. His focus became the mission and nothing else. If he let up even a little, he knew his mind would wander back to Polly and the kids.

Pappy Gunn was not a man who gave up hope. All his life, he

sought opportunity when none seemed there. He made things happen, dared and executed when others quailed. If MacArthur did not scrub their mission, he would soon be back in the Philippines. That meant he would be less than a thousand miles from the family. If he could only find out their location, he might be able to pull a rabbit out of his hat once again.

He set his sights on that slender thread of hope and pulled himself from his cot to go make it happen.

Though the reason for the Royce mission no longer existed, MacArthur ordered the planes north anyway. They might not be able to force supplies through to Manila Bay, but they could show the remaining defenders of the Philippines that they were not forgotten. Fourteen bombers seemed a paltry morale boost compared to the surrender of seventy thousand troops, but it would have to do.

From saviors to symbol. It didn't matter to the pilots and crew. They just wanted to help those embattled men left behind and surrounded by the enemy.

At 0100 on April 11, 1942, the planes departed for Darwin, where they refueled and flew north, ten B-25s and three B-17s strong. It wasn't much of a strike force compared to what came later in the war, but this was the best they could do under the circumstances. When volunteers were asked to crew the B-25s, almost every member of the old Twenty-Seventh Bomb Group begged to go along. So did Jack Fox, who tried everything to get a seat north on one of "his" beautiful North Americans. Not getting to go remained a disappointment for the rest of his life.

They lost a B-25 at Darwin to a damaged tire; the rest of the planes refueled and launched for Mindanao by 1030. The mission was so urgent that they decided to risk flying through a thousand miles of Japanese-held territory in daylight to pull it off.

The B-17s led the way with two flights of B-25s in their van. The weather, which had started out fine, soon turned into a nightmare.

They ran headlong into a huge storm front, complete with towering cumulous clouds that rose to twenty thousand feet. The formations dispersed, the crews navigating on their own. Pappy's was the only B-25 not to carry a navigator, but he found his way back to Mindanao without any trouble.

Pappy's B-25 refueled at Del Monte, then flew to an auxiliary strip where the crew went right to work getting their aircraft ready for the next day's missions. There was so much to do and so little time to do it that Pappy could hardly take a moment and revel in the fact that, against all odds, he made it back to the islands. One look at the situation at Del Monte convinced him this would be his last chance to get his family out. The mood there was desperate, grim and resigned. Morale was low, and Pappy saw a lot of people loitering at the field hoping to catch one of the few remaining rides out of the Philippines before the Japanese came.

Now that he was back, he needed two things to fall into place. First, he needed to know where his family was. Once he established their location, he would somehow make contact with people he knew through PAL and find a way to get to Polly and the kids.

From the first moment they landed on Mindanao, though, the demands on the crews taxed them to the limits. The B-25s needed basic maintenance after their long flights, and while there were ground crews on the island, none were familiar with the airplanes. Pappy and the other pilots had to pitch in to help get them ready to fly again. It proved an arduous task given the primitive nature of the auxiliary strip.

As Pappy and the others who reached the island first labored under their aircraft, the rest of the raiders straggled into Del Monte throughout the late afternoon. Some of the B-25s didn't arrive until sunset, and the last one got down only after spotting Cagayan through a hole in the overcast.

That night, Royce and the pilots met with Gen. William Sharp and his intelligence staff to discuss the latest developments in the island, pick targets, and plan the morning's raids.

The news was bad. Cebu had fallen. The Japanese had captured Cebu City on April 10, where much of the stores meant for Bataan and Corregidor fell into their hands. Sharp's intelligence officer reported that the Japanese amphibious task force remained in Cebu Harbor, and the general selected those ships as the Royce Raid's primary target for the next morning. The port at Davao would be hit as well, while the B-17s were assigned targets on Luzon.

Then a curious thing happened. For months, Colonel Elsmore and General Sharp had gone to great pains to prepare landing grounds throughout northern Mindanao. A secret base at Maramag, fifty miles from Del Monte, had been purpose-built for B-17s. Ground crew from the Nineteenth Bomb Group manned that base, and they had just finished building well-camouflaged revetments large enough for the big bombers. Sharp and Elsmore planned to send Royce's trio of B-17s over there as soon as they arrived.

For reasons known only to himself, Royce refused to disperse the B-17s, choosing instead to leave them at Del Monte. One of the three had limped into Mindanao on three engines, and it would require considerable work to get it in the air again. That might have influenced Royce's decision.

The B-25s were a different matter. Royce ordered Pappy and about half the crews to take their bombers down to another secret strip at Valencia, while the remaining five stayed at Del Monte along with the trio of B-17s, one of which was deemed unfit to fly after mechanical failure had crippled one engine on the flight from Darwin.

At Valencia, Pappy and the other crews went back to work prepping their planes for the morning missions. They ran into serious problems. The bomb bay tanks did not come out easily, and it took hours that night as they struggled to get the fussy things out of the bomb bays. When they finally cleared the bays, the crews discovered that the release mechanisms on several of the B-25s no longer functioned, which made loading the ordnance impossible.

Pappy was the Royce Raid's most proficient mechanic, and his skills were needed everywhere at once. Together with the other men, he worked through the night to troubleshoot each issue that arose.

Pappy worked right alongside both American ground crews and Filipinos. Beneath their B-25s, Pappy began asking about the fate of Allied civilians in Manila. He probably had learned earlier that the Japanese were locking them up at Santo Tomas, but if he did not know this already, he found out that night. Were his wife and children at Santo Tomas? Nobody could tell him for sure.

Where are they? Would Polly have stayed in Manila after I didn't show up? Could she have escaped into the countryside? Is she hiding out with the children someplace? Or are they in Santo Tomas?

Pappy hoped to find familiar faces among the men on the ground at Mindanao. No doubt he knew some of them, but they didn't know his family's fate, either.

By dawn, most of the B-25s were at last ready to go. None of the aircrew managed to get much sleep. Some had been awake since leaving Australia and had to be utterly exhausted. Others grabbed a few fitful minutes around or inside their aircraft, battling mosquitoes and the noisy clank of mechanics hard at work on these incredibly complex machines.

Pappy got no sleep at all. As the sun rose, he stowed talk of his family, at least for the time being. The hour for revenge was at hand, and the crews were eager to wreak all the damage they could on the Japanese. They grabbed whatever rations they could find, washed them down with some coffee, and headed back to their waiting birds.

The two Forts took off for Luzon first. On the way, they encountered a ship the crews identified as a tanker. One of the B-17s attacked it, expending its bomb load and claiming it as sunk. Frank Bostrom flew the other B-17 to Nichols Field, where he completely surprised the Japanese. They were using the former American base for missions against Corregidor, and a marauding B-17 was the last thing they expected. Unharried by flak or fighters, Bostrom made a textbook attack on Nichols. His bombs struck a hangar and exploded in the operations area, starting fires that the crew could see burning as they turned away from the target area. Flying out over Manila Bay, Bostrom made a single pass over Corregidor, dipping his wings as a final farewell salute to the men and women trapped on that island, now surrounded by the full might of the Japanese empire. The Fort gradually disappeared from view to the south, leaving the Rock to its inevitable fate.

As the B-17s flew north, the B-25 crews manned their aircraft and turned their engines over. At Valencia, Pappy's Mitchell suffered mechanical failure. Seething with frustration, he threw himself into fixing the problem, but their plane was scrubbed from the morning mission against Cebu. The crew, dispirited and angry, hoped they could get the aircraft fixed in time to make the afternoon attack.

While Pappy, Jack Evans, and the rest of his men furiously repaired their B-25, mechanical failure knocked Colonel Davies out of the first mission, too. Equally frustrated, the Third Attack's commander stood on the flight line watching the other Mitchells make their takeoff runs. It had to be an agonizing moment for him to come all this way only to miss out on leading them into battle.

The bombers that did get aloft from Del Monte and Valencia rendezvoused over northern Mindanao before setting a course for Cebu. Eight B-25s—five in one flight, three in the other—reached the harbor and caught the Japanese by surprise. Ships lay anchored offshore while several others were tied up to docks where sailors were unloading supplies.

The eight Mitchells streaked over the serene scene below and peppered it with bombs. Three ships took direct hits, sending up billowing clouds of smoke from their damaged decks. Part of the strike group aimed for the warehouses adjacent to the docks, blowing several of them up. Those warehouses were probably still full of American supplies intended for Bataan.

The Japanese made a belated attempt to intercept the raiders with float planes. The Third Attack's gunners claimed three of them shot down. All eight B-25s returned safely to Mindanao, where ground crews quickly dispersed and camouflaged the aircraft, then began refueling them by hand.

The two B-17s returned to Del Monte, their crews pleading with Royce to let them move to a more secure area. Royce refused. They still were working on the nonfunctional Fort, and while the engine was repaired, a Japanese reconnaissance plane flew overhead shortly after lunch. The sight left little doubt in any American's mind that they would soon be attacked.

As that ominous development took place, Pappy's crew finally solved their B-25's mechanical problems, as did Colonel Davies's crew. Just in time, too, as the rest of the Third Attack was ready for the second mission of the day. They lifted off from their jungle strips and sped north once again, hoping to deliver a double punch to the Japanese at Cebu.

At four thousand feet, Davies's men thundered toward the harbor, formation tight, gunners scanning the sky around them for signs of Japanese interceptors. As they closed on the target, Japanese float planes dove down to attack them. Gunners called their targets and snapped out bursts at the onrushing aircraft.

Jim McAfee, who had been Pappy's tentmate back in Australia, watched the Japanese planes make their attack runs as he held his B-25 in tight formation for the final rush to target. Suddenly, one Japanese float plane arrowed out down on McAfee's flight leader. Ignoring the tracers filling the sky around his fragile craft, the pilot held his course until he realized he was about to overshoot the lead Mitchell. He rolled inverted and pulled through his dive in a remarkable turning half loop and came right down on McAfee's B-25, guns blazing.

McAfee's crew fought back furiously with all available guns, but the Japanese pilot refused to quit. He zoomed through the American formation and dove out the other side. Once clear of the defensive fire, he pulled back up into a steep climb. McAfee's gunners called it out in utter astonishment. Here was a Japanese pilot flying an awkward-looking float biplane, pulling his nose up into a classic World War I fighter maneuver known as an Immelman. In seconds, the plane was behind and above the B-25s, its pilot inverted and coming back for another pass. As he sped back for the Americans, he half-rolled to right himself—directly on McAfee's tail.

It was an extraordinary display of agility and aerobatics from a pilot whose aircraft was designed for such pedestrian duties as artillery spotting and short-range reconnaissance. Fortunately, for all the fancy flying, the Japanese pilot failed to inflict any damage, but it was a stark reminder that they faced excellent-quality aviators.

Fighting their way through the Japanese float planes, the Third Attack's B-25s reached the harbor, where smoke still coiled over the ships struck earlier in the day. This time, the Americans went after the docks, planting a string of bombs that damaged another Japanese ship.

In the middle of the bomb run, Pappy Gunn suddenly broke formation and winged over after one of the vessels in the harbor. Diving down onto the wave tops, he bored in after his target with throttles wide open and his nose gunner hammering away at the ship with his single machine gun. Pappy was channeling his early Naval aviation days, when he'd learned to make torpedo runs in squat, slow biplanes. Except he didn't have a torpedo. Instead, his crew waited until the last possible moment before toggling their bombs at the ship while passing bare feet over it.

Back at Mindanao, Colonel Davies sought Pappy out and furiously dressed down his friend for breaking formation. Pappy's response was never recorded, but he was probably unrepentant. His experience in the Dutch East Indies convinced him that level-bombing ships, even from as low as four thousand feet, simply could never be effective. The four vessels hit in Cebu represented a better total than just about any single antiship raid launched by FEAF aircraft to date, but those targets were stationary and easy prey. Pappy believed the future lay in wave-top attacks.

No other source describes this incident, and the veteran may not have actually been on the mission that day, but it does ring true. Pappy found level bombing to be almost useless against ships while flying Miss EMF in the Dutch East Indies. His final attacks with her had been down on the water. Clearly, ideas were percolating in his head on how to increase the effectiveness of these antishipping attacks. He'd get several more opportunities in the days ahead to test those ideas out.

The scene at Del Monte may have contributed to Colonel Davies's mood. When they returned that evening to refuel and disperse, they found a disaster. The Japanese reconnaissance plane returned to its strip, where the crew reported sighting aircraft at Del Monte. The Japanese Army Air Force promptly launched a strike force against it.

General Royce's refusal to move the B-17s to another field proved costly. The Japanese raid singled out the crippled B-17 and blew it to pieces. The other two Forts suffered significant blast and shrapnel damage as well.

These three planes were the last ticket out of Mindanao for many of the Americans left in the Philippines. They saw their ride go up in flames and raged against the stupidity that caused its loss. For some of those men, the B-17's destruction probably meant a death sentence while in Japanese captivity.

Bitter and dispirited with General Royce, the B-25 crews went back to their assigned auxiliary strips to prepare their aircraft for the next morning's missions. Once again, they would get little sleep. Some of the men grabbed quick catnaps under the wings of their aircraft. Most of the others labored long into the night to fuel and arm their mounts. Mechanical issues needed attention, oil levels had to be topped off, and a myriad of other systems required checks or basic maintenance.

Pappy was right there in the mix throughout the night, working himself to the brink of collapse again. So far, there was no time to plot a rescue; he was maxed out trying to keep the bombers flying while getting his licks in at the Japanese. Perhaps tomorrow, there would be an opportunity. For now, he focused on getting his squadron back in the air.

Meanwhile, General Royce seemed to lose what little enthusiasm he shared for the mission. Concluding the B-17s could no longer operate safely on Mindanao, he ordered the two remaining ones back to Australia as soon as they could fly again. Just before dawn the next morning, loaded with as many Americans as they could carry, the two big bombers winged south for Darwin.

The morale boost would be left up to Davies and the Mitchell pilots now. But for all the effort and dedication, what effect were the Royce Raiders having?

On April 17, a few days after the first day's raids, a Filipino spy reported to General Wainwright that Frank Bostrom's solo attack on Nichols Field was a spectacular success. The spy learned that a conference was being held at the time of the attack with some three hundred aviators, including the notorious flight commander Wolfgang von Gronau and his band of German pilots. Bostrom's bombs struck the conference, killing von Gronau and many of his aviators. Bombs then hit Grace Park and destroyed a fuel dump (probably one stashed by Pappy) and supplies there, which may have caused the fires Bostrom's crew had observed.

At the outset of the war, the American high command had refused to believe that Japanese pilots could be as skilled and aggressive as those encountered over Luzon. The conclusion many came to was that a German expeditionary force was flying with the Japanese. Rumors of white pilots being shot down and captured abounded in December. Somehow, intelligence reports picked up the supposed German expeditionary leader's name: Flight Commander von Gronau was a well-known Luftwaffe pilot whose prewar record-setting exploits included landing the first European plane in New York Harbor in 1930.

The rumors were inaccurate fantasy. No Luftwaffe crews had flown in combat with the Japanese, though reports of German pilots or German aircraft fighting in the Pacific would persist until 1943.

Still, in the moment MacArthur must have gained some small satisfaction reading Wainwright's report of von Gronau's death, the man who some credited with much of the carnage wrought on FEAF at Clark Field on the opening day of the war.

To the crews laboring to get their B-25s ready that night, the color and race of the pilots they faced over Cebu didn't matter a whit. They saw their skill, and they knew that if they'd been in more capable aircraft, the B-25s might have taken losses. As it was, the gunners, working together in their flock-of-geese V formations had come out on top that day. In the morning, the Japanese would be alerted and ready for them. The surprise they pulled on the Japanese that day would not be repeated. From that point forward, things were destined to get rough.

29

Secrets, Spies, and
Mystery Holes

April 13, 1942
Davao, Mindanao

Before breakfast, they hit Davao. Nine B-25s sped into the target area at only a few thousand feet. Two cargo vessels and a warship filled the harbor and channel, and the men could see a line of aircraft on the ramp at the nearby airfield as they approached. That was PAL's field; the hangar there and other facilities had been built under Pappy's direction. Now, the Japanese used them to tend to their own planes.

A float plane caught one B-25's attention. The pilots broke formation and dove on the Japanese aircraft to turn the tables on its pilot. The bombardier manning his machine gun in the nose shot it up along with the top turret gunner. Bullets stitched across its fuselage and wings until one found its mark in the aircraft's fuel system. The craft exploded, and the wreckage spiraled down in flames as the Mitchell rushed back up to rejoin the rest of the group.

Five of the B-25s bombed the shipping in the harbor and channel. One pilot dove down and made a low-level run on one ship, his light, hundred-pound bombs throwing up sheets of shrapnel in his Mitchell's wake.

Two others dropped a string of hundred-pound bombs on the docks and warehouses. Pappy and one other B-25 lined up on the airfield and pounded it with twenty hundred-pounders. The bombs fell in tight strings along the ramp, blowing up aircraft and setting fires. The hangar that Pappy had built met its ironic end, care of one of his own bombs.

Later, Pappy quietly told a reporter, "I was there when that hangar was built. I was there when it was destroyed."

The destruction of part of his life's work affected Pappy deeply. He tried not to show it, but after the loss of NPC-56, taking out one of PAL's newest facilities seemed like a cruel twist of the knife. He took the blow and internalized the damage. With all his guilt, rage, and moments of self-loathing, though, that damage was changing him. He was building to a boiling point, and he couldn't keep a lid on it forever.

The B-25s made it back to their bases safely by 0900. As they refueled and rearmed, Pappy received a special mission. MacArthur personally ordered two Japanese-American counterintelligence agents to be rescued from Corregidor before the end came, knowing that if they fell into Imperial Army hands, they would be tortured and killed. Worse, one of the spies once had worked at the Japanese consulate before the war, and his family still lived in Japan. There could be retribution to them if his role as a counterintelligence agent ever came to light.

The spies had escaped from Corregidor aboard one of the last planes left to the Bamboo Fleet the previous night. Before they could reach Mindanao, though, their plane had suffered mechanical trouble and they force-landed on Panay.

General Royce ordered Pappy to go get them.

"You want them dead or alive?" Pappy asked, probably only half in jest. The damage within him was feeding a growing hatred of the Japanese—even ones supposedly on his side.

When he recovered from the comment, Royce told him to bring the spies to him unharmed.

Pappy took off as soon as the ground crews finished fueling his B-25. Keeping low, he darted north to the rendezvous point 220 miles away. Just after lunch, he dropped his landing gear and set down on a golf course outside of Iloilo in a magnificent display of the B-25's versatility, not to mention his skills as a pilot.

They rolled to a stop and four men climbed aboard. To Pappy's astonishment, he recognized the spy at once as Arthur Komori, a Nisei he'd taught to fly in Hawaii when he worked as a flight instructor for K-T Flying Service. With Komori was war correspondent Frank Hewlett, a Chinese Army liaison officer to USAFFE named Col. Chih Wang, and Clarence Yamagata, the agent whose wife and children lived in Japan.

Komori told Pappy he copiloted the Bamboo Fleet's plane down from Corregidor, using the skills his old instructor taught him. Their flight down left them in a constant state of fear that they would be intercepted and shot down in their defenseless craft. Plus, their forced landing was a hairy one. After Pappy learned the details, he told his old acquaintance that he would stay so low no Japanese planes would see their shadow from above and detect them. They'd make it through just fine.

Getting Komori and his associates off Corregidor was only part of the mission. With him, Komori brought two folders full of top secret documents from USAFFE Headquarters. The first was the USAFFE operations journal detailing every significant action on Luzon and elsewhere since the start of the war. The other was the intelligence journal that noted all Japanese actions, reported sightings, and discoveries made of their capabilities. Pappy was good to his word. He stayed on the wave tops, racing south as fast as the Mitchell would go. Komori later wrote that when they crossed islands in the Visayans, Pappy didn't let up. He dove into canyons and scraped the trees, as was his usual style before they set down safely at Del Monte.

After delivering his passengers and offering a hasty good-bye, Pappy went off to learn what Royce and Sharp were cooking up for the rest of the day.

Half the B-25s were to hit Davao again. The others were told to go search for a Japanese aircraft carrier reported to be somewhere north of Mindanao. Royce assigned Pappy to the search, which meant he would be heading north.

This was his opportunity. With his crew's collusion, they could slip away, find a patch of flat ground on Luzon, and go get his family.

Except he didn't know where they were, he had no way to contact them, and he couldn't just land and leave a B-25 in enemy territory while he searched for them. If he was going to do this, he needed somebody on the ground in Luzon to help him out. At the moment, there was no time or way to set up a line of communication through Japanese lines.

Pappy stalked back to his B-25 after the impromptu mission briefing, silently agonizing over the situation. There was no solution, except to fly the mission per Royce's direction.

He left just before 1700 and flew clear to the southern coast of Luzon that evening. Through his windscreen, he looked out over the familiar terrain. He knew every curve of coast, every stretch of black sand beach. This was the coastline that always beckoned him home before the war, one of those welcome milestones on his way from Davao north to Nielson. The sight took him back to those days where he would land in Manila, tired and cranky and smelling of stale cigarettes. Polly would be there, waiting for him in their walled compound home. The boys would open the gates, and he would park and rush inside to find the girls and his wife ready to embrace him no matter how filthy he was. Food on the table, wine and music playing on the Victrola—that was what this horizon once meant to him.

Once warm and familiar, it now felt cold and taunting. There was no home on the far end of this flight, just an army of occupation tearing apart everything he loved and built.

He flew on, ignoring his copilot and Jack Evans in the top turret behind him, lost in the most profound loneliness he had ever known.

They saw no sign of any Japanese carrier; the flight seemed like a wasted trip to a past life that served only to salt his open wound. A last look at the island ahead, then he grimly wheeled the B-25 around to the south. Though the search was a bust, they would not be going home just yet. They headed to Cebu Harbor instead, Pappy seething at the controls.

This time, the Japanese were ready for them. As the small formation of Mitchells sped into the harbor, they discovered three more warships anchored there. The Imperial sailors quickly filled the sky with flak, rocking the B-25s as they jinked and juked through the fusillade.

Pappy picked out a ship and keyed his intercom microphone to tell Jack and his bombardier to suppress the antiaircraft guns aboard it. He plummeted out of the sky in another solo attack, Jack blazing away from his top turret while the bombardier struggled to keep the handheld .50-caliber on target as Pappy maneuvered wildly through the flak.

Pitching and bucking, they dropped onto the water again, the sky rippling with tracers. Pappy ignored it all, boring in with reckless intensity. The vessel he selected looked like a cargo carrier. Dodging the warships, he lined up on her and leveled his wings. Throttles wide open now, he told his bombardier to stay on the gun; he would release the bombs.

The ships swelled, filling their windscreen as the B-25 roared flat-out along the placid harbor's surface. Their bomb bay doors swung open; still Pappy held the plane just above the water. Dull black explosions peppered the sky as streams of antiaircraft shells burst above them.

The hull of the cargo ship rushed toward them as the two gunners laid on their triggers, lacing the deck with ropes of red tracers. At the last second before a collision, Pappy pulled up and toggled the bomb release. The Mitchell leapt over the cargo ship's mast before Pappy threw the controls forward, dipping the nose sharply. They plunged for the water, pulling out just before impact and streaking away as their bombs exploded behind them. Several struck home, others sent gigantic plumes of water upward as they detonated on either side of the vessel's hull.

When they left her, she looked to be listing, afire and sinking. The sight of their success stilled the torment inside Pappy, at least for the moment. As they raced out of the target area, he felt only a fierce thrill of victory that was part exultation, part bloodlust.

In that attack, he found his safety valve. Combat was the only outlet that relieved his inner turmoil. He wanted more of it, *thirsted* for it. He flew the B-25 back to Del Monte, exhausted but driven to keep striking the Japanese.

Postwar research by the U.S. Strategic Bombing Survey does not list any ships sunk in the Philippines during this time period, though that compilation was never considered complete.

When they returned to Del Monte, they learned the Japanese had bombed the base repeatedly throughout the day. General Royce, who remained at the main field through the entire mission, recorded in his diary that he had to run to bomb shelters five times in the morning alone. The general was just finishing dinner when the B-25s returned.

Given the number of attacks on Del Monte that day and the loss of the B-17 the day before, Royce decided it was time to stop tempting fate and return to Australia. He gave the word to load the bomb bay tanks back in the bombers. They would leave as soon as the crews completed that and had refueled.

The men were astonished. They had only just arrived on

Mindanao, and they'd assumed they would stick around to use up the remaining stocks of bombs and fuel on the island as planned. There were still plenty of bombs and lots of fuel, and the men wanted to fight.

General Royce did not fly a single combat mission, choosing instead to remain behind at Colonel Elsmore's headquarters and quarters at Del Monte. That resulted in much grumbling at the time and afterward.

Big Jim Davies and Pappy decided to try and talk Royce into staying. They went to see him and did their best to persuade him. Pappy became highly emotional at the thought of leaving the Philippines again. The Japanese were slowly closing the noose on the remaining outposts. Soon they'd be in control of all the Visayan Islands. After that, Mindanao would be next.

If they left now, there would be no coming back. Not anytime soon. Not with what few planes FEAF still possessed in Australia. Given the low priority FDR made the Pacific Theater, who knew if they'd even make it back at all?

Combat reenergized Pappy. He wasn't about to run away if he could help it. He passionately urged General Royce to stay, let the crews use up the bombs, keep hitting the Japanese. Everyone in that room knew that Pappy was also arguing for his own personal reasons.

Royce, well aware of Pappy's situation, refused to budge. They were going home, and that decision was final.

Staying behind during every combat mission destroyed much of Royce's credibility among the aircrew. Whispers about it circulated among the men, and many concluded the general didn't have any stomach for the fight.

That combined with the order to run away to Australia convinced Pappy that was the case. When Royce wouldn't move from his decision to leave, they began to argue. Royce was taken aback by a captain willing to challenge his authority. The old Navy hand didn't give a damn about rank. He cared about character, and he finally blew his stack.

"You're just a goddamned coward!" he shouted at the general.

"Well," Royce said flatly while ignoring the accusation, "the order stands."

Davies heard the words come out of Pappy's mouth, but he couldn't believe he said them. He talked about it for years afterward, remembering how he turned to his friend and stared at him in complete shock. Pappy held his ground. He didn't care. As far as he was concerned, Royce was yellow, and the stars on his shoulders were no reason for restraint. General Royce took no immediate action against the impetuous captain's accusation, but Pappy's words permanently destroyed their relationship.

Discussion over. The men of the Third Attack went to work getting ready for the fifteen-hundred-mile-flight back to Darwin. They reinstalled the bomb bay tanks and handed out all their remaining cigarettes, supplies, and other offerings to the ground crews they would be leaving behind. They straightened out who they could take along, and each B-25 was soon filled with passengers. Just after midnight, nine Mitchells lifted off at Del Monte, heading south into the protective darkness.

Pappy Gunn remained behind.

When he went to get his bomb bay tank reinstalled, he found it full of holes. The official story he told later was that the Japanese bombing raids damaged the tank beyond repair. Given Pappy's personal mission, it seemed a convenient way to disobey a general's direct order and stay in the Philippines. Davies even wondered if the holes were caused by Pappy's Colt .45s, which Pappy never denied.

Pappy spent the night searching for some way to load enough fuel into the B-25 to get back to Darwin. There were no other long-range fuel tanks available on Mindanao—there was hardly anything besides bombs, fuel, and men with ample courage left on the island by this time. He took to searching through the wrecks around the field and stumbled across one of the old B-18 Bolo bombers the Twenty-Seventh had flown into Del Monte months back. It was almost completely destroyed, but as Pappy scoured it for salvage, he found its two wing tanks intact.

He and his crew pulled them out of the broken bomber's wings, dragged them over to their own B-25 and went to work trying to figure out how to make them fit. Jack Evans had come along as a gunner on the mission, but he also doubled as Pappy's crew chief. He'd worked beside Pappy for days back in Brisbane during the desperate time in January, assembling aircraft and stealing parts with the old man when necessary. He rolled up his sleeves and got to work alongside him, and Pappy was glad to have his experience.

The tanks wouldn't fit in the bomb bays, so they had to change their shape. Carefully, they beat them flat and reconstructed them so they were four inches on a side. By the time they were done, dawn was approaching and they needed to get out of Dodge. Pappy and his crew piled into the B-25 and hid at Valencia while the Japanese bombed Del Monte.

They spent the fourteenth under the trees, Pappy searching for any additional information on his family. The problem he faced was insurmountable, and as he talked with everyone he could find who had been on Luzon, he chain-smoked incessantly. Eyes ringed with bags and lines betrayed his fatigue and stress. He walked like a man in pain and looked sixty years old.

Nobody knew his family's fate. The best they could do was speculate that the Japanese took them to Santo Tomas. What about finding a way to communicate with anyone on Luzon? Surely his Filipino friends were still in Manila, right?

Yes, but with the fall of Bataan, Luzon went dark. Bands of Filipino and American soldiers who had escaped in the chaotic aftermath of the surrender would eventually coalesce into an active guerrilla movement, one that created its own communication network throughout the islands right under the nose of the Japanese occupation authorities. That was months from taking shape. In April 1942, those networks simply did not exist. Rumors swirled, and occasional escapees from Bataan or Corregidor brought news from the north, but there was no substantial or sustained communication with anyone left behind Japanese lines up there beyond the occasional radio message from a spy or two.

Pappy's luck had simply run out. The window to rescue his family was closed, but he couldn't admit it. While he continued to look for ways to make contact with anyone on Luzon, the phone on the other end of that line was dead. He needed more time, and that was something the Japanese would not give him.

After nightfall, they flew back to Del Monte and continued work on the fuel system. The B-18 tanks still didn't entirely fit in the bays, and they would have to leave the doors open for the duration of the flight to Darwin. That would slow them down and consume more fuel, and as Pappy ran the calculations, he found he still wouldn't have the gallons to get to Australia even under optimal conditions.

He spent the night scrounging for more ways to hold fuel, but the pickings were slim. The crew fanned out, looking for anything. They came up with three small tanks that Pappy wedged into the narrow tunnel the bombardier used to crawl from the cockpit into the nose. It was a tight space that required a man to flatten out and scoot his way along. But even with the tanks shoved up in there, they were still not going to make it to Darwin.

They were getting desperate. Finally, Pappy went back out to the B-18 wreck. One of its oil tanks still remained in it, and it seemed intact. Together with some of Elsmore's men, they figured out how to stuff it into the B-25's nose and connect it to the jury-rigged feeder system.

Dawn came, and they were still not finished. They left Del Monte for the safety of Valencia, but as they flew south, they ran into a fierce thunderstorm. They'd installed the B-18's wing tanks the night before, tying them into the bomb bay with Manila rope. The weather was so bad and the aircraft so thoroughly Rube Goldberged that he decided not to risk flying through the scud to get to Valencia. Instead, he flew north. Exactly where he went will probably never be known. He landed later that day at a small, primitive fighter strip near Cagayan on the north coast, the B-25 throwing up a fan of mud as it touched down.

At dusk on April 16, they loaded up to fly back to Del Monte to finish the modification. Take-off at Cagayan was a true gut-check moment. The B-25 lurched through the mud there and barely scrabbled aloft at the end of the strip. The bomber almost struck a grove of palm trees, but Pappy managed to squeeze just a bit more out of the plane and got it up and over safely.

Back at Del Monte, Elsmore's men met them in the dispersal area, and they worked with singular devotion to put the final touches on the B-25. Pappy added up the extra capacity they'd stowed aboard. He was still 140 gallons short of what they'd come in with from Darwin the week before. He didn't know the B-25 all that well yet and didn't know what kind of margin he had with the original fuel load. Going out that short could drop them in the drink somewhere between the Dutch East Indies and the Australian coast.

They didn't have a choice. There wasn't any other place to stick a tank, and they didn't have anything else to work with anyway.

They started gassing up the B-25. Pappy realized his plane might be the last one out of Mindanao, which meant a lot of Americans would be left behind to face the full wrath of the Japanese Army. Given his fuel situation, nobody would have faulted him for simply heading south as soon as the tanks were topped off, taking only his crew to keep the plane as light as possible.

He wasn't that man. He sent word around that he would take as many people out with him as could fit in the B-25. One by one, desperate men with orders south but no ride save this Mitchell squeezed into the back of the aircraft. They crammed eighteen men into the B-25 that night. They were so sardined in there that the fuselage must have looked like a fraternity phone booth stunt.

As they finished fueling, one last man secreted himself aboard. He was one of the mechanics who had helped to install the oil tank in the B-25's nose. As he had done so, he left a little crawl space beneath it. Now, he slipped inside and stowed away.

They taxied out to the runway, overloaded, overcrowded, dripping fuel from tiny leaks in the makeshift tanks. The fuselage reeked of gasoline, and the bomb bay doors still couldn't be closed. One spark and the vapors would have roasted them in place. Once again, Pappy would have to go the entire flight without a smoke.

Pappy gave it throttle and the Mitchell lurched into the night's sky. Slowly, they gained altitude and turned south. Come dawn, he dropped down to a hundred feet and stayed there for the rest of the flight. The B-25 usually cruised at 230 miles an hour. They'd never make it to Darwin at that speed—the fuel consumption would run the tanks dry and they'd end up in the ocean. Getting on the step wouldn't help much, either. So Pappy leaned out the fuel mixture and backed off on the throttles until they were barely hanging above a stall at 130. The engines were supposed to operate between fifteen hundred and twenty-one hundred RPMs. Pappy slowed them to fourteen hundred.

Low and slow, they inched their way through the Japanese-held Dutch East Indies. As they flew along, every man aboard knew they were the lucky ones. At least they had the chance to get out. Mindanao was doomed. Elsmore's men would either die defending those fields, or they would fall into Japanese hands. The thought of so many dedicated, overworked Americans left behind played heavily on their minds.

For Pappy, every second those props spun, the B-25 took him further away from his family. This had been it; there'd be no bases to fly into after this, nobody on the ground to help him. Polly. Julie. Connie. Nath. Paul. If only he'd known for sure where they were, or if they were even still alive. He faced only a return to Australia to renew the fight against the FEAF brass and the bureaucracy that hampered the war effort at every turn.

He could feel himself coming apart. No support, working for people he hated in a service that couldn't do anything right, led by men like Royce who were yellow dogs as far as he was concerned. He wasn't just flying away from a nightmare, he was flying back into one.

He held the control yoke steady, eyes on the horizon ahead as the eastern sky turned pink with the morning sun. His eyes may have been locked on the way ahead, but he left his damaged heart far behind.

30

Survival Versus Sin

Spring 1942
Santo Tomas Internment Camp, Manila

Down the third floor hall of the main building, in the classroom marked "46" over the doorway, Polly Gunn stood before her bed in the far corner and stared at the package Guyenne Sanchez had just delivered to the front gate.

Loyal to the Gunns, he took special care to bring them food, clothing, and little treats almost every week since they had gone into the camp. Given the qualities of the meals they received each day, these tokens were godsends to Polly's family.

She unwrapped the bundle and extracted each item carefully. A few extra pieces of clothing lay at the bottom. Guyenne had picked them up for her at the duplex, knowing they would be much needed in the weeks ahead.

Many of her fellow inmates believed their internment would last only a few weeks, perhaps a couple of months. The war, they assured everyone around them in their blind confidence, would be a short one. The Navy would break the blockade and come to MacArthur's rescue. The Japanese would get it for sure then.

At the beginning of April, the army trapped on Bataan had laid down its arms. When news of that disaster spread, it struck at the heart of the camp's morale. The mirage of a short war disintegrated. The Japanese, who had behaved as if they were constantly looking over their shoulder for the rest of the American army, suddenly swelled with confidence and pride. They trumpeted the victory with exultation; to the inmates, it felt as if the Japanese were rubbing their noses in it.

No. It wouldn't be a short war. They were in Santo Tomas to stay for a long while. Years, maybe. Without access to new clothes, shoes, or even decent food except through the episodic packages, life was bound to get more difficult for everyone.

Already, Polly noticed Julie dropping weight. Always a finicky eater, the sixteen-year-old barely managed to down the bug-infested breakfast mush slopped onto her tray every morning. They sometimes ate tinned sardines for lunch that first spring, but the stock of those soon ran out. Dinners consisted of little better fare, some rice and vegetables and little else. The vegetables were getting scarce, and the internee committee decided to divert much of what did arrive to the youngest children in the camp.

Polly set aside the food Guyenne included and extracted the clothes. When she entered the camp in February, she had worn hiking fare. Her small suitcase included only a few extra shirts and slacks—enough for days but not months of captivity. Now, she regarded the things Guyenne selected for her with great relief before placing them with her meager wardrobe.

In the bottom of that suitcase lay a beautiful, light-colored dress. Ever the optimist, she brought it with her as the one frivolous item in a place of threadbare basics. She wanted something nice for the day of their liberation, and thought often of how she would wear it to the camp's chapel to thank God for their salvation.

That salvation seemed so distant, like a pinpoint of light in a tunnel miles long. Really, it was just hope now, a resolve to keep going, day in and day out, despite the depressing, dreary reality of life with freedom stolen.

The dress was her beacon. Someday, she would slip it on and revel in the moment of freedom restored. She would see P.I.; he would be there with the first wave of troops, they all knew him and knew he would find a way. She would look her best, complete with a red hibiscus flower in her hair.

She had found the plant growing beside the area where she hung her laundry to dry. Somebody always watched over the clothes, and she spent hours out there guarding them from thieves. They learned the hard way that one careless moment of inattention could cost them their literal shirts.

While she waited for the clothes to dry, she noticed the broad petals of those hibiscus flowers, so out of place there in what the rest of the campus looked like now.

She pulled one off and put it in her hair, a splash of color in a world that had taken all the other trappings of beauty from her. The red hibiscus would be her talisman, her reminder that P.I. was out there somewhere. He would be back, and all this would end.

In the meantime, it was her duty to not lose Faith. It was her duty to keep the family together and live a righteous path, no matter how many "every man for himself" moments they encountered through the course of their day. It was her duty to make sure their new circumstances did not change them. The dress symbolized that as much as the hibiscus flower. She had sewn it herself on the Singer that P.I. had brought home as a "just because" gift.

She did her best to end each day on a positive note. More than once, she said to the girls that they would be better for this experience. "We needed some refining," she had said. For sure they appreciated the little things now. Basics like soap and privacy, a life lived without waiting in long lines for anything; they missed those things.

Her days, once passed within her home, children close at hand, were now spent waiting in lines. There were lines for everything: showering, toilet, food lines, medical lines, and lines to talk to the internee committee. When she wasn't trapped in a line, the internee committee gave her a uniquely grim job. Assigned to the kitchen staff, she and a handful of other women spent hours every day plucking insects from their food. Weevils, worms, and countless other bugs infested the wheat delivered to the camp. Ultimately, keeping them out of their food proved impossible, and diners were left to pick them out on their own. As hunger increased in the camp, younger inmates learned to eat the bugs, too. Anything for a bit of extra protein. For most of the adults, going to those lengths even in the face of starvation was beyond them.

She returned each day from such work bone weary and exhausted, wanting only a moment for herself. There would be no such moments, with twenty-eight women in room forty-six. Most of them were English; the room monitor was a scrappy Britisher with a perpetually cheerful demeanor named Florence Rimmer. She was elected by the other women and carried out her duties with a deft touch. Her mood matched Polly's efforts to put the best possible face on things. Together they were a bright spot in a room where each inmate had twenty-three inches of personal space.

They were so cheery that one visiting Japanese officer saw them and remarked that he couldn't understand such people. Didn't they realize they were prisoners?

Polly took that as a moral victory. She needed those desperately. Even as she did everything she could to not let the camp change her family, she could see it changing her babies. She tried her best to maintain the prewar sense of order and values that the family lived by, but they were tested every day, and Polly could not be with the children beyond the short intervals in work and chores that they shared.

One morning, Nath stood in the breakfast line with Paul, waiting their turn with Polly's food chit, when two men came by carrying a ten-gallon tub of hot mush between them. One of them tripped and the steaming mush slopped out, splattering Nath's bare legs. Instantly burned, Nath howled in pain and dove for a nearby mud puddle to try and get the stuff off of him. He succeeded, but covered himself in grime and pebbles in the process. When he stood up, his burned flesh peeled right off of him. Paul and others carried him to the hospital, where Connie worked as a janitor. She was the first to find him and check on his condition. Polly didn't hear about what had happened for several hours. By then, she was elbow deep in vegetables, washing them before they were served for the next meal. She worked the rest of the day, desperate with worry over her youngest boy. Finally, as soon as she could, she rushed to his side and found him in bad shape. The doctor and nurses were still picking gravel out of his wounds, and the pain left him in wrenched agony. The clinic did not have much medicine; even aspirin was a luxury.

He stayed in the hospital for about ten days, his bandages sticking to his weeping burns. Changing them was a dreadful experience. He endured most of it alone. Connie could check on him only periodically. Polly juggled so many responsibilities that she simply could not make it the three quarters of a mile to the hospital every day to see him. Plus, they needed to set their schedules so one of the family members always remained in room forty-six to watch over their small cache of food, cash, and clothing. Whatever the cost, those had to be closely guarded, even if it meant Nath did not see his mom when he needed her most.

On his first morning in the hospital, a strange clanging roused him from fitful sleep. He looked around in time to see a young boy, his legs in metal braces, running down the aisle in their ward. He ran with crazed intensity, his legs awkwardly flying about as he moved. He carried a metal crutch in each hand, and as he ran he banged them against the ends of the hospital beds. Others shouted at him, some ignored him. The staff indulged him. At first, Nath did not understand that. The kid, perhaps seven or eight years old, seemed possessed. Then all at once, his energy abandoned him. He collapsed in a heap, unable to stand, let alone run. A nurse rushed to him, picked him up, and carried him to his bed. She gently laid him down as he looked up at her with despair-filled eyes. He lay listlessly in his bed, his malformed legs beneath a sheet for the rest of the day.

The next morning, the same thing happened. He struggled from his bed, fell. Got up. Fell again, then finally found his footing. As he did, he unleashed all the energy he possessed, racing up and down the ward again with furious intensity. His expression said it all: These few moments of freedom from his bed made his life worth living. He embraced every second with all his heart, and the passion that seized him as he ran poured out of him in yelps and cries. Each step was a personal victory. But whatever had afflicted him always got him in the end. After an hour or two, he'd lose his balance and crumple to the floor. The staff would find him, exhausted, panting, drained, and they would return him to the hell of his hospital bed.

After seeing this twice, Nath understood why the staff treated him so gently, even if some of the patients did not. The boy left a profound impression on him, reminding him that no matter how bad things were for him, he was still better off than some. In this new world, complaining just seemed self-indulgent.

The hospital ordeal toughened Nath. He dug deep within himself and found reservoirs of strength he did not know existed within him. He watched others around him grow more infirm and weak. He wanted out desperately—becoming one of them terrified him.

Fortunately, the pain gradually diminished. His burns weren't fully healed, but he returned to Leake's, driven by his duty to take care of Polly and his siblings. That was his sacred charge from P.I., and he meant to honor it.

The time away from Polly forced both Nath and Paul into premature independence. There was no teacher or school to supervise them. The camp made an early effort to educate the children, but that soon fell by the wayside as everyone focused on survival. That left Nath and Paul outside the only two structured environments they'd ever known: home and classroom. Tossed into an upside-down version of real life, they came to their "sink or swim" moment quicker than Polly did.

Polly saw this erosion of youthful innocence and tried to stem its tide, though she was worn down physically, weakened by dysentery and beriberi. A few months after Nath emerged from the hospital, she was bitten by an insect. The bug bite grew infected, and her strength failed her. One day, Connie and Julie found her barely able to sit up, long crimson-red streaks coursing up her arm.

There were no antibiotics in the fall of 1942. Even if there had been, there would not have been any at a place like Santo Tomas. The family got Polly to the hospital, where she recovered from the infection, though when she returned she remained desperately weak. Paul, who worked in the kitchen carrying heavy cauldrons of rice around, knew his mother needed extra food to regain her strength. One afternoon, he took a terrible risk and stole a few handfuls of rice for her. If he had been caught, the punishment would have been severe. He risked it, worried that without it she could die.

When he reached her later in the day and offered her the rice, he was astonished by her reaction. Instead of being grateful, Polly lost her temper, railing at Paul for committing the sin of stealing. The Gunn family did not steal. How could he do such a thing?

Paul recoiled, deeply hurt at her words. This place ground up good values. Good values could get you killed. Polly didn't realize it. She clung to her precamp morality while her kids realized, as Julie put it later, that there was a difference between "sinning and survival."

The Bible and its teachings were not worth dying for, at least not to Paul and Nath. That first half year in the camp turned them from boys to survivors—tough and hard, willing to do whatever they could to protect themselves and take care of the family. Much was done outside the sight of their mother. They learned to trade with adults, and found unlikely sources for things to trade. The seminary building on campus housed a museum that the Japanese declared off limits to the internees. The priests still in the camp turned the space into a storage room for the duration of the war. One day, Nath, along with a few close friends he trusted, broke into the building and discovered hundreds of Bibles stashed inside.

The adults could sometimes get tobacco, but they always needed paper with which to roll cigarettes. Nath saw immediate opportunity. The Bibles became a prime source for such homegrown smokes. Quietly, they opened these holy books and tore out a few pages before creeping out of the building. Sure enough, they found an eager market later that day. They traded their ill-gotten Bible pages and brought their bounty back home to their families.

Getting those pages became a semiregular enterprise, though the risks they took to get them never waned. Had Polly known what was happening, she would have been appalled. But the bits of food and toiletries they bartered for helped keep the family going.

Whether or not their mom approved, Nath and Paul resolved to do anything to keep the family alive. Nath learned to box that spring and summer. Even before his burns fully healed, he returned to the ring. He discovered that he could take a punch and learned not to be afraid of getting hit. He also developed a wicked array of strikes that dropped nine opponents. He lost his only match to a close friend.

The adult men still preyed on Leake's boys. They took things; they ordered them around. They cut them out of lines and dismissed their complaints. One man, whose family lived in the main hall that year, would spend hours bouncing a tennis ball against a wall while his son looked on forlornly. The father ignored his son's desire to join him and kept the ball for his own amusement. The few times the boy worked up the courage to ask if he could play, too, his father cut him down with angry remarks.

Nath witnessed such moments and reflected on that day his father had handed him the broom handle. The meaning of the lesson he taught that day started to sink in, and he found ways in the camp to apply it.

His dad showed him how not to be a victim. If you always played by the rules, others would come along and exploit you. The bully who knocked Nath down that day had done just that. No way could Nath have taken him on equal terms. The bully was simply too big, too tall, and too strong. The broomstick and a surprise attack leveled the playing field, even if it was considered fighting dirty.

The point was: Nath was never victimized again by that kid. Smacking him in the head wasn't a matter of revenge, it was a matter of showing the bully and his ilk that messing with Nath was going to be painful. Nobody wanted to risk that level of pain again, and Nath never became a victim while they lived on Eighth Avenue. Word got around quickly that to pick a fight with a Gunn boy was complete folly.

The boys couldn't start carrying clubs around the internment camp, but they found a way around the strength and size of the adults who tried to exploit them. Strength in numbers was the answer.

The boys in Mr. Leake's care coalesced into an organized gang that watched out for each other. They conceived a special whistle that served as their distress call. When an adult confronted one of them, the boy would whistle; the others would pick up the call and then rush to his aid. The adult would find himself surrounded by angry bantams, willing to stand up to him.

Gradually, those showdowns turned the tide. The boys found that the men always backed down. Those victories built confidence in the boys, and they grew bolder and more willing to take risks for each other. They spoke out in ways they never would have done before the war. Some, at times, grew insolent and unrepentant. They saw those same men treating their own families with such disregard that the respect they were taught to accord adults by their parents dissolved into contempt.

The father who bounced the tennis ball for hours sometimes ended up in the food line with Nath and Paul. He would carry his family's food chits down and get their rations for them. At first, it seemed like a noble thing to do, sparing them the long wait in the line. Yet, it seemed out of character; the man was quick to berate anyone and was suspected of beating his wife and son. Why would he go through the trouble?

Nath discovered the answer one day as they walked from the chow line to the main hall to eat with their mother. Tennis Ball Man walked ahead of them glancing around furtively. When he thought nobody was looking, he scarfed down some of his wife's rations. He took a few more steps, then stole some of his son's.

Nath couldn't believe it. He and Paul exchanged glances and felt nothing but scorn for him. Already they couldn't stand the man for the way he treated his family. Now they witnessed him stealing his own son's food. It was the lowest of the low.

Over the weeks that followed, food grew increasingly scarce. A new, stricter camp commandant took over and banned package deliveries. Food and items that had been tossed over the main wall to waiting internees were also banned. To make sure the Filipinos could not do that any longer, the Japanese built an inner wall about twenty feet inside the main one. Anyone caught receiving outside contraband was severely punished.

Without the food parcels brought by loyal friends and employees on the outside, the inmates lost weight. The Japanese, in what some saw as a senseless act of cruelty, installed a scale on the first floor of the main building just so the inmates could track their weight loss. Polly weighed herself every day, watching the number drop as her body slowly wasted away from malnutrition and bouts with diseases.

Several more times, Nath and Paul showed up with breakfast from the chow line for their mom after following the Tennis Ball Man up the stairs. They spotted him stealing from his family's rations each time. They told their mother, but Polly refused to do anything about it. It was their internal family business, and to get involved would have borrowed trouble she didn't want. Best to let it go and not make waves.

One afternoon, Nath was in the hallway outside room forty-six. Tennis Ball Man was out there, bouncing the ball as his son watched. He dropped the ball, and Nath quipped, "You ought to keep your eye on it."

Tennis Ball Man turned on Nath with sudden anger, "Don't you think I know how to catch this ball? I've been throwing this ball for hours every day. I know what I'm doing!" A year before, Nath would have recoiled at such an outburst by an adult. Not now. He'd learned the central truth of the Eighth Avenue rules: Most bullies are cowards, even adult ones. If you stand up to them, they will be the ones recoiling.

Nath nodded at Tennis Ball Man's son. "You ought to let him have a turn."

The man turned bright red and raged at Nath, "You can't speak to me that way!"

Nath fired back, "I'll speak to you however I want. I've seen what you do every day from the breakfast line. How would you like me to tell your family?"

The man froze, face contorted with fury. He picked up his ball and stormed off, ordering his son to follow.

Polly, who watched the exchange from a table set outside room forty-six, called Nath over after Tennis Ball Man had left.

"Nath, you shouldn't have done that," she admonished. "Now you have an enemy."

Nath shook his head. He never stood up to his mom before, but this time the lesson was hers to learn. "Mom, I already had an enemy in that guy given the way he treats his family." After all, how would he treat the Gunns if given half a chance?

The old rules simply no longer applied. Of all the family members, Polly was the last to let them go.

31

The Death-Dealing Sweetheart with the Jack Dempsey Crouch

April 1942
Archerfield, Brisbane, Australia

Pappy Gunn lay exhausted on his bunk in his modest Brisbane quarters. The town was a circus at the moment with reporters swarming all over the place, interviewing the Royce Raiders and writing stories about their exploits that ran in hundreds of Stateside papers. Pappy didn't care about that crap. He had talked to a few journalists in the Dutch East Indies, and he consented to an interview after he got back to Australia, but the press coverage did not help his cause.

The unknown dogged him every moment he slowed down. Lying there in his bunk, his mind played over the events of the last four months, returning again and again to the decisions he made and the missed opportunities.

There was also the constant fear for Polly and the girls, the worst a husband and father can face. Pappy possessed a powerful and vivid imagination, one that fueled so much of his problem-solving abilities. In moments like this one, his imagination felt like a curse.

What have they done to my wife and girls?

His mind shifted back to those grainy horrific images from China. Mass rapes, lines of naked women standing before open pits with bodies piled atop one another. Photos of Japanese officers delighting in using their swords to behead innocents. He had seen those, their faces beaming as if striking a pose during a vacation snapshot, while at their feet lay the heads of their victims.

Twenty thousand women were raped in Nanking alone. Brutalized, tortured, murdered right in front of their families. Children and the elderly were raped right alongside their parents and daughters. It was a carnival of horrors so beastial that at least one American who witnessed these atrocities later committed suicide.

Pappy saw all those images again in his mind, and his dread for the safety of his daughters and wife surged anew. When they needed him most—he was not there.

He flung himself out of the bunk. There was no escape from such thoughts, only a descent toward madness as he suffered. If only he *knew* where they were. If they were okay, or not. Instead, the unknown became the playground of his worst-case imagination.

He walked to the shower, struggling to drive these thoughts from his mind.

What about Nath and Paul?

Images flashed before him. Paul, bookish and calm; Nath, the brawler and always willing to stand up for what was right. He met fist with fist, Pappy knew Nath would die fighting to protect his mom and sisters. Paul would do his best, but he was not a fighter.

Entire families raped and killed in front of each other. It was a game to those Japanese soldiers. Something unleashed the worst, most primal instincts in those men in 1937, as if their power over life and death became a drug, and the more despicable the act, the greater the power rush.

It didn't just happen in Nanking. Or in 1937. Where the Japanese Army marched, butchery followed.

Pappy turned the shower on and stepped inside.

I have to believe they are still alive.

There would be no redemption if they weren't. The guilt and anguish would kill him just as surely as a bullet.

The water poured over him as he scrubbed gingerly. Patches of prickly heat caused rashes on his skin, something he could have avoided if he stripped down to shorts like most of the other aircrew. He didn't do that, wearing his long-sleeved shirts even when the temperature spiked over a hundred and the humidity caused sweat to drip off him incessantly.

Every night, his imagination plagued him. Every morning, he rose from his bed with red, puffy eyes and a little more hate. The occasional shower he managed around his otherwise nonstop schedule served as the bridge to his day. He washed out the nightmares and returned his brain to problems he could solve.

He dried and dressed as he went through that transition, stowing away his dread and guilt as best he could while preparing for another day working for the people who had betrayed him in the first place.

He hated them, almost as much as the Japanese. But it was the Japanese he wanted to suffer.

Since returning from the Royce Raid a few days before, Pappy wanted to take all the lessons he learned and apply them. For all the attacks they made up in the Philippines, the truth was they didn't inflict much damage. As good as the B-25 was, it could be made better. They needed new tactics, new ideas. The Japanese war machine showed no signs of slowing, and the Allies showed no ability to stop it. The planes had been built to prewar specs. The tactics manuals had been written by officers who'd never flown in combat, whose priority had been not how to damage a future enemy, but how to get Congress to give them more money for B-17s.

Things needed to change, and he recognized that any hope of going back into the Philippines depended on the Allies turning things around. Defeat would simply push him farther from Manila. Victories could reverse that trend. He knew MacArthur hungered for the same thing; MacArthur's ego had been wrecked by the Japanese success in the islands, and getting back to liberate the Philippines had become his obsession from the first moment he arrived in Australia.

The way they were fighting didn't work. What they were fighting with was often ineffective, obsolete, or easy prey for the Japanese. Bad tactics, bad equipment: the twin pillars of defeat. It drove Pappy crazy to watch his friends ordered to go do the same thing over and over just because some book said to do it that way.

We either adapt or lose. We don't have the planes or the equipment, and we don't have replacements for the aircrew who are dying trying to prove the manuals were right.

The B-25 was the best ship in Australia, but it could have been better. Before the war, he tinkered constantly to improve the Beech 18s, and he couldn't wait to get his hands into the guts of those Mitchells to see what he and Jack Evans could do to wring a little more performance out of those airframes. Maybe Jack Fox would help out.

In the meantime, he wanted to apply things he learned in the Navy to the way the Third Attack went after targets. The B-25s were designed to bomb targets from between eight and ten thousand feet in level flight. Standard doctrine called for the planes to be in wingtip-to-wingtip tight V formations of three planes each. One V would be stepped down below and behind the next, the idea was to have everyone release their ordnance simultaneously to maximize the number of bombs put on the target by keeping the pattern small. Meanwhile, the close formations would mass their defensive firepower as well, keeping enemy fighters at bay.

The Royce Raid did some damage, but most of it was symbolic. He thought they could do a lot more—really hurt the Japanese, if only they adapted to the situation. Stately parades at eight thousand feet when the bombers didn't have fighter cover or anyone to suppress antiaircraft fire was going to get a lot of men from the Third Attack killed in the months to come. They were lucky not to run into any Zeroes in the Philippines. That luck would not hold in New Guinea, or anywhere else, at this point.

Pappy drove over to Archerfield, eager to get back to see Jim Davies and pepper him with these thoughts. He was a man who would listen—maybe the only one.

When he reported in, he discovered the headquarters brass expected him to go back to the Twenty-First Transport Squadron. Yes, his knowledge of the Philippines had proved invaluable to the Royce Raid, but that was over now. They saw him as an over-the-hill middle-aged pilot who had no business flying combat missions with young men half his age. So it was back to the Squadron of Misfit Aircraft for the old Navy vet. Maybe he could fly a few staff types between bases to keep his flight pay.

His desk awaited him, a mountain of paperwork needing his attention.

Since December, Pappy had made a living operating outside Army Air Force conventions. He broke rules, launched solo attacks, ignored chains of command, went rogue on supply clerks, and always got away with his lone wolf behavior because his motives were pure. He wanted to fight—he *needed to fight*.

He spent the first days back dealing with schedules for mail aircraft and cargo deliveries, all the while ready to explode with rage and frustration. This was not his place; he didn't care what headquarters said. Running toilet paper between Brisbane and Townsville certainly wouldn't get him back to the Philippines and his family, either. For the moment, he was stuck and left to stew over the situation.

One day, he returned from one of these flights to find several brand-new airplanes, called A-20 Havocs, lined up on the tarmac at Archerfield.

They looked fast just sitting on their tricycle landing gear on-ramp at Archerfield, like thoroughbred racehorses waiting for the bell. High shouldered with stubby engine cowlings, one *Popular Science* writer of the era described them as looking perpetually coiled in a "Jack Dempsey crouch." A pair of machine guns protected the tail; four more .30-caliber light machine guns graced the nose around the bombardier's glass birdhouse. With that firepower, the *Popular Science* article called the A-20 a "regular death-dealing sweetheart of an aircraft."

Designed by one of America's greatest aviation geniuses, Ed Heinemann, the Havoc was officially known as the Douglas A-20A. Heinemann had made a career out of making rocket sleds for bomber pilots who dreamed of flying fighters. The A-20 straddled both worlds; in fact, later versions served in combat as night fighters. They were that fast.

The British used it in battle first and loved the plane's speed and agility. They dubbed it the Boston.

Pappy saw those beautiful new airplanes and rushed to his office to call Jim Davies to tell him about them. Davies told him they belonged to the Third Attack Group, which was still struggling with both manpower and aircraft problems. At the moment, the unit possessed an odd mix of dive bombers and Dutch B-25s, but not enough of either. The A-20 would be the group's third aircraft type for its four squadrons.

The A-20s fascinated Pappy. He saw great potential in them—if they were used the right way. In his mind, the right way was down on the deck, trimming the treetops at full power. Forget altitude. Altitude would just get men killed, he was convinced of that.

Abandoning his desk, he flew up to Charters Towers to bombard Davies and the rest of the Third Attack with the ideas he wanted to try.

Without a doubt, he thought, going in low after ships was far more effective than trying to carpet bomb them in B-17s from twenty thousand feet. If they went in low enough, they could actually slip under the ship's ability to shoot at them. From his Navy days, he recalled how antiaircraft guns could not be depressed beyond a certain angle. That left a blind spot the ships could not cover just above the wave tops.

Going in low gave them another opportunity to inflict damage. As he attacked the ships in Cebu Harbor, his bombardier had strafed their decks with his single machine gun while Pappy made his attack run.

A single machine gun didn't do much damage. But what if more could be stuffed in the noses of those A-20s? Pappy told Davies he wanted to experiment with one airframe and see how many .50-calibers he could put in it to give the plane some real punch. Stuff enough guns in the nose, the pilots could suppress AA defenses as they made their runs into the target. They wouldn't need fighters to do that for them. There weren't fighters available to do it anyway.

Davies listened skeptically. He told Pappy he didn't think it could be done. The engineering challenges were daunting, to say the least, and any modification of aircraft needed to be done in prescribed depots with Air Force Materiel Command's express permission. Air Force Materiel Command was at Wright Field (now Wright-Patterson Air Force Base), Ohio. Trying to get official approval for such a modification, given the red tape already crippling them, seemed unlikely at best.

Besides, Davies argued, even a few extra nose guns wouldn't be all that effective given the way the tactical manual required them to fly. They'd be up at five to ten thousand feet, bombing with their Norden sights.

"Forget the book, Jim. Set fire to the goddamned book!" Pappy erupted. It was time to go in low. How low? Ten to fifty feet off the trees.

Capt. Don P. Hall, one of Davies's squadron commanders, listened to Pappy's ideas. Hall was an old member of the Third Attack group. Like Davies in the 1930s, Hall had spent hundreds of hours flying strike aircraft, buzzing treetops while dropping sacks of flour on a simulated enemy. He came up through attack aviation at a time when the rest of the Army Air Corps was obsessed with high-level precision bombing of factories. It was not the fastest career track, but he loved the flying and the mission. Now seemed the time to resurrect those old ways and go work over the Japanese with them.

Pappy talking about staying low and shooting the hell out of things with a lot of guns was right in D.P. Hall's wheelhouse. Pappy saw an ally in Hall. He worked on him until finally he came around. Faced with a united front, Davies caved. He gave them the nod to take one of the precious new A-20s and experiment with it.

Don was a slender, twenty-eight-year-old Texan who'd been in the Air Corps since 1937. Never an establishment sort of officer, he was eager to try new ideas and buck standard thinking. He loved the unorthodox and pushing envelopes. He and Pappy formed a formidable team, a perfect combination between tactical, practical, and mechanical skills. They dropped their other projects and made this one their priority. Pappy neglected his day job commanding the Twenty-First and threw himself into this task. Victory was the only path back to his family. The Twenty-First could win no battles, but squadrons of gun-laden bombers could.

Right away, Pappy and Hall plowed headlong into such red tape and supply depot politics that their experiment was nearly derailed.

They acquired their A-20 and drew up a list of things they needed. First, they needed .50-caliber machine guns. They couldn't get them. Mounts for the guns—nope. The supply types would not give those up, either.

From the chaos of the first months of 1942 came a hardening of the supply arteries as the quartermasters and depots became more organized and better stocked. Many of the officers running these depots were absolute by-the-book types who categorically refused to release anything to the combat units that was not part of their table of allotment.

Each group received a prescribed amount of materiel, equipment, tools, and supplies based on a complex formula created in the prewar days. It wasn't realistic in combat conditions to begin with, but now the modifications would require parts, machine tools, drill presses, and metal.

The depots refused to give Hall and Pappy anything. In fact, the supply types around Charters Towers who were supposed to be taking care of the Third instead grew to detest Davies and his men, because they pestered them so relentlessly. When the Third couldn't shake anything loose from the warehouses, they took to "midnight requisitions" and stole what they needed. The supply guys knew, or at least suspected, that the Third was behind these thefts. In retaliation, they blocked shipments, stole equipment bound for the Third, and refused to turn over things expressly sent to the bomber crews. They almost seemed to glory in the frustration they caused Davies and the rest of the Grim Reapers.

In later years, the passionate hatred expressed for these rear-echelon types formed a universal thread among those members of the Third who endured this fledgling period.

Davies finally blew his stack over it and wrote to headquarters, "Instead of being all out to keep us supplied with everything we need, the supply organization makes obvious efforts to obstruct our getting anything."

Pappy grew so furious with the air depot commander at Charters Towers that he couldn't contain his anger any longer. He found out where a particularly noxious colonel lived, then roared over his tent in a three-hundred-mile-an-hour, haircut-level pass in a B-25. The massive propwash flattened the colonel's tent and scattered his belongings. While that must have been satisfying, if anything, such revenge just reinforced the petty embargo on one of the few bomber units flying combat missions at the time.

When Davies and Hall failed to get what they needed, Pappy tried to wear his Twenty-First Transport Squadron commander hat and demand things for his unit—of course intending to give them to the Third. That didn't work, either. What did airline pilots need with machine guns? The supply clerks rejected each request, insulting his intelligence with frequent uses of the old stand-by, "Not in Stock."

When all else failed, Pappy still carried his pair of .45s—and a fat wallet.

If this experiment was ever going to take place, they needed machine guns before anything else. With the supply types blocking their every move and watching their caches like mother hens, Pappy found another way to get the weapons.

Since they first arrived in Australia, scores, if not hundreds, of factory-fresh American aircraft ended up wrecked in accidents or shot to pieces in combat. Ground crews dragged those too damaged to repair into boneyards, where they cannibalized the wrecks for spare parts that kept other planes flying. Those were not as carefully guarded as the depots were these days. Pappy and D.P. Hall saw opportunity there, and they raided several nearby boneyards and stripped the guns they needed off wrecked P-40s. Like grave robbers, he and Don returned to those boneyards in the dead of night, carrying acetylene torches to hack out chunks of metal that they needed for the gun mounts they decided to build from scratch. They stole, built, and bought with Pappy's deep pockets whatever they needed to keep their project going, even after headquarters lost its mind over the fact that they were tearing apart a brand new A-20 without any official approval.

Pappy's cash proved incredibly helpful, and the project never would have moved forward without it. Exactly where his roll of cash came from remains a mystery. He may have carried it out of the Philippines with him, or he may have been able to tap into Soriano's network of businesses to get the funds. Either way, when they couldn't steal or fabricate what they needed, Pappy found some Australian firm that could do the job—for a price. Out would come his wad of cash to ensure the work got done with haste.

The experiment nearly ended when General Royce discovered what Pappy and D.P. were doing. Pappy was not only not running his air transport squadron, but he was hacking apart one of the General's brand new A-20 Havocs and making unauthorized changes to it with materiel illicitly acquired. He picked up the phone from his headquarters in Melbourne and kicked Pappy out of Brisbane, taking his squadron away in the process.

Pappy flew straight to Charters Towers, where he wanted to be in the first place. Davies, glad to have him, got him assigned to the Third Attack again and put him in charge of the group's engineering section.

Despite General Royce's wrath, Pappy and Don continued their work without missing a beat.

The work proved a godsend to Pappy. At night the dread returned, and he often lay awake captive to his worst imaginings. Worst-case scenarios would play out in his head until he couldn't stand it any longer. Any hope for sleep forgotten, he would fling himself out of bed and return to the field and the work that now gave him purpose. At least he was doing something tangible to get back to Polly and the kids. Other men might have turned to liquor as the answer to inner torment. For Pappy, working on the A-20 became his shield from guilt and the distraction from all the pain.

Day and night he labored, and the other Grim Reapers were simply astonished at his capacity to keep going, hour after hour, with minimal sleep. Truth was, he was trapped in a *Nightmare on Elm*

Street–esque life where sleep was a mortal enemy. There were no happy dreams and refreshing morning wake-ups anymore, only the darkest thoughts and fears.

He worked to collapse more than once. Jack Evans and his other enlisted men would help him to some spot around the Dutch aircraft where he could catnap long enough to regain his strength. Occasionally, his legs swelled up again. His skin broke out in rashes, and he itched constantly.

He kept going, convinced that his path back to Manila lay in the devastation airpower could inflict—if only the crews went into battle with the right equipment.

After much trial and error, they finally completed the first modification. They managed to mount four of the eighty-four-pound, .50-caliber machine guns in the lower half of the A-20's nose, arrayed two over two in a tight, boxlike format. The ammunition and bracing for the guns to handle their recoil added substantial additional weight.

Hall insisted on test-flying the plane first, which didn't sit well with Pappy. He figured that as the more experienced pilot, he should have first shot at it. Plus, he didn't want anyone else to risk their lives in something he conceived.

Don refused to budge, and Pappy grudgingly gave in. Don took off in the A-20 and found right away their modifications transformed a thoroughbred into a plow horse. Sluggish, slow, and nose heavy, the massive weight they dumped in the bombardier's compartment crippled the Havoc's performance. Far from being the lethal machine they hoped, their Frankenhavoc was only going to get more aircrew killed with its poor maneuverability and speed.

Back to the drawing board they went, even as another problem developed. One night, they were sitting around discussing the targets the Eighty-Ninth Bomb Squadron would attack with the new bombers. They would not be going back to the Dutch East Indies, or making Hail Mary flights to the Philippines. The war moved on; New Guinea and New Britain had become the focal point of the fighting now. The Japanese established more bases on the north coast of New Guinea and on New Britain, each base moving them closer to the Allied airfield complex at Port Moresby. Lose Port Moresby to the Japanese, and the last barrier between the Empire of the Rising Sun and Australia would be lost. Everyone sensed that the war out here at the end of America's supply line hung in the balance. Losing New Guinea could open Australia to invasion. At the very least, it would make a drive back to the Philippines almost certainly beyond MacArthur's means.

Holding Port Moresby meant holding the springboard back to Manila.

That night, somebody grabbed a map of New Guinea and New Britain, and Pappy began calculating the flying distances between Port Moresby and the latest Japanese bases. As they did the math, they realized that their A-20s lacked the range to get to almost all of those targets.

If the A-20 would be of any use to Davies's aircrews, they would have to figure out a way to increase its fuel capacity. After spending so much time modifying the PAL Beech 18s, figuring out where to put more gas tanks was Pappy's specialty. He went right to work fabricating a 450-gallon fuel tank, which he and his confederates installed in the A-20's forward bomb bay. That not only helped with range, it also counterbalanced the heavy nose guns.

After further test flights, Pappy installed weights in the tail to move the center of gravity further back along the fuselage. Then, they extended the range even more by pulling out the wing tanks and replacing them with ones pinched from wrecked B-26 Marauders and B-25s. Altogether, those fuel mods almost doubled the range of their test A-20. Yet Pappy found a way to retain most of the A-20's performance. They would not be overloaded, nose heavy and limping into battle unable to escape Japanese fighters. The crews would have their cake and eat it too: a thoroughbred with unparalleled hitting power.

Davies loved the results. The A-20 now had the legs to reach the Japanese bases around New Guinea and sported four heavy and four light machine guns in the nose. Eight guns pouring lead in one narrow cone of fire could potentially do a lot of damage to ground targets. They decided to find out just how much damage such firepower could do.

They took turns flying the A-20 over to a gunnery range outside of Charters Towers, where they made simulated strafing passes on ground targets.

The results were devastating. Each second on the trigger spewed over a hundred bullets into an area the size of a truck. Anything in their path simply disintegrated. Run after run, they watched whatever they shot vanish into countless pieces.

The firepower awed them. Pappy talked incessantly about what they could do against Japanese vehicles, parked aircraft, and even ships. Why, with such firepower, they could wipe out antiaircraft emplacements around airfields, and even armored mounts on ships.

At last, the Third possessed a weapon that could savage the Japanese.

Davies gave the word to start converting more so the Eighty-Ninth could get into action with a full squadron of these strafer A-20s. Pappy and D.P. orchestrated the modifications, bringing in more personnel to get the job done, even as they encountered more resistance from the brass above Davies's head.

The modifications on the A-20s continued through the spring and summer, both at Brisbane and at Charters Towers. The Third's isolated base turned into an advantage. It became a sort of petri dish where they experimented like mad scientists, far away from the prying eyes of those married to regulations. What worked went into production at Brisbane, overseen by other members of the group after Royce banned Pappy from the city and its many supply depots. What didn't work led to other avenues and new developments. Through trial and error, they improved the A-20s even further.

While the A-20s underwent these transformations, the other squadrons in the group went into action over New Guinea. Port Moresby remained under constant Japanese air attack, so it wasn't safe to base more than a few bombers at a time there without risking the destruction of what aircraft they did have.

The A-24s flew up first and went straight into action. The Japanese shot them out of the sky whenever they caught the dive bombers without fighter escort. The B-25s went up next, staging out of Townsville then flying up to Port Moresby to conduct a few missions before ducking back down to Australia.

As great as the B-25 was, their small numbers meant they could do little more than pinprick damage to the Japanese. For all the effort, such raids proved incredibly costly to the group. The Japanese fighter pilots in the area belonged to the legendary Tainan Air Group. They included many aces and veterans of the China War. They were some of the most capable opponents Americans ever faced in aerial combat.

In May alone, thirty-five Grim Reapers died in action. Six more died in accidents. In one two-week stretch, they lost twelve B-25s. At times, 30 to 50 percent of the bombers sent out failed to return. Morale plummeted. The A-24 was a death trap, and Japanese fighters made level bombing with B-25s from ten thousand feet a bloody mess.

It would be several more months before Don Hall and Pappy's squadron of modified A-20s were ready for combat. In the meantime, they needed to do something, or the group's other squadrons would be bled to destruction.

Every plane lost meant the Japanese came a little closer to

scoring their final coup in New Guinea. On the ground, their troops advanced closer and closer to the vital base, throwing back the Aussie troops sent to stop them. The issue hung in the balance, and the margin between defeat and victory seemed to grow every day.

The crisis intensified. Pappy knew he was racing the clock. He was one man caught up in a cataclysm engulfing tens of thousands, yet never once did he ever doubt he could make a difference. He worked with an eye to a larger picture few saw, with a skill set and range of experience nobody else possessed. As the losses mounted, Davies grew nearly frantic. His men—his friends—went into battle and never returned. Day after day, his squadron commanders reported more deaths. Empty spots in the mess hall became a cruel reminder of the odds they faced in New Guinea. The Reapers were being bled white, and the brass offered little support and no answers.

Finally, Jim Davies sent a personal message to General Brett explaining the severity of the situation. "Japs now attacking B-25s from front killing pilots STOP They got five B-25s out of eight yesterday STOP until protection afforded can expect same ratio of losses."

Brett could not have missed the underlying point of the message: Keep ordering missions without fighter escort or more firepower, and my men will keep dying.

Brett offered no solution. FEAF headquarters seemed lost in a torpor, filled with prewar officers who owed their promotions more to their political agility than to their competence. If things were going to change, that change would have to come from the bottom up.

Pappy Gunn, Jack Evans, and the rest of his engineering section rolled up their sleeves. They had some B-25s to modify.

32

"The Gun-Craziest Man I Ever Met"

June 1942
Charters Towers, Australia

In a grungy hangar on the edge of nowhere, surrounded by a sea of dust, Pappy Gunn sweated through his long-sleeved shirt. When he first proposed his modification ideas for the B-25, some of the men in the Third Attack laughed at him. Pappy believed he could install eight forward-firing machine guns inside a B-25's nose, each with five hundred rounds of ammunition. The naysayers said it simply couldn't be done. How would the guns be fed? Where would the ammunition be stored? How could the airframe take the sort of recoil eight heavy machine guns would produce? No way. Four guns on the A-20 was a stretch. Eight in the B-25 would make the plane an uncontrollable death trap to fly. Some of the men even vowed they wouldn't risk their skins in it even if Pappy succeeded in getting one built.

Ignoring the "it can't be done" crowd, Pappy sat down and designed the mounting system. The sketches took shape, and with Jack Fox's help, they created a set of blueprints for their new creation.

Between work on the A-20s, Pappy's crew got ahold of a B-25, and their latest experiment began to take shape. Their first modifications made the B-25 so ponderous that Pappy couldn't even get it off the ground. Whispers of Pappy going a plane too far began to spread. He thumbed his nose at these naysayers by renaming their B-25 guinea pig *Pappy's Folly*. Just to make sure any passing supply guys knew which Pappy, somebody painted a wild-eyed aviator toting a pair of .45 Colts under the plane's name.

He worked like a man with a demon on his heels, and anyone who slacked off or got in his way felt the furnace of his wrath. The men of the Third who had never met Pappy saw him as a borderline fanatic. At times, he worked seventy-two hours straight without sleep, pushing himself against an inner clock whose tick only he could hear.

The pace wore out the younger mechanics and maintainers. Some saw him as ruthless; others couldn't believe the pace he set. Once again, his body was not the measure of his spirit. His legs swelled, and his skin seemed always covered in rashes. He endured prickly heat and dysentery, dropped weight as the bad Aussie Army rations they received went straight through him. At times, his system would just give out, and he'd collapse from complete exhaustion again.

Sometimes at night, he gathered with Big Jim Davies and other members of the Third, including one of the group's medical officers, Dr. John Gilmore. Davies pitched his tent under a couple of scrub trees surrounded by bushes so the entrance looked more like a cave than a military encampment. Out in front, somebody scrounged a small square table and some folding chairs. Pappy would join the men there, passing on the latest developments and hurdles they faced. As he got to know these men, the less serious side of his personality began to emerge. A drink or two with them, and Pappy would start spinning yarns. They were funny and often self-deprecating, frequently crazy tales of twenty years' worth of flying in the most extreme conditions.

Some of the men who didn't know Pappy that well in the spring of 1942 considered him a braggart. They listened to his ridiculously over-the-top tales of flying and dismissed him as a blowhard. Yet, as he got results, they began to listen more closely to his yarns. They were full of wild moments and absurd humor; he was always accidentally blowing something up or ending up in a totally improbable situation. He never made himself to be the hero of the story; usually he was the goat. Those moments where he was the hero—he kept those close and to himself.

Instead, they heard tales of flying with legendary air race pilot Jimmy Haislip in the Philippines, and of the time Pappy bashed face and teeth while being craned aboard his light cruiser. He talked freely of his days as a rumrunner and how the local law brought him to justice. How when he went before the judge, he didn't even own a suit. He ended up wearing one borrowed from Haz.

He never talked about the time where a pilot from Fighting Squadron Three went down at sea off the California coast and Pappy landed his float plane beside him and saved the man's life. Instead, he regaled his audience with the time he tried to loop his two-seat biplane, only to have a toolbox break free in his cockpit and smash him in the face when he got the bird inverted. The sudden blow caused him to jerk the controls so hard the plane stalled, and they spun two thousand feet before Pappy was able to right the aircraft and get down safely.

As the men of the Third flew with Pappy, they realized he wasn't just a talker. Here was a man twice their age who could fly better than any of them. He was a combat pilot ten years past his expiration date for such things, and while the brass kept trying to keep him in the rear, he kept finding ways to join frontline units.

One thing they all understood: Pappy Gunn knew aircraft and could fly anything to the edge of its envelope—then push it just a little farther. He navigated like a bird, relying on instinct, and never seemed to have a map. Yet, he always ended up exactly where he wanted to go with more fuel left in the tank than anyone else. Pappy Gunn possessed an almost preternatural feel for getting to where he wanted to go, something that his fellow pilots always remembered about him. After seventeen thousand hours in the air, seat-of-the-pants navigation became part of his aviator DNA.

Those who got to know him discovered that beneath the brashness beat an empathetic, giving heart. On trips to Brisbane or Melbourne, he would never let anyone pay for drinks or food while out on the town. When the group sent detachments up to Port Moresby to live in rugged jungle conditions, he took a well-abused former Dutch B-25, named it *Not in Stock* and ran morale missions up to the men there. He brought them fresh meat, vegetables, and fruit at a time when they were eating little more than canned Aussie army rations. For a while, he delivered beer, too. Then he decided the hard stuff packed more punch per square foot inside the B-25's fuselage, so he started buying scotch, whiskey, and bourbon with his own cash and would load the bottles in duffel bags for the Moresby resupply runs.

During those runs to Moresby, he often ditched his clothes. Gone was the concern for revealing his tattoos to those around him—nobody cared what graced his muscular arms. The heat left him constantly covered in rashes; he developed crotch rot and a host of other conditions that plagued the other pilots as well. Somehow, Pappy's skin seemed more sensitive to these things, and when the rashes grew particularly bad, covering them with cotton only made the itchiness even worse.

After weeks of working long hours in stiflingly hot hangars, those flights to Moresby afforded him the chance to air himself out a bit, much to the astonishment of the skeleton crew who ran with him.

He donned an aboriginal loincloth and would stretch his shirt and slacks out behind the pilot's seat to let them get some air, too. This cost him dearly once when somebody opened a side window in the cockpit somewhere over the Coral Sea. The sudden jet of the slipstream into the cockpit blew his clothes into a whirlwind. Before he could catch them, they spun right out the side window. Normally, that would have just been an aggravation, but Pappy's pocket contained at least a thousand dollars in pay and poker winnings. The actual amount varied on the telling and retelling by his pals, but even worse was his arrival at Port Moresby in nothing but a loincloth.

As they parked at the airdrome there, a group of females—either Red Cross workers or nurses—showed up with coffee and snacks for the crew. Pappy refused to get out of the cockpit. Always modest, the idea of a woman other than Polly seeing him in such a state roused him to panicked fury. He demanded somebody get him a change of clothes, and when his crew wouldn't stop laughing, legend has it he threatened to shoot them. Somebody finally got him a shirt and a pair of slacks. He dressed while muttering a constant stream of invectives, then dropped out of the B-25's hatch and stormed off.

During one trip up to Moresby, Japanese aircraft struck the base with a surprise bombing raid. He was traveling with his receipts for all the work he'd requisitioned from the Aussie machine shops. While he was taking cover, a bomb blast blew up his receipts. He unintentionally ended up donating more than sixteen thousand dollars to the Allied cause as a result of that very untimely example of Japanese accuracy.

Around Davies's table at night, such stories engendered a lot of laughter. Bill Smallwood, one of the pilots who got to know Pappy around this time, recalled him as fitting right in with the group's "live for today" culture. The men sent to Port Moresby to fly missions against the Japanese rarely returned unscathed. In that first month and a half after the Royce Raid, Pappy's copilot from that mission had vanished in a storm, and one of the other leaders had been shot down and killed by the dreaded aces of the Tainan Air Group. Every man sitting around Davies's table knew they were all short-timers with long odds of seeing this through. So they lived in the moment as boisterously as they could. Pappy played to that, did what he could to make their lives a little better in the time they had. In those gestures, they realized the old man of their warrior clan genuinely cared about them.

He spoke often of his family to his new friends. He woke up every day with a severed heart, the anguish of separation serving as the backdrop to everything he did. At times when it got the best of him, he turned sentimental. On at least one occasion, he teared up talking about his wife in front of a Twenty-Seventh Bomb Group veteran who'd escaped from Bataan just before the surrender there.

He never slowed down, not even after he broke his right pinky finger while working in the bomb bay of an A-20. The cast Doc Gilmore put on for him kept getting in the way while he worked and flew. As a result, it was difficult for him to operate the B-25's throttle quadrant, so he finally just tore off the cast. Doc Gilmore was appalled. Pappy ignored him. He generally hated doctors and referred to Gilmore as the resident "veterinarian." Though Pappy was a bad patient with an attitude, somehow he and Gilmore ended up becoming very close friends.

He kept rebreaking the finger while tearing into the B-25. At night, he'd come in to chow, or to report the latest progress, his pinky sticking out at such a weird angle that the men would remark on it. "That's my Society Tea Drinking Finger," Pappy would say proudly, holding it up as if he were daintily sipping like an English lord. The pain must have been terrible, but he never seemed to respond to it. If anything, he saw it as an annoyance, a necessary part of everyday life.

As Pappy made friends within the group, the scope of his personal mission began to change. Building a better B-25 became more than finding a way to hit the Japanese harder and start winning the air war. It became a matter of survival. These young men were going out every day and dying in airplanes not the measure of their courage. The Japanese drove that point home after every mission, when the group would sit around Davies's table and try not to look at the empty chairs. At one point, some of the pilots did the math and concluded at the current loss rate, they would run out of aircrew in just a couple more months.

The situation grew so extreme that the Third finally looked outside the AAF for warm bodies to put in their cockpits. Several dozen Aussies joined the group and served as copilots through the summer of '42.

They died valiantly right alongside their American brothers. They burned to death, were crushed to death, were blown apart by cannon fire, or were dismembered by antiaircraft shrapnel. Some bled out on the fuselage floor as they struggled back to Moresby, their planes full of holes. It was a dark time that the laughter and raucous behavior back at Charters Towers could only paper over. At night, alone, the men dwelt on their fate. Life expectancy for these twenty-somethings boiled down to weeks.

Pappy was determined to give them the means to survive and thrive in the Japanese-held sky. He never strayed from his work for long. Sticking eight machine guns in a bomber never designed to have such firepower might have looked easy to the uninitiated nonaviator, but there were huge obstacles to overcome.

While D.P. Hall prepared to take the A-20s north to Moresby as the Eighty-Ninth Squadron's commander, Pappy and Jack Fox puzzled through each problem with their B-25 modifications. At each step, Pappy tested the latest changes with short flights as they went along. It was the ultimate trial-and-error process—no wind tunnel tests, no computer models and simulations. With Pappy functioning as a sort of shoestring test pilot, they discovered solutions to every problem they encountered. He wouldn't let anyone fly *Pappy's Folly* until he had ensured it to be safe; no way did he want to lose a man because of something he'd done to the aircraft. He took the risks himself, trusting in his mechanical skills, but falling back on his flying prowess when something went wrong. Things often went wrong.

They started with the nonessential stuff inside the B-25. The retractable turret designed to protect the underside of the bomber was one of the first things they'd stripped out. Those two guns wouldn't be needed with the way they envisioned the bomber would be used—on the treetops. Besides, the turret rarely worked as advertised.

They played around with the idea of mounting two or three machine guns in the back of the fuselage at an angle firing downward and to the rear. That way, as the Mitchell passed over the target, the pilot could keep the AA gunners' heads down and continue to strafe as the Mitchells fled the target area.

They tore apart the bombardier's compartment. They pulled out the seat and much of the equipment around it, including the flexible machine gun and its mount. Then they constructed a carriage to hold four .50-calibers, and stuck four more .50s on side packs along the outside of the fuselage beneath the cockpit windows.

On the first test flights, Pappy fired the guns and all hell broke loose. Rivets popped, aluminum crumpled under the crushing force of the recoil. The plane shook so ferociously that part of the landing gear system in the nose failed. Instead of being deterred, they looked over *Pappy's Folly*, gleaned the lessons learned, and went to work troubleshooting each issue. They reinforced the B-25's metal hide, used more durable rivets, added rubber grommets, and extended each gun's blast tube to dampen the vibrations and protect the landing gear system.

Pappy and Jack Fox did not do this work alone. Jack Evans kept pace with Pappy and rarely left his side. His loyalty never wavered from combat missions to 120-degree hangars; he swung in orbit around Pappy and played a significant role in the modification process. Davies also gave them a cadre of engineering and materials men, mechanics and armorers—whoever they needed. They worked with almost the same feverish intensity as their boss.

Meanwhile, the situation in New Guinea grew worse. The Japanese Army captured the entire north coast of the island. Now, they pressed inland on Port Moresby. A naval invasion of the critical Allied base was turned back in May during the Battle of the Coral Sea, which saw the Japanese sink Pappy's beloved old home, the aircraft carrier USS *Lexington*. Though the seaborne force was turned back, the Japanese Army on the north coast seemed unstoppable. Marching from their enclaves on the Bismarck Sea, they advanced across the rugged Owen Stanley Range along a narrow track known as the Kokoda Trail.

As the Japanese pushed the front lines closer to Port Moresby and their Zeroes savaged the Allied air squadrons sent to blunt their advance, the Third licked its wounds through June, then returned in force to the New Guinea skies in July using all available aircraft. Often without fighter escort to protect them, they waded into the hornet's nest of Lae, where the Tainan Air Group's aces shot them out of the sky. In just a few missions that month, the Grim Reapers lost seven planes, twenty men killed or missing, in 146 sorties.

They flew these missions over the most inhospitable terrain imaginable. Those who crashed or bailed out faced primordial swamps, triple-canopy jungle, razorback ridges towering thousands of feet, all teeming with deadly insects, spiders, and diseases. There was no search-and-rescue service, no helicopters that could hover over the jungle to extract a downed airman. Those who escaped the Japanese largely died in the jungle unless they happened upon friendly natives.

Don Good, an Oregon-born A-20 pilot who served under Don Hall that summer, got hit on one mission and crashed on the northern New Guinea coast. He was one of the lucky ones who evaded the Japanese and caught the attention of a passing U.S. Navy PT boat. He was picked up and returned to Port Moresby, but that was like winning the lottery.

What happened to 1st Lt. Robert Cassels and Sgt. Loree Le Boeuf at the end of July was depressingly more common. Shot down in one of the Third Group's A-24 dive bombers, the two men bailed out over New Guinea and fell into Japanese hands. The Japanese tortured them for information before executing them.

Later that summer, the first rumors of atrocities against the Aussies defending the Kokoda Trail began to circulate. Among them was a persistent rumor that the Japanese were resorting to cannibalism. More than once, intelligence reports detailed such incidents where prisoners of war were ritualistically eaten—and eaten slowly while still alive. Some thought this nonsense—simply propaganda or exaggerations coming from unreliable sources. Yet it was the truth. The Japanese were eating Allied POWs.

As the battlefront closed in on Port Moresby, the Third received orders to send a full squadron up to the base's defense. Up until that August, they used the battered airfields around the Moresby largely as staging points to bomb up and refuel for missions before slipping back south out of the range of Japanese airpower. Now, Davies told Don Hall to get his men ready for the move. They'd be taking their freshly modified A-20s up to see what they could do to help the jungle-bound Aussie troops make a last stand. Meanwhile, as Pappy labored in the hangar at Charters Towers, discussions about his future were taking place at the highest levels in MacArthur's headquarters.

The Philippines fell in May when the Japanese assaulted and captured Corregidor. General Wainwright tried to surrender only the troops on the Rock, but the Japanese refused to accept that. They told the aging American cavalry officer that if all Filamerican forces in the Philippines—including those on Mindanao—did not surrender, the men on Corregidor would be massacred. The word went out, and the majority of the U.S. and Filipino troops laid down their arms. Some refused to submit. Violating orders to surrender, they escaped into the jungle to form the nucleus of a guerrilla warfare movement against the Japanese.

Even as the Imperial Army threatened to capture Port Moresby, MacArthur's headquarters began to try and organize support for the guerrillas. In June 1942, the Allied Intelligence Bureau was established with the purpose of stoking those behind-the-lines fires. The AIB included Dutch, British, American, Aussie, and Filipino agents, and in time it would grow into one of the most successful special operations headquarters of WWII. Commanded by Colonel C.G. Roberts, AIB's main priority was to find capable, courageous men with diverse skill sets and a knowledge of the Japanese-occupied areas.

That summer, Colonel Roberts learned of Pappy Gunn's unique background and knowledge of the Philippines. Roberts sent one of his officers, Maj. Joseph McMicking, to see MacArthur's chief of staff, Gen. Richard K. Sutherland, and inquire on Pappy Gunn's availability.

Roberts and McMicking wanted to offer Pappy a job in AIB. The exact role is unclear, but Roberts planned to send him back into the Philippines to work with the guerrilla movement in some capacity. With Sutherland's approval, he dispatched McMicking to Charters Towers to offer the job to Pappy.

Not long afterward, Pappy flew down to Melbourne, where he spotted a familiar figure at the airfield there climbing out of a P-40. He hurried over, excited to see an old friend.

It was Jess Villamor, the Filipino fighter pilot who had become a national hero the previous December. He was so short he was having a hard time getting his feet down into the toe slot below the cockpit and the P-40's wing roots. At the moment, he was almost dangling from the cockpit, focused on not falling.

"I am here," Pappy said to his back, and helped him down.

Jess got his feet on the tarmac and greeted Pappy warmly. He had escaped out of the Philippines in April, only to face the indignity of racism in Australia. When he got to Melbourne, he tried to check into a hotel, but was turned away because he was Filipino.

Now, seeing a familiar face lit Jess up as much as it did Pappy. They stood beside the P-40, chatting with happy animation. Pappy told Jess about the modification work he'd been doing: "I want guns not only in the front of my plane but in the rear too, so I can mow 'em down not only on my way in but also on my way out."

Combined with the signature pair of .45s strapped in Pappy's shoulder holsters, the discussion prompted Jess to call the middle-aged Arkansan "the gun-craziest man I ever met."

At length, Pappy said, "They're getting me ready to go back to the Philippines. How about you join me?"

He didn't need to be asked twice. Jess went up to Brisbane not long after to meet with Major McMicking and talk it over. Jess was pulled into AIB a short time later.

Pappy returned to Charters Towers, determined to finish the B-25 modification project. As soon as it was done, the two old friends would return to their Philippine home together. This time, instead of going as pilots they would be going back as secret agents.

33

Bust 'Em George, the Undocumented Renegade General

August 1942
Charters Towers, Australia

Maj. Paul Irvin Gunn looked over the B-25. His recently acquired, foot-long lizard, Sam, perched atop his shoulder and dozed on his owner, his tail wrapped partway around Pappy's neck.

Jim Davies could keep his foul-mouthed albino parrot. Real aviators flew with reptiles.

Pappy was the only human Sam liked. The Arkansan, like Polly, had a touch with animals, and they were drawn to him. Pappy had found him in the scrub somewhere around the tent he shared with Jim McAfee these days, and he'd picked him right up. The lizard felt at home on his shoulder and seemed totally unconcerned when Pappy took him for his first flight in a B-25—an aircraft not particularly animal friendly, given the two massive engines blasting out Mötley Crüe–worthy decibel levels of noise. If anything, Sam grew more sedate, and he would creep down Pappy's arm to sack out, with his chin resting on the back of Pappy's hand as he worked the throttles.

Pappy grew protective of Sam, perhaps because of losing Dingo and Chi-Chi and Amos the cat back in Manila. While at work on the B-25 or some other project, Sam had a tendency to hiss at passersby. When he did, Pappy would eyeball whoever had violated his lizard's airspace and growl with faux menace, "Don't touch my lizard."

Nobody touched Pappy's lizard.

The B-25 experiment, meanwhile, was progressing, and Pappy knew he would be heading over to AIB soon. The Mitchell was too nose heavy thanks to the four thousand extra rounds of machine gun ammunition they'd crammed inside the fuselage. It was also about twenty miles an hour slower with all the extra weight. Still, they'd been executing successful gunnery runs on the range for days now without any major structural damage. On one of those strafing passes, Pappy "accidentally" machine-gunned some rancher's wandering steer and ended up sixteen bucks out of pocket for its replacement. On the plus side, legend had it they ate steak at the Third group mess hall that night instead of canned mutton.

They needed to work through the nose heaviness, but he and Li'l Fox—Pappy's nickname for Jack Fox—would puzzle through it. Some extra counterweight in the rear of the fuselage would probably help. It was always going to be a little out of balance, but Pappy figured some extra training with the pilots plus some extra elevator trim fed into the controls would be enough to overcome it.

Today, Colonel Davies mentioned they would be getting a visit from some brass. New brass. MacArthur had grown weary of General Brett and the lack of performance of his air force to date. Morale in FEAF was generally low. Living conditions were barely tolerable outside of Melbourne; missions were sporadically flown and losses were high. Plus, the crazy-quilt layers of headquarters Brett had implemented had made getting anything accomplished almost miraculous.

So Brett was out. MacArthur had his pick of a couple of other air generals and he selected somebody named George Kenney. Pappy had never heard of him, but assumed that this new guy would be as clueless and obstructionist as the rest of the den of thieves at FEAF HQ. The thought of yet another new brass hat to deal with, after slamming his head into their bureaucratic wall for so many months left Pappy with no patience for the dog and pony show they'd have to put on for the new general. It would only delay work on the strafer conversion, which was intolerable.

Pappy figured the general would order him to stop hacking up perfectly good aircraft anyway. Government property was not to be experimented on, after all. Pappy decided to do what he usually did with the brass: ignore them. Inside, he burned with frustration. Fighting the war on two fronts, never knowing who had his back and who was out to get him, was grinding him down. By August 1942, he knew he was on the edge of a breakdown.

He stayed at work in the hangar while Davies and the other officers in the group did the glad-handing, wanting only to be left alone.

George Kenney was anything but a typical American Army Air Force general. For one thing, he technically wasn't even an American, though he bristled at any suggestion otherwise. His Canadian parents moved the family from his birthplace in Nova Scotia and settled in a Boston working-class neighborhood when he was a young child. Later, as an adult he covered up the nature of his heritage by telling reporters that he was born of American parents who had happened to be vacationing in Canada when he arrived in the world. Whether or not Kenney ever formally became a naturalized citizen of the United States is unclear. But nobody identified more as an American, and as a patriot, than George Kenney.

After high school in Boston, he went on to study civil engineering at MIT. During his sophomore year, his father abandoned the family, which ultimately forced him out of college when his family's financial resources gave out.

Kenney returned to Canada for two years, and he found work in Quebec as a surveyor for a railroad company. Two years later, his mother died during an operation, and he moved back to Boston to be closer to the remainder of his family. He found a job at one of the top civil engineer firms in the city, and worked there until he started his own general contracting firm.

World War I changed everything for him. He'd always had an interest in aviation, and had even tried to build an airplane with some college buddies at MIT. Now, as the U.S. mobilized for war, he joined the army in the spring of 1917 and became an observation pilot. Deployed to the Western Front the following year, Kenney saw extensive combat over the trenches in French-made, two-seat biplanes. He and his gunner shot down two German planes, and Kenney displayed tremendous courage in many air battles. In the spring of 1918, he was badly injured in a crash, but returned from the hospital to keep flying. His fellow pilots nicknamed him, "Bust 'Em George" after that.

In the final weeks of the war, he was shot up by German fighters. A bullet pierced the sleeve of his flight jacket, his instrument panel was shattered, and his wings were riddled with holes. He limped back to base, set down on the grassy runway—and the left wing promptly fell off the aircraft. For that mission, he earned a Distinguished Service Cross.

The civil engineer had become a war hero, and he chose to stay in the Army after the war and make a career out of flying. He proved to be a free-thinking officer, unafraid to speak his mind and criticize the dominant thinking prevalent in the brass during the '20s and '30s. At times, he even took aim at the Air Corps' sacred cow: the B-17. He spent much of his time in trouble with his superiors, earning something of a reputation as a rebel in uniform. For a few years, he was sent to command the Third Attack Group, and the experience of tear-assing around the treetops with the Air Corps' misfits inspired him to invent a small parachute fragmentation bomb designed to destroy aircraft and unarmored vehicles. He convinced the service to build a small number of them, but the bombs ended up in a warehouse unused and untested.

Though he had not drunk the same strategic bombing Kool-Aid as the other senior air officers of the era, Kenney's enthusiasm, energy and competence kept him in the game. He was steadily promoted and even jumped the rank of major in the mid-1930s, becoming a lieutenant colonel and given a staff position at General Headquarters.

That didn't last. After he roundly criticized the Air Corps for purchasing more B-17s, he was busted down to the rank he'd never held—major—and sent to the aviation equivalent of Siberian exile, the Army's Infantry School at Fort Benning, Georgia. There, he taught young officers soon to be commanding rifle platoons advanced tactics.

He hung in there despite the career sidetrack and eventually earned a transfer to Wright Field, where he served as the chief of production engineering. It was a good slot for him; all through his career he had tinkered with ways to improve the aircraft he flew. On one occasion, he even rigged up extra forward firing guns on an ancient WWI-era De Havilland biplane.

A visit to France in 1940 opened his eyes, and he concluded the Army Air Corps was far behind the Europeans. He recommended a host of changes and engineering upgrades to existing aircraft, and wrote a highly critical report of the AAC's capabilities compared to the Luftwaffe. Again, he rankled the senior leadership with his bluntness, and he was ordered out of France in response.

Trying to find a slot for his rebellious engineer, Gen. Hap Arnold, head of the Army Air Corps, sent Kenney to command an experimental and testing school, where he earned his general's star.

When the war broke out, Kenney was not one of the generals

tagged for early overseas command. He was put in charge of a training operation on the West Coast and languished there until Arnold offered him to MacArthur.

To the top air officers, being sent to a backwater theater to work with MacArthur was the wartime version of exile. MacArthur disdained his air generals, and he earned a reputation for being non-air-minded and almost impossible to work with, as Brereton and Brett would later attest.

Kenney reached Australia in July 1942 and quickly established an excellent relationship with MacArthur. He then set out on a whirlwind tour to see the true state of the command he would soon inherit.

He was not impressed.

The first visits to bases around Australia convinced him a whole lot of people needed firing. Everywhere he looked, he saw incompetence, ridiculous layers of bureaucracy, and a disastrous lack of support for the aircrews actually doing the fighting. He spent July and early August gathering information and getting ready for the housecleaning to come.

On August 5, 1942, Kenney flew into Charters Towers and met Jim Davies and some of the other senior members of the Third Attack for the first time. Over lunch at the mess hall, they talked over the hardships the group had faced, the aircraft situation and the combat losses. Somewhere in all that, Pappy's name came up. Kenney listened as Davies and his men brightened up as they spoke of what their mad scientist had been doing. Stories of his flying ability and engineering skills tumbled out until finally, Kenney decided he needed to meet this guy.

Davies told him that Pappy had spent the last two days straight closeted away in the hangar. He'd been having coffee and sandwiches sent down to his crew there so Pappy wouldn't starve them all to death as they worked on their A-20s and the B-25.

"Shall I send for him?" Davies asked.

Kenney replied, "No, I don't want to interrupt his job that much, but after lunch I would like to inspect his show and meet this legend of yours."

Davies drove General Kenney over to Pappy's hangar. When they stepped inside, the stifling heat struck both officers. The hangar was made of canvas—it was really just a huge tent. It had no ventilation to speak of, and the desert sun of Charters Towers turned it into an oven by noon every day.

There was Pappy, the only one with a shirt on. Unless he was flying, he still wore his shirt as much as he could stand it. On this afternoon, instead of his crushed officer's hat, he sported a mechanic's ball cap with his major's oak leaves pinned to its front.

Davies made introductions. Pappy shook the general's hand coldly, while Kenney began to ask questions. The questions jolted Pappy. From them, he could tell this new general was different from the other ones he had battled with around Australia. Kenney spoke the language of engineers, and he made it clear from the first moment they met that he was as fluent as anyone else in the hangar that day.

The two formed an instant connection; Pappy saw in General Kenney a man open to new ideas. Kenney saw Pappy's almost fanatical levels of energy, his knowledge and unorthodox ideas, and knew that he was going to be a very useful officer to have under his command. That first meeting gave Pappy hope that things might actually change for the better.

Pappy walked General Kenney around the hangar, introduced him to all of the enlisted mechanics working with him and told the general a bit about each man. Kenney found the gesture both surprising and telling. It said a lot about Pappy's character to ensure those working with him received recognition as well.

The meeting broke up, and General Kenney headed off.

Later that day, Pappy flew to Port Moresby in his B-25. Things in New Guinea were quickly reaching a crisis point. The Japanese army was poised at the threshold of victory. One more push would carry them into Port Moresby itself, and General Kenney would have to begin his war fighting from Northern Australia.

It was an all-hands moment, and everything that could fly was soon en route to the strips around Moresby. The Eighty-Ninth started north for the group's first permanent move to New Guinea as part of this desperate reinforcement effort. Don Hall flew in with an advanced echelon behind the controls of one of the modified A-20s, while his group of mechanics in Brisbane, working under Capt. Bob Ruegg, worked around the clock to finish the modifications. They managed to send about fifteen strafer A-20s, all based on Pappy and Don's prototype, up to join the fight for Port Moresby.

During an inspection trip about this time, Kenney found the Australian commander at Port Moresby almost resigned to defeat. His half-trained troops managed to slow the Japanese advance, but they lacked the strength and firepower to make a stand. What he didn't realize was that the Japanese situation had grown equally desperate. With a tenuous supply system that crossed the formidable Owen Stanley Range and required every bit of gear to be moved either by humans or pack animals, the Japanese slowly ran out of food and medicine. Now, on the brink of victory, their frontline troops faced starvation. They were wracked with disease and were low on everything they needed for the final assault on Moresby. About thirty miles from their objective, the Japanese had reached the limits of their endurance.

Don Hall and his Eighty-Ninth Squadron pilots made things even worse on the soldiers struggling through the jungle. Using their nose guns, the A-20s roared through narrow canyons no other bombers could operate within, shooting up strong points and Japanese troops. Other Allied units, particularly several Aussie squadrons, joined the fight to stem the enemy advance, and for the first time in the South-west Pacific, a Japanese land offensive was stopped.

In the climactic days of the Kokoda Trail battle, Don Hall flew six missions a day from Kila Kila Drome outside of Port Moresby. Some flights took less than twenty minutes between takeoff, attack run on Japanese troops, and landing.

Pappy flew into this chaos without any orders to be there, or to fly combat missions. Orders didn't mean anything to him. The Japanese were close, and he thirsted for some revenge. Over the next three days, he flew at least five ground support missions, strafing and bombing Japanese troops to ease the pressure off the beleaguered Aussies. He went in low, using one of the modified A-20s to hammer targets with the nose guns before lacing the area with antipersonnel bombs.

During one run, ground fire struck Pappy's A-20. A chunk of shrapnel burst through the side of the cockpit and struck Sam, who was perched atop Pappy's throttle arm. The metal impaled the liz-ard, went clean through Pappy's arm, and pinned it to his seat's arm-rest. He couldn't pull it clear as he flew back to Moresby, Sam dying on his hand. Once back on the ground, the ground crew rushed to his aid when Pappy didn't emerge from the cockpit. They found him bloodied and still impaled by the shrapnel, groaning, "They got Sam. The goddamned bastards got Sam."

Losing his lizard, after all the other heartbreak he'd suffered since December, added to his near-fanatical will to keep working, keep doing, keep bombing the Japanese. He was relentless and spent only the bare minimum time with the medical staff at Moresby before being flown back to Charters Towers to continue his work.

There, Pappy discovered General Kenney had given him a spe-cial assignment. Kenney's arrival in theater came with an added bonus. As he left his Stateside post, he'd asked for the supply of three thousand fragmentation bombs he'd designed earlier in the 1930s. Arnold was happy to oblige, as nobody else had use for the weapons.

Kenney explained their purpose to Davies, and Pappy's crew went about modifying the bomb bay cages that held these small, twenty-three-pound weapons. They were cumbersome devices, and too often in tests they malfunctioned. Kenney gave them only two weeks to fabricate a solution and prepare enough racks to equip the Eighty-Ninth Bomb Squadron.

Meanwhile, thanks in part to the influx of airpower and fresh reinforcements, the Japanese drive to Port Moresby fell only a few miles short. The Aussies made their stand, and when the Japanese could advance no further, they began to starve in place. Slowly, the Allies began to push them back across the Owen Stanley Range, a retreat that became a hellish ordeal for the emaciated, disease-wracked Imperial soldiers.

MacArthur's springboard to the Philippines had been saved.

At the end of August, as Pappy's crew labored away in the hangar at Charters Towers, Don Hall's A-20s went into action against the Tainan Air Group's home at Lae Airdrome, where they used the new strafing tactics to great effect. Six Havocs roared right off the jungle treetops and completely surprised the Japanese, who were servicing both fighters and dive bombers for flight. Hall's A-20s swept overhead, their new nose guns pouring lead into the Japanese as they scrambled for cover. In seconds, the Havocs strafed the length of Lae Airdrome, extended out away from the target before turning for Moresby.

They suffered no losses. In fact, over the course of the next month, Hall's squadron didn't lose a plane whenever they stayed on the deck, though they lost two in other attacks. Given the meat grinder the Third Attack had been through since April, this was nothing short of miraculous.

In record time, Pappy's team finished the new honeycomb rack for the A-20s. He and Jim Davies tested them on the gunnery range and watched as the frag bombs fell out of the Havoc in a long stream.

They struck the scrubland with such devastation that both men were momentarily awestruck. The bombs carved a swath right through the trees, tearing them apart like they'd been through a wood chipper.

After the flight, Pappy grinned at Jim. Thinking a leap ahead, he quipped that in a B-25, "you can carry a hundred parafrag clusters in the bomb bays. You'll have the most devastating air weapon that ever came to the Pacific."

A few weeks later the Third discovered just how devastating the parafrags could be to the Japanese. Hall's A-20s went after ground targets at over three hundred miles an hour, their propeller tips mere feet over the trees. Raking the Japanese with their nose guns as they made their approach to kill any antiaircraft gun crews, they released scores of these frag bombs, their tiny chutes blossoming like a trail of white mushrooms behind each A-20. The chutes slowed the bombs down just enough to let the A-20s escape their blast radius. As the Havocs fled, the bombs detonated, throwing hurricanes of shrapnel in 360-degree arcs. They scythed through men, AA guns, trucks, aircraft—anything not armored or buried in the ground.

After September, Kenney's light and medium bomber units adopted the low-level tactics wholesale. Pappy's strafers were in business to stay.

Yet, one more problem needed to be solved. In eight months of trying, the Army Air Force managed to sink only a handful of Japanese ships. The B-17s couldn't get the job done. The B-25s and A-20s did not have much success, either. The final victory on the Kokoda Trail stopped the Japanese threat to New Guinea, but if the tide were to be turned in the Allies' favor, MacArthur's aircrews would have to become ship killers.

34

Clara Crosby Comes of Age

Fall 1942

Santo Tomas Internment Camp, Manila, Philippines

It took Julie almost dying of malnutrition for Polly to find the limits of her strength and courage.

The symptoms manifested in different ways in different people. With Julie, malnutrion's effects afflicted her spine. As she lost weight she became increasingly debilitated by pain in her back. She had been part of the camp census team, documenting who was interned when the family first had arrived. But as her condition worsened, she spent more time in her narrow cot, in agony.

Seeing her daughter suffer changed everything for Polly. For years, she was content to let P.I. take charge of everything. When he was gone, she would come into her own and manage the household's daily affairs, but she still deferred to him on any major issues, even when he was away at sea. In some ways, she lived in P.I.'s shadow, and almost from the first day they met, she allowed him to redraw the scope of her life so thoroughly that she even let him give her a new name.

Her real name was Clara Crosby, but P.I. decided Clara didn't fit her. "You look like a Polly to me," he exclaimed early in their courtship. She'd been Polly ever since.

Now, she faced the pivotal moment in her life. She had no support. She couldn't call on her parents or husband for help and guidance. What needed to be done for her babies, she would have to do herself. In the upside down world of Santo Tomas, she knew nobody would have her back. If Julie was going to be saved from a slow, torturous death, Polly would have to be the one to fight for her.

Not that she lacked strength. At times, she did not hesitate to stand up to P.I., but she always did it with a deft and nonconfrontational touch that left him powerless to resist. After they moved to the Philippines, she and P.I. were unpacking in the bedroom of the Villamor Court house when Polly found the corporal punishment device P.I. had fashioned for use on the boys. It looked like a miniature cat-o'-nine-tails, and he would slap it across their hindquarters instead of spanking them whenever they had gotten into serious trouble. He did not use it often, but Polly always felt uncomfortable about such methods of punishment. She was the nurturer, after all.

She withdrew the lash from a box and stared at it. P.I. paused and turned to see what she was holding. They made eye contact. Deliberately, she said, "We will no longer be needing this out here."

No discussion. She threw it in the trash, and P.I. never disciplined the boys with physical punishment again.

Defending her boys gave her the strength to stand against P.I.'s force of character. It didn't hurt that he was totally in love with her, and he would do whatever she wanted if she made that want clear.

Getting Julie help would be far more difficult a journey. Polly had no connections in the committee, no ability to influence decisions made that affected her daughter. That had already been driven home when word reached the camp that a prisoner exchange would soon be conducted between the U.S. and Japanese governments. Three hundred and fifty people from the camp were to leave aboard a ship and return to America. Many of those 350 people had already been chosen by Washington. They were State Department types or high-priority civilians. Most of the remaining slots, it was decided, would go to the infirm.

Polly tried to get Julie on that boat. The committee denied her request, telling her that if her underage daughter left the camp, the whole family would have to go as well. That meant five slots, and the Gunns weren't worth five slots as far as the committee was concerned.

That disappointment lingered for months and felt especially bitter when, in September 1942, the first group to be repatriated left the camp for the first leg of their journey. It seemed most were picked by ingratiating themselves to Earl Carroll, the head of the internee committee. By the time the lucky 350 departed, Julie could hardly walk. The camp hospital's chief, Dr. Fletcher, told Polly they did not have the equipment nor the expertise to handle her case.

Red flower in her hair, Polly went to war for her girl. She started with the internee committee. The members had already blown off her other request, but this time she probed around until she learned who was in charge of recommending outside treatment for camp patients. The man was Mr. Holland, and Polly made it her personal mission to badger the man until he acted on her behalf. She dug deep and shed her timid, sweet persona. She harassed Holland so thoroughly that he started calling her "Mrs. Two-Gunn."

At last, he allowed her to have the camp's Japanese doctor take a look at Julie's condition. The Japanese doctor was known to grant passes for those cases too severe for the camp hospital to cure. He was a bizarre, mercurial man who inspired fear in the inmates. He held their medical fate in his hands, and his decisions seemed capricious and random. No matter; this man was the next step in the bureaucratic ladder that Polly needed to climb.

A few days before the Japanese doctor was to examine Julie, Polly sought to get a one-day pass so that her daughter could get x-rayed at St. Luke's Hospital in Manila. Dr. Fletcher had made it clear that without them, trying to diagnose her condition would be almost impossible.

To get that pass, he needed both Holland's approval and the signature of one of the senior Japanese camp administrators, a man named Mr. Ohashi. Polly met him in his office one morning, bowed formally, and set the tone with the respect she showed him. He was a civilian businessman pressed into his role as one of the senior administration officials. He tried to throw roadblocks in front of Polly, but she refused to be dissuaded. She kept pushing him to issue the pass without anger, just a relentless respectful pursuit of what she needed.

Her touch worked. He issued the pass, plus one for Polly, too. Upon their return, Dr. Fletcher reviewed the X-rays and saw some abnormalities in her lower spine. A dark mass of some sort. He was unsure what it was, but he knew it was still beyond the capabilities of the camp hospital. She needed to be seen by an orthopedic specialist. He promised Polly he would recommend that Julie be released for treatment in Manila.

The next day, Dr. Fletcher, Polly, and Julie went over to meet with the Japanese doctor. He gave Julie a cursory exam, then held up the X-rays. He looked at them blankly for a long moment, then Dr. Fletcher quietly took them out of his hands, turned them right side up, and gave them back. The doctor nodded his head absently. Clearly, the Japanese had not dropped their medical A-team into Santo Tomas for the prisoners.

He finished with the X-rays and that apparently concluded the exam. The doctor walked out of the office without another word.

What did that mean? A bolt of fear struck Polly. She could not let this happen. She ran out of the room, leaving Julie alone as she chased after the Japanese doctor. She reached him, but he ignored her and kept walking.

"My daughter," she said. "Can she go for treatment?"

No answer. The doctor kept walking, face inscrutable.

Polly kept pace with him and asked again, "My daughter, can she go for treatment?"

He continued walking.

She wasn't going to beg. Weakness would only get exploited in this freedomless world, and Polly knew it. She was not the begging kind anyway—she had too much poise, too much adroit charisma and pride, for that. But she refused to give up.

She asked again. Same exact words. Same tone, respectful but insistent.

The man did not slow down.

One more time, controlled. She wasn't going to panic. "My daughter, can she go for treatment?"

He now eyed Polly. A moment later, he finally said, "Yes."

She'd won the first battle, but many lay ahead. Julie went to St. Luke's and Manila General Hospital, where her case continued to puzzle doctors. Polly returned to Holland and Mr. Ohashi to get Julie's passes extended, and to get one for herself so she could be with her daughter as she endured the battery of tests and the poking and prodding of exams.

At last, an orthopedic surgeon named Dr. De Los Santos took on her case. He concluded that she needed to be placed in a full body cast from her neck to her hips to stabilize her spine and diminish the pain. With proper rest and food, she would be able to walk again while in the cast, but the recovery would be a long one.

Polly went back to Mr. Ohashi to secure another pass for herself so she could be with Julie during the cast procedure. Again, another round of negotiations with him ensued.

"How is your daughter's condition?" he asked politely.

Polly, exhausted from all the bureaucratic battles, debilitated by bad food and sleepless nights, blurted out, "She is very bad from her treatment."

She looked on, horrified that she may have just ruined the most important relationship to her daughter. She had meant to say that the treatment the doctors were giving her was painful. Instead, it came out as an indictment.

Mr. Ohashi apparently did not take offense, much to Polly's relief. He gave her the pass needed to be with Julie. During their many back-and-forths, he finally said to her, "You are a very determined little woman."

A short time later at a hospital in Manila, Polly stood nearby comforting her daughter as Dr. De Los Santos suspended Julie between two tables. She hung there in agony as the doctor constructed the cast around her. It took hours, and after they were finished, her spine had not yet settled into place. Julie lay in bed, Polly helplessly watching her daughter's agony until her spine finally cracked and moved into position. When it did, Julie cried out and laughed hysterically at the same time.

Polly stayed close to Julie over the ensuing days, her thoughts torn between her daughter's well-being and the fact that the boys and Connie were still at the camp without her. She could feel the family being torn further and further apart, but she could handle only one crisis at a time.

At length, she returned to Santo Tomas, determined to wring another concession from the Japanese. Julie would never recover in room forty-six. The doctors in Manila had told her she needed healthy food and extended bedrest. Earl Carroll had arranged for some wealthy internees to live off-site in sanatoriums around the city, but to get such a waiver required pull, social standing and resources she did not possess.

She tried a different tact. She returned to Mr. Ohashi and told him she wanted a long-term pass for Julie so she could convalesce with the Gurevich family. She would go to Manila General for treatment when needed, return to the camp every few weeks to get her pass renewed, and be examined by the Japanese doctor whenever necessary.

This was stretching Ohashi's goodwill, but he eventually gave in to her relentless refusal to take no for an answer.

Julie remained in the hospital until she was able to walk with the cast on. When she could move around, she was taken to the duplex and placed under Eva Gurevich's warm care. She ate borscht and many other Russian meals in the middle of Japanese-occupied Manila. Gradually, over many weeks, she regained her strength.

Guyenne and the Garriz twins, the family friends whom Polly came to trust so thoroughly, came round to visit several times a week. Some of the Spanish in Manila were anti-Japanese, and this trio had developed ties to the Filipino guerrillas operating in and around the capital. Exactly what their roles were in the nascent insurgency is unclear. They probably operated as couriers, carrying messages between different cells. The Japanese secret police were aware of one Garriz brother, but they never figured out he had a twin. Many times, the boys would establish an alibi by making sure one twin was seen in public while the other carried out business for the insurgency.

Just as Polly got Julie on the road to recovery, Nath fell ill in late 1942 or early 1943. By then, Nath had outgrown his shoes, which had fallen apart anyway, and he had been forced to go barefoot. Now, after bouts with dysentery, beriberi, and dengue fever, Nath found his feet suddenly swelled up so badly that he couldn't walk. The dreaded red streaks of infection shot up his right leg, as if he'd been bitten by an insect or suffered a cut while working in the recently established internee garden.

Dr. Fletcher didn't have the means to help Nath, so Polly went to war with the camp bureaucracy again on his behalf. She got him on the morning bus to Manila General Hospital, where Dr. De Los Santos treated him. Nath was in so much pain he wanted them to just cut his feet off. De Los Santos thought he might need surgery, but decided to try a course of medication, hot wraps, and massages first. Nath's feet responded immediately, easing his pain considerably.

Two days later, Polly wrangled yet another pass out of Mr. Holland and Mr. Ohashi so Nath could convalesce at the Gureviches' with Julie. The longer her kids stayed out of the camp, the better chance they'd survive this ordeal. Nath was taken back to the duplex, and for two weeks Eva fed him all the rice and borscht he could handle.

While there, Guyenne and the twins showed up quite often. Though Nath was only a preteen, he saw them meeting at the house and wondered if something was afoot. Occasionally, a couple of priests came over as well. Exactly what they were up to he did not know, but it all seemed very clandestine to him. During their gatherings, they sometimes spoke in hushed voices in elliptical ways. It leant an aura of mystery and excitement to the duplex that left Nath intrigued.

He'd already been resisting in ways only kids could do. Nath and his pals would walk past guards at intervals, forcing them to return their preteen bows with similar politeness. That left the guards bowing constantly and became such a problem that the administration changed the rules. Prisoners then needed to bow only when in groups of three or more. When some of the friendly guards asked the kids to sign autograph books they carried, the boys scrawled horrible things in English that the guards couldn't read. Later, when an interpreter translated some of the books, they disappeared and the guards stopped asking.

Outside the camp, the Japanese treated the Filipinos roughly, especially out in the provinces. Word had filtered into Santo Tomas of the Bataan Death March and the horrible conditions in the Allied POW camps at O'Donnell and Cabanatuan. The wives of some of the soldiers there would sometimes receive letters smuggled into the camp by daring friends. The letters routinely begged the wives to send food and money. What little they had, they tried to get to their prisoner husbands, but often their packages were intercepted or proved too little too late. All too often the wives would get the dreaded call to report to the camp commandant's office, where they were told their husbands had died of some unspecified disease.

The treatment of Filipino civilians and the Filamerican Army lit the fuse for a long and bloody guerrilla war throughout the islands. In Manila resistance was coalescing around determined patriots and Filipino soldiers who had escaped from the mass surrenders in the spring of 1942. Guyenne and the Garriz brothers were drawn into the underground almost from the beginning. As Julie convalesced at the Gureviches', she joined their inner circle and became a teenage spy. P.I. was always overprotective of Julie, and at times she bucked against the boundaries he established. Had he known what she was doing and the risks she began to take, he would have erupted and put an end to it.

Of course, he could not know Julie was fighting her own way, as he was in his own. While daughter turned spy, father labored thousands of miles away to put the finishing touches on the plane that he believed would give them the best chance to get back to the Philippines and decisively defeat the Japanese.

35

Margaret, Pappy's Radical, Scrappy, Lethal Engine of Death

October 1942
Brisbane, Australia

Pappy and Jess stood in a long hallway within an ordinary building, staring at a blank wall in front of them. A young officer escorting them slipped between the pair, found a hidden latch, and popped open a small door concealed in the wall. They stepped through and found themselves in a dark, narrow alley. They followed the officer until he came to another wall. He pushed another hidden button, and the wall swung open. Inside lay the inner sanctum of the Allied Intelligence Bureau.

Pappy and Jess Villamor followed the aide until he delivered them to Col. Allison Ind's secret office. A small, bantam-like officer, Ind had been at Nielson Field at the start of the war, working as the intel officer for Fifth Fighter Command. He had survived the retreat into Bataan and stayed with the men trapped there until he'd finally been ordered out. He escaped south, probably expecting to rejoin FEAF. MacArthur had other ideas for him; he served as Colonel Roberts's deputy at AIB.

As a spy master, he'd already made a difference. When the Japanese landed at Buna and pushed across the Owen Stanleys along the Kokoda Trail, Ind inserted teams of "coast watchers" into the jungle around Buna. There, they identified where the Japanese had stored their supplies. That information was passed to General Kenney, whose bomber pilots then had blown their stockpiles to cinders. The Imperial troops on the trail had run out of food, and after their desperate push on Moresby, they had retreated back to the coast, hundreds dying of disease, exhaustion, and starvation.

Ind hoped for similar success in the Philippines, and he had a difficult assignment for Jess. He welcomed his guests and offered them chairs on the other side of his desk, upon which Pappy dropped his feet. Leaning back, he regarded the spy master. Jess, much more formal, sat quietly.

"Pappy," Ind began, "General Kenney says you can't go on this mission."

Pappy looked at him a moment. The war had become more organized since Kenney had arrived. He had stomped on the supply people, fired the ones responsible for hoarding the stuff the frontline units needed, then ordered the quartermasters north to Townsville so their stockpiles would be closer to those who needed them. He'd streamlined organizations—gone were the layers of headquarters all competing with resources. FEAF remained the overall air headquarters, but now there was Fifth Air Force, Fifth Fighter Command, and Fifth Bomber Command below. Pappy had thrived by maneuvering through the administrative cracks; those were gone now. The war had gone corporate, and Pappy had been snatched up by Kenney, who had seen his genius and needed its fruits. He would not allow him to become a spy now.

Pappy felt the opportunity to go back slipping through his fingers.

He asked, "Does that mean he won't let me, or that there are technicalities in the way?"

Jess would be going into Cebu with a covert operations team. He and Pappy had hatched a scheme where the Arkansan would extract him at the end of the mission in either a B-17 or a B-25.

"He said he wouldn't let you—yet."

Yet. Still hope. Ind went on to say that Kenney had no available B-17s for such a scheme, and the B-25s didn't have the range.

Pappy waved his right hand dismissively. He'd rebroken his finger yet again and had pulled Doc Gilmore's cast off to fly down. His pinky stuck out at such an odd angle that Ind asked about it. Pappy brushed him off saying it was a flying mishap.

Then he got back to the point. "I'll fly it there and take a payload, too."

He sat up, his boots slapping the floor, and pulled a pencil out of his shirt pocket. He looked around on Ind's desk, saw a piece of paper, and reached for it. Ind saw it was an intel report from MacArthur's headquarters and pulled it away, handing him a blank sheet instead.

Pappy wrote some numbers down as he said, "We'll want a B-25 to start with. Well now, we got to lighten her, so we take out her guns."

He scratched another set of numbers down. Villamor looked surprised. No guns? Fly to Cebu in a plane without any guns?

"Then we take out the armor plate, then her radio. See, that lightens her up a bit, don't it?"

"But Pappy," Villamor stammered, "no guns, no armor plate, no radio? Are you taking the engines, by chance?"

Pappy went on to explain his plan. No guns, no ammo, no oxygen system. Thoroughly lightened, he'd stick rubber fuel tanks in the bomb bays and in every nook and cranny until the B-25 was little more than a gas bladder with wings. They'd fly right on the water, as was his usual MO, and sneak north from Darwin. There were plenty of places to set a B-25 down on Cebu. He calculated the fuel consumption versus weight saved and concluded that he'd have just enough of a cushion to pull off the mission.

Ind was doubtful. He later wrote Pappy had "enough safety factor to be seen with a good microscope."

Pappy thrived with a razor's edge of a margin. No worries there. He finished running the numbers and announced, "So Jess, you're practically picked up."

His idea was not dismissed, and the three plotters set in place the mission's emergency extraction plan. Jess and his team would be going in by submarine in December; they could need Pappy any time after that. He'd keep the mission in his hip pocket, his ticket back to the Philippines and his family. Maybe Jess could use the guerrilla network to locate Polly and the kids. Then, once he arrived, they'd know where they were and could figure a way to get them out.

The minute Jess radioed for him, he'd strip a B-25 and go north.

In the meantime, Kenney had pulled the Arkansan up to Fifth Air Force Headquarters and made Pappy chief of special projects. His first assignment was just now coming to an end. Kenney sent him to the massive aircraft boneyard at Eagle Farm, outside of Brisbane, with orders to get as many of those wrecks flying as possible. Working with the air depot and service squadron personnel there, the effort yielded dozens of patched together P-40s, P-39s, and B-25s. They cobbled together Frankenplanes; wings from one went onto the fuselage of another. Parts were cannibalized freely until barely anything on the airframes were factory original. It was ugly and certainly violated dozens of prewar guidelines, but none of that mattered anymore, thanks to Kenney. The mechanics and maintainers at Eagle Farm gave the Fifth Air Force an infusion of fighters and bombers right when the men in the front lines needed them most.

The experience at Eagle Farm lifted a huge burden within Pappy. For the first time, he had pull. With General Kenney giving him clearance to go do whatever needed to be done, much of the resistance to his ideas and methods vanished. No longer did he need to rob supply depots—Kenney fired all the ones who thought a job well done meant a warehouse properly stocked and combat units starved for parts.

Now, whatever he needed, he got. The work was still long and arduous, but the real signs of support lifted Pappy's spirits and erased much of the bitterness he wrestled with every day before Kenney's arrival. "Kenney saved me," he once said about this time. "I was losing my sanity, and he came along and believed in what we were doing. That made all the difference."

The Allies still did not have control of the air over New Guinea. If they were ever going to start the long road back to the Philippines, they needed to defeat the Japanese air forces. That fall, a sort of parity had been achieved thanks to the additional aircraft sent north from Eagle Farm. But the air war still hung in the balance.

At the same time, MacArthur was gearing up for his first land counteroffensive. Seeking to capitalize on the Kokoda Trail victory, he was marshalling Australian and freshly arrived American troops to attack the Japanese base at Buna. This would be the first tangible step up New Guinea's northern spine. Tomorrow, Buna. After that, the march back to the Philippines would begin in earnest.

In early November, an intelligence report landed on Kenney's desk that proved of great interest. The report contained the lessons Felix Hardison, a B-17 squadron commander with the Nineteenth Bomb Group, had learned while his unit conducted a new type of ship-killing technique.

Kenney and one of his aides, Maj. William Benn, had brought the idea to MacArthur's air force. Benn had seen it tested in Florida, and both men had read the follow-up reports. The British, Australians, and Germans had all tinkered with the concept, but Kenney would be the driving force behind making it a practical reality.

Every kid has stood by a lake and tried to skip rocks across its surface. Aviators discovered the same principle could be applied to bombs. If done right, they could be slung right into the sides of ships by fast-moving planes flying at extreme low altitude. The British even tried it in the North African desert, bouncing bombs into the sides of German tanks.

It was dubbed "skip-bombing." Benn and Kenney tested it out for themselves during a stop en route across the Pacific to Australia. Both men agreed the tactic had some merit, and when they arrived in theater, Kenney put Benn in command of a B-17 squadron and turned him loose to develop the attack methods.

Taking a gigantic four-engine bomber designed to pound targets from twenty thousand feet and putting it on the deck was a radical departure that raised a lot of eyebrows at first. Benn took his B-17s into Japanese harbors at night, hugging the wave tops while trying to bounce their bombs into merchant ships. Hardison's B-17 squadron soon followed. His report detailed how his pilots had made individual attacks on Japanese ships by diving down from medium altitude to gain speed, then releasing their bombs at no steeper than a twenty-degree angle. The Fort pilots would pull out at between one hundred and five hundred feet, their few forward-firing guns blazing away to try and suppress the ship's antiaircraft defenses.

Hardison concluded the B-17 wasn't the aircraft for such tactics, but medium bombers would be far more suited to them. Even lighter planes, he argued, faced a very difficult attack run. He wrote, "The attacking aircraft is necessarily so vulnerable to anti-aircraft fire that this method appears practicable for use only against lightly armed merchantmen, auxiliaries...or [with] heavy strafing by escorting aircraft..."

Benn's crews had come to similar conclusions. The attacks were much more accurate than anything the AAF had tried before, but to carry them out required getting low and close to Japanese AA guns.

The solution to the AA problem lay with Pappy Gunn. Kenney

had seen the A-20 strafers he'd built, and Pappy wanted to get back to his B-25 project, which the work at Eagle Farm had derailed. That November, Kenney gave him the green light to build twenty-eight gunned B-25s. The general called them "commerce destroyers." He wanted these gunships grouped into a single squadron of elite crews who would be thoroughly trained on skip-bombing tactics.

The new ship-killing mission was given to Capt. Ed Larner's Ninetieth Bomb Squadron, one of the units in Davies's Third Attack. The pilots learned the news and at first felt great enthusiasm. The A-20s had more than proven their worth, and now they would be going into battle as a squadron with 120 forward-firing machine guns threshing anything before them. The firepower and the new tactics seemed like a perfect marriage.

They went to work learning how to skip bombs into the side of ships. Using a wrecked merchantman that had run aground in 1923 in Port Moresby Harbor, the Ninetieth made hundreds of practice runs, puzzling through the smallest details. They learned that they stood the best chance of getting the bombs into the target if they stayed around 250 feet and kept their speed around two hundred miles an hour. The bombs would sometimes skip high and actually bounce over the target ship. Other times they'd fall short, having been released too early or at the wrong angle.

They discovered that they could blow themselves up as they passed over the ship at the same time the bomb struck home. So they turned to delayed fuses, some Aussie made, some American. Pappy had a role in their selection and may have even acquired the first batch of eleven-second Australian fuses for the Ninetieth.

With the new fuses, the bombs would skip, hit the side of the ship, and either puncture it to explode inside, or slide down the hull and explode beside it under the waterline like a supertorpedo. Either way, the blast would cripple a merchantman.

As the crews practiced, Pappy, Li'l Fox, and Jack Evans worked furiously to build the commerce destroyers. It was one thing to complete a prototype like *Pappy's Folly*, but it was quite another to work through a series of modifications that could be standardized and quickly made by the air depots at Brisbane.

They threw themselves into the task with furious intensity. They'd worked through some of the initial issues already but encountered many more obstacles along the way. For starters, the guns had to be racked and charged before they could be fired. They could have set up a hydraulic system to do this, but that would have added more weight. They settled on a simple system of cables and pulleys that ran through the nose to handles bolted to the underside of the instrument panel. Pilot and copilot would have four each, and before the guns could be fired, they'd need to rack those handles back to get rounds chambered.

When Kenney came to visit and see what they were doing, Pappy gave him a tour. When he finished, the general asked, "But Pappy, what about the center of gravity?"

"We threw that out a long time ago, General!"

And they had. The planes would be nose heavy no matter what they did. They did put weights in the rear of the fuselage and made other modifications that minimized the deficiency, but if a crew had to land with no bombs and a full ammo load for some reason, it would be a tricky proposition requiring great skill.

They finished four commerce destroyers by the end of November. Three of them were Dutch B-25s taken over by the Americans.

Margaret was the name of the first B-25 delivered to the Ninetieth that month. The men, some of whom had scoffed at *Pappy's Folly* in the summer, turned out to have a look at their future. Four guns now jutted through the glass nose right where the Norden bomb site would normally be mounted. Four more guns sprouted from side pack blisters set back along the fuselage below the cockpit. Pappy and Jack had originally installed the side packs farther forward, but that had caused havoc with the center of gravity. Moving them back helped that considerably.

Gone was the single flexible machine gun the bombardier would use. Gone was the oxygen system—no need for the weight of all those tanks in a plane designed to fly at two hundred feet. They'd pulled the bottom turret out. In time, that would be replaced with an extra, droppable fuel tank.

The bomb bays could handle thousand-pound demolition bombs, five-hundred-pounders, or scores of Kenney's parafrags. They'd built the aircraft with an eye to versatility; heavy bombs for ship killing, parafrags for ground targets. Pappy had taken the honeycomb rack designed for the A-20s and modified them for the larger bomb bays in the B-25.

They could fly farther, hit harder, and drop more versatile loads of ordnance than anything else in the Southwest Pacific. The pilots regarded *Margaret* with amazement. Maj. John Henebry, one of those who had set eyes on her at Charters Towers that November, described the feeling of that first encounter and what they thought of the new weapon. "Radical, scrappy, lethal," Henebry dubbed the aircraft. "Pappy's engine of death."

Boys being boys, they promptly took *Margaret* over to the gunnery range and blasted another wandering cow into utter oblivion. The infuriated rancher threatened to sue the U.S. government. Of course, it might have helped to keep his herd from grazing on the gunnery range. A payoff was arranged, and the rancher went away mollified, while the pilots went away at once appalled and awestruck over the gruesome power of those .50-cals.

Over the next few weeks, more of Pappy's engines of death reached operational status. As December wore on, they completed twelve more. Kenney had his squadron of ship killers.

Just in time, too.

MacArthur unleashed his first land offensive in New Guinea on November 16, 1942. The ill-trained and equipped Aussie and American troops blundered through the jungle straight into well-camouflaged machine guns protected in palm log bunkers. Attack after attack was thrown back with heavy losses, while thousands of men went down from the heat, poor diet, and disease. In a war where movement reigned supreme, Buna became a jungle version of the First World War's Western Front. Progress wasn't measured in miles but in mere yards.

Kenney's planes supported the suffering men as best they could, but the Japanese were so skilled at concealing their positions that sometimes the men in the jungle didn't see them until they were only a few feet away from them.

The Japanese fought with ferocious skill. Tenaciously, they held each defensive position to the last man. Their willingness to die before retreating shocked the Allies and served as a huge wake-up call to MacArthur. They were not facing a Western army, versed in the merits of surrender rather than needless further sacrifice. These soldiers of the Rising Sun would die before suffering dishonor.

And they fought on with virtually no food, their stockpiles of ammunition giving out, ravaged by disease and the depredations of jungle life. MacArthur committed almost twenty thousand fresh troops to the battle, about half his available combat power. They faced about six thousand starving, unsupplied, and unsupported Japanese troops, some of whom were survivors of the Kokoda Trail.

And those six thousand desperate, resolute Japanese held off the Allied force for over a month. In the final stages of the battle, they stacked their rotting dead atop their trenches and used their comrades' bodies as cover. The stench of the battlefield grew so horrific that some of the Allied troops donned gas masks before each attack.

Both sides were riddled with malaria cases, dengue fever, crotch rot, tropical ulcers, scrub typhus, dysentery, and some diseases that didn't even have names. They suffered profoundly and died anonymously in this remote jungle, which few had ever heard of before their nations flung them across the Pacific.

The battle raged until the end of January, and even then Japanese holdouts continued to snipe at Allied troops for days after. The butcher's bill appalled everyone. Of the thirteen thousand Aussie troops sent in, almost thirty-five hundred became battle casualties. The Americans suffered similarly, and a postbattle study determined that the GIs who had fought in this campaign had had a one in eleven chance of being killed during those three months. When those who fell ill are factored in, almost 14,500 of the twenty thousand men engaged became casualties. Buna became the most costly campaign to forces deployed in the Pacific War for the Allies. As such, it burned itself into the psyche of MacArthur and his ground leaders.

Worst of all, that one battle had cost MacArthur almost half his available combat troops. It was a Pyrrhic victory at best. One more such win would essentially wipe out the Allied ground forces in New Guinea.

For MacArthur and his commanders, the most sobering takeaway from that terrible ordeal was the nature of the enemy at Buna. All this carnage had been inflicted by a trapped, desperate, and isolated force that had already endured unimaginable suffering for much of 1942. They lacked heavy weapons like artillery. They had no tanks and few weapons that could destroy the ones the Allies employed. They had no supply lines, little food. They were a starving, spent force penned in against the Bismarck Sea that had fought virtually to the last man and last bullet without their morale ever crumbling.

What would happen if Allied troops came up against a fresh Japanese force, well supplied and supported? That question dominated GHQ after Buna, and the answer was clear: It would be a bloodbath.

The Japanese knew it, too. At Rabaul, they gathered thousands of hardened veteran soldiers and reinforced them with extra artillery and engineer units. They would go into New Guinea in fast convoy runs, complete with all the supplies, ammo, and food they would need to fight in the jungle for months. If they arrived intact, the whole balance of power in New Guinea would change. The drive back to the Philippines would be delayed or completely derailed.

Those convoys had to be stopped at all costs. Yet in a bloody year of trying, MacArthur's airmen had never been able to do that. Pappy's radical, scrappy, lethal engines of death would soon be put to the ultimate test.

36

The War on Hope

Early 1943
Santo Tomas Internment Camp, Manila, Philippines

The Japanese military took on a greater role in the camp at the end of 1942. As the war started to go badly for them, their treatment of the internees grew increasingly harsh. The civilian administrators saw their authority diminished as new Imperial Army officers arrived and went to battle against the one thing that kept the internees going: hope.

Hope was survival currency in the camp. It fueled endless rumors about victories and imminent arrival of help. MacArthur was coming back. Hitler was dead. The Japanese were being thrown back all across the Pacific—these and countless other whispers spread like wildfire every day. Where they started, nobody seemed to know or care. Just exchanging these stories gave them a sense of spirit and resistance. The Japanese tried everything they could to isolate the camp from the outside world and control what trickle of information reached the prisoners. To start a rumor was to be subversive; it was the chance to strike back against those who had stolen their freedom in a way that could not invite retaliation.

The rumors were often based on real sources of news that prisoners took great pains to procure. Manila newspapers floated around the camp for many months. This at first was not discouraged by the Japanese, because they controlled the papers and had turned them into propaganda organs for the occupation. But as the announcements of great Japanese victories continued to dominate the front page, those battles seemed to be unfolding closer and closer to the Philippines.

Everyone knew what that meant, and the Imperial Army soon cut off that news outlet. Official announcements and a Japanese propaganda rag called *Nishi-Nishi* became the only legal sources for word of what happened beyond the university's iron bars.

Don Bell became the great hero of this struggle. He'd been interned in early 1942 with his family under his real name, Clarence Beliel. Clark Lee, one of the reporters who'd covered the 1941–42 campaign on Luzon, later reported Don had been captured, tortured, and killed. To America, the Voice of Manila was gone forever. In reality, he'd become the Voice of Santo Tomas.

The Japanese had installed a speaker system for morning announcements. Don was one of several who woke the camp up with a bit of music and whatever the Japanese wanted the prisoners to hear that day.

Don proved endlessly creative and would send subtle messages to his fellow inmates with very particular song selections. He'd use elliptical word choices to tell the camp something important, and he usually made it so nuanced the Japanese translators missed his real intent.

When Jimmy Doolittle's Tokyo Raiders bombed Tokyo in April 1942, the camp awoke to the song "It Looks Like Rain in Cherry Blossom Lane." Word circulated around the camp as to its significance, as Don would whisper into the rumor net what it meant.

Another time, he played "Ding Dong! The Witch Is Dead" after a false report of Hitler's demise. He turned out to be wrong about that one, but usually his news was solid gold and spot on.

The Japanese couldn't figure out where the information leaks were coming from, but they assumed there must have been hidden radios in the camp.

The war on hope began with a campaign to ferret those radios out. Japanese troops started descending on the living quarters in the middle of the night in surprise inspections in search of those devices. They turned the camp upside down and didn't find a single radio. Then they started all over again.

Sleepy-eyed, half-starved prisoners would be roused from their bunks and forced to stand at attention outside their rooms while the guards did their work. As always, most people had food, money, or valuables squirreled away in some bolt hole. Waiting to see if the Japanese found their personal stash left everyone frayed, stressed, and trembling with fear. Polly took these moments especially hard. Between some of the food she'd hoarded and the outlawed cash she'd used to keep the family going, she had a lot to lose. If they'd been found, surely Mr. Ohashi at the very least would cancel Julie's passes. It could mean her death after all. Yet, she couldn't give her stash up without compromising her family's ability to endure. Stuck between two bad consequences, she trusted in God and her sewing skills to ensure the mattress was never too closely examined.

Despite the ramped-up surprise inspections, news continued to flow into the camp. The battles unfolding in the Solomon Islands and New Guinea became daily topics of conversations. Word of new planes, new warships, and their nation's mobilizing to fight its way back to the Philippines kept spirits up even in the worst moments.

One day, Nath and Paul decided to make a run to the storage room behind the seminary. Such adventures now were increasingly dangerous—the Japanese troops and their inmate informers were hypervigilant. Still, they'd run out of bartering material and they decided it was worth the risk. They slipped into the storage room and moved like barefoot wraiths through the stacks of random stuff in search of more Bibles to cut up for tobacco paper.

The darkness was punctuated by bolts of light spearing in through small windows. As they crept along, they stayed in the shadows, weaving through the room until they found the holy books. Quietly, they each opened a Bible, started pulling pages out of the binding and tucking them away in their short pockets.

A noise froze them in place. They glanced around and saw nothing. But then they heard it again, closer this time. They ducked and went to ground, praying there wasn't a Japanese guard searching for them.

The noise resolved into footsteps. Light, quick. They traced a course from the door straight for them. Hearts pounding, the boys could only wait and trust their ability to hide would prove better than the guard's ability to seek.

The footsteps ceased, replaced by a rustling.

Nath ventured a look, hardly daring to take a breath. Peering over the Bibles, he saw a figure crouched beneath the silhouette of a stuffed gorilla, part of the museum's collection that had been stored here.

It wasn't a guard. It was Don Bell. He waited beside the gorilla, listening and glancing around the darkness while Paul prairie-dogged beside Nath to see for himself who had joined them.

Don did not see them. The man whose words had brought the Pearl Harbor attack home to everyone in the Philippines, who had stood on rooftops during air raids to give blow-by-blow accounts to his audience, now looked furtive and alert.

At last, satisfied nobody had followed him, he reached for the gorilla. The boys watched, astonished, as first Don's hand disappeared in the animal's bum, then his forearm and elbow. Pretty soon, almost his entire arm vanished into the gorilla.

He extracted a small radio a moment later. He flipped it on, keeping its volume low. It hummed to life, and a tinny English voice whispered into the storage room. Ear to the small speaker, the sound of the broadcast traveled only a few feet. The boys couldn't hear its words, but could make out the reporter's tone.

They'd stumbled across Don Bell's secret source.

He listened to the broadcast, shut the radio off, and tucked it back up inside the gorilla. With a last look around, he slipped away as he had come.

One by one, the boys crawled over to the gorilla, plunged their hands inside its rear and felt the secret device. This was power. The Japanese would surely reward them for revealing this. Don Bell would be seriously punished. He might even be dragged off to Fort Santiago and turned over to the Japanese secret police. The boys had the chance to curry favor and gain extra food and privileges for their families.

They would never do that. They hated informers more than they hated the Japanese. They'd seen how their own people had turned against each other to score an extra scrap of food, and it disgusted them. Those days when they once believed adults to be virtuous and noble were gone. Now, the boys of Mr. Leake's rooms had their own code and values. Most important—they would never be rats.

Besides, hope for all of them lived inside that gorilla. Those glimpses of the world beyond the walls kept everyone going. Hope and the code won out. The boys vowed to protect Don Bell's secret, and none of them ever revealed it to anyone else inside the camp.

Because of Don Bell, they knew the tide had turned against the Japanese. They knew America was on the offensive. They were coming, and they believed with all their heart that their dad would be leading the way through the front gate when their hour of liberation finally arrived.

They believed in that day; it was their talisman against the oppression of the present. But they all had their own moments of doubt. P.I. was not a man to stay out of a fight. The thought of him dying in combat and that reunion never happening plagued their worst nightmares.

It was the unknown that preyed on them.

They knew P.I. was still alive, out there somewhere doing his thing up to the spring of 1942. After the fall of the Philippines, internees arrived from the Southern Islands who told tales of Pappy Gunn, the man who could do anything with an aircraft. They spoke in hushed tones to Polly, relating what they knew and had seen. He'd become a hero, and the tales of his exploits lingered in the islands long after he had been forced to flee them. But their latest knowledge of his whereabouts was a year old by the spring of '43.

One day, a boy approached Polly and told her a man needed to see her in the hospital; he had news about her husband. She nervously entered the ward. A screen had been erected around one bed, and the staff looked nervously around while some Japanese walked through the facility. When they had their backs turned, a Filipino motioned to Polly and gestured to the screen. Polly saw her chance. She slipped behind it.

On a cot lay a man on his stomach. He had been beaten and tortured by the Japanese and was in such bad shape he could barely move. Polly looked down at the pitiful wreck his body had become and eased to her knees beside his cot and waited for him to speak. He was in such bad shape, the words would be an effort.

The stress of the not knowing P.I.'s status or whereabouts would crush her if she let it. She could not afford that; she had to remain strong for her children. *Gone with the Wind* had been a favorite film of hers. Polly took a lesson from the privation the Southerners faced after the war. She forced herself to put P.I.'s well-being out of her mind. She focused all her energy on the daily issues of survival. It was her Scarlett O'Hara coping method. Deal with it later; other things have to be handled in the moment.

This was the later.

Behind the screen, their captors not far away, she would learn something. Be it bad news or good, at least she would *know*. She could pray for him as she pictured where he was—if he was still alive.

When he was out on nocturnal flights before the war, the family used to pray for P.I.'s safe return. Polly used to say, "My prayers flew P.I. in on the beam." The beam was a radio signal pilots would use to navigate with at night or in bad weather.

In Santo Tomas, in her few alone moments, she prayed for P.I. to ride the beam home to her. At times, during midnight storms, the lonely sound of a plane's engines would come to her ears. She would know out there above the city, a Japanese pilot sought some way down through the clouds. Polly didn't hate; she didn't blame. There was no malice in her, and she did everything she could to keep bitterness from infecting herself and her children. She'd listen to the plane and say a prayer for its pilot, too. Enemy or not, that was still somebody's loved one up there who needed help getting home.

Now, seeing this broken man must have tested both Polly's faith and sense of forgiveness. He was wracked with pain, his body ruined by barbaric acts. Exactly who he was, Polly never learned. He looked Filipino, and somehow he'd been in touch with the guerrillas or had been one himself. Why he'd been taken to Santo Tomas instead of someplace else was anyone's guess.

How he had information about P.I. also remained a mystery. Perhaps he'd picked up the message from Jess Villamor on Cebu. Whatever the case, who he was and how he got his information did not matter. The message did.

His head lay on the cot, lips a few inches from Polly's ear; she waited breathlessly for the words to come.

"Your husband," he whispered weakly, "your husband lives."

37

Blood and Fire

January–March 1943
Australia

While the crisis brewed in New Guinea, Pappy lost Jack Fox, who returned to California to show the North American Aviation engineers just what they'd been doing to the B-25s at Eagle Farm. Pappy wasn't happy about this development. He and Li'l Fox had become close friends as they worked to achieve what others thought impossible. As a joke, they'd unofficially incorporated as "South American Aviation Corporation," and all of the letters Pappy later sent to North American were signed "President, South American Inc." Their friendship and engineering collaboration had yielded amazing developments. Pappy was eager to do more with him.

When Jack Fox hadn't returned by mid-January, he dashed off a missive to North American that concluded with:

Another great error committed by your command has been the failure to return to this company its inefficient, illiterate, and broken down operations manager who answers to the name when called like a dog "Jack Nero Fox." An urgent request was made upon delivery to you to have this specimen stretched or blown up to normal size and returned to this Company. Realizing you will take due note of these demands we will expect immediate action to be taken.

> Respectfully Yours,
> P.I. Gunn
> President, South American Inc.

As work continued at Eagle Farm without Li'l Fox, the Ninetieth Squadron's pilots stepped up their training pace. Their commerce destroyers functioned well, and as they got used to the new feel of the aircraft, they began pushing its envelope to see just what it could do in flight.

While they skipped practice bombs into the Port Moresby hulk, the Japanese snuck two reinforcement convoys into rear area bases in New Guinea. Neither suffered any losses. A smaller third one sped to Lae with a few thousand troops and some supplies. MacArthur needed that convoy at the bottom of the Bismarck Sea. Kenney ordered it attacked, and his B-25s and B-17s tried to knock it out with conventional tactics. They succeeded only in sinking one ship. The others delivered the supplies and men ashore.

MacArthur had been failed by his airmen yet again. Kenney knew they couldn't fail the next time. The stakes were simply too high.

In mid-February, reconnaissance planes detected another shipping concentration at Rabaul. Intelligence gathered from decoded radio transmissions indicated the Japanese were planning a massive resupply effort, probably for their men at Lae. The Fifty-First Infantry Division and a force of elite Japanese Marines, complete with artillery, vehicles, food, ammunition, and fuel had been tasked for this new mission. They would be carried aboard eight transports and eight fast, well-armed destroyers. Sixteen ships would bring in at least eight thousand men with all their gear and supplies to keep them in fighting shape for months.

Kenney read the reports and alerted his leaders, telling them to cut back on missions and get as many aircraft ready to fly as they could. No more going in against Japanese ships in penny-packet strikes. The Canadian-American wanted to hit them hard with everything his squadrons could get in the air. Pappy wanted nothing more than to fly north and join his old outfit, but Kenney expressly ordered him to remain out of combat. That didn't matter; according to Kenney, Pappy went north anyway.

On March 2, 1943, the convoy was spotted at sea. All of the Fifth Air Force squadron leaders met in one epic briefing. Nothing like that had ever happened before, and it generated a sense of excitement and purpose the aviators had not felt.

The briefing detailed the convoy's composition and probable destinations. They'd all be going after it the following morning. There were sure to be Zeroes overhead, but Kenney had a solution for that. He now had a handful of fast, long-range, twin-engined fighters known as P-38 Lightnings. They'd fly cover for the entire strike force.

The B-17s would lead the way, but instead of lumbering along five miles above the swells, Kenney ordered them to stay below ten thousand feet. Next in would be a squadron of recently arrived level-bombing B-25s. Behind these two waves would come Ed Larner's ship killers, escorted by a squadron of heavily armed Australian fighters who would strafe the enemy warships to suppress their antiaircraft defenses.

The Aussie escort was welcome, but Larner's men had read stories of the low-level torpedo attacks launched against the Japanese at Midway. They'd seen the newspaper photos of Ensign George Gay, the sole survivor of a squadron of fourteen planes. In fact, almost all the Navy's low-level torpedo bombers had been wiped out in one morning.

Going after lightly armed transports and coastal shipping was one thing. They were confident they could take out those kinds of targets. But Kenney was ordering them in against men-of-war. They expected to lose half their number at least. Few men in the Third Attack slept well that night.

The next morning, the go order came just after breakfast. Larner didn't have time to give his men a thorough brief; besides, he'd already done that the night before. He simply said, "Rendezvous at Cape Ward Hunt—let's go!"

Pappy's engines of death rose from their jungle airdrome and sped north. They reached Cape Ward Hunt in clear blue sky and saw a beautiful sight. Gone were the days they'd take on the Japanese in formations of three or four planes. Now, they linked up with almost a hundred bombers and fighters flown by Aussie and American alike.

The B-17s led out, thirteen of them guarded by flights of fork-tailed P-38 Lightnings. Below and behind came a squadron of B-25s. And behind them came the Aussie fighter-bombers and Ed Larner's ship killers, broken into two flights of six strafers each. Larner commanded one; John Henebry had the other six.

Zeroes hit them just before ten o'clock. The Lightnings waded into them, and a sprawling air battle raged over the bombers. For once, the Zeroes couldn't get through to do serious damage.

The convoy came into sight. One ship had been sunk the day before. Now, the remaining fifteen steamed in a long rectangular formation, three heavily armed destroyers on either side, the vulnerable transports in two parallel lines in the middle. Two large destroyers led the way to Lae.

The Japanese, used to being bounced around by near misses from bombing B-17s, trained their heaviest guns on the Forts. As Larner's men rushed toward the convoy, they saw the destroyers erupt in sheets of flame as scores of antiaircraft guns thundered to life. The sky filled with arcing tracers and exploding black clouds of flak.

Next came the level-bombing B-25s, pelting the Japanese ships with strings of demolition bombs. The vessels twisted and turned to avoid their fall, and soon their stately formation devolved into pure chaos as every ship captain maneuvered on his own.

The Aussies dove into the fray, guns blazing. The destroyers protecting the south side of the convoy spotted them coming down to wave-top level, and their crews assumed them to be torpedo bombers. They turned bow-on to the attackers, the standard counter to such an attack. It was a disastrous move. The ships masked their own AA guns while giving the Aussies the chance to rake the destroyers from bow to stern. Their decks exploded with cannon strikes and light machine fire. Sailors and Japanese soldiers dove for cover and were torn apart by the fusillade.

Then the Aussies were over them, racing for the merchant ships whose decks were crammed with men and cargo.

Larner broke radio silence and announced, "I got the cruiser. You guys pick your own targets."

He banked left and dove from two thousand feet onto what was actually the destroyer *Shirayuki*. Armed with almost three dozen anti-aircraft machine cannons plus six dual-purpose five-inch guns, the ship threw up a formidable wall of lead and fire. Flak bursts exploded less than a hundred feet from some of the Aussies and Americans as they closed the distance, but then at fifteen hundred yards, Larner tapped his gun trigger—and in that moment, everything changed.

The Japanese saw his B-25 boring in on them seemingly explode with fire. Flames jetted from its nose, and some on decks that morning thought it had been hit by flak. They had no idea they were witnessing eight closely placed machine guns unleashing ten bullets a second. They sped across the divide between plane and target at 2,750 feet per second. Each belt had its own rhythm: one tracer for sighting, two armor piercing rounds for punch, two incendiary rounds for fire and mayhem.

A second and a half later, the hail of heavy machine gun bullets struck *Shirayuki* with unimaginable force. The decks splintered; gun positions simply disintegrated. The men manning them didn't just die: The velocity and mass of these .50-caliber bullets pulverized them, blew limbs off, and left in their wake such carnage that nobody who bore witness to it ever forgot its trauma.

Larner walked the rudders from left to right, and the bullet storm sawed across the destroyer's length, demolishing the bridge and killing or wounding everyone there. Fires broke out; secondary explosions went off as the .50s detonated ready ammunition. In seconds, the *Shirayuki* went from a fighting man-of-war throwing up its own wall of steel to a broken ship of death.

John Henebry and the rest of the Ninetieth saw the destroyer's antiaircraft guns cease firing and thoughts of suicide missions evaporated. This wasn't Midway; the Navy didn't have this kind of firepower. These B-25s were ship killers. Below them, the Japanese quailed before their firepower.

They piled in, their Mitchells spewing sheets of flame as they strafed and maneuvered down to the whitecaps. Incoming fire hit two B-25s, but neither went down. The rugged birds stayed in the battle, their crews skipping bombs and barreling over mastheads.

They attacked from multiple angles at once, intertwined now with the Aussies. Confused and overwhelmed, some of the Japanese panicked as their ships fell victim to bombs and bullets.

Larner reached the waves, leveled off and drove for his destroyer target. His copilot toggled two bombs. One hit a five-inch gun turret, the other exploded right alongside the ship, heeling it over even as an ammunition magazine belowdecks blew up and vaporized the destroyer's stern.

Larner still had two bombs and he meant to use them. He banked around and barreled back into the convoy, destroyers on either flank. This time, he landed a bomb in a transport, and near missed another destroyer as he egressed from the target area.

Around him, his other ship killers scored hit after hit. One strafed the transport *Teiyo Maru* until less than forty yards from its crowded decks. The pilot, Chuck Howe, could see Japanese soldiers in full battle rattle being swept away by his hurricane of bullets. They died by the dozen before his bombs ever left their racks.

All through the convoy, juking planes danced across the wave tops as ships exploded and smoke poured skyward. The bomb hits blew men like matchsticks into the air. Arms flailing, they fell like rain into the Bismarck Sea.

Aboard the destroyer *Tokitsukaze*, a nightmare scape unfolded. A survivor recalled how a strafing attack pinned him in a compartment, riddling it with over a hundred holes. As he came out on deck, he found dead and dying littered everywhere. Then a bomb skipped into the hull, pierced it, and speared through the heart of the ship's engineering spaces before exploding through the other side of the ship. The blast killed dozens and the ship went dead in the water. As it slowly sank, blood poured over the decks and through the bomb hole, tinging the water red around the doomed ship's hull.

The blood in the water attracted sharks. As the Japanese abandoned their burning ships, the sharks began to feed.

Robert Chatt had painted the nose of his engine of death with menacing eyes and a terrifying shark's mouth that grinned fanged teeth around the .50s. It must have been a fearsome sight, bearing down with its guns afire, its wicked grin flashing over its target. He strafed and bombed the destroyer *Arashio* and hit it with three of four bombs. One completely demolished the bridge and flung the remains of the navigator against a broken, shredded window. A survivor emerged from belowdecks and was confronted with the sight of the man impaled on the glass and twisted steel.

With no bridge and no officers left alive there, the ship ran out of control. The other bombs had jammed its rudder, destroyed a gun turret, and left the decks awash in blood and gore. Now, it ran through the convoy out of control and slammed full speed into the supply ship *Nojima*. The collision touched off ammunition and fuel in the ship's hold, and in minutes *Nojima* was wreathed in the flames. Both ships went down.

Behind the Ninetieth came Pappy's other creation, the Third Attack's Eighty-Ninth Bomb Squadron. The A-20s, operating at the limit of their range, strafed and bombed their way through the shattered convoy, contributing hits and tearing up men and materiel with their nose guns. The B-17s and level bombing B-25s contributed hits that morning, too, and the Aussies inflicted tremendous casualties with their furious strafing runs. Larner's commerce destroyers inflicted the vast majority of the damage. Twelve B-25s claimed thirty-nine bomb hits on a convoy of fifteen ships.

They went back in the afternoon, the B-25s arrowing over a sea of blood and ruin. Debris littered the wave tops, and amid them Japanese survivors struggled feebly as hundreds of sharks circled their helpless prey. Those who bore witness to the sight later swore the Bismarck Sea ran red that afternoon.

They finished the ships off. All eight transports went down along with four of the eight destroyers. The ones that survived had largely fled the area after rescuing as many men out of the water as they could.

It wasn't over. The next day, the Allied planes reappeared over the stranded sailors and soldiers in the water. They'd spent a tortured night at sea, watching as great whites and hammerheads tore their comrades apart while clinging to anything that would float, praying for salvation they knew would not come.

And the Allies raked them again and again. Desperately, they fought back with whatever they had. A few rifles, a machine gun in a landing craft or two—but these paltry weapons could not save them. Exactly how many men died in the water will never be known, but the attacks were justified based on the toll those Imperial soldiers would have taken on Allied troops had they reached New Guinea.

Buna had taught the Allies that even a starving, half-dead Japanese soldier would fight with unparalleled tenacity. There would be no mercy shown to such resolute and courageous troops. They needed to be killed.

Pappy watched the strafers carry out their grisly work from above in a B-17. General Kenney prohibited Pappy from flying combat with the Third during the battle. He considered him too valuable to lose in a fight, no matter how crucial that fight was. Pappy obeyed the spirit of the order at the outset of the battle, but he could not contain himself. He needed to see what his commerce destroyers could do to the Japanese.

He hitched a ride on a B-17 during one of the last days of the battle. From its perch about ten thousand feet over the Bismarck Sea, Pappy saw the wave tops littered with debris, lifeboats, and men. The B-25s and A-20s made their gun runs, and he watched the carnage with cold eyes. When he wanted to win, he never fought fair. He instilled that in Nath—deliver the blows however you can to ensure your opponent can never hurt you again. After the Philippines, after Java, after losing so many friends in futile raids that did no damage to the enemy, here at last was the payoff.

It was horrifying. Pappy stared at the scene but never felt a sense of exultation, of victory. After he returned to Moresby, he never spoke of the battle or the things he witnessed during that flight. There were limits, even for him, and while he knew the crisis demanded a desperate response, the slaughter of so many helpless men in the water was something he never cared to remember.

Pappy's strafers poured over a quarter million bullets into the Japanese convoy and its survivors during the battle. Prior to Bismarck Sea, high-level bombing against ships scored a 3 percent hit rate by Allied estimations. The number was actually even smaller. Pappy's ship killers put almost 40 percent of their bombs into their targets. Masthead bombing was the wave of the future.

Those survivors drifted all over the region in the days and weeks ahead. One group actually blew ashore on Guadalcanal Island on the far side of the Coral Sea, where an Allied patrol found and shot them. Others straggled ashore at Kiriwina Island, where Aussie troops took a few prisoner, killed the others. In the process, they discovered entire caches of prime intelligence material, one of the lesser known outcomes of the battle. One batch of documents included the names of every senior Japanese officer in the Imperial Army and the unit he commanded. It turned out to be a gold mine; the Allies hadn't had a decent picture of the size and number of units in the Japanese Army. These pages gave them its complete order of battle.

Kenney's air force came of age that day in March. Pappy's gunships played the central role in the destruction wrought upon the Japanese. Casualty estimates vary wildly from three thousand dead to upward of ten thousand. The exact toll will never be known.

What MacArthur knew at the time was this: the ship killers had wiped out an entire reinforced Japanese infantry division, a force larger than the one his twenty thousand infantrymen had fought at Buna for three months. The cost of this victory in the Bismarck Sea? Thirteen Allied airmen, two bombers, and four fighters. After juxtaposing this against the fourteen thousand Aussie and Americans killed, wounded, or enfeebled by disease at Buna, MacArthur became a born-again air power true believer. His aviators finally came through, and the victory they gave their general turned the tide irrevocably against the Japanese in the Southwest Pacific. The strafers and the new tactics made the difference. Pappy's experiments had succeeded beyond his boldest boasts. Now, his gunships would be mass-produced, and the drive to the Philippines would be kicked into high gear. That success came with an unintended cost. In mid-March, Kenney ordered Pappy to the States to meet with the Army Air Force engineers at Wright Field, who still insisted such modifications could not be done. Then he wanted him to go to Inglewood and work directly with the North American staff at the B-25 factory there to standardize the mods so they could be churned out.

He left Australia around March 20, 1943, just as Jess Villamor and his team ran into trouble on Cebu. The Japanese had closed in, and they were on the lam now. From his isolated guerrilla's nest in the Central Philippines, Jess radioed back to MacArthur personally and pleaded for Pappy Gunn to come and rescue them in his stripped-down flying-fuel-tank of a B-25. While nobody was willing to take a Mitchell north through thousands of miles of Japanese-held territory, the Navy ultimately retrieved Jess and his team via submarine later that spring.

While Pappy winged eastward for the California coast, the inmates of Santo Tomas had begun to slowly starve to death.

38

Reconnections and Revolutions

March 1943
Stateside

Pappy Gunn reached San Francisco in the dead of night, a briefcase handcuffed to his wrist. He stepped off the plane that he had
caught in Hawaii and headed for the terminal to find a phone. As
he walked, he checked his BUSHIPS watch. Two in the morning,
Texas time. The call he needed to make was nine years coming.
It could have waited until morning, but patience was not Pappy's
strong suit. He found a phone and asked for a long distance operator,
to whom he recited the number he had never called before.

Time to make amends.

He had not spoken to his sister, Jewell, since the day he had said
good-bye to their dying mother in 1933. Jewell sent word to him
in San Diego that he needed to come home, and he hurried back
on emergency hardship leave. It was his first time in Quitman since
he'd brought Polly home after their wedding. Though he hadn't visited, he'd spent his entire Navy career sending his mom the bulk of
his paycheck so she would never have to experience privation again.

The call clicked through as the operator made the connection.

Through the handset, Pappy heard Jewell's husband, Haz, sleepily say hello.

Pappy's voice shocked him into silence. The family did not have a clue as to where Pappy was or even if he was still alive. For months, Jewell suffered terribly, frantic with worry over his fate.

Before the war, Haz had moved his family to Texarkana, Texas, from Searcy, Arkansas. He still owned the hotels and a brothel or two that his pious wife did not know about, but his days of rumrunning were long over.

Pappy listened to the quick update, then learned Jewell wasn't home. She was in South Dakota visiting one of her sons, who was in the Army Air Force now. Pappy told Haz he would be in Dayton, Ohio, for a few weeks, and they agreed to work out a way for Jewell to come and visit.

In the meantime, Pappy needed to cover a lot of ground in little time. He said his good-byes, hung up the phone, and headed east.

Exactly where Pappy went from San Francisco remains unclear. He popped up next at Eglin Field, Florida, where one of his cousins picked him up and drove him to Pensacola. According to the family, he showed up in a rumpled, reeking khaki shirt that he'd worn since leaving Australia. He was still carrying the briefcase cuffed to his wrist. When his cousin asked about it, Pappy only told him, "I've been ordered not to take it off until I deliver it personally to General Arnold in Washington D.C."

Hap Arnold was the commander in chief of the United States Army Air Force. Pappy's response awed his cousin, who drove him home to Pensacola and the house that Polly's father had built on Navy Boulevard. It looked the same as when he'd last seen it years before, in the 1930s. Standing right on the water and stoutly constructed with ship spikes for nails in its thick foundation, it had weathered countless storms that blew flat other homes.

In Pensacola, Pappy learned the fate of his loved ones. Sometime in 1942, the Japanese allowed Polly to write one short postcard to her parents, telling them of her location. It took months for the postcard to travel the globe aboard neutral vessels and find its way into the mailbox affixed beside the Crosbys' front door in Pensacola. Now, that spring, Pappy read her words with a twin sense of relief and anxiety. At least they were alive at Santo Tomas. They survived the bombings and the fall of Manila. That was the good news. The bad news was the Japanese held them captive, and captives he knew were never treated well by the land of the Rising Sun.

Pappy spent only a night with his in-laws. Still rumpled, in need of a shower, he departed the next morning with his cousin, who drove him back to Eglin. After hasty good-byes, Pappy later recounted, he flew on to D.C. to meet with Gen. Hap Arnold, and it was a meeting he'd dreaded.

General Kenney flew into D.C. about the same time for several high-level meetings following the Battle of Bismarck Sea. According to Kenney, when he met with Hap Arnold, a discussion ensued about Pappy's modified gunships. Arnold brought several aviation engineers from Air Force Materiel Command into the meeting who argued that such modifications simply could not be done. Kenney assured them they already had been, which left them stunned. Arnold asked Kenney who made the modifications, and how they were carried out in the field. Kenney related Pappy's story, and Arnold decided to send him to Air Force Materiel Command headquarters in Ohio to document how he carried out the mods. Kenney wanted B-25 gunships coming to him straight from the factory so he wouldn't have to modify them in Australia. If that was to happen, it would require changes to the North American Aviation production lines, and that might affect the production rate in the short term.

Kenney grudgingly accepted the arrangement, but he was eager to get Pappy back to Australia after his sojourn in the States. In the meantime, he asked Arnold for more aircraft and combat groups, a request that the senior American air general denied.

Not long afterward, Kenney secured a meeting with President Roosevelt and detailed for him what the Fifth Air Force had accomplished at Bismarck Sea. Making an end run around Arnold, Kenney asked the president for reinforcements. He needed more planes and more people. Roosevelt agreed and later told Arnold to make it happen. Being outmaneuvered by one of his theater generals could not have sat well with Hap Arnold, and Pappy was set to meet with him after that dustup.

Pappy arrived in Washington fearing that Kenney might have thrown him under the bus if the Stateside powers-that-be took issue with his modifications. He considered this likely, especially after all his encounters with engineering officers so resistant to making any changes to the airframes. As he reached Arnold's office in the Pentagon, Pappy wondered if he might even be court-martialed.

Pappy was ushered into Arnold's presence, where a number of engineering officers greeted him coldly with demands to know what he was doing in those depots in Australia. The engineers already heard Kenney's descriptions and remained highly skeptical. After they vented, Pappy said simply, "Look, I'm not an engineer. I'm not even an educated man. But what we have done works."

He put the briefcase he carried all the way from Australia onto the table. Opening it, he pulled out a sheaf of photographs taken with cameras installed on the gunships. Some depicted the tests and practice attacks on the hulk at Port Moresby, but some apparently included stunning scenes from Bismarck Sea. Pappy explained that he'd wanted to document these aircraft and the new tactics, so he had installed three cameras in each plane—one in the tail, one in the nose, and one in the belly. The combat imagery was unlike anything

Arnold or the engineers had seen before. Along with the photos were probably some of the blueprints for the modifications.

The engineers stared, jaws open. The gunships would go into mass production.

On March 23, 1943, Pappy returned to Florida and piloted a reconnaissance version of the B-25 between Eglin and Orlando. He carried aboard with him several staff officers from Air Force Materiel Command, with whom he would be working in the weeks ahead. The Army Air Force had first tested skip-bombing tactics at Orlando earlier in the war, so it is quite possible Pappy was taking the brass down to the Orlando gunnery range to give them a demonstration of what the Fifth Air Force had developed in theater.

En route to Orlando, the B-25 suffered total hydraulic failure, and Pappy couldn't get the landing gear to extend and lock into position. He ended up dumping fuel over a nearby lake then belly-landing on a grassy patch between two runways at Orlando—his fourth known crash since December 7, 1941. He set the bird down so gently that it suffered minimal damage. Only the props, engines, and bomb bay doors needed to be replaced afterward, and nobody was hurt. Pappy filled out some paperwork after the crash, then headed for Ohio without giving the incident a second thought.

Wright Field outside of Dayton served as the engineering and testing hub for the Army Air Force. The engineers in uniform there were conformed, cautious, and meticulous. They were bureaucratic and paperwork friendly and devoted to routine. Pappy blew into town like a Pacific typhoon, all ad hoc, make-it-work and get-her-done. It didn't take but a few days for him to blow fuses over the nine-to-five culture and obsession with documentation. Out in the Pacific, nobody cared if you could write a report. What mattered was flexibility of thought and the ability to make things work.

He worked insane hours, growing increasingly restless as he tried to impart his knowledge to an unwilling audience. Fortunately, he found an ally in Maj. Tom Gerrity, who was one of the Twenty-Seventh Bomb Group originals and among the last to make it out of Bataan. Gerrity had returned home just before Pappy and received an assignment to a staff post at Wright. When Pappy showed up, he and his wife offered him a place to stay. Jewell came into town a few days later via train, and after a tearful reunion she stayed with the Gerritys as well.

Each night, Pappy returned from the field boiling with anger at what he considered the straitjacketed environment there. At the same time, he must have felt even more and more cut off from his family. He spoke of them constantly to Jewell, often getting emotional. He was suffering, using work as an escape while flaying himself at night for leaving them behind. Pappy perseverated over his family for a year, swallowing most of the guilt and pain to hide his feelings from the men of the Third Attack. Back in the States, something changed in him. He couldn't hold the pain in any longer; it poured out of him to anyone who would listen. Every surviving account by those who met Pappy on this trip mentions this.

Tom and his wife finally concluded Pappy needed a night out on the town to get him out of his head, at least for a few hours.

They hit one of the local Dayton hot spots for dinner, drinks, and dancing with some of the Gerritys' friends from around the post. Pappy's naturally festive spirit percolated to the surface. By the time dinner had ended, he had become the center of attention, spinning stories and laughing through them.

At length, he asked a married friend of the Gerritys' to dance. She tried to defer, saying she wasn't particularly adept at it. "That's okay," Pappy said brightly, "I dance in seven languages."

Sure enough, he took over the dance floor, stomping out a New Guinea native ritual dance as onlookers gawked. By the next song the band played, Pappy was doing a jig peppered with polka steps. He and the entire family had taken hula lessons in Hawaii, so he started swaying island style as his audience laughed and cheered. Mrs. Gerrity later wrote, "[Pappy] created quite a sensation and enjoyed himself hugely."

When they got back home later that night, Tom and his wife went to tuck their son in bed. Pappy followed them and watched from the doorway as they kissed their boy good night.

When they turned around, they saw Pappy standing there, tears welling in his eyes.

Unabashed, Pappy said, "This reminds me of the evenings when my wife and I have been out having fun and then coming home and tucking our children in bed."

The devotion evident in his voice moved the Gerritys. Pappy held his gaze on them and added, "You know, all four of our children and Mrs. Gunn are at Santo Tomas, and I'm going to get them out if it is the last thing I ever do."

The remaining days at Wright Field passed quickly. Pappy helped the staff create the documentation needed to get the field modifications of both the A-20s and B-25s into production. Those changes were then sent to the corporations building the aircraft and the bomb racks for them.

As the final part of getting these birds built the way Kenney needed, Pappy was sent to North American's headquarters in Southern California, where for three weeks he worked closely with owner Dutch Kindleberger and his team of engineers. He received a much different welcome at the factory there, probably thanks in part to Jack Fox's consistent updates on what they had been doing in Australia. Not only were the North American folks receptive to the new modifications, they wanted to take them even further. Together, they worked out different armament configurations and even increased the B-25's nose gun armament to ten .50s. Still later, they'd up that to twelve. Another variant, which North American began experimenting with in October 1942, included a 75mm cannon in the nose. Pappy loved that idea; there was no such thing as too much firepower as far as he was concerned.

He made many friends at North American during those three weeks. They saw him work relentlessly hard, pushing himself and everyone around him to create, innovate, and push past the boundaries of conventional thought. That flexibility ensured North American would become the world's premier aircraft corporation for the next decade, producing some of the greatest airplanes ever built. Pappy found kindred spirits at North American and remained close to them long after his three weeks in Southern California came to an end.

As rewarding as this last stop proved to be, Pappy's personal suffering kept boiling to the surface. He spoke openly of his grief to his new North American friends. While Pappy surely knew the importance of his trip back to the States, he felt he was in the wrong place. He needed to be back in the Southwest Pacific, flying and fighting, creating and improvising, as MacArthur continued his campaign to return to the Philippines. By the time he finished up at North American Aviation, he was like a caged animal.

When Pappy departed for Australia in June, he left behind an indelible mark at North American. The B-25 had been in danger of being eclipsed by the Martin B-26 Marauder as the standard USAAF medium bomber. Pappy's innovations gave the Mitchell a new lease on life. The company made minimal changes on the production line to accommodate the gunship changes, but established modification centers at Kansas City and several other places around the country in former airline overhaul facilities. There, the finished bombers would be tailored to whatever theater of war needed them. The Pacific-bound B-25s frequently emerged with gunship configurations and then were flown to the West Coast for shipment to Kenney's crews.

A revolution had begun at home. Now it was time to see what a gunship air force could do to the enemy abroad.

Part Three

Homeward Bound

39

Later Legends

Hear about Pappy? Stuck a 75mm cannon in a P-38 and sank a cruiser with it!

That's Pappy Gunn. He shot down sixty Japanese planes over Rabaul with those strafer B-25s we helped him build.

Pappy went behind enemy lines. Stole a Japanese bulldozer and got it working so he could finish the airstrip on Leyte...

Craziest thing he ever did was fly across Southeast Asia, no guns of course, dropping propaganda leaflets and "I Shall Return" matchbooks.

Saw him in China once. Just showed up at our airfield. On his way to Mongolia, I think, to help set up some sort of weather station for the Fifth Air Force.

He was supposed to be promoted to colonel, but he pissed off General Whitehead, who looked him in the eyes and scooped his eagles off his desk and dumped 'em in a drawer. That was that.

Heard him say we could survive in the jungle no problem if we went down. Just eat bugs, like centipedes. Said all you need to do is strip off all their legs, hold him up and lower it in your mouth and sort of just suck the juices right out of him.

He told us to look around rocks and caves. "Find a nice vampire bat. Them's good eatin'."

Looked at that staff guy and said, "How the hell would you know anything about flying? You've never been higher than a flight of stairs!" Made a bunch of Hollywood starlets faint with one of his Buna stories. He was back at North American then, working with Dutch and his engineers. Sitting around a pool, he started talking about strafing the Japanese, how it makes a man sweaty and thirsty. Then he got shot down. Joined an Aussie infantry attack, fighting his way forward with pistols. Killed eight Japanese, which made him really thirsty, and hungry too. So as he bayonetted the ninth, he took a bite out of his shoulder, and sucked a bit of blood.

Pappy captured a Zero once. Snuck up behind it in a P-40. Jumped out onto the Zero's tail, yanked the pilot out. I heard he flew it to Tokyo and strafed the Emperor's palace with it.

Pappy got bored one day and went out looking for Japanese submarines. In a rowboat. Found a periscope, painted the glass green. The sub skipper kept ascending, thinking he hadn't broken the waterline yet. By the time he realized his mistake, the scope was a hundred feet in the air, and Pappy cut it down with a Browning Automatic Rifle.

Ballad of Pappy Gunn

He sank six battleships at one time
With a hundred big bombs tied to a line
He strung it across them all as a joke
Then watched the whole fleet go up in smoke.
Gunn Happy Pappy
Yes it's Gunn Happy Pappy who's making the run
His planes are just bristling with cannon and guns
The Japs are unhappy, without any chance
If they run into Pappy, and to his tune dance...

40

Gunship Summer

July 17, 1943
Dobodura Airfield, Papua New Guinea

The B-25 swung into the pattern over Dobodura, a long, wide dirt strip carved out of the New Guinea jungle just south of Buna. It served as home for the Third Attack Group, as well as for the fighter squadrons that escorted the Third's A-20s and Mitchells. Now, Kenney would use the vital base as a springboard in a major new air offensive.

The B-25 touched down and taxied to the Third Attack's dispersal area. Those who saw it land noticed it looked different from any other B-25 they'd ever seen. The solid nose looked stubbier somehow, and almost seemed to have a chin. Anyone who looked particularly closely would have seen under that chin rested the huge barrel of a 75mm cannon.

The B-25 rolled to a stop and the pilot cut the engine. Under the pilot's side of the cockpit, somebody had painted the plane's name: *Lil' Fox.*

Lt. Col. Pappy Gunn dropped out of the aircraft and walked up to the first man he saw.

"Well, when the hell do we leave?" he demanded.

Taken aback, the man replied, "Sir? You just arrived, where do you want to go?"

"Leave??" Pappy bellowed. "Why, you damn fool, I want to go to Rabaul. I'm here to show you young whippersnappers how to shoot the hell out of Rabaul five times a day!"

Pappy calmed down when somebody told him the weather was bad, though he stalked off in search of Don Hall and John Henebry muttering about the terrible weather he'd flown through over the years.

He'd returned to the Southwest Pacific and found himself stuck in Australia working as Kenney's chief of special projects again.

Not acceptable.

After being so far away for so long, he was almost rabid with the need to get back in combat and feel like he was making progress back to Polly and the kids. When Doc Gilmore examined him that summer, he was alarmed by his old friend's physical and mental state. He wrote a report that documented Pappy's high blood pressure, the constant swelling of his legs, and the rashes that continued to afflict him. When describing Pappy's mental state, Doc Gilmore flatly stated he possessed "psychopathic tendencies" as a result of his desire to kill the enemy.

Pappy's thirst for killing Japanese only increased after he learned of Ed Larner's death at Port Moresby. He wasn't going to be left behind in Australia tinkering on aircraft for long if he could help it. When one of the first cannon-equipped B-25G Mitchell bombers arrived in Australia shortly after he returned from the States, it gave him the opportunity he needed.

Gilmore's report painted a picture of a man living on the edge of a physical and mental breakdown. The months of endless work, distressed over his family's plight, the battles with the Japanese and the brass, pushed the man almost as far as he could go. Yet Gilmore did not recommend grounding his friend. He knew better than to do that; Pappy would have turned his full wrath on the local "veterinarian." He remained on flight status, though Kenney insisted he stay out of combat. Pappy always found the cracks in the rules.

He requested clearance to take the new bomber up to New Guinea and demonstrate its capabilities to the strafer pilots there. A demonstration was tolerated, and he was given the green light. Of course, Pappy figured the best way to demonstrate the plane's firepower was to blow holes in something flying the Rising Sun.

Starting in the middle of July, he visited first the Thirty-Eighth Bomb Group and gave each pilot a chance to fly *Lil' Fox*. Things had changed since March. Gone were most of the glass-nosed B-25s. The modification facilities in Australia had produced almost two hundred gunships, and they'd made their way to New Guinea. They'd been in combat for months now, doing tremendous damage to the enemy.

When he finished up with the Thirty-Eighth, he bounced over to the Third Attack to do the same thing. Accounts differ, but it appeared that some of the old guard in the Third Attack did not have much confidence in the new aircraft. The cannon was a modified version of the classic French-designed "75" that had played such a vital role in World War I. The U.S. Army used it in WWII as a man-portable infantry gun, as well as the main armament for its medium tanks.

There was good reason to be hesitant about such firepower in an airplane. If the .50-cals tore rivets loose, the fearsome recoil of the 75mm cannon could not possibly do good things to a B-25's airframe. Plus, the weapon had a slow rate of fire—it had to be loaded by hand by the flight engineer. Pappy resolved to demonstrate the weapon in combat and set everyone's mind at ease.

Before dawn on July 24, 1943, Pappy climbed into the cannon-armed B-25 with three other crewmen, one of whom was listed as "Bowling Fox." That was probably Jack Fox. Both he and Pappy were convinced that the 75mm would give the gunships an entirely new level of firepower and was the wave of the future. This would be their chance to prove it.

Maj. John Henebry led the mission that day. In the darkness, the pilots struggled to link up and get into the proper formation. They encountered squalls and thunderstorms that spread them out even further. They stayed low and made their way to the southwest coast of New Britain.

The Japanese situation in Papua New Guinea grew increasingly desperate after the Battle of Bismarck Sea. Supply convoys could not be risked in the face of the Fifth Air Force's commerce destroyers, but the Army defending the coastal enclaves at Lae and Salamaua were running out of food and ammunition. The Japanese squadrons based on the airstrips there long since retreated north to Rabaul or westward to Wewak, leaving the Japanese troops exposed to constant air attack that whittled away at their remaining stockpiles of supplies.

To at least get something to those starving men, the Japanese started running barge convoys along the coast of New Britain and New Guinea. Dubbed by the Japanese as "ant freight" runs, they used thirty-meter-long landing craft that plodded along at a few knots. At sea, they were vulnerable and easily destroyed; their one defense to air attack was their ability to duck into narrow inlets and hide whenever Allied planes appeared on the horizon.

MacArthur wanted the Japanese in Papua to starve. He planned to invade Lae later in the summer and needed its defenders as weak and ill prepared as possible. Taking out the ant freight convoys became a priority given to the strafer squadrons.

On this day, Henebry's crews tumbled across an ant freight convoy chugging along the coast off Cape Bushing. The Grim Reapers firewalled their throttles and barreled into the columns of landing craft. Pappy quickly blew one in half with a direct hit from his 75mm. Pulling off target, he zoom-climbed above the scrum while the other B-25s made strafing passes or dropped hundred-pound bombs. The barges were twisting and turning in all directions, frantic to evade the terrible slaughter unfolding.

Overhead, Pappy's *Lil' Fox* suddenly rolled on its back and came down in a near-vertical dive. He fired a single shot from the 75mm. The aircraft shuddered violently as flame shot from the weapon's muzzle. The high explosive shell blew a barge to smithereens. Pappy pulled out of the dive at the last possible second, racing over the beach and barely managing to avoid the trees at the edge of the waterline.

He waded back in, cannon blazing. The other B-25s were racing in all directions, making attacks, pulling off runs as streams of tracers streaked into the barges. What few machine guns the barges possessed were soon snuffed out by all the firepower in those Mitchells. The greatest danger the Americans faced was from other Americans. A blue-on-blue tragedy was so narrowly avoided that after the crews returned to Dobodura, both Henebry and Pappy sat everyone down and discussed the need for better discipline and formation flying.

Sloppy flying aside, Pappy and his crew demonstrated the killing power of the 75mm cannon. He fired twelve shells during the course of the mission, sinking two barges and setting fire to an ammo dump ashore.

Four days later, Pappy was in the air again. This time, he joined a sixteen-Mitchell barge hunt mission, again along the coast of New Britain. They found a lot more than barges that day.

The group swept up north from Cape Bushing toward a small Japanese airstrip right on the coast of Cape Gloucester, New Britain's westernmost tip. Along the way, bad weather caused their fighter escort to abort. The Third Attack continued on alone.

As they reached Cape Gloucester, the Americans discovered two Japanese destroyers off the north coast. Above them circled a formation of Zeroes, and below the fighters a single Japanese transport plane was about to land at the nearby airfield.

Don Hall, Pappy, and a couple of other B-25s bored in after the transport aircraft. The first passes on it missed, and the plane hurriedly touched down on the runway. The B-25s chased after it, props practically cutting the grass they were so low as Japanese anti-aircraft gunners hammered away at them. Fifteen hundred yards out, Pappy started lobbing cannon shells at the transport plane as it bounced along the dirt strip. One of his shells exploded directly beneath the right wing, stopping the aircraft and setting it afire even as Don Hall started strafing it. Suddenly, a bunch of Japanese officers piled out of the aircraft and started running for safety. Pappy took careful aim and put a shell right in the middle of them from less than four hundred feet away. The blast shattered bodies and blew them skyward, and Pappy's B-25 flew right through the carnage as bits of human remains rained down around it.

They sped on, crossing the runway as both Don and Pappy set their sights on one of the destroyers. This was the *Ariake*, 359 feet long, a sleek and modern warship built in the mid-1930s. She and her consort, the destroyer *Mikazuki*, had both run aground while delivering troops to the area. *Ariake* had freed herself earlier, transferred all of the troops off her sister destroyer, and transported them to the beach. She'd just come back to protect the *Mikazuki* when the Third Attack Group arrived.

Both destroyers threw up considerable antiaircraft fire, but the B-25s could not be stopped. One ship was helpless; the other, outnumbered. Already Henebry and the other pilots scored hits and strafed decks with their .50-cals. Now Pappy swept on Don Hall's wing, ready to add to the carnage.

He opened fire with the cannon and managed to get seven shots off in that first pass. His first two shots missed—"Buck fever," he later wrote. His third struck the ship in the stern near the aft five-inch gun turret. The blast suppressed or demolished a number of AA guns and the incoming fire diminished.

He kept shooting, hitting the poop deck and the smokestack just behind the bridge. By now, the B-25 was under a thousand feet from the destroyer. Pappy and his crew had enough time to reload and send a shell into the bow. From just over a football field away, he triggered one final shell and watched it explode on the bridge. The captain of the *Ariake* died in the attack, and this shell may have been the cause.

Then he was over the destroyer as Don Hall skipped bombs into the vessel's side. At least one hit and exploded within the doomed warship. The B-25 crews continued to rake and skip bomb the ships until both were left wrecked and burning.

The next day, the Third went back out and found the *Mikazuki* still grounded on the reef. Between skip-bombs and 75mm cannon strikes, they made short work of her. The *Ariake* had already sunk.

The destruction of two destroyers earned several men of the Third Attack Group decorations. Pappy received a Distinguished Flying Cross for his role in their destruction. The medal meant little to Pappy; despite his many enemies at headquarters—at least one of whom probably blocked a Distinguished Service Cross that Jim Davies had put him in for—he already had a pile of awards sitting back in his quarters in Australia that included the Silver Star and several other DFCs.

All he cared about in 1943 was delivering a better weapon to the guys doing the fighting. That July, the middle-aged Arkansan proved the 75mm cannon could be a devastating weapon in combat, but the revolution he'd foreseen with it never materialized. The 75mm was either loved or hated by the crews. It was hard to use and difficult to aim, and it took a very good pilot and crew to employ effectively. The Thirty-Eighth Bomb Group tended to like it better than the Third, and it saw useful service in the China-Burma-India Theater, but it remained a supplement to the .50-caliber strafer staple, the revolution that Pappy had already started.

In the summer of 1943, the gunship came of age. Solid nosed, ten- to twelve-gun B-25s began arriving straight from the United

States, and the depots in Australia continued to modify more. They filled the air above New Guinea, hunting barges, strafing airfields, tearing up targets wherever they went.

Bill Runey, a quiet and reserved Fifth Air Force P-40 pilot, often covered the strafers from above. He was mesmerized by them, sweeping phalanx-like over their targets with all guns lit. The combined firepower of the .50-cals and occasional 75mm shell made it look to Bill as if everything in front of the bombers was simply melting away under the fusillade.

That summer, the Japanese Army Air Force attempted a full-scale redeployment to New Guinea. The Imperial Navy would be responsible for the Solomons, Rabaul, and the rest of New Britain while the JAAF would defend New Guinea. Entire squadrons were flown from Burma, the Dutch East Indies, and China all the way through the Philippines and down into north-central New Guinea, where the planes congregated at a series of primitive strips at Wewak. The Japanese had picked that location because it was out of Allied fighter and medium bomber range, yet was close enough that it would give them a good springboard from which to hit Allied targets in Eastern New Guinea.

Kenney's intelligence unit detected the buildup. Instead of being worried by it, the general saw an opportunity. Through guile and creativity, the Fifth Air Force had secretly built a fighter strip in the Markham Valley that was within range of Wewak. To do it, Kenney's air transport crews figured out how to fly in everything the remote strip needed, from miniature bulldozers to two-and-a-half-ton trucks. Of the latter, they cut each truck in two, shipped them into the secret field in two C-47 transports, then welded them together in the field. It was a model of American ingenuity, and by midsummer, the strip was up and working.

Thanks to Pappy's earlier experiments, there was a way to deliver the gunship B-25s to Wewak, something the Japanese never expected.

When he removed the belly turret out of the earlier B-25s, Pappy conceived a way to replace it with a droppable, three-hundred-gallon fuel tank. While sitting at an outdoor café in Australia one day, he watched a waiter push open a spring-loaded screen door, and in a flash of inspiration, he realized he could do the same thing with the Mitchells. He and his team installed a spring-loaded trap door over the belly turret hole. When the three-hundred-gallon tank was emptied, the crew could eject it through the trap door. The bombers were hastily modified, and most were ready to go by early August.

Just in time, too. The Japanese air strength at Wewak now totaled almost two hundred planes. Since it had been out of fighter range, the Japanese could sneak convoys into that section of New Guinea from the Philippines, and they had painstakingly accumulated considerable amounts of aviation fuel, spare parts, lubricants, and other supplies that were pivotal to sustaining any air operation.

By this time, the gunship crews had developed their own sense of esprit de corps. They called themselves "strafers" and wrote songs about their peculiar form of warfare, which they gustily sang during evening fish frys on their off-duty hours. They were veterans now, too. Men who had destroyed the Bismarck Sea convoy now led squadrons and groups. They'd been blooded at places like Buna and Lae and Gasmata, learning through trial and error the best way to machine-gun ground targets.

In short, they were the deadliest and most effective Army Air Force bomber pilots in the Pacific.

On August 17, 1943, they struck Wewak at dawn like rolling thunder. The Grim Reapers of the Third Attack surprised the Japanese completely. Two years removed from Pearl Harbor, they had lined up their aircraft almost wingtip to wingtip to conduct inspections and engine tests.

The target was a strafer's dream. They sped down the long rows, flames spewing from their noses as their .50-cals boomed. A collective twelve thousand rounds per minute poured from Reaper weapons into the fuel-laden, ground-bound Japanese planes.

The cream of the Japanese Army Air Force was torn to bits in a matter of minutes. At the other fields around Wewak, other strafe squadrons discovered the same scene and wrought havoc with merciless efficiency. They dropped parachute fragmentation bombs in their wake, blowing apart whatever their guns missed.

Follow-up raids continued through the rest of August. When it was over, conservative postwar estimates placed the final count at 175 Japanese planes destroyed. In concert with high-level attacks by four-engine B-24 Liberators, the strafers destroyed most of the fuel and supplies built up around Wewak to sustain air operations. In the wake of the raids, U.S. signal intelligence intercepted multiple calls from Wewak asking Tokyo for gasoline.

The raids crippled the Japanese Army Air Force. Kenney's crews smashed every other attempt to build up airpower in the South West Pacific Area, as the initiative they seized over Wewak in August ensured the Japanese would never regain a foothold in the air over New Guinea.

With the destruction of the JAAF, MacArthur was now poised to make big leaps up the spine of New Guinea in preparation for his final return to the Philippines. The Fifth Air Force secured one of the most complete and least expensive victories in airpower history. Pappy's strafers paved the way for it. The total cost to Allied forces during the Wewak raids? Two B-25s, three B-24s, and six escorting P-38 Lightning fighters.

The gunship's ascendancy was complete. From here on out, they would lead the way back to the Philippines.

While Pappy chafed at being out of the front lines, General Kenney gave him an additional set of duties. The general occasionally had to accommodate VIP tours sent from the United States. Some of these VIPs included pop culture stars touring with

USO shows designed to improve troop morale, while others were fact-finding trips by politicians or other senior Army brass. Whenever these developed, Kenney usually assigned Pappy Gunn the task of flying these VIPs around, since he was one of the most experienced pilots in the theater. This was old hat to Pappy, who had done the same thing for politicians and top brass in the Navy while stationed outside Washington, D.C., in the early 1930s. It was a duty he suffered with a firm grip on his temper. Every moment he wasn't fighting or creating better weapons was an opportunity lost as far as he was concerned.

Pappy met some interesting people in the course of these flights, including silver screen legend Gary Cooper. In September 1943, he flew Eleanor Roosevelt around Australia when she arrived on a fact-finding tour. Though she visited hospitals and Red Cross centers and met with various Australian dignitaries, Pappy was frustrated by her seeming fixation on the condition and treatment of the African-American troops in the SWPA. To Pappy, the men who needed the First Lady's attention were the combat troops fighting, dying, and falling ill with all manners of tropical diseases, not the rear echelon battalions living in relative safety in Australia. Her attentiveness to the plight of the African-American units convinced him yet again that Washington's elite continued to focus on the wrong things.

Pappy may not have known it, but the year before, in the spring of 1942, while he and the Third Attack Group furiously modified A-20s, one of the first African-American units to deploy overseas arrived at Townsville. The Ninety-Sixth Engineers was a segregated outfit with white officers whose men were treated extremely poorly by the Australians. In April, just after reaching Townsville, a wild fight erupted in town that involved more than a hundred of these African-American engineers. White American troops surrounded the men from the Ninety-Sixth and even drew down on their officers when they rushed to resolve the situation. After that incident, the Ninety-Sixth was banned from going into Townsville, which left them few options for R&R. They spent their days carving out airfields by hand in the Australian outback. Their nights they languished in primitive living conditions with few creature comforts. Combined with the racism endemic in the Army and in Australia at the time, the situation destroyed the Ninety-Sixth's morale.

Tensions boiled over a month later, on May 22, 1942. After an African-American sergeant was physically assaulted by a white officer, two companies from the Ninety-Sixth mutinied. Seizing machine guns and other heavy weapons, some of the African-American troops opened fire on their officers. Some accounts state there was one death and multiple casualties; others state at least nineteen men were killed as bullets flew. Local Australian combat troops were called in to surround the Ninety-Sixth's encampment with orders to shoot on sight any African-American soldiers.

Some of the mutineers escaped into the outback and "went bush." They were hunted by Australian troops for weeks, and local authorities attributed several crimes, including a rape, to these men.

Shortly after the disastrous incident, the two companies involved were sent up to New Guinea, where they helped build the airfields Kenney's aviators depended on to strike the Japanese. Meanwhile, back in Australia, the U.S. Army went to great lengths to cover up the incident, and the mutiny was lost to history for seven decades.

Fortunately, Robert Sherrod, a war correspondent for *Time* and *Life* magazines, discovered what happened and wrote a long article about it. The censors crushed the story, but Sherrod was determined to get the word out somehow. In June 1942, Congressman Lyndon B. Johnson flew into Townsville on a fact-finding mission, and Sherrod gave him his article. Johnson took it back to Washington with him and delivered it to the White House, which may have been part of the reason for Eleanor Roosevelt's visit to Australia.

In fact, Pappy flew the First Lady up to Townsville during her visit; there she visited the North American Services Club, the only African-American recreational facility in the city. Staffed by some of the first black Red Cross women to be sent overseas, the club opened in October 1942. There was considerable resentment among the locals, who preferred to keep African-Americans out of Townsville altogether.

The dreadful state of race relations in Australia held strategic implications for the Allies in the SWPA. Throughout 1942 and into 1943, when MacArthur and Kenney were absolutely desperate for men, material, and machines, they both asked Washington not to send any further African-American units into the theater. The mutiny of May 22 was probably a defining factor in their decision. Kenney went so far later as to refuse a bomber squadron crewed by the legendary Tuskegee Airmen.

41

Miss Priss Strikes Back

Late 1943
Santo Tomas, Manila, Philippines

Julie Gunn approached the iron gates of Santo Tomas and made eye contact with the guards on watch. Leo Gurevich had just dropped her off after a long kalesa ride through a city of growing shortages. Fuel, food, and basic necessities had long since become scarce on the shelves of Manila's shops. The place had a downcast, oppressive feel, made worse for Julie and Leo because the Japanese now forced them to wear identifying armbands. Those allowed them safe passage through the city, but it also made them a target to pro-Japanese Filipinos resentful of Americans, who would shove her or make cutting remarks.

At the front gate, the guards stared at her, this seventeen-year-old girl dressed awkwardly around her full body cast. She lurched forward a few steps, then paused to smack her chest. The hollow sound of her cast resonated. The guards all knew about this one, the girl trapped in plaster. They waved her through.

Eyes straight ahead, she limped through the gate as they regarded her. A few more steps and she was inside the camp, approaching the second wall built to prevent friendly Filipinos from throwing supplies over the main one.

There was a blind spot here they'd discovered weeks before. The guards at the gate couldn't see her, and there were no other nearby posts where prying eyes would be upon them. Waiting in that blind spot were Paul, Nath, and Connie.

She moved to them, and even as they said hushed words of greeting, the boys reached down the back of her cast and began fishing out small packages. Connie did the same to her front. Without another word, the three siblings scattered to deliver the packages to their recipients.

Julie continued on to the commandant's office, hobbling bravely. She once had been a boy-crazy teen craving attention before the war. P.I. affectionately nicknamed her Miss Priss for her fussy ways. Now, hardened by her experience in hospitals and prison camps, she discovered reserves of strength and courage she'd never needed to tap before the Japanese came. She was resourceful, flexible, and able to think on her feet. Whip smart and coldly calculating, she took risks lesser souls would never dare to attempt. She grew into the role and came to inhabit it. Not only was she helping her family and friends, she was striking back at the despised Japanese.

Cool as ice, she reached the Japanese commander's building and stepped inside.

Polly was waiting for her on a narrow bench in front of Mr. Ohashi's office, looking wan and ragged. She practically disappeared within her threadbare clothes, which were many sizes too big now.

They exchanged subtle nods, then Julie eased herself down onto the bench beside her mom. Quickly, Polly's hand slid across the bench. Julie covered it with her own. It looked to the Japanese like a sign of affection, mother and daughter holding hands as they waited to see Mr. Ohashi. On one level that was true. But beneath their flesh lay notes of hope and need, penned by only the most trusted friends of the Gunn family. Polly palmed them to Julie, and she casually concealed them with her fingers before stuffing them down her cast. To anyone looking, it appeared she was just trying to get comfortable. A second later, her hand quit readjusting the cast and returned to the bench. Polly covered it with her own and made the second handoff. Money for other families and incoming notes.

Gone were the thoughts of sin with such subterfuge. Polly had come of age just as her daughter had; no longer wed to the prewar conventions she'd clung to well past their prime. She would do whatever it took to keep her family alive.

Mr. Ohashi called them in, and they politely stepped inside to bow and wait for him to offer them a seat. He wore, as usual, a severe black suit totally out of place in the Pearl of the Orient Seas. He looked like an undertaker, though he'd been a businessman in Manila since 1938, representing a Japanese corporation's interests there.

He served as a buffer of sorts when the camp gradually came under control of the Japanese military. Rumor had it they would soon get an Imperial Army officer as a new commandant. If true, that would surely mark a turning point for the worse for the internees.

They exchanged pleasantries and Mr. Ohashi renewed Julie's pass. A few more months and Dr. De Los Santos planned to remove the cast and put her in a brace. Until then, she would stay in the care of the Gurevich family, reporting every few weeks to have her pass renewed.

These trips into the camp became a source of news and information, food, and money for those Polly most trusted. Eva Gurevich's father and stepmother were also interned at Santo Tomas. Though Russian by birth, they gained Polish citizenship after World War I when the frontiers were redrawn. Since Poland was an Allied nation, the Japanese ordered them into the camp. To repay the Gureviches for taking care of Julie and Nath, Polly passed notes from Eva's folks to her youngest daughter whenever Julie returned to renew her pass. That grew into a two-way operation, with Julie bringing packages of food for them along with money and messages.

As the situation in the camp worsened, Julie took greater and greater risks as Polly allowed trusted friends access to this network. Julie traveled all over the city to deliver their notes, meeting some very unsavory characters at times. She developed steel nerves and remained calm even in the most stressful situations.

Some of those notes went to guerrilla cells, possibly associated with the Spaniards the family knew. Incoming messages that Julie passed to Polly included not just words of love and care but news of the outside world that the Japanese did not want known. After the Japanese stopped allowing packages to be delivered, Julie's smuggling operation became the only way some families could communicate with the outside world.

Polly reminded the kids never to speak of what they were doing. There were a lot of bitter Americans who felt abandoned by their government and were using that bitterness as justification to collaborate with the Japanese. They'd be only too happy to reveal their operation and give no thought to the fate of the Gunn family.

Though Polly chose carefully whom to admit into their circle of confidants, she made one mistake. A man friendly to the family asked Polly to get him some bacon. She slipped the request to Julie, and a couple weeks later, she came into the camp with a few slices wrapped and stashed down the back of her cast. When she arrived in room forty-six after getting through the gate, Nath reached down and extracted the meat. He had the smallest hands in the family and could get them all the way down her cast. Doing so always sent jolts of pain through Julie, but she sat through it in stoic silence. Out of necessity, Julie, like the boys, was leather-tough now.

Nath handed the bacon over to Polly, who delivered it to the man. Instead of being grateful, he grew bitter and angry.

"What's the matter with you?" Polly asked, taken aback by his reaction.

"That's it? That's all of it?" he demanded. Then he accused the Gunns of stealing some of his bacon. They had done nothing of the sort. Julie couldn't find any more in town. Besides, her hiding spot in her cast would not hold more anyway.

Polly laid that all out, but the man remained bitter. Finally, she gave up and said, "That's what they gave us. We gave it to you. Don't you ever come back to us again."

For a while, they feared he would blackmail them for more contraband, threatening to go to the commandant if they didn't get him what he demanded. Nath stayed alert for any betrayal, ready to ensure the man "slipped" on a bar of soap in the shower should he squeal. Fortunately, he kept his mouth shut. Still, the experience made Polly even more cautious. She knew Julie was probably risking her life each time she came through the gates.

After that dicey moment, Julie continued to bring the family small packages of food, along with notes to Connie from Guyenne Sanchez, who was still deeply in love with her. The camp was down to about fifteen hundred calories of food a day from the kitchens, and everyone was growing weak and sickly. They supplemented their meals any way they could, hoping for the day Red Cross packages might arrive. Or MacArthur.

In December 1943, the Japanese did allow Red Cross packages into the camp. Every internee received two bundles, one small and one a little larger. After almost two years of bland diets and slow starvation, many of the internees fell upon their Red Cross manna and devoured everything without thought to the future. They mowed through coffee, salted meat, canned food, and chocolate with total abandon. For some, the food lasted only a month, and then the party was over. Back to boiled rice and the occasional vegetable. Meat had become almost nonexistent after the summer of 1943.

Polly rationed everything with strict fairness. She secured the family's Red Cross packages in room forty-six and made sure they were guarded at all times, by either a family member or a trusted confidant. Polly knew that theft of these precious items could cost them their lives if the food situation grew any worse.

It did grow worse. In February 1944, the Japanese military took full control of the camp. The civilian commandant was replaced by a succession of oddball lieutenant colonels unfit for duty in combat. One was particularly quirky, seemingly spending more time playing baseball than running the camp.

A new officer in charge of the camp's guards also arrived with the transfer of control. Lt. Nanukazu Abiko stayed on as the one constant over the next year while the commandants came and went. He was a buffed and broad-shouldered officer who fought on Guadalcanal in 1942. Most of the men he served with on the "Isle of Death" never made it out of the jungle. He escaped at the very end of the campaign when the Imperial Navy evacuated the island. Ill health or wounds restricted him to rear-area duty, a status which embittered him.

For two years, the guards mostly left the internees alone. That changed with Abiko's arrival. From the outset, he personally took over the evening roll calls and through interpreters went to every room and ordered the prisoners to show him the proper respect by bowing with regimental precision. He was a meticulously dressed officer, a martinet stuck behind the lines thirsting for a return to combat so he could kill Americans. Instead, his army forced him to watch over them. He vented at the prisoners and reveled at humiliating them any chance he could. His hatred spilled out in every encounter, and his internee victims despised him with singular passion.

When he forced the internees to bow repeatedly to him in subservience, not respect, he would chortle and laugh to himself. Once, he told a gathering of prisoners through an interpreter, "Remember, you belong to a third-class people."

If somebody defied him, he was quick to slap or rain blows on the person. More than once, he beat internees unconscious when they failed to grovel thoroughly enough for his liking. Age or gender didn't matter; he was an equal opportunity sadist.

One eleven-year-old boy in Mr. Leake's rooms discovered the hard way the level of violence the lieutenant could inflict. Outside near the main building one day, he noticed Lieutenant Abiko emerge from his quarters and tried to pretend he did not see him. The boy turned his back to the lieutenant and called out to a friend. In a flash, Abiko jumped him, threw him to the ground where he kicked him and beat him with his sword's scabbard until it broke.

Another time, a sickly, elderly woman was sitting in a line in front of the main building's infirmary, hoping to get some medicine the Red Cross had delivered in December 1943. Abiko appeared, and everyone but the elderly woman stood, turned, and bowed to him.

Seeing the old lady still seated on the ground sent Abiko into a rage. He pulled his scabbard off his belt and flailed it down on her again and again as the other internees looked on in helpless horror.

The Americans called him "Shitface" behind his back. Many of the internees quietly vowed that someday, there would be a reckoning and the lieutenant would be at their mercy.

They would give him none.

As the war continued to go badly for the Japanese, Abiko drank his sorrows away. Often, he appeared out of nowhere, reeking of sake and full of pent-up fury, which he would unleash with fists, kicks, and scabbard on any prisoner caught in the midst of some minor infraction.

Paul and Nath managed to avoid his wrath that spring and summer of '44, but the violence in the camp seemed to escalate as food grew scarce. Sometimes, fights between prisoners broke out. Other times, a guard would mete out vicious punishment. Nath, who worked in one of the internee gardens by that point, sometimes stole from it. He and his band of toughened teens learned they could sneak out after curfew, crawl along a drainage ditch into the garden, and poach a few potatoes or peanuts if they dug them up then replaced the topsoil. Nath would bring his bounty back to the main hall to share with the rest of the family.

Others tried to steal from the vegetable gardens, only to be caught and punished. Such ventures were always laden with risk, as the guards and internees watched this vital food source like hawks. Sure enough, Nath got caught one night, and a Japanese guard rushed over to stop him.

Before Nath could escape, the soldier boot-stomped him in the stomach and chest so hard it left a permanent indentation on one side of his body.

The beating didn't discourage Nath. He just planned his foraging missions more thoroughly. Keeping his family alive was worth risking a beatdown by a guard, as far as he was concerned.

By the summer of 1944, the family wasn't doing well. Paul injured his back while carrying the heavy cast-iron rice pots in the kitchen. Too proud to stop and let it heal, he hobbled through his daily chores in growing pain. Connie's health deteriorated as well. Wracked by continuous disease, she lost so much weight she looked skeletal. One day, she developed a fever and her stomach ached. It rapidly grew worse, and soon the pain localized on her right side. They took her to the hospital, where she was diagnosed with acute appendicitis. There was no time to haggle for a pass and get her to Manila General—passes were not forthcoming anymore, anyway, now that the military ran the camp. They carried her into surgery, but there was no general anesthetic left for the internees. They gave her a weak local, and cut out her appendix while she remained awake.

It took her several weeks to recover, and she remained weakened by the ordeal and the accompanying pain. Fortunately, she burned with her father's spirit: She was a fighter and refused to give up on herself. That was no easy emotional feat—pain wracked, starving, she lay in bed surrounded by the dying and infirm. She saw how their suffering broke some of them. They gave up and let death overtake them.

The oldest and most infirm went first, victims of tuberculosis, beriberi, malaria, or simple starvation. The hospital ward swelled with patients and exhausted what little remained of the Red Cross medicine sent with the packages in December 1943. The docs and nurses could do little for them but provide a little extra comfort in their final hours.

In the midst of this growing horror, the internees glimpsed hope. On June 8, 1944, Nath was in the main building with his mom when multiple formations of planes flew over the camp. Some passed over into Manila Bay, others headed for the airfields around the city. This was not unusual; the Japanese flew overhead all the time. Then, they heard a sound absent from their lives since December 1941. Everyone in the camp froze to listen, even the Japanese.

It was the sound of antiaircraft fire.

The family rushed to the nearest window and watched planes dive down over Manila Bay. Bombs exploded in the distance, flak bursts filled the sky, their concussions rattling the building. Soon, antiaircraft shrapnel began tinking off the rooftops and landing in the open spaces of the camp.

The planes were navy blue with bright white stars. Cheers swelled around the camp and people began to shout, "The Americans are back!"

The Japanese guards ran about chaotically as the commandant rushed out, barking orders. It seemed like he feared a parachute assault. Then Abiko stormed onto the scene, his bullish face twisted in rage. As the planes passed overhead, he grabbed his saber, raised it over his head, and shook it at them while raging in Japanese.

Polly pulled Nath close and said to him in a hushed voice, "No matter what, don't believe anything you don't see for yourself. Okay?"

"Yes, Mom."

"It may be years before American soldiers get here," she added. That reality killed some of the joy in the moment. Together, they stared out the window, watching the planes dive and wheel, and wondered if P.I. Gunn was at the controls of one of them.

The sight of American warplanes confirmed all the news they'd received about Japan being pushed back on all fronts. Morale soared among the internees, only to slowly degenerate again as everyone realized the bombing raid did not signal their salvation. Food grew even scarcer. Rations were cut yet again. And the camp settled back into a tense routine.

Abiko drank even more, and he vented his wrath on the weakest internees. The other guards, fearful of what the future would bring, grew edgy, nervous, and often nasty. Perhaps they knew the fate of so many of their friends and comrades in New Guinea, in the Solomons, and at Rabaul. If they did, they knew they would probably never escape from the Philippines should MacArthur make good his return.

One day, Nath returned to Mr. Leake's dormitories and found Abraham Zelekofsky, the young musical prodigy, in a state of utter despair. Pale, fragile, and unathletic, he looked completely out of place in a room full of boys made lean and hard by years of work.

Nath asked what was wrong, and Abraham related how his mom gave him a small package of crackers. He rationed them out carefully to himself, stashing the rest away for as long as he could. Inevitably, a larger boy discovered his hiding place and ate everything left.

"Who took your food, Abe?" Nath asked.

The musician told him. Nath stood up and went looking for the boy. He found him in the third room used as a dorm in the education building. When Nath confronted him, he fired back, "What are you, his mommy?"

"No," Nath said slowly, "but his mom asked me to look after him."

The bigger boy turned to Abe, who was behind and off to one side of Nath. "Is that right, little Jewboy?"

"Yes it is," he said softly.

The boy scoffed at Nath, "So you really are his mommy."

Fourteen years old now, Nath possessed reserves of energy and strength few retained. He ate anything he could find—even bugs—to stay that way, and as he matured from preteen to teen, he grew into a formidable physical opponent.

He didn't hesitate. Nath punched the thief in the chest, and the boy toppled over backward, stunned by the force of the blow.

Eighth Avenue rules. Make it too painful for anyone to mess with you or those you're tasked to protect.

As the thief got to his feet, Nath stepped forward in a boxer's stance, poised to strike. The boy swung at him, but Nath nailed him with a hook to the side of the head and dropped him back to the floor.

Just then, Mr. Leake rushed in to break up the fight. He listened to Nath's explanation, punished the bully, then took Nath aside to have a one-on-one talk. Nath noticed that Leake looked wan and terribly thin. Like the other men in the camp, he had dropped at least 20 percent of his body weight by this time. Yet, he carried himself with a calm dignity that always commanded respect. The boys were loyal to him, as he was to them. Some owed Mr. Leake their lives.

Mr. Leake told Nath he'd done the right thing. Abe needed protecting, but he would see to that now. Nath and Paul had grown up under his care, and he told them they were ready to rejoin the men in the main building. Mr. Leake knew they could take care of themselves. Most of the men did not have any energy left these days, thanks to the starvation diet. The fighting between them gradually disappeared as hunger sapped their strength. Nath and Paul would have the upper hand now.

The Gunn boys had made the transition from naïve and trusting kids to hardened survivors. They shed their idealism, something that others never managed to do. As they learned the ways of survival in the camp, they took different paths. Nath was the risk taker, the muscle. The protector. Paul was steady and calm in a crisis, the thinker whose determination in the kitchen earned the respect of everyone there. Despite his size and his injury, he never missed a day since it materially aided the family. If Nath was the protector, Paul was the provider. Together, they were the yin and yang of their dad's character, a perfect combination of calculated action and steadfastness.

That night, Nath and Paul packed their things. With people dying throughout the camp, finding a bunk in the main building close to their mom's room would not be an issue anymore. They walked over side by side in silence, determined to be the wildcats that nobody wanted to tackle. They were no longer the rabbits—adulthood had arrived.

After the first U.S. air raid, the Japanese ordered all internees living outside the camp to return. Julie, whose cast was replaced by a metal brace by this point, made one final run through the gate. With her brace, she couldn't hide packages as she used to with the cast. Instead, she stuffed them in her clothing and tried to conceal them as best she could. The money and notes she tucked down her shirt.

On this last mission, she reached the gate and saw the guards staring at her as usual. They waved her through, but as she walked beyond the checkpoint toward the drop-off point with her brothers and sister, the guards began to follow her. A moment later, they stepped beside her, escorting her to the commandant's office.

Under the guards' watchful eyes, Polly appeared in Julie's path. Her face betrayed nothing. She smiled at her daughter, who was trying not to look petrified. Both knew they were in trouble here. But Polly was not about to abandon her. She stepped forward and grasped Julie's hand. Side by side, they walked into the commandant's office, their enemy's bayonets on either flank.

Mr. Ohashi greeted them, and the women bowed to him with the usual respect. Then the guards searched Julie. One by one, the concealed food items emerged. Polly saw them and her stomach groaned. She was desperately hungry, and even the mere sight of these vital treats left her sighing out loud for them.

The guards did not search under Julie's shirt. If they had, they would have found notes and money secreted there in her bra, a far more serious offense. Had the notes contained anything that could have connected Julie to the insurgency, she almost certainly would have been whisked off to face the secret police at Fort Santiago.

Instead, Mr. Ohashi looked over the food, considered the situation, and decided to give most of it back to Julie and Polly. It was a unique act of mercy.

They were released, and Julie moved into room forty-six again with her mom and sister. She was never allowed to leave Santo Tomas again. Her days as a teenage spy came to an end; her days of survival had just begun.

42

The Pinky and the Lungs

March 1944
New Guinea

The Japanese tried one more time to reinforce Wewak in the spring of 1944. The strafers returned to it and another airfield complex at Hollandia, several hundred miles up the coast. Once again, the painfully hoarded Japanese aircraft were simply pulverized on the ground at minimal cost. In the middle of March, they sent a convoy down the coast from Wewak toward Hollandia. The Fifth Air Force pounced on it, and a mini–Bismarck Sea ensued. Warhawk pilot Bill Runey took part in escorting the gunships that day, and from his perch above, he watched the Mitchells tear into the ships. When the first wave of bombers passed over the convoy, Bill saw nothing but broken vessels, burning oil spewing from ruptured hulls. One vessel rolled over, its side ripped open by skip bombs. As he passed over it, he thought the water around it was covered with oil. Then he realized with a shock it wasn't an oil slick at all—it was a people slick composed of hundreds of soldiers and sailors, clustered together around bits of wreckage.

Once again, the sharks fed.

The successes of March culminated with a surprise onslaught at Hollandia. Scores of Japanese aircraft were destroyed in two consecutive days of attacks. Three weeks later, MacArthur launched a surprise amphibious invasion at Hollandia. As American troops poured ashore and seized the airfields, Japanese pilots, ground crews, and support troops fled into the jungle.

The air attacks followed by the ground assault ensured that some of the Japanese Air Force units in New Guinea suffered 95 percent casualties. Those men who did not perish in their planes or on their air bases were cut off by MacArthur's advancing troops and left to die slowly in the jungle. Some reverted to cannibalism to stay alive. They died of disease and malnutrition, attacks from indigenous people, or from roving Allied patrols. Almost none survived the war.

As the revolution he unleashed destroyed Japanese airpower in New Guinea, Pappy Gunn worked as furiously as ever. He juggled a dozen special projects at once, never wavering in his quest to improve and make better and more survivable the equipment sent from Stateside factories. Everything from better fuses and bombs to new racks and even a searchlight mounted on a B-25 for night operations occupied his time. As usual, he rarely slept and kept pushing his aging body past the breaking point.

His pinky became a casualty of that work ethic. For years, it kept breaking under the strain of Pappy's frantic work. He would go to Doc Gilmore to have it reset, only to break it again. By this point, it hung useless at an odd angle, and it only got in the way when Pappy dug into a mechanical project.

Finally, he had enough. He sought out Doc Gilmore and demanded he amputate the broken pinky. Doc told him he was a flight surgeon, not an actual surgeon, and he couldn't operate on it.

"Well, goddamnit, Vet!" Pappy shouted. "Take me to somebody who can do the job."

Doc Gilmore knew his friend well enough by now to realize arguing was pointless. He brought Pappy to a field hospital and found a surgeon. The man looked over Pappy's hand, pronounced the digit salvageable, and refused to cut it off.

Wrong answer, sawbones.

Pappy had stuff to do and wasn't going to waste time with this egghead. He pulled out his Colt .45, pressed it to the broken pinky, and announced, "Either you cut the goddamned thing off, or I'll blow it all over the place and you'll have to clean up the mess."

The surgeon glanced at Doc Gilmore, who made it clear Pappy would do it.

The surgeon caved. "Okay, come with me."

After the amputation, Pappy carried the pinky around with him in a jar for some time. It became known as the "wicked digit," and it ended up in weird places. Once, while visiting the Third Attack Group in New Guinea, somebody crafted a statue of Buddha and stuck the wicked digit in his belly button. Parties were held around the finger, and much lore emerged from the Fifth Air Force about it. Legend has it that the finger was finally laid to rest with a full and proper burial.

That spring, Pappy flirted with the AIB again. This time, MacArthur's spies conceived a plan to have the Mindanao guerrillas build a complete airfield complex in the island's interior. Pappy could then run supplies to the guerrillas in modified aircraft. There was even a plan to get the guerrillas their own bomber force to use off those strips, but that plan never came to fruition as the Japanese overran the proposed airfield site in June 1944.

Frustrated that the Japanese had blocked his latest opportunity to return to the Philippines, Pappy returned to work with renewed vengeance—and even less patience for those not operating in high gear. On the Fourth of July, Pappy showed up at a supply depot in Australia, needing material for one of his projects. To his outrage, the place was closed for the holiday.

In recent months, word of the Bataan Death March and of the horrific treatment accorded Allied prisoners of war in the Philippines was filtering into the press. As the Americans advanced closer to the

Philippines, that treatment only grew worse. Pappy was frantic with worry again, his head filled with worst-case scenarios. Even as the tide turned and the march to Manila kicked into high gear, he grew even more merciless in his efforts to help speed the advance onward.

Taking a holiday off was unacceptable to him. Pappy got out of his vehicle and stormed up to a guard standing watch over the supply dump. The guard saw this furious lieutenant colonel coming and braced himself for the tongue-lashing sure to follow. His orders were clear: Nobody gets into the supply dump. Not even angry field-grade officers.

Pappy tore into the guard with righteous fury, but the soldier refused to budge. No admittance.

Pappy drew one of his .45 Colts, pointed it at the guard, and asked once again for him to open the gate.

As usual, the pistol did the trick. The guard opened the gate, and Pappy got what he needed. Yet, this was not the chaotic months of early 1942 when such things could be overlooked. The AAF of 1944 was much more organized and disciplined. Robbing a supply dump could not go unpunished; not even if the robber were none other than Pappy Gunn.

Pappy received a stern official reprimand in writing, along with a disciplinary letter for his personnel file. He could not have cared less. He had poached the needed parts, and that was all that mattered to him.

While stuck in Australia, he learned of a new strafer aircraft coming into theater called the Douglas A-26 Invader. He barraged General Kenney with requests to combat-field-test the A-26 and report on its capabilities. Eventually, that request was granted. It is not known how many missions he flew in the aircraft, which began arriving in June 1944. The first four test aircraft went to the Grim Reapers, and Pappy rejoined his old outfit to run combat missions with them in the new aircraft.

At first glance, it looked like a beautiful new addition to the gun-ship lineup. Incredibly fast, rakish, and factory armed with eight .50-calibers in the nose, the A-26 could carry six thousand pounds of bombs. That was more than Miss EMF could carry in 1942 as America's premier heavy bomber. The technological potential was amazing.

Yet, the combat tests proved disappointing. Pappy and the other strafer pilots found the cockpit totally unsuited for low-altitude fly-ing. They couldn't see over the nose; the layout of the instruments and controls was cumbersome and counterintuitive. Pappy recom-mended that the Fifth Air Force reject the aircraft until modifi-cations could be completed. Kenney agreed and did so. The A-26 would later become one of the great gunships of aviation history and would be used in Korea and Vietnam by the USAF, but for now, the Grim Reapers wanted more B-25s and A-20 Havocs.

While back with the Third, Pappy was reunited with Big Jim Davies, who returned from the States and was back in New Guinea again. It was just like the old days, and the pair teamed up at night to drink and reminisce—and remember old friends long dead now. Doc Gilmore joined them, as did some of the other old hands still left in the group.

One night, Davies and some confederates got to drinking with-out the Arkansan and decided to prank Pappy while he slept in a general-purpose tent. Off they went to secure some explosives and more booze before rendezvousing on a hill above Pappy's peaceful jungle bedroom.

Gathering on a hill above Pappy, somebody produced the explo-sive charge used in one of Kenney's fragmentation bombs. They wired it with a fuse and rolled it down the slope toward Pappy's tent. Thinking it would only wake him up and scare the socks off him, they were appalled to see the explosion blow Pappy clear out of the tent. They raced down the hill to his aid and found him crit-ically injured. Dazed from a concussion, one lung collapsed, he was having trouble breathing as Doc Gilmore went to work on him. He got Pappy stabilized, then rushed him to the nearest field hospital, where he made a speedy recovery. Later, Pappy credited Doc Gilmore with saving his life.

Pappy took the prank in stride; he knew they meant to do no harm and things had just gotten out of hand. He was not much of a prankster himself, but he lived in a culture steeped in it, and he knew that the aviators chose only targets they liked. If you weren't victimized by pranks, it usually meant the other men in the outfit didn't respect you. Pappy understood that, and the incident never affected his friendship with Davies.

Fifth Air Force HQ took a different view of the incident. Davies was a full colonel, up for promotion to brigadier general. The lack of judgment combined with the severity of Pappy's injuries almost cost Davies his general's star.

Once Pappy recovered, he showed up at Kenney's headquarters hoping to get approval for his latest return to the Philippines plan. He started with a whopper: He wanted to take a single, modified B-25 loaded with fuel and incendiary ammunition up to Manila on a one-way mission.

He'd heard that there were hundreds of Japanese aircraft being sheltered on Dewey Boulevard in downtown Manila. He figured one B-25 strafer down low could wreck them all.

Of course, he wouldn't have enough fuel to get home, so he proposed to crash-land elsewhere on Luzon and make a rendezvous with a Navy submarine for extraction. He probably really wanted a way back to Manila to try another rescue attempt. The strafing run was just the cover.

Didn't matter. Kenney vetoed it. But Pappy was persistent. He came back with the same idea with a twist: He'd go in without bombs or a top turret, and with extra fuel tanks everywhere they'd fit. That way, he'd at least be able to get to the Southern Philippines.

No dice.

In September 1944, as the invasion of the Philippines was about to be undertaken, Pappy tried again. This time, he wanted to go ashore and recruit a guerrilla army to attack the Japanese in the rear while MacArthur's troops landed on the beaches.

Kenney told him that the half million men assigned to the operation might resent him trying to win the war all by himself.

Still, Kenney decided he did have a spot for Pappy in the coming invasion. The original conception of MacArthur's return to the Philippines started with an amphibious assault on Mindanao. After securing airfields there, the next jump would be in the Central Philippines, then Luzon eventually. The entire drive up the New Guinea coast was predicated on the need to have bomber and fighter bases within range of the Mindanao beaches so the first rung on the Philippines ladder could be taken.

That plan went out the window in September 1944. Intelligence reported that the Japanese were particularly weak on Leyte Island in the central Philippines. If Leyte could be taken and airfields quickly constructed, they could shave months off the entire campaign to get back to Luzon.

Given that there were thousands of POWs and internees still on Luzon enduring the hell of Japanese incarceration, every day they could speed up their liberation would save lives. Yet Leyte was a gamble. It would be out of Fifth Air Force fighter and bomber range, which meant the invasion force would not have USAAF air cover. That would have to come from the U.S. Navy and its fast aircraft carriers. Only once before, at Hollandia, did MacArthur rely on the Navy for air cover.

The troops would need to get ashore and seize suitable ground for airfields, then the engineers would need to build them in record time. Once ready, Kenney's air units could fly in and join the fight.

There would be a fight. The Japanese concentrated almost nine hundred aircraft in the Philippines. If the U.S. Navy's fast carriers ended up in a battle with the Japanese Imperial fleet—rumored to be ready to intervene in any Philippines operation—things could get dicey for the beachhead. The troops would lose their air protection and air-ground support. In a worst case, the Japanese might actually control the sky over Leyte.

The landing would take place around Tacloban, the island's capital. A small airstrip stretched along a narrow peninsula a few miles from the town. That would be the first objective of the landings. Take it, get engineers onto the strip to expand it, lay metal planking down so it could be used in bad weather, and build aircraft revetments. Kenney's P-38s and B-25s would be standing by to fly in once the strip was declared operational. It would be one of the most critical components of the initial liberation of the Philippines. Tacloban had to be functioning within a matter of days. It was a tall order.

Kenney wanted it done right. He told Pappy to put together a crew of capable men with an array of skills, fifty at most. They would be the troubleshooters, the men on the ground he could trust. They would go into Tacloban as part of Col. David Hutchison's 308th Bomb Wing to help finish and run the airfield. Kenney told Pappy to pick men of action who could handle themselves in a fight.

Pappy loved this new assignment. It would get him back on Philippine soil on day one of the invasion. He'd be within reach of Polly and the kids at last. Of course, Kenney knew that, and he wanted his mad genius safe. After Pappy left his office, Kenney contacted Colonel Hutchison and told him not to give Pappy an airplane once Tacloban was operational. He would tolerate no midnight runs to Manila or solo flights to take out Japanese targets. Santo Tomas could wait. For now, getting the troops and ships some air cover to protect them from the nine hundred Japanese planes in the area was all that mattered.

43

On the Tail of Custer's Ghost

October 20, 1944
White Beach, Leyte Island, Philippines

Forty-four-year old Lt. Col. Paul Irvin Gunn gazed out across the placid cerulean sea, awed by the sight playing out around him. Battleships steamed off White Beach, their main gun batteries belching flames and smoke. Cruisers and destroyers loitered nearby, awaiting their turns in the morning sunlight. Overhead, Navy fighters orbited protectively while dive bombers streaked down on targets behind the beach Pappy's men would soon be storming.

His landing craft rocked in the gentle swells as it churned around its mother ship, its crew awaiting the order to drive in on the beach. Around him, hundreds of ships and boats and craft of all sizes filled Leyte Gulf. It was power he'd never before seen, the awe-inspiring fruits of a total war economy and a united country with industrial power never seen before in human history.

If only such ships and planes existed in 1941. If only this moment had come in 1942 instead of two and a half years after he'd left Manila on that dark and chaotic Christmas Eve.

He was here now at the tip of the spear, helping to ensure MacArthur made good his promise to return. Instead of being thousands of miles from Polly and the children, Pappy was only a few hundred now.

For two hours, three battleships pounded the invasion beach and its rear areas. The massive shells blew meters-deep craters in the soft Leyte soil. They blasted trees to splinters, demolished buildings, bunkers, pillboxes, and supply dumps. Then the battlewagons gave way to their smaller consorts. The cruisers closed on the beach, their guns bellowing in a rapid-fire cacophony. A line of destroyers finished the job just as the order was given to send in the assault waves.

As one, the hundreds of landing craft wheeled for White Beach, a small spit of sand edged by coconut trees and backed by a swamp. The Seventh Cavalry would be the first ashore, eager to redeem their regiment's honor and erase the stain of Lt. Col. George Armstrong Custer's defeat at the Battle of the Little Bighorn two generations before.

Pappy Gunn and the engineers assigned to get Tacloban airfield operational would land just behind the Seventh. Once ashore, they would pivot right and start working on the strip as soon as the cavalry troopers cleared the area of Japanese.

The waves of landing craft approached the beach as gunboats rippled salvos of rockets into Japanese positions. Their impacts created an overwhelming roar as they tore apart both man and nature. A few hundred yards out, and every available machine gun threw lead at the beach to force the Japanese to keep their heads down.

The first waves grounded ashore, ramps dropped, and hundreds of well-armed American cavalrymen poured onto White Beach. The Japanese defenders were able to respond with only sporadic rifle and machine gun fire.

The Seventh pushed into the tree line, moving fast with tanks in close support. Half the regiment drove west toward Tacloban City. The other half swung right for the Cataisan Peninsula, fighting their way past Filipino shacks and the swamp until they reached the road to the airfield.

Right behind them, the engineers and Pappy's force of fifty can-doers splashed ashore and chased after the Seventh. Pappy outfitted his team with pistols and submachine guns and packs of extra ammunition on top of an assortment of gear he thought useful once they reached the airfield. They looked rugged and ready, like modern-day pirates on a raiding mission.

They reached the road at the base of the peninsula and made their way north, encountering dead Japanese soldiers sprawled in the sand on either side of the blacktop. By 1600, Custer's old command had finished clearing the airfield, and Pappy's crew arrived to assist in any way they could. The engineers set to work lengthening the runway. It would have to extend almost to the base of the peninsula to handle the kind of planes Kenney wanted to base there.

They needed heavy equipment, but their bulldozers and graders had not yet arrived. Pappy and part of his team went off to search for whatever might be of use while the rest of his men began repairing some buildings that could be used as repair shops.

While foraging for gear, Pappy's crew wandered behind Japanese lines west of the peninsula and found an abandoned dozer. It wouldn't start at first, but Pappy dug into it and got it fired up. They drove it back to the airfield and turned it over to the engineers.

As they worked, the Japanese attacked. Low-flying fighters strafed the beaches, setting freshly landed supplies ablaze. Others machine-gunned and bombed the men building the runway, and more than once Pappy had to dive for cover. He quickly ordered some of his men to start digging slit trenches on either side of the runway, even as more Japanese aircraft broke through the aerial cordon to bomb ships offshore.

Kenney reached the airfield and found a scene of complete chaos. Incoming Japanese fighters sent men scurrying for cover. Much of what the engineers needed had not yet been landed, including the critical steel mats they would need to lay down and lock into place on the runway to make it usable after rainstorms. The peninsula was only three hundred yards wide, and the strip took up most of that. There'd be no room for revetments or much else, and Kenney quickly calculated he'd be lucky to get seventy-five fighters based there when it was done.

This was the best field they had. Farther to the south, American troops captured a flat stretch of ground near Dulag that was supposed to be turned into another strip. But one look at the boggy place, and the engineers realized it would take herculean efforts to get it functional.

For now, the 420 aircraft aboard Adm. Thomas Kincaid's twelve tiny jeep carriers provided air cover. That number seemed large, but the Navy pilots needed to patrol above their own flight decks to keep them safe, plus provide antisub missions, scouting runs, and other operations. At any given time, only a few dozen fighters could be overhead to protect the hundreds of vessels in Leyte Gulf.

The Japanese quickly overwhelmed that fighter cover with a myriad of small attacks. The Americans simply could not be everywhere at once, and on that first day, the Japanese set the tone for the invasion. Their pilots would not give up without a fight. In fact, two of them crashed their planes into a pair of Allied cruisers in what was one of the first dedicated kamikaze attacks of the war.

Kenney's men needed to get Tacloban up and running without delay. Col. David "Photo" Hutchison arrived later that day with the headquarters of the 308th Bomb Wing, the outfit that would form the tip of the Fifth Air Force's spear in the Philippines. His was a command without aircraft at the moment, but Hutchison made Pappy his airdrome officer. From a fire brigade leader, Pappy was now responsible for the most important piece of real estate in the Philippines.

The engineers reported that they needed something to grade the runway with so that it could withstand use by heavy aircraft.

The field had been cut straight out of the jungle before the war and had been used only by light aircraft. Now, before they could lay the steel mats down, they needed a more rugged layer than just the existing sand and dirt. Pappy set off late that day in search of something usable. He returned and reported that a source for crushed coral lay only two miles away. That was good news, and trucks were dispatched to go tap the source the next morning.

The next day, the first deliveries of steel planking arrived. Called Marston mat, these heavy planks were an ingenious and little heralded American invention that ensured airfields could be constructed almost everywhere in the world. They were modular, Swiss cheese–looking planks of steel that could be interlocked in different ways to form a sort of puzzle-piece airdrome. Used all over the Pacific for runways, taxiways, and dispersal areas, these products of North Carolina became one of the keys to victory over the Japanese.

When the first load of Marston mat arrived, Pappy showed up with almost two hundred Filipino volunteers to help carry them into place. Each plank was ten feet long and fifteen inches wide and weighed sixty-six pounds. To build a three-thousand-foot-long runway required thousands of these mats. Getting them into place was always manpower intensive. Pappy had foreseen that and had gone off in search of old friends among the civilian population to ask for help. Over the coming days, he eventually recruited almost fifteen hundred Filipinos for the job.

Nothing went right at first. Only five hundred feet worth of Marston mat arrived. While Pappy's crews laid it down and the engineers hooked it together, another wave of air attacks hammered the ships offshore. The landing craft crews became so spooked that they didn't want to deliver their supplies and troops to their assigned beaches, where they would be vulnerable as they disgorged the cargo in the surf. Instead, they made for the nearest point of land—which happened to be the Cataisan Peninsula.

While everyone at the field worked frantically, the Navy's landing craft suddenly began dumping piles of equipment destined for other units right in the middle of their work space. By the time Kenney arrived for another look at progress on the twenty-third, two dozen landing craft had dumped their loads atop the airfield and construction had all but ground to a halt. Some of the stacks of supplies towered over ten feet high.

Kenney was beside himself. He went up to Tacloban to take a look for himself. As he was driving up the peninsula to the edge of the runway, a Japanese bomber streaked overhead and clobbered a nearby landing craft. It burst into flames only a few hundred yards offshore.

At the strip, Kenney saw the problem needed a high-level solution. Somebody with major pull had to get those Navy boat crews to stop gumming up his airfield with stuff his guys couldn't use. He contacted the Navy, and MacArthur, and said it needed to stop at once. Even then, twenty-eight more craft were about to offload on the airstrip. Desperate to stop this insanity, Kenney ordered Hutchison to bulldoze into the sea any supplies still clogging the airfield on the morning of the twenty-fifth. In the meantime, Pappy volunteered to make sure no other boats would land—by setting up a line of machine guns along the peninsula's beaches. He kept watch over them, figuring since he was an old salt he'd be able to talk to the Navy crews in their language and convince them to go find another place to dump their stuff. The machine guns would back up his words.

Amid all the logistical issues, the Japanese continued their attacks. Speeding fighters roared over the runway at treetop level in surprise strafing runs every few hours. Other attacks came in at higher altitude, and a radar set that had made it ashore gave the men a bit of advanced warning before their bombs began to fall.

During each attack, everyone would scramble for cover. Kenney witnessed many attacks during his visits to the strip. Pappy and the others endured them all. Once, while standing beside a jeep with Colonel Hutchison, a lone Japanese fighter pilot flashed over the field in a surprise strafing run. Together they dove under the jeep as bullets raked past them.

No matter how close the call, as soon as the Japanese had passed, Pappy would bound up and order everyone back to work. They got so good at it that they squeezed a few extra minutes of work between air raid warnings and the actual arrival of level bombers. Every minute counted when men offshore were dying in this onslaught.

On the twenty-fourth, far out to sea, American scout planes and submarines discovered the Japanese fleet had sailed against the Leyte invasion force. Coming in from multiple directions in several task groups, the Imperial Navy hoped to overwhelm the Americans and break through to the vulnerable transports and cargo ships. They would stand no chance against Japanese battleships, and if they could be destroyed, the entire invasion would fail. It was one of the great gut-check moments of American military history. The Japanese nearly pulled it off.

Throughout the day of the twenty-fourth, American carrier planes bombed the incoming Japanese battleships and cruisers. These attacks sank numerous ships, including the *Musashi*, the largest battleship ever built. That night, the last battleship versus battleship encounter in naval history took place in Surigao Strait to the south of the Leyte beachhead. The Americans ambushed and annihilated the Japanese task force.

By dawn of the twenty-fifth, it looked like the Americans had scored a great victory.

Then the *Yamato*, *Musashi*'s sister ship, and her consorts steamed right into Adm. Thomas Kincaid's force of baby flattops. Those vulnerable escort carriers and their attending destroyers were the only American ships between the Japanese battleships and the transports off the Leyte beaches. In one of the epic naval engagements of World War II, the escort carriers launched their planes and tried frantically to evade the guns of the Japanese fleet while brave destroyer crews made suicide runs to buy the flattops time.

The Navy pilots made desperate attacks against the Japanese behemoths, strafing their decks and dropping bombs. They even launched dummy torpedo runs when they ran out of ordnance and ammo. The Japanese, unable to tell the difference between the real and fake attacks, maneuvered against each one. That threw off their aim as they fired at the fleeing carriers and bought the American sailors a little bit more time.

With their ships twisting and turning to dodge car-sized battleship shells, the pilots could not land and refuel on their decks. The fast carriers, the ones that could hold up to a hundred planes each, had sailed north earlier in the day to attack another Japanese task force. There were no more decks for these courageous aircrew to use.

Except for the unsinkable one at Tacloban and a barely functional strip at Dulag. The pilots flew south even as the jeep carrier USS *Gambier Bay* went down in flames under a deluge of shell hits. The bombers needed fuel and weapons to help stop this onslaught until better help could arrive, and they prayed they would find it at Pappy's airfield.

Stacks of abandoned supplies no longer cluttered Tacloban, and the Filipinos were able to lay eighteen hundred feet of Marston mat by the morning of the twenty-fifth. Still, the strip was barely halfway complete. Nevertheless, Navy planes began landing by midmorning. Many of the first ones down crashed at the end of the Marston mat as their tires sank into the soft Leyte sand. The engineers bulldozed them out of the way to make room for others. A joint Army-Navy air control team using radio-equipped jeeps made contact with the pilots overhead and began to guide them in properly. One by one, they dropped down and skidded to a halt, the crews piling out to help refuel and rearm them.

They quickly discovered they faced the same problem the Twenty-Seventh Bomb Group found with its dive bombers back in

Australia in the dark days of 1942. Even after three years of war, Army and Navy bomb shackles were still not compatible. Pappy saw the problem and rounded up some of his fire brigade troops. Together, they modified the bombs on the fly with blow torches, welding and cutting tools then sent them back to the waiting aircraft. Loaded aboard safely, the planes took off north to south as others landed in their wake.

The operation continued at a manic pace at Tacloban as the Navy bombers sped north to attack the Japanese in reckless solo runs. Soon more planes streamed in after 1000 when a furious kamikaze attack sank another of Admiral Kincaid's flattops and heavily damaged three others. In just a few hours, almost half his flight decks had been put out of action. There'd be no Navy air cover for the invasion fleet anchored off the Leyte beaches now. In fact, the dependency inverted as a result of the surprise Japanese onslaught. Kincaid's pilots were depending on Tacloban and the army now.

Almost a hundred planes landed at Pappy's field that morning and afternoon. Of the first sixty-five to land, twenty crashed. A few others tried to get down at Dulag, but there were no facilities, fuel bombs, or ammo there yet, and they ended up marooned on the island as a result. Somehow, amid all the broken aluminum and confusion, not a single naval aviator was killed.

The constant air attacks broke the Japanese commander's resolve, and the battleships turned for home, their escorting cruisers and destroyers providing antiaircraft cover from the ongoing American aerial charges.

While all this unfolded, Adm. William "Bull" Halsey's fast flattops were fighting a different battle against a Japanese carrier task force to the north. The Imperial Navy counted on that, and they dangled some of their last remaining aircraft carriers in front of Halsey as bait. He took it and steamed north away from the landing area to sink them.

Now, that afternoon, he sent part of his carrier force under Adm. John McCain to go back and help Kincaid out. Late in the day, he launched his bombers at the Japanese battleships fleeing San Bernardino Strait. He did so at their maximum range, knowing full well that many of those planes would never make it back to his ships.

McCain radioed Tacloban and asked if his bombers could divert to the field there. Hutchison calculated that they would arrive after sunset and said no. He had no landing lights, no way to illuminate the runway, and besides, the place was still a mess, with piles of broken Navy planes scattered along the length of the strip.

He thought no more of it until he and Pappy were talking over the events of the day in his tent and his field telephone rang. An air controller told him they had Navy planes in the pattern requesting landing instructions. They were low on fuel and some of them were shot up. It was either Tacloban or the waters of Leyte Gulf.

"I can bring 'em in," Pappy said. Before Hutchison could ask how, he stood up and bolted from the tent to go scrounge what he needed. He found a couple of metal frying pans and strapped a flashlight to each one's handle. The light reflected into the pan, creating an instant beacon. Satisfied, he raced to the edge of the runway through a growing rainstorm.

During his Navy career, Pappy spent many years aboard aircraft carriers. He made countless landings at night on pitching narrow decks in all manners of weather and knew that the secret to such dangerous operations lay in excellent coordination with the ship's Landing Signal Officer (LSO). The LSO stood at the edge of the deck with a pair of brightly colored paddles. As the planes made their final approach, the LSOs would guide them in with arm signals. The LSOs were always experienced pilots and they knew what the guy in the cockpit was going through as he prepared to land aboard. It was an incredibly effective system that remained in use until the dawn of the digital age.

Those flyboys overhead needed an LSO. The weather was growing worse. They were up there, scared, orbiting in darkness, with the half-finished strip their one chance. Pappy gave the word to bring them in, and the air controllers passed it along.

Standing alone at Cataisan Point, face to the sea, Pappy flipped on the flashlights. Instant LSO paddles. He stretched his arms out, like mimicking a bird soaring through the air. Ahead of him, he could see the landing lights of an approaching plane coming down toward him. The pilot saw his lighted pans and knew instantly there was a Navy pilot on the ground guiding him in. He watched Pappy's arm movements and followed his signals. He banked and slipped to line up on the runway, then Pappy gave him the cut engine sign—a paddle raked across his throat. The pilot throttled down and dropped safely onto the runway.

No time to celebrate. Another plane was coming in. Pappy lined him up and got him aboard safely. A third followed. By then, he'd been standing in the open for quite a while, exposing himself to any lingering Japanese snipers as the rain soaked through his uniform. It didn't matter. All he cared about was getting those boys down safe. If any of the Japanese snipers still lingering in the area took potshots at him, so be it.

He brought two dive bombers from USS *Hancock* down safely. They were part of a squadron of twelve that had tried to attack the Japanese battleship task force. Then something totally unexpected happened. An aircraft in the pattern swung onto its final approach. Its landing lights blazed, and its gear was down. Pappy started bringing it in. Down the strip, Hutchison and Kenney watched as the pilot didn't seem to react to Pappy's directions. Suddenly, the pilot slammed the throttle forward, pulled the gear up and sped over the edge of the runway. He banked hard left and extended out over the water—directly toward the darkened shape of a landing craft anchored offshore. The vessel suddenly exploded in flames as a bomb struck her and put a torch to a cargo of aviation fuel.

It was a Japanese bomber. The crew sneaked into the pattern and pretended to be a landing American plane until the last possible moment. The pilot pulled off quite a coup, but the attack ended up benefiting the other American planes overhead. The flames from the ship cast a yellow-orange glow across the entire peninsula, and Pappy's paddles were no longer needed. One by one, the remaining planes touched down safely. Not a single one crashed, and there were no casualties among the crews. Sources vary on how many Pappy brought home, but it was probably somewhere between nine and twenty. He saved a lot of American lives that night with his quick improvisation.

Two days later, Tacloban officially opened for business. Maj. Gerald R. Johnson, one of the Fifth Air Force's great fighter aces, brought in the first twenty-five P-38 Lightnings. They landed, refueled, and went to work searching for Japanese raiders.

In six and a half days, the men at Tacloban pulled off a near-impossible feat. They built a usable airfield in the middle of a chaotic war zone while under constant air attack and hobbled by innumerable problems nobody had foreseen. Work on the strip virtually stopped through the twenty-fifth as everyone focused on getting the Navy planes down, refueled, and rearmed, and bad weather hampered their efforts after that. It was an incredible achievement. With the strip open for business and Lightnings buzzing overhead, Pappy returned to thoughts of getting to Manila. Since landing at Leyte, he grew increasingly paranoid that the Japanese would either kill his family or move them out of Santo Tomas if they should discover he was back in the Philippines. He kept a low profile as a result, avoiding all reporters and staying out of the limelight.

The Filipinos who came to work at the airfield for him included a number of guerrillas. Pappy knew some of them, and one of them tipped him off on where the insurgents thought Gen. Tomoyuki

Yamashita had located his headquarters in downtown Manila. He was the Japanese commander in the Philippines. Pappy went straight to Colonel Hutchison with this intel and demanded a plane so he could go kill him.

Hutchison turned Pappy down. Kenney concurred, telling him he was more valuable alive than any dead Japanese general was to the air force. Besides, if he was shot down, he could be tortured into giving up information that could get his family killed. That thought sobered Pappy. He realized they were right. If the Japanese learned his identity and checked the internee rolls, he had no doubt they would execute his family along with him.

He would go in with the ground troops and be with the first ones through the gate. At this point, that was the only way to be sure he wouldn't get them killed if another aerial rescue attempt failed.

Hutchison didn't know quite what to think of Pappy's change of mind-set. Just to be sure, he told everyone on the airfield that the mad Arkansan was not to fly on any combat missions. Nor was he to be given a plane under any circumstances. Even then, he worried Pappy would try to steal one.

Pappy went back to work around the airfield. His old band of pirates busily constructed a control tower from palm logs cut and dragged up from the base of the peninsula. He oversaw the construction of antiaircraft emplacements and the storage locations for bombs, fuel, and ammunition. The repair shops were now working overtime to keep Johnson's P-38s flying. Already they'd been scoring victories, knocking down dive bombers over the invasion fleet only a few hours after arriving on the field.

A typhoon blew in on the twenty-eighth and offered them a short break from the relentless hit-and-run air attacks. But the weather turned the strip at Dulag into a swamp and made the living conditions at Tacloban even more miserable. The next day, with the skies clear, the Japanese returned.

This time, a single Ki-43 Hayabusa fighter raced over the wave tops of Leyte Gulf, evaded radar detection and surprised everyone at Tacloban. It barreled down the runway bare feet off the ground, its twin machine guns spraying bullets into a line of P-38s. Jerry Johnson's crew chief, Jack Hedgepeth, was killed instantly in the cockpit of the great leader's P-38, where he'd been cleaning the windscreen before the morning's mission.

Even with the arrival of one of the best fighter units in the Pacific, Tacloban remained a very dangerous place.

The next day, Kenney was back at the field when four Japanese fighter-bombers appeared over the water, heading straight for the runway. The antiaircraft gunners opened up, but the four were fast and low. None were hit.

They machine-gunned their way down the airstrip, dropping light, sixty-pound phosphorous bombs as they went. They scored a direct hit on an antiaircraft gun crew, killing two men. Farther down the runway, a pair of P-38s erupted in flames. Kenney was standing next to a jeep with a map spread on its hood, talking to an engineer officer when the attack began. As the fighters strafed their way to him, he and the engineer ducked behind the vehicle. Ten feet away, a burst of machine gun fire tore into a truck, wounding the driver and setting it afire.

Pappy was caught in his jeep in the middle of the attack out in the open. One of the planes zoomed right over him, guns blazing. A split second later, a bomb landed a few feet in front of the jeep. The explosion blew him out of the driver's seat and flung him to the ground. He lay sprawled there, unconscious for several moments. Then he sat up and climbed shakily to his feet. He took a few jerky steps, crying out in agony, then collapsed facedown, unmoving, on the cold steel runway he had done so much to build.

44

The Vow of Last Resort

Late October 1944
Santo Tomas, Manila, Philippines

Good morning everyone, it is six-oh-one. I'm sorry for being late, but better late-ey than never!" Don Bell's voice happily announced to the camp. He was so used to getting away with passing news surreptitiously through his daily broadcast with impunity that MacArthur's return to the Philippines made him reckless. The reference was so obvious that even the Japanese got it. Not long after that broadcast, the Kempeitai dragged him off to Fort Santiago.

The internees lost their beloved voice of Santo Tomas, but the last piece of news he shared with his fellow prisoners swept through the camp like a firestorm. They knew for weeks something big was afoot. American planes raided the Manila area almost every day. The Japanese now ordered the internees to remain away from windows and stay inside during the raids. Part of that was to protect them from shrapnel or errant bombs, but the internees also suspected it was their way of avoiding humiliation. From lords of this dark and twisted realm, the guards stood as powerless observers to the full might of a resurgent and rearmed America. They knew their time was running out.

The Imperial Army appropriated all available food as it geared up for a last stand on Luzon, triggering starvation within the civilian population. Inside the camp, the Japanese cut rice rations to less than a handful a day per inmate. They supplemented with bulbs and weeds and a plant called talinum that Julie pointed out were what Filipinos fed their pigs. After eighteen months of life at the Gureviches', the sudden change in diet left her sickened and revolted. Even though she was desperate with hunger, she could not bring herself to eat much of what the boys scavenged to supplement their rations.

By early November, the situation in the camp grew truly grim. The number of deaths continued to rise. Starvation slowed everyone's mental abilities. They talked slower, processed things slower. The adults became lethargic, and productivity in the gardens and kitchens suffered as their bodies failed. By this point, most men were down an average of fifty pounds, almost 33 percent of their body weight. A loss of 40 percent was almost always fatal. Survival hung on a knife's edge, and the gulf between the haves and have nots grew ever wider.

Those who had not self-rationed their Red Cross packages or squirreled away some small cache of food fared the worst. They watched jealously as neighbors and roommates included tidbits from their stashes with their daily rations. Even little things like salt, or a quarter teaspoon of rancid coconut oil, meant the difference between another day of life and complete collapse. Those who planned for the leanest of times felt guilty, but they could not share with those who ate through their windfalls without risking their own health. It was every family, every man, for themselves that fall as death stalked the camp.

Polly ruthlessly rationed out what remained of their five Red Cross packages. At dinner, she would produce one of the few chocolate bars left, and in front of the family she would break off a single square, then cut it into fifths. Even the shavings were shared, as nothing went to waste. Polly tried to short her own rations for the sake of her kids, but they put a stop to that. She had lost too much weight already, and they were terribly worried about her. Julie noted with horror that the last time Polly stepped on the scale downstairs, her mother weighed seventy-eight pounds.

Nath took greater risks to get anything extra he could for the family. He and his confidants ran their own version of the bait and switch on the Japanese. During one of their many prowlings, they discovered the guard's kitchen had barrels of dried fish and other goods stacked beside a hog-wire fence. If they could distract the guards, one of them might be able to reach through the hog wire and grab some extra grub.

They enlisted Ruski for the job. He was one of Nath's crew, a kid with British citizenship and Russian heritage, who lived in China long enough before the war to learn some Japanese. Nath first ran into him one day as the boy sat outside carving wooden biplanes and chess pieces. He introduced himself, and they became friends, playing chess together whenever time allowed. Ruski was a master at the game, and Nath never could beat him.

Nath knew that to pull this caper off, they would need his strategic thinking and language skills.

They talked over their plan in detail. There were three of them: Ruski would be the decoy; Nath and one other kid would be the thieves. Ruski went to the gate to the guard's living area and said something in Japanese. The soldiers let him in, and they began talking to him. Ruski's ability to speak Japanese made the young boy a favorite among the guards, and they would often stop to talk to him. That coziness convinced a lot of people that Ruski was an informant. He was anything but—he despised the Japanese for what they inflicted on his friends in China, but his relationship with the guards often proved useful.

The guards handed Ruski some food as they chatted. Meanwhile, Nath and the other boy crept to the side of the kitchen area. Distracted, the soldiers did not see them. They reached through the hog wire and began grabbing the dried fish, stuffing them into their pockets.

They escaped without notice. After they cleared the area, Ruski said his good-byes and slipped back to the main hall to share the bounty even stevens. Then they each took their share to their families.

They only carried that plan out a few times. Each time was a huge risk that could only be done in broad daylight. The last time, Nath thought one of the guards noticed him pilfering the fish but chose to let it slide. There were Korean conscripts among the guard detail. They tended to be more friendly and lenient than the Japanese ones. Probably, the guard who'd noticed Nath with his hand in the fish barrel was one of the Koreans.

As things grew worse, Dan Stickle abandoned all pretense of not knowing the Gunns and would sometimes bring his wife, Marie, to room forty-six to share meals with Polly and the kids. Polly returned in kind, and they began to work together to survive. One of the big coups Dan scored was a bit of caribou meat, which Polly boiled into a watery soup. Julie could barely stomach it, but the boys and Connie ate every bit.

Not long after, Nath caught and killed a cat that belonged to one of the Japanese guards. He loved cats, and couldn't help but think of Amos and Chi-Chi. Meat of any kind was needed, though, even if it was one of the hardest things he'd had to do since getting imprisoned.

Polly, the biggest animal lover in the family, dressed it and turned it into soup. They tried to hide from Julie the nature of the meat, but she suspected what it was and refused to take more than a sip or two.

Meanwhile, American air strikes hit the Manila area almost every day. When rain or clouds kept the bombers away, morale in the camp dipped. The sound of bombs and ack-ack fire may have terrified some at first, but they turned into a vicarious way the denizens of Santo Tomas struck back at the Japanese. Besides, every time an American plane appeared, it reminded them that their ordeal would not last forever. Someday soon, hopefully, Uncle Sam's soldiers would be at the gate, and freedom would be theirs again at last.

On November 13, 1944, some of Kenney's B-24 Liberators rumbled over Manila. Though forbidden to do so, many of the internees watched these planes with fascination, peering through windows despite the risk that entailed. These were marvelous, amazing craft none of them had ever seen before. They'd all known and seen the B-17s MacArthur possessed before the war. These four-engine bombers seemed so much larger, with narrow, elegant wings and broad, twin rudders that made them look as if they had forked tails. They paraded overhead in close formation, seemingly invulnerable to Japanese flak and attacking fighters.

Then the Japanese scored a lucky hit. Nath, Connie, and Polly saw it burst into flames and drop out of formation. As it fell, men began to bail out. The Japanese concentrated their antiaircraft fire on them, and to their horror the airmen were blown out of their chutes by the exploding shells.

Polly gasped and teared up. Nath stood, spellbound with horror by the sight. "Mom?" he managed.

She couldn't look at her youngest. She just held him and Connie close. After it was over, she whispered her pain, "That could have been P.I. That could have been P.I."

Nath had never thought of that. Neither had Connie. They hugged their mom hard and together, they said a prayer for those brave men whose deaths they witnessed.

A few days later, during another air raid, the camp got peppered with antiaircraft fallback. A chunk of shrapnel fell into the main yard and sizzled in the soft soil. Nath, watching from a nearby window, saw it land. Without thinking, he jumped up and ran for it, wanting it as a souvenir. Another boy, perhaps seventeen, ran out after him. Nath reached the piece of shrapnel first, and was about to pluck it out of the ground when a shadow passed over him.

He looked up, thinking it was his competition. Instead, he found himself staring at Lieutenant Abiko. Scabbard in hand, face full of fury, he pounced on Nath. Abiko jammed the scabbard into his chest, knocking him over. He swung it back and forth, the hard metal striking home as Nath struggled vainly to deflect it until he fell into the dirt, dazed and aching with pain. Abiko saw him slump to the ground and wheeled on the other kid, slapping his face repeatedly then raining blows down on his head. He collapsed next to Nath, bloody and barely conscious. Abiko studied them a moment, a look of triumph and satisfaction on his face. Without another word, he attached his scabbard back to his belt, turned and strutted away.

One mistake. That was all it took at Santo Tomas. Don Bell made that one mistake and now languished in the secret police dungeon at Fort Santiago. Nath had defied the rules recklessly without need, and it could have cost him more than a bad headache and a knot on his chest. After that, he broke the rules only to serve the survival needs of his family.

At least he and Paul were close to their mother again. They could watch out for her, protect her. The men in their new room left them alone. They were weak from malnutrition, listless, and depressed. The boys possessed more strength, more energy. The tables had turned. They were the ones feared now, and nobody tried to steal their belongings. In the land of *Lord of the Flies*, they all understood the Eighth Avenue rules.

Meanwhile, at Fort Santiago, Don Bell wasn't talking. Furious, the Kempeitai raided the camp repeatedly in search of clandestine radios. They even tossed the hospital, examining the mosquito netting and all the electrical fixtures in hopes of finding a hidden antenna that could lead them to the device.

When that didn't work, they surprised the camp with a full-scale search in December. They went through every room, pulling out each internee's personal belongings and scattering them around wildly. They left behind an array of luxury items, carefully preserved by the wealthy members of the white Manila elite. Fur wraps, fine suits and dresses, and linens were thrown all over the rooms like broken memories of better times. Everyone clung to those little bits of the good life despite the stark realities they faced.

The secret police did not check the gorilla's bum. Don Bell's concealed radio was never found. There were a few others scattered around the camp, and they remained expertly hidden as well.

December rains pummeled the camp, and morale plunged to an all-time low. In the grip of a starvation torpor, survival went from a daily struggle to an hourly one. Make it to the next meal, live a bit longer.

Polly, wracked by beriberi, her strength rapidly eroding, could only walk short distances now. Connie was little more than a scarecrow draped in rags. Julie's health started to fail again, and even steadfast Paul was suffering. Carrying the pots in the kitchen required a daily test of will. Boy-man versus indescribable pain. The boy-man won every time, but the margin of victory grew ever slimmer.

Then, Nath went down right after Christmas. It started with a fever; he'd suffered through plenty of those over the years. This felt different. It wasn't the rhythmic fever that came with dengue. It wasn't the flu or malaria or the dreaded TB. By the next day, his stomach burned. It grew so bad that standing left him panting and weak from pain.

His mother saw his flushed and sweat-covered face and led him to the hospital. They made the quarter-mile trip through the rain, leaning on each other, each step draining their last reserves of strength. They made it, as they survived everything else: together.

The doctors were harried and overworked. The ward was packed with dying, suffering men. Polly shuffled Nath, now nearly bent over from pain and exhaustion, to an empty bed and a nurse helped ease him into it. Her youngest looked up at her with eyes aged beyond his fourteen years. He was her lionheart, a mirror of P.I., her man cub made hard by circumstance and duty.

A doc diagnosed him with acute appendicitis. Nath needed surgery immediately, just as Connie had not long before. His mother watched as the nurses carried him into the barren surgery room, where they numbed the incision site with ice. The cold hit him like needles on his swollen flesh. A moment later, they gave him a pill that made him dizzy and disoriented. He lay there, the room spiraling around him as he struggled to keep a grip on his fear. A nurse appeared over him to drape a sheet in front of his chest so he could not see the surgeon work. Still, he tried to look. Masked faces appeared, half concealed by that white piece of linen. He felt a ripping bolt of pain, and a spurt of blood splashed the sheet crimson. He stared at it in shock, realizing dimly that it was his blood. A second later, his brain switched off and he passed out.

He regained consciousness in the ward, a nurse beside him. There were no painkillers to give him, and his right side seemed afire. The nurse gently told him the surgery had been a success. He would recover. Left unsaid was that he would survive only if infection did not set in. Without antibiotics, or even rubbing alcohol to sterilize the incision, all bets were off.

Connie came to visit. His mother limped the quarter mile each way to visit him, too. For the most part, he was on his own. Unable to even sit up at first, he slept fitfully as much as he could, telling himself he had to get his strength back to be there for his mom and siblings.

A rapid-fire banging roused him from sleep the next morning. Metal on metal. He couldn't see what it was, but some sort of commotion had broken out in the ward. He wanted to sit up to see what was happening, but he couldn't even raise his head. A moment later, he caught sight of movement coming down the ward's main aisle. With effort, he turned his head and saw the little boy in braces, run-staggering along, crutches smacking the metal grills at the end of each hospital bed.

He was still alive, living the only life he could amid the rows of dying men. He lurched past Nath, his braced legs flailing crazily, eyes hollowed. A moment later, he careened into something and crashed to the floor. A nurse rushed to his aid and carried him back to his bed.

When his own nurse came to check on him, Nath asked about the boy. He was amazed he was still here, still alive two years later. The nurse didn't know that Nath had seen him in 1942 and understood. She assumed he was annoyed with the boy, like so many other patients had been.

"Don't mind him." she said. "That's just what he does."

She paused, then added, "That's all he has."

It was more than Nath had. He wondered when he would be able to run again.

A week later, Paul arrived to get Nath, who was still too weak to make it all the way back to the main building on his own. Two men had died in beds near Nath, and all he wanted to do was get out of there as fast as he could.

Arm around his brother, he hobbled weakly through the ward and out into the morning. As they walked, Paul told his brother of the latest rumors circulating through the camp. The American army landed at Lingayen Gulf in almost the same place the Japanese used in December 1941. They were driving south for Manila now, and the Japanese in the camp were behaving oddly.

Since the summer, they'd heard rumors of POW massacres in other camps. The Japanese, knowing they were going to lose, chose mass executions rather than letting the POWs be liberated.

Word was, the Japanese were about to do the same thing at Santo Tomas. There were maybe fifty guards to the three thousand prisoners, and perhaps if they were in better shape, they could overpower them as a last resort to stave off a massacre. But nobody was in any shape to fight; they were all too sick, too hungry, too debilitated. The camp was ripe for slaughter.

As Paul half-carried his brother back to the main building, the boys made a solemn promise to each other. They would stay close to Polly in the days ahead. If the Japanese did start a massacre, they would defend her and the girls with whatever they could. No matter what, they would not let their mother and sisters be violated. They would die defending them, as they knew their father would do.

The brothers staggered into the main hall and slowly made their way up the stairs. Each one seemed a small mountain that left Nath cursing his weakened state and wondering how much time they all had left.

45

Pappy's Final Battle

January 1945
Forty–Second General Hospital, Brisbane, Australia

Pappy lay, sweat soaked and weak, dreading the moment about to come. A nurse frowned down at him as she checked his vitals and looked over the plaster cast that covered his wounded arm. In the background, the Forty-Second General Hospital's PA system played big band music. "Begin the Beguine" was the song of the moment. In better days, it would have brought Pappy back to those nights in Villamor Court dancing with Polly as the children watched and laughed.

Now it brought him only torment. Every low note sent a new surge of pain up his wounded arm. He writhed from it, pleading with the nurse to have it turned off.

"You know I can't do that, Colonel. We've been through this before," she said with a bite of contempt in her words.

She finished checking him out and reached for the covers. Pappy knew this was coming. In the past, he explained, begged, shouted, and screamed for the hospital staff to stop. They ignored him. More galling, they seemed to think he was a psychiatric case.

The covers descended on him. He felt them hit his body like a bed of nails. The sudden contact between skin and sheet sent a rush of fresh anguish through him. Back arched, face grimaced in pain,

Lt. Col. Pappy Gunn passed out. The nurse hurried on to her next patient.

Pappy had slipped into a coma by the time he reached the Forty-Second General Hospital at the beginning of November 1944. He spent five weeks drifting between darkness and sudden moments of pain. Twice, he awoke as somebody injected Novocain into his neck. Another time, he grew dimly aware of the staff as they put the cast on his arm. Yet these moments never lasted. The intensity of the pain overwhelmed his system, and each time he awoke the pain quickly drove him back into unconsciousness.

A dentist examined his teeth and found nothing out of the ordinary. He missed the fact that Pappy wore dentures. Before the war, a Japanese-American dentist in Hawaii who was a friend of the family's pulled his teeth and forged a set of false ones for him. Later during the war, he was among the few Japanese-Americans in Hawaii sent to an internment camp on the mainland. While imprisoned there, something compelled him to make another set of dentures and mail them off to Pappy's Stateside family. Eventually, they reached Australia in a moment of pure serendipity—Pappy had just broken his original set. When he retrieved his mail and discovered the box of teeth along with a note from his old friend, Pappy was rendered momentarily speechless. It became one of his favorite stories to tell.

The hospital dentist missed the false teeth, and Pappy's gums were virtually destroyed as his dentures remained in his mouth through his coma.

Around Christmas, just as the camp doctors operated on Nath's appendix, Pappy woke up. The pain in his arm had subsided. The dentist returned and pried his dentures out. With his gums blistered and torn, it was days before he could eat.

At first, he appeared to be slowly getting better. The doctors expected a full recovery. The wound, they judged, was not serious.

Then strange things happened. A nearby fan used to cool the

ward was pointed his way, and the air current over his body sent him into convulsions of pain. When people wearing boots clomped across the ward's wooden floor, the drum beat of their soles resonated in his wounded arm. It swelled under the plaster cast until the pain knocked Pappy out again. He would awake hours later, weak and limp from the ordeal.

Ten hours a day, the PA system played music. Every moment tormented Pappy. The low notes played particular havoc on his arm. He didn't understand the connection, only knew there was one. He asked the nurses to move the ward's high-powered speaker somewhere else. They refused. He went up the chain of command, barraged the doctors and the colonel in command of the hospital with requests to get rid of the thing.

They all refused, saying the other residents of the ward enjoyed the tunes. Pappy lapsed in and out of consciousness as the music tortured him. He awoke one morning determined to secure better treatment for himself. He couldn't go on like this; he knew in his weakened state if something didn't change, the pain would eventually kill him.

He went to war with the hospital staff. Every day, he harangued the ward boys and nurses. Every other day, he went after the Forty-Second General Hospital's commanding officer, demanding to see him and then barraging him with demands to be moved to a quieter ward.

The campaign initially failed to have any effect. The nurses and doctors simply came to believe that Pappy was either a malingering malcontent inventing phantom pains or he was a psychiatric case. As Pappy's anger increased, their position on him solidified. They ignored his calls for help, and they blew off his descriptions of the pain.

The hospital's doctors removed his cast and could not find any reason for his pain. The shrapnel went clean through Pappy's arm. It didn't hit anything vital.

Still, when Pappy was conscious, the pain was almost ever present.

He lived with it every moment at some level. Every loud noise sent it spiking to levels that often overwhelmed him again and knocked him out. When he awoke, the cycle would repeat.

Embittered, he raised hell whenever he could. At last, the hospital's commander, a Colonel Gundrey, consented to move Pappy eighty feet down the ward, away from the other patients whose noisy conversations fueled Pappy's arm pain.

He was fighting a war he couldn't win. The colonel outranked him by one grade, and he knew what the staff thought of him by this point. He changed tactics—and tried to escape.

One day, he forced himself to get out of bed. He couldn't get shoes on without help; he couldn't dress without a ward boy's attention. Yet, he got his feet on the floor and took a few unsteady steps around his bed before collapsing with exhaustion.

The next day, he tried again. This time, he made it a few more steps before his strength failed. He refused to give up. He knew if he stayed in that bed, his fate would not be good.

He demanded that he be released from the hospital so he could pay for his own treatment in a civilian one elsewhere in Brisbane. Colonel Gundrey shot this down. Pappy tried again, requesting to be moved to an unused section of the base where he could hire outside help to tend to him.

Request denied.

He made his escape anyway.

One day, he staggered outside the ward's main entrance. Not far, but enough to get the lay of the land around this side of the base. A few buildings stood nearby, but he saw off in the distance a thick stand of trees. Slowly, each morning he made it a little farther toward the trees before turning back for the ward.

He reached the woods one morning. It took him an hour to limp the mile to those trees, and he was so spent from the effort that he collapsed between two fallen logs. He lay there, surrounded by forest and relaxed in the silence. Gone was the music. Gone were the sounds of boots on hardwood, the laughter of the other patients as they waited for orders sending them Stateside.

He lay in the woods for hours, at ease within himself again at last. The colonel wouldn't discharge him. He wouldn't let civilian doctors examine him. This would have to be his sanctuary.

Pappy made the hour-long trek to the woods every morning after that. He lay between the logs, dozed, and escaped into his thoughts. After lunch, he staggered back for the full course of his rehabilitation—a cold pack and a light tissue massage—before returning to the woods until dark. He spent as much time out there as he could, still bombarding the staff with demands to be moved.

After Pappy threatened to go to the Army's surgeon general and report everyone for the way they treated him, Colonel Gundrey finally allowed Pappy to move over to Ward Six. It was an empty building on the edge of the hospital. Pappy found solace there in the quiet for two weeks. The swelling in his arm vanished, the pain went away, and he speedily recovered strength.

It lasted only two weeks. Then, the hospital's band began practicing next door to him. The music sent waves of pain into his arm again. It swelled up to twice its normal size. The doctors could not figure this out and again blamed it on psychiatric issues. It was all in Pappy's head, they reported.

The band practiced every day, and Pappy's torment worsened. His condition deteriorated, and he pleaded with the hospital commander to have the musicians play somewhere else. Colonel Gundrey's response was, "They've been moved all over the base because nobody likes to hear them practice."

For a short while, the band moved elsewhere, but not for long. The musicians returned one day to Ward Six itself and blasted Pappy out of bed. His arms swelled suddenly and the pain struck him with such force he could hardly function.

He called Colonel Gundrey, who assured him the band would be moved again. It wasn't. By this time, the staff was sick of this lieutenant colonel's constant badgering and—as they saw it—demands for special treatment. From that point on, they mostly ignored him.

Pappy quickly figured that out after he requested a meeting with the hospital's chief of surgery. It was denied. He protested again that band practice was destroying his recovery. Nothing was done. Then one day, after struggling out to Eagle Farm to see if he could get back in the cockpit with this bizarre reaction to sound, he returned to Ward Six to discover the hospital staff had installed a high-powered speaker just outside his building. Once again, he was subjected to ten hours of living misery as the PA system blared out dance music.

Pappy Gunn never wavered from a fight. Wounds did not keep him out of combat, nor did long odds or desperate situations. When knocked down, he always found his feet and came back with twice the power and energy to batter whatever obstacle lay in his path.

This was different. He was fighting a battle for his own health against people who controlled almost every aspect of his life now. He was a prisoner to a system that not only didn't care about him but seemed to go out of its way to crush him.

It was starting to work. His energy waned. The pain took over as his arm swelled from the music's effect. His morale plummeted. He began to wonder if his outcome would be a good one. At best, he might lose his arm. At worst, the pain was going to kill him. He didn't see any other endgame.

For the first time, his heart went out of the fight. Listlessly, he complained to Colonel Gundrey about the new speaker. The officer, charged with the well-being and recovery of his patients, shrugged at Pappy and said, "The other patients enjoy it. You will be compelled to stand it."

There seemed no way out.

46

The Sweet Georgia Peach

February 3, 1945
Santo Tomas, Manila, Philippines

The sky above Santo Tomas buzzed with airplanes. Blue and gray, they sped this way and that over Manila but did not attack any targets. If P.I. had been there, he would have told them they were Marine dive bombers, the same kind that he had helped assemble back in the desperate weeks of January 1942. Instead of being called A-24s, the Corps went with the Navy's moniker of SBD Dauntless.

One suddenly broke ranks and dove down on the camp. Silent eyes watched it from windows all around Santo Tomas. Down it went, lower and lower, almost as if on a strafing run. At the last minute, the pilot pulled up and disappeared behind the main building. Nath, still very weak from surgery stood in the shadows beside a partially open window and saw the pilot waving as he streaked past. Violating rules, the prisoners cheered and clapped as if their salvation flew wing on that glorious SBD.

The plane electrified the camp. In room forty-six, the women erupted in joy, energy spiking from the adrenaline rush. Similar scenes unfolded throughout the main building as the internees began chattering at once, trying to decipher what that maneuver meant.

A few minutes later, somebody came into the main hall with

more news. The dive bomber's gunner had thrown his goggles overboard when the plane buzzed the building. They landed on the patio behind the main hall, and several courageous prisoners rushed out to retrieve them before the Japanese took notice. Wrapped with the goggles, they found a handwritten note: "Roll out the barrel. Christmas is coming today or tomorrow."

When the news broke on the third floor, the place turned into sheer bedlam. Exultant cheers, shouting and back slapping, rivals and enemies now suddenly hugging and shaking hands—it was a moment unlike any other they'd been through. That was until the room monitors tried to restore order. In Paul and Nath's room, their monitor's name was Henry Pyle. He finally got everyone quiet by shouting, "Calm down and shut up! Do you want the Japs to come up here?"

That quieted things quickly. The boys slipped into the hallway and went to go be with Polly and their sisters. The ladies were huddled and talking in hushed tones now, delighting over the prospect of liberation.

A man appeared in the doorway to room forty-six. The women turned their attention to him as he said, "Stay together—try not to move around more than absolutely necessary."

This seemed logical. Then he added what was in the back of everyone's mind, "Be ready for any reprisal."

Nath and Paul took station next to their mom. Out the window, fires burned on ships crippled in Manila Bay by the recent air attacks. Smoke coiled up from them like signals of Japan's imminent defeat. The man was right. Lieutenant Abiko was volatile enough already. This could push him and others like him into a murderous frenzy.

Rumors swirled, whispered from room to room or passed between friends in the hallways of the main building. The Japanese were planning to kill all the men. The whole camp would soon be taken to Fort Santiago, the Kempeitai's dreaded torture lair. Others heard they would all be killed.

These rumors sent dread through the prisoners. Nobody had any doubts the Japanese were capable of such action. In the fall, the Imperial Army disbanded the internee committee and turned three of its members over to the Kempeitai. At Santiago, the Japanese tortured them for information before executing them in December.

Don Bell somehow survived his ordeal there, and for some reason the Kempeitai returned him to the camp. He was not the same after his experience there, and his stories of the horrors unleashed on the prisoners circulated through the camp for weeks.

No. Nobody had any doubts that the Japanese were capable of the most barbaric acts. Around the camp, the outbursts of joy evaporated as the prisoners went to ground and waited for their captors' reaction. To some, it felt like being on death row, the clock ticking down before that final rendezvous as the inmates prayed for the governor's call.

Late that afternoon, they decided Paul needed to get to the kitchen. The Americans hadn't arrived, and they would need whatever he could pilfer from the rice stocks there. Even with the news, the basic needs of survival still needed attending. Reluctantly, he hugged his mom and disappeared down the hallway.

Things remained tense until after dinner. Just as darkness began to fall, the sunset breeze carried the sound of distant gunfire to the camp. Everyone listened, trying to divine meaning in their reports.

Nath went back to his room just before nine. Paul returned a short time later after completing his kitchen duties. He walked into room forty-six just as a tremendous roar filled the air. Unlike anything the prisoners had ever heard, it seemed to be coming from the main gate. The window in the boys' room overlooked that part of the campus and was perhaps 150 yards from the checkpoint Julie had gone through so many times.

Without a second thought, Nath rushed to the window in time

to see a flare suddenly shoot skyward. It exploded overhead, bathing the gate in an eerie, wavering orange glow. A second later, Paul and the rest of the family joined him to watch the scene with a mix of awe, hope, and fear.

As the flare slowly sank earthward, a tank crashed through the wall. Wrought iron and masonry went flying everywhere as the vehicle thundered onto the grounds of the camp, a spotlight mounted on its turret shining its beam directly into the main hall.

Behind the tank came soldiers scurrying through the hole. Everyone came to the window at once, staring at the running figures.

They didn't look like Americans. The American soldiers they knew wore World War I–style tin helmets and khaki uniforms. These men had a style of helmet nobody had seen before and olive drab uniforms.

"They're Germans. Oh my God, they're Germans!" somebody cried in horror.

"I speak German," somebody else said.

"Then listen to them. I tell ya, they're Germans. Look at the helmets!"

The tank paused, its spotlight sweeping along the main building. As its beam passed the boys' room, they saw an American flag draped on its front glacis. On its side was the name *Georgia Peach*.

One of the soldiers yelled, "Why, hell yes! Move 'em up!"

"They're Americans!" somebody shouted. A sudden round of cheers erupted. Nath and Paul threw open the window, screaming at the top of their lungs, "Here we are! We're here!"

Where was P.I.? Each member of the family squinted down at the scene unfolding at the gate, searching for his familiar shape and gait. He was nowhere to be seen. Polly and Connie felt their euphoria drain away, replaced by foreboding. They knew P.I. wouldn't have missed this moment for the world. Something must have happened to him.

The tank moved forward into the campus, a ragged line of soldiers following in its wake, rifles and tommy guns on their hips. Just then, two figures emerged from the commandant's office. Mr. Ohashi stood in his severe black suit, arms raised, caught in the glare of *Georgia Peach*'s searchlight. Behind him, another civilian administrator raised his arms as well. Soldiers approached them both warily.

An internee shouted, "Don't shoot them! They're decent men!"

The soldiers grabbed them and pulled them behind the tank. A minute later, Lieutenant Abiko stepped out of the commandant's office wearing a backpack and his sword. He started for *Georgia Peach*, reaching for something in his pack. Some who saw him thought he was drawing his sword.

An American soldier saw Abiko pull a grenade from the backpack. He fired a burst from his tommy gun even as other GIs cut loose around him. Abiko spun around, gut-shot and winged by multiple bullets. He collapsed in the yard, still breathing but unable to move.

Seeing their tormentor fall triggered a sudden rush from the main hall. Men, once bankers and respected businessmen, miners and engineers, now reduced to little more than subjugated walking skeletons, erupted with pent-up violence. As the Gunn family stared on from the third floor, a crowd of angry, starving men began kicking and beating the mortally wounded Japanese officer. Somebody cut the ribbons of his tunic as souvenirs. Another grabbed his sword. Abiko was stripped of everything of value, picked clean by the most bitter and baseless human motivations. He lay in a pool of blood, helpless before their onslaught, too weak to even raise an arm and deflect the blows raining down on him. Several women whom he'd abused pushed their way to him and reveled at his incapacitation. They lit cigarettes given to them by the GIs and burned Abiko with their tips. He screamed and tried to resist. The smell of his burnt flesh filled the air.

Eventually, the American troops carried him to the small dispensary inside the main hall, where a doctor tended to his wounds. While stitching him up, Abiko somehow summoned enough strength to grab another hand grenade secreted on his body. He pulled the pin, but the weapon was a dud. A GI grabbed it and carefully took it outside.

That act of attempted immolation destroyed any hope of mercy for the Guadalcanal veteran. A crowd of angry internees appeared and pulled him off the examination table. They dragged him to a broom closet under the stairwell and threw him inside. Internees would come by every few minutes to gawk at him, kick him again. Some flicked cigarette butts at him as he pleaded in vain for water.

Meanwhile, the other guards fled to the education building, where forty of them took Mr. Leake and the kids hostage. Altogether, they had two hundred internees, and they threatened to shoot them if the Americans came into the building. Instead of a clean and joyous liberation, the kind of which would fill the imagination of those back home, used to seeing dancing crowds in French towns and cities, Santo Tomas had turned into a nightmarish stand-off.

The tanks and soldiers belonged to the Eighth Cavalry Regiment, First Cavalry Division. Ordered by MacArthur to save the internees at Santo Tomas at all costs before the Japanese could execute them, they broke through Japanese lines and plunged deep into enemy territory to get to the university, supported along the way by the Marine dive bombers that the internees had seen overhead that morning.

Now, eight hundred American cavalrymen and a few tanks were the only American combat troops in Manila. The rest of the army was dozens of miles away, fighting its way south against growing resistance.

Around them, sixteen thousand Japanese sailors and soldiers occupied Manila. It would be days before American reinforcements arrived, and the men of the Eighth Cav faced a terrible situation: a hostage crisis inside the compound, and hopeless odds outside. They bunkered down for the night, as did the internees.

Nath, still weak from his operation and unable to run, realized that the fighting might impact their ability to eat. The kitchens might cease functioning, or be destroyed in what was to come. The Red Cross packages were just about empty, and the family's food reserves had dwindled to almost nothing.

After midnight, he set out alone to see what he could do. Limping down the stairs, he stepped outside. The campus had been blacked out for months because of the air raids. Now, all the lights blazed brazenly, as if to dare the Japanese elsewhere in Manila to come and do their worst.

Sporadic shots rang out. Troopers were sharing their food with internees. They didn't have much, just K and C rations—the World War II iteration of Meals Ready to Eat (MREs). Some people still danced and celebrated, but that was petering out. Nath made his way through the scene toward a small storage room close to the front gate.

An internee grabbed a trooper, hugging him close and crying, "God, I hope you're real!"

The soldier hugged him back, speaking to him in a thick Texas drawl. Many of the men, it turned out, had belonged to a Texas National Guard unit before the war, and Southern accents abounded.

A cavalryman saw Nath limping along and suddenly scooped him into his arms. The man was sweaty and hot. He'd been fighting for days with little sleep and no chance for a shower, but to Nath he smelled fresh and clean. The internees reeked of death and disease. After a year of marinating in that stench, a healthy human, even a sweaty one, smelled divine.

The cavalryman let go of Nath and fired off something in a deep Texas accent. Nath couldn't process what he had said. He stared at him uncomprehendingly. The man repeated himself. He talked so fast, moved so fast, that it felt overwhelming. Starvation slowed the internees into an almost sort of hibernation. Nath hadn't realized it until that moment. Even their speech slowed down as their minds processed at a snail's pace compared to a well-fed human's. Nath tried to communicate with the man, but he made no progress. They were citizens of the same nation, humans of polar opposite experience, and for the moment, that gulf could not be crossed.

Nath continued to the storage hut. He found a way inside and shuffled between the barrels stored there. He pulled the lid off of one, dipped a hand inside, and discovered it was full of rock salt. He put an entire handful in his mouth. It burned, but tasted so delicious he did not care. He poured handfuls into his pant pockets knowing his family needed salt desperately. He stepped to the next cask, opened it, and found it full of salted fish. He stuffed as many as would fit in his pockets, then wrapped even more in his shirt tails.

He made his way back to room forty-six and turned his haul over to his mother. She passed the food out with the other residents as Nath went back for more. He made two interminably slow trips to the storage shed that night. By the time he got back, he was utterly wasted. He collapsed in his bunk and fell into an exhausted sleep.

47

War Made Animals of Men

February 5, 1945
Manila, Philippines

Guyenne Sanchez picked his way through shattered streets and burning buildings, dodging roving Japanese patrols as he made his way to the Gurevich duplex. The Japanese had descended into madness, killing anyone they found on the street. They bayonetted civilians, set them afire, and played death games with them, knowing they themselves were doomed to a terrible fate. The Americans were coming, and the city would soon become a charnel house, fought over like a corpse between two predators.

Bodies lay scattered in the street. Most were Filipino civilians caught outside by the Japanese patrols. Guyenne passed them, growing ever more anxious. He loved Connie; he had hoped the Gunns would be family one day. He would do anything for them, and a gesture to prove that was what set him forth into the streets.

The spool post bed. Polly once told Guyenne of its significance, how it was their cherished wedding gift. Wherever it was, the Gunns had made it a home. It was the one constant in their itinerant Navy lives. No matter where P.I. was assigned, they found a way to get that beautiful work of art, lovingly crafted by Polly's woodworking father, to whatever place they had rented.

Guyenne turned onto the last street, moving quickly now. He wanted to save the spool post bed, break it down, and get it somewhere safe.

A dog lay dead in the street. With a shock, Guyenne realized it was Eva's beloved pup. He moved closer. The duplex stood smoldering, partially burned. Leo Gurevich was sprawled in the front yard. The fun-loving pianist who loved boogie-woogie and lived to play music, lay motionless, his slender fingers cold and still. Guyenne rushed to his side. He'd been shot repeatedly and had been dead for at least a day.

The Japanese had been here.

Guyenne found Leo's dad next, dead in a pool of congealing blood. The Spaniard checked for a pulse, knowing there would be none. Then he rose from the corpses of his friends and looked around for Eva. Had she escaped?

No.

He spotted her a few yards away, facedown in the street.

Guyenne gently knelt beside her, praying silently that he would feel her heartbeat. He could see she had been shot in the head. Dried blood matted her hair, and the roadbed around her was stained red with it. He checked her pulse, and when his fingers touched her neck, she twitched.

Eva was still alive. He scooped her limp form into his arms and struggled to his feet. Holding her as gently as he could, he began to walk toward Santo Tomas.

How he got her across a city turned battlefield is anyone's guess. Somehow, on foot he managed to evade incoming artillery, the Japanese, and small-arms crossfires as he carried Eva toward the only safe place he knew of left in his beloved city.

He reached the gates of Santo Tomas and delivered her to the doctors and medics now congregating there. He went in search of the Gunn family heirloom. He saved Eva Gurevich's life instead. He left her in the care of the surgeons and went off to find Connie to tell her the news.

In room forty-six, Polly dug into her suitcase and found her elegant liberation dress. She hoped to wear it for P.I. as they went to the chapel together to thank their Lord for their freedom, but P.I. had not come. Now, weak and sick, she slowly unfolded the dress and laid it on her bed. It was one of the most beautiful she had ever sewn, the one she'd saved from a wardrobe of clothes she had created with her own skills while sitting at that "just 'cause" Singer P.I. had given to her.

She wanted to put it on and head down to the chapel anyway, then make her way to the dispensary to see Eva. But the effort seemed too much for her at the moment. She decided to wait until after lunch to struggle into it.

Some army field kitchens had arrived that morning. Lunch was delayed as a result while the camp waited for the army cooks to finish their work. No more watery rice. No more weeds and bulbs and bugs. The thought of actual food again filled all of them with hope.

A few minutes later, Paul and Nath went down to get lunch for the family from these new field kitchens, where they waited in line and heard the latest scuttlebutt. The hostage crisis was over. Ernest Stanley, a Japanese-speaking British citizen widely considered to be a collaborator, negotiated safe passage into the city for the guards and the commandant. In return, they released all two hundred hostages. The Japanese guards streamed out of the university in a nervous column, Stanley walking with the commandant. They made it through the gates, but rumors later circulated that a guerrilla cell ambushed and killed all forty of them.

With that resolved, the cavalry set to work saving as many of the starving internees as they could. One could not be saved. Mr. Leake, whose tireless efforts saved so many fatherless children at Santo Tomas, died of starvation the day the camp was liberated.

The wait for food seemed to take forever. But finally, they reached the front of the line and filled their plates with steaming hot army chow, the likes of which they had not seen since New Year's Eve, 1942.

The boys returned to the main building, climbed the stairs to the third floor and found Polly and the girls seated at a table in the hallway beside room forty-six. They joined them, laying the food down on the table and pulling up chairs.

Around them, other families began to eat as well. One of the ladies who slept only a few feet from Polly stood in the doorway of room forty-six. She stepped into the hallway beside Nath, regarding the meal they'd just brought up.

A tremendous explosion rocked the building. The floor shook, the sound like a freight train roaring past deafened everyone in the hallway. Nath looked up just as something struck Polly's neighbor in the back. It exited out the left side of her chest, tearing her dress.

Her face contorted in surprise. She muttered, "Oh," in a soft and breathless voice. Then she fell to her knees between Nath and Paul and sank facedown onto the hallway floor.

Bedlam erupted all around them. People running, screaming, cries of help filled the air. The family looked around wildly, unsure what had happened. They rushed to their neighbor's aid, Paul kneeling beside her. Nath stared down at her, his mind racing, but there was nothing to be done. She had been killed almost instantly.

Outside on the grounds, the irrepressible Don Bell was giving a live film report of Santo Tomas and the liberation of the camp with gear brought by journalists embedded with the First Cavalry Division. While sitting and talking into the movie camera, a Japanese artillery shell exploded behind him. He ducked down for a moment, composed himself, then continued on as if nothing had happened.

Inside, casualties lay bleeding and calling for help. The shell captured on camera behind Don Bell had gone into room forty-six, blowing out the wall and spraying shrapnel everywhere. It turned hunks of masonry into projectiles, and a jagged piece of concrete struck a woman in the head with such force that it tore away part of her face and skull.

Suddenly, army medics appeared from the stairwell, rushing through the throngs of panicked internees. One ran to the neighbor lying beside the Gunns' table. He checked her, saw she was dead, and moved to the next casualty.

Nath stepped toward the woman hit in the head. The medic reached her first. She was still alive, but bleeding badly. The medic looked around. "Hey, you," he said pointing at Nath. "Get over here."

Nath went over. Others gathered as well. Dimly, he sensed Paul was beside him. The medic pointed to the woman's ruined face. Her eye was gone.

"Hey, you with me?" the medic asked sharply.

"Yeah."

"See that thing squirting?"

"Yeah."

"Hold it. Don't let go no matter what."

"Okay."

Nath slid his fingers into place. The masonry had severed an artery in her neck. It was slick and slippery, and he lost his grip for a second.

"You have it?" the medic demanded.

Nath nodded.

"Let's lift her up," he said to the others around her. "We need to get her downstairs, *now.*"

Paul and other internees lifted her up, Nath still holding the artery.

"Let's go," the medic ordered. They carried the woman to the stairs and worked together to get her down to the main floor infirmary, where Lieutenant Abiko had been stitched up.

A doctor flew to her side as they laid her on a gurney. He grabbed a clamp and told Nath to let go as he slipped it onto the artery. Nath held on, almost paralyzed by the scene. The doctor quietly told Nath again he could stop. He released his fingers, pulled them to his side. They were covered in the woman's blood.

He stepped outside into the hallway by the stairs, dazed by what was unfolding.

From the closet under the stairs, he heard a noise. He walked over and opened the door. Peering inside, he saw Lieutenant Abiko lying on the floor, surrounded by cleaning equipment. His wounds were infected, and he smelled of gangrene. Cigarette butts flicked at him by bitter prisoners covered his bloody tunic.

Weakly, he motioned for water with one hand. Nath stared at him, remembering the beating this dying man inflicted on him only a few months before. He remembered the look of triumph on his face after he beat both boys senseless. Nath had looked up at the officer's polished boots, at his immaculate uniform, through a haze of pain.

Now he was no threat, a man reduced to begging for a bit of mercy from the very people he tormented.

Nath stepped back, shut the door, and walked away without another thought. The lieutenant lingered for a few more hours before finally expiring.

Upstairs, Julie followed Polly into the wreckage of room forty-six. Blast damage had destroyed most everything in there, but Polly saw her liberation dress still lying on her bed. She went to it, reached down and lifted it up. Shrapnel had cut it to ribbons. Strips of torn fabric hung limply from the dress as she held it and looked it over.

Julie saw something happen in her mother. Perhaps it was a delayed reaction to the sights in the hallway. Perhaps the ruined dress symbolized the broken dream of how they would be liberated.

Polly had governed herself with an iron grip for three years. She had fought every fight; she had given her last measures of strength to protect and care for her children. Now, as more shells rained down on the university, sending everyone diving for cover, trauma broke that iron grip. In the days that followed, she grew passive, quiet. Compliant. Gone was the fire of resistance sparked by the need to stand up and protect her babies. Instead, she slipped into their care and the care of others. Every person has a breaking point. Polly reached hers in the hallway that afternoon.

48

Ward Six

February 1945
Ward Six, Brisbane, Australia

Paul Gunn Jr. stepped out of the Australian car wearing other people's clothes. High-waist khaki slacks several sizes too large cinched with a belt that was too big, a gingham shirt that he fairly floated in, and a dark pair of shoes given to him somewhere along the way were his only worldly possessions.

He stood next to the car, waiting for his mom and sisters to get out. Nath, clad in a pair of shorts, a diagonally striped belt, and a shirt that didn't fit him climbed out and took station next to him.

The Army Air Force had taken the family to a hotel after a journey of thousands of miles. Paul peered up at its beautiful edifice with a tangle of emotions. How many times had he thought of this moment? How many times had he created scenarios in his head, complete with eloquent speeches that he would give? Those thoughts often sustained him through some of the worst nights in the camp.

The last few days had been such a whirlwind that he did not take the time to find the words he wanted to say. It made him feel unprepared and vulnerable. The return to civilization added confusion, shock, and an air of unreality to the emotions at play within him. The world around him seemed indistinct, dreamlike, and vague.

Perhaps part of that was due to starvation's effects, but part of it, he knew, was waiting inside the hotel.

Polly shakily emerged from the car wearing a dress over her gaunt, stick-figure-like form. She braided her hair and put on makeup for the first time in years, but she found no red hibiscus here in Australia. She shrugged it off. Didn't matter now anyway; the symbol was no longer needed.

She gathered her flock. Paul moved to her in his dreamlike state. He wanted to shake himself out of it, find the words he needed to find, prepare himself for what was to come. He cursed himself, focused, searched, but his mind simply had no words.

He floated along on the current of his family, following them as they went up the front stairs and entered the hotel. The opulent lobby disoriented them even more. Three days before, they'd barely escaped the hell of Manila. The city had died in an orgy of violence so barbaric it would keep war crimes investigators busy for years. The streets they loved, the shops and churches—all gone. Burned to the ground or blown to bits by artillery fire as two armies fought house to house, room to room. A hundred thousand Filipinos died, trapped between the armies.

After their rescue from Santo Tomas, a lieutenant assigned by Fifth Air Force to escort the family out of Manila chose instead to take them sightseeing. He drove them in a jeep through the rubble thinking it would be a fun little outing for the freed internees. With occasional sniper fire sounding in the distance and bursting shells, it was anything but that.

For most of the drive, Polly and the girls averted their eyes at the innumerable horrors. Humans defiled in death lay everywhere. Burned. Shot. Blown to pieces. After everything they'd been through, the family had not needed to see their city's fate. Nath and Paul, too young and too curious to know better, looked at everything. The images they saw were seared on their memories, never to be forgotten.

When the lieutenant returned with them after their macabre sightseeing trip, a colonel stormed up and screamed at him, "Do you have any idea what Pappy Gunn would do to you if he knew you just risked his family like that?"

Pappy Gunn. They heard him called that earlier when a cousin from Texarkana assigned to the First Cav came through the gate at Santo Tomas looking for them. Six four and 250 pounds, he belonged to the Owen side of the family. Kenney and Colonel Hutchison had made sure he was sent along with some field-grade officers to find the Gunns and get them out of harm's way.

Paul held the front door open, peering inside at the spectacle while his mom and sisters passed through it. The lobby was bustling with people—fresh faced, clean and well dressed. They never faced starvation, never faced beatings and businessmen turned feral by captivity. The genteel scene underscored the great divide between realities. Paul realized then that the transition from one to the other would not be an easy one.

Their cousin was the first to call P.I. a war hero. He told them Pappy was a legend to everyone fighting in the southwest Pacific. Polly was not surprised; she'd expected nothing less from her full-throttle husband.

Then their kin broke the news that Pappy was wounded at Leyte. He didn't have any details. Over the next three days, Polly asked everyone she could to tell them what happened to her husband. Nobody knew.

The Army Air Force flew them out of Manila to Mindoro, where they met some of Kenney's strafer crews. The family was overwhelmed by the reception as the young men treated them like royalty. Pappy stories tumbled out. Everyone seemed to have one. But nobody there knew how badly he had been wounded. Or at least if they did, they did not want to say.

Pappy. The name was so foreign to the family. He was always P.I. or Daddy. It was like these friends of their father knew a totally different person.

The next day, they had climbed into a transport and found two waiting nurses equipped with bottles and formula. When Polly asked what they were doing, the nurses had replied, "We've been sent by General Kenney to take care of Pappy's babies."

Polly had grinned and pointed at Nath. "That's Pappy's baby."

Paul was the planner, the thinker in the camp. Now, as they crossed the lobby, still moving a half speed slower than all the healthy people around them, he felt utterly lost. He had no plan, no outline of what to do or how to react to what lay ahead. It made him feel unfit to face it.

They reached the stairs and slowly climbed them as Paul's head filled with random memories cannonballing around. The last time he had seen his father, that Christmas Eve in 1941. Strong, capable, filled with confidence, P.I. had kissed him on the lips and promised to get back to them.

The children learned from their youngest moments that a promise from a Gunn was a bond that could never be broken. A promise was sacred.

P.I. had broken the most important one he ever made. It left Paul alternating between anger and anguish for three years. He wanted answers. He wanted to know why their father had abandoned them to such a terrible fate.

The transport plane flew them on to Biak Island, where more pilots mobbed them and plied them with food they couldn't eat and stories of Pappy they could not really understand. It was as if they'd spent the previous three years living at the bottom of the ocean. The world had moved on. Technology had taken gigantic leaps they could not even fathom. Events, trends, movies, and radio shows had all changed. Now, the transport plane had thrown them back into this new culture without context. They felt rootless, disoriented.

All the while, they heard the same refrain: Pappy was a legend, a hero, a myth, who had helped win the war in New Guinea.

They reached a landing, and Doc Gilmore, who had escorted the family from the Brisbane airport to the hotel, told them this was the floor. The family slowly entered into a hallway. Doc motioned to a door and said, "He's in there. I'll wait out here if you need anything."

Polly had been on autopilot since the day the shells first had fallen on Santo Tomas. Through that door waited the man who had always taken care of her. She needed that more than anything right now. Her body was wrecked by their experience. She was weak and spiritually wounded. She needed him to take the wheel for a while.

She looked around at her children to see if they were ready. They were all struggling with the same range of emotions. None of them could speak. Their reunion was finally at hand, and the family would be whole again at last. What would that look like? They could never go back to how it was before, that they all realized. Beyond that—?

Polly opened the door and stepped into the room, the children streaming in behind her.

It was a small suite with a bed in the far corner and a table next to the door, upon which some fruit was placed in a bowl. On the far side of the room, an old man, shoulders hunched, sat in a chair, a blanket draped in his lap.

They'd gone into the wrong room.

The old man stirred. His eyes glittered with tears as he looked up at them. His left arm was in a sling, and his right had only four fingers. His face was lined and drawn so thoroughly he looked withered, and flecks of gray now colored his hair.

No. Right room. They realized it simultaneously and tried to hide their shock.

Polly stared at the man the war made of her husband and found no words. He looked pitiful, far worse than she did in her wasted state. Beside her, the kids struggled to reconcile the last images of their father with the man seated before them now.

Gone was the energy, the man who had only two speeds: full and off. The strapping, youthful father they said good-bye to on Christmas Eve had been transformed into an unrecognizable shell.

Pappy tried to stand. He clenched his teeth and rose slowly with obvious effort. When he finally got to his feet, he looked hunched like a question mark. Paul had quietly harbored profound pain over being left behind. For three years, he'd battled its bitterness. Now, as he watched his father fight his wounded body for the dignity he once possessed, that anger vanished. How could he be bitter when his father had clearly given so much?

He had looked upon his dad with pity when they first walked into the room. Now, he knew pride. His dad might have broken his promise to them, but he did not abandon them. He had given everything to the war. He was the hero those pilots described. The pieces fell into place, and the man Paul knew as his father stood before him now as the hero he had become while trying to make good his promise. No son could ask for more.

As Pappy stood, waiting for them to come to him, Polly realized he would be the one needing care. Her needs would have to wait. That realization made this long-sought moment bittersweet. No more autopilot; she would have to be the advocate.

The vibe in the room trended toward awkward. Nobody said anything, the shock of the war's effects on both father and family churning emotions in each person. Polly knew she needed to save the moment. The iron grip she had on herself in Santo Tomas returned. She took the lead.

Bright and cheerful, her voice rang out, "Well, I know where we've been for the last three years. Where have you been?"

She paused, then grinned. "And it better be good."

The spell was broken. Tears streamed down Pappy's leathery face as he welcomed his wife into his one good arm. They embraced gently as the kids looked on, each awaiting their turn. The girls went next, saying a few quiet words as they held their dad around his wounds.

Nath, as the youngest, would be last. He waited by the door, anxious for his turn. His stomach growled with hunger, distracting him, until finally he snatched a plum out of the fruit bowl. One became four; after he finished each one he held on to the seeds.

Paul went to his father after the girls shared their moment with him. His left side was obviously so painful that they had all half-hugged his right. Pappy's one arm wrapped around his oldest boy and Paul moved into it. They held each other as Paul felt a surge of emotion. Pride over the hero P.I. had become. Sadness over the cost. Pure joy to have his father back at last.

Paul feared he would be speechless, overcome by the moment. Instead, the joy swelling inside him burst out in a long torrent of chatter. Pappy listened, said little for a change, and pulled him even closer.

And then, it was Nath's turn. Doc Gilmore slipped into the room beside him to see how things were going. Now, the youngest Gunn had a fistful of plum seeds and a long-lost father to greet. Not knowing what else to do, he turned to Doc and handed the seeds to him.

He wiped the plum juice on his shorts and went to his dad. Theirs was a shared heart, their characters a mirror. They were protectors, doers. Achievers, these two. In time, this would cause conflict between them. When it did, Polly would always say they fought because they were so much alike.

Pappy hugged his youngest boy as he said weakly, "You made it. You made it," like a mantra of joy and relief.

As they began to catch up, Pappy told them he booked rooms for the family in the hotel.

"Where will you be?" Polly asked.

"The Forty-Second General Hospital. Just down the street."

Polly asked him why they met here at the hotel. Pappy told her he didn't want the family's first sight of him to be in a hospital bed.

Not good enough. Polly took over right then. "We're staying with you," she announced in a voice that brooked no discussion. Pappy was too worn and pain-wracked to argue anyway.

Doc Gilmore disappeared for a few minutes, then returned with a wheelchair. Pappy could only stand for a couple of minutes, and even that proved exhausting. He would have to be wheeled back to the Forty-Second.

The reunion ended. Life together began anew. They headed out into the hallway to the elevators and discovered they'd need to take two trips to get the family down, given the size of the wheelchair. Nath and Paul stepped into one, and everyone else got into the other. The boys got stuck in their elevator, and a hotel employee had to get the elevator functioning for them again. The delay led to a revelatory moment for the rest of the family.

When Pappy was wheeled into the lobby, they found the place filled with bagpipe players fiddling with their instruments. Doc Gilmore looked around nervously. A piper standing nearby began to play, and suddenly Pappy wrenched in agony. Polly and the girls stared in alarm. What was going on? Doc rushed to the musician and sharply ordered him to stop. The bagpipers looked annoyed. A few others started playing, but Doc shut them down with orders furiously barked.

Quickly, they wheeled Pappy out of the hotel and back to the Forty-Second General. Several months before, the staff had placed him alone in an outbuilding known as Ward Six, where he remained isolated from the rest of the hospital population.

Doc explained to Polly that the phosphorous bomb that blew him out of the jeep sent two pieces of shrapnel through his left arm above the elbow. The doctors at Leyte saw the clean entrance and exit wounds, sewed him up, treated him for an infection, and believed he would make a full recovery. They sent him back to Brisbane to get healthy.

He didn't heal as expected, though. He had lingered for months in the ward, writhing in agony as the staff all but ignored him. They didn't know who he was or all that he had given to the cause. Instead, the nurses and doctors considered him a field-grade malingerer who did nothing but complain.

The family moved into Ward Six with Pappy to heal together and get reacquainted. It didn't take long for Polly to discover the pain was not in Pappy's head as the doctors kept telling her. She brought this up with the staff, but they dismissed her outright, including the hospital's chief doctor, an irascible colonel who clearly did not like Pappy.

One day, Gen. Enis Whitehead came to pay a visit. Pappy was not in good shape, and the general was astonished to see his transformation. Jittery from pain and painkillers, he looked like he was wasting away. Polly seized on this chance and told the general everything that she had seen and how the doctors continued to insist that Pappy's agony was all psychosomatic. She told Whitehead she witnessed his arm suddenly swell up while Pappy was sound asleep. A bus braking hard in the street outside triggered it once. Another time, Nath whistling in the bathroom caused it to happen. Polly wanted the doctors to put her husband to sleep and play music next to him. If the arm swelled, it couldn't be in his head. They rejected the idea outright, considering the whole thing a farce.

Whitehead walked to the nearest phone and demanded to see Pappy's doctors immediately. They came on the run and Whitehead unleashed hell on them. The general was well-known for his profanity-laced ass chewings, and this one was as epic as they came. By the time he was finished, the doctors had been utterly cowed.

Whitehead turned to Polly and apologized for his graphic language. Polly quipped, "General, I've been married to a sailor for years."

The medical staff wheeled Pappy straight into surgery. They put him under and tested his arm. Sure enough, sound waves caused it to swell. Something far more serious than a clean-through shrapnel wound had happened, and everyone had missed it. The surgeons went to work and operated on his arm.

Inside, they discovered a single phosphorous fragment lodged in his arm. It had burned out much of the tissue around the site and torched the nerve to a brittle mess. Loud noises, especially music, caused the damaged nerve to vibrate like a tuning fork. That was the source of the swelling.

They cleaned the site, removed the phosphorous fragment and sewed him up. When he returned to the ward later that day, the difference in his demeanor astonished everyone. Gone was the old man imprisoned by pain. Back were the bright eyes and humor of the man they knew and loved. He recovered steadily and soon began walking short distances.

A few weeks later, Pappy was ordered to a hospital in California for more tests and rehabilitation. He flew out of Brisbane while the family followed him aboard a passenger ship. In the summer of 1945, after eight months in hospitals, Pappy was released. He would need a final surgery in 1948 to completely eliminate the pain, and his arm would never be fully functional again. It was not the total recovery he wanted, but it was as close as medical technology could get him.

After his release, the family retreated to Pensacola and the bayside house on Navy Boulevard. There in the Florida sun that summer, they regained their strength and learned how to be together again. That would be a long process; things had changed, the kids had grown, and in the months to come they needed to establish their own new sense of normal, as well as their own postwar identities.

The war had robbed them of their prewar lifestyle. It wrecked Pappy's livelihood and had stolen all their possessions, including the spool post bed. It took their health, denied them the joys of shared experience. It destroyed the city they loved, and forced them to confront realities that would have broken lesser souls. For all it inflicted on them, the war never demolished the love they held for each other. That was indestructible.

Afterword

The revolution that Pappy Gunn started with the A-20s and B-25s helped ensure that over two hundred and fifty thousand Japanese troops would be cut off and left behind in New Guinea. That was almost as many men as the Germans lost at the Battle of Stalingrad. It was the largest force to be isolated during the Pacific War. Less than ten thousand of those Japanese remained alive to return to their homeland following the end of World War II.

Many have said that Pappy did more than anyone under the rank of general to win the war in the Southwest Pacific. His legacy is more than that, and it endures to this day. Gunships have remained an integral part of the American military ever since the Battle of Bismarck Sea. Today, when A-10 Thunderbolts and AC-130 Spectres prowl the battlefields of the War on Terror, the spirit of Pappy Gunn rides on their wings.

Big Jim Davies, John Henebry, and David Hutchison all earned their general's stars. One other Third Attack alumni, Dick Ellis, rose to become the vice commander of the USAF. Kenney went on to become the first leader of Strategic Air Command. He struggled in the job without the crazy band of misfits and innovators that had made the Fifth Air Force so successful.

After Pappy was wounded, Kenney sent Jack Evans to flight

school in the United States. He was killed during a training flight in an AT-6 Texan in early 1945.

Two weeks after Santo Tomas was liberated, Don Bell talked his way onto a Navy bombing raid along the Chinese coast. He embedded with VPB-118 and flew one combat mission with them. His aircraft was shot down and the crew marooned at sea off Japanese-held beaches. He and the other members of the bomber made it ashore, escaped, and evaded the Japanese for weeks until found by a Chinese guerrilla unit. Eventually, Don returned to friendly lines and brought yet another epic story to the American people. He ranks as one of the bravest and most capable journalists the United States has ever produced.

The Gunn family later returned to Manila, where Pappy helped stand up the new Philippine Air Force and reestablished Philippine Air Lines. Connie fell in love with a Navy officer and married him. The news broke Guyenne Sanchez's heart, and even though he also married and found happiness, he carried a torch for her for the rest of his life.

Julie went to work for the CIA. Nath and Paul went to work for their father, and the three Gunns later started their own air transport company together. Nath, perhaps wanting to live up to his father's legend, spent fifteen years as an aerial mercenary; he was wounded multiple times and shot down during the Indonesian War of Independence. His father taught him to fly, and while he spent thousands of hours in the air flying everything from P-51 Mustang fighters to cargo craft and Beech 18s, he never officially received an American pilot's licence.

Paul served as a sergeant in the Army during the Korean War. Afterward, he came home and settled into the quiet life of a high school history teacher.

Eva Gurevich made a full recovery. She immigrated to the United

States, remarried, and worked as a translator for various governmental agencies before retiring in the San Francisco Bay area.

A decade after the war, Nath ran into the woman whose face had been torn away in the bombardment of Santo Tomas. She had a glass eye and walked with a cane, but the plastic surgeons had done what they could for her. She told Nath how she learned what he had done for her and thanked him with a long embrace.

One night in 1957, Pappy was at the controls of a Beech 18 running a charter flight between Mindanao and Luzon. Flying low as always, his plane was struck by a crippling microburst over Cebu Island. The downdraft slammed his Beech into the ground. With supreme effort, Pappy was able to get airborne even after the impact. The 18 was badly crippled, and he turned for the nearest airstrip. As he did, the aircraft struck a coconut tree and crashed. All aboard were killed.

Polly never remarried, though she had opportunity. One of the oldest family friends came to visit one day years after Pappy died. He confessed he had always been in love with her, and now the circumstances and timing were finally right. He proposed to her in Nath's kitchen.

"I can't marry you," she told him. "I've had the love of my life."

Acknowledgments

This book began with a birthday wish in the spring of 2014. My daughter, Renee, said to me, "Dad, this year for my birthday gift, I want you to write a book by yourself." I've had two tracks to my career—books I've written on my own and in collaboration with combat veterans. I had not written a book on my own for years, having been tied up with *Outlaw Platoon*, *The Trident*, *Shock Factor*, and *Level Zero Heroes*. So when Renee made her birthday wish, I thought, *Couldn't you have just asked for a car?* It would have been easier.

A short time later, I drove home to California. Along the way, I thought about the internal bucket list I've made of people and subjects I want to write about before I die. At the top of that list were Pappy Gunn and George Kenney. Back in the '90s, when I first started researching fighter ace Gerald R. Johnson's combat career in the Fifth Air Force, many of the veterans I interviewed for my master's thesis would drift from talking about Kenney's great aces to the legendary Pappy Gunn. I heard many stories about Gunn and his time with the Third Attack from two close friends of Johnson's who also flew in the Third—Don Good and John Henebry. Don and Gerald went to the University of Oregon together before the war, where they competed for the affections of the same girl. Johnson won that courtship and later married her. But one day, Don and Gerald bumped into each other at Dobodura and discovered they'd been on many combat missions together. The old romantic rivals now became a one-two punch against the Japanese, Don in his Pappy-modified A-20 raking ships and grounded aircraft while Johnson hovered protectively overhead in his P-38. Through

Don, Gerald met John Henebry, and the two became fast friends for the rest of the war.

I interviewed both men in graduate school, then later while I wrote Johnson's biography as my second book, *Jungle Ace*. The stories they told of Pappy's exploits and the Third Attack resonated with me. Later, another Fifth Air Force veteran, Billy Runey, described for me watching the strafers make their runs against a convoy off Wewak in 1944. The destruction wrought in that attack was something that remained vividly in Bill's memory until he passed in July 2015.

Needless to say, the story of the mad professor of aviation and the strafers he created was something I wanted to write about for almost twenty years. To me, it illustrates the best of the American can-do spirit and serves as an exemplary tale of creating greatness out of disaster and shortcomings.

In April 2014, I locked myself away in a hotel near Santa Cruz, California, and just let the Pappy stories flow into a proposal. That became the genesis of *Indestructible*.

In one of those serendipitous moments of life, at the same time Jim Hornfischer brought the *Indestructible* proposal to market, Mauro DiPreta started at Hachette Books as its new publisher and vice president. The partnership between us has been an extraordinary personal and professional experience. Mauro, thank you for taking a chance on me, thank you for sharing the vision for this book, and thank you for your friendship. You've made it so much better with your guidance and counsel that whatever success it has will be your achievement. Thank you for all the pep talks, the long calls in the middle of your workday, and your flexibility, empathy, and compassion after Bill Runey died. Those are the marks not just of a skilled and talented editor, but of an exceptional human being. It has been an honor working with you on *Indestructible*.

A huge shout out to Betsy Hulsebosch, Mandy Kain, Ashley Yancey, Melanie Gold, David Lamb, the rest of the staff at Hachette, and copy editor Mark Steven Long. Working with all of you has been a tremendous joy. Thank you for all the hard work and effort you've put into making *Indestructible* the homage to one American family in a time of war that we envisioned two years ago.

In the summer of 2014, I flew to Texas to meet Nath (now Nat) Gunn and his wife, Vera. Over the years, many people have approached them with the intent of either making a movie or writing a book about Pappy, and Nat had been burned more than once. I'm not sure why they rolled the dice with me, but I will never be able to express enough gratitude that they did. What developed from that first meeting has been an enduring friendship built on near-daily calls between us for two years now. The insight, memories, and material provided by Nat and Vera have been vital to breathing life into *Indestructible*. Nat, you have been more of a friend to me than almost anyone else in my life since I returned from Afghanistan. You've been a mentor from whom I've learned much about how to govern myself in life. You and Vera, the love you share for each other—it is Indestructible, and inspirational to me. You both aren't just friends; this journey has made you part of my family. Thank you for everything you have done for me. Looking forward to seeing you again soon.

I need to thank Renee next. Sixteen years old at the time of her birthday request, she has grown into an eighteen-year-old college freshman now. I read much of *Indestructible* to her aloud along with the rest of my family, watching her emotional reaction carefully and noting the areas where the technical aviation stuff lost her in the weeds. I wanted not just a story for engineers and aviation grognards (like myself) but one that was accessible and meaningful to anyone who has a family and has known separation from or hardship with their loved ones. Renee's comments, insights, and reactions helped shape the narrative to achieve that goal. Thank you, Cricket. I'm looking forward to more road trips and lemur photos with you. The two of us narrate a podcast series called *John and Renee Do History*, which can be found on the web here: https://soundcloud.com/john-r-bruning/.

Ed is my budding aviation grognard. Fourteen now and a freshman in high school, he spends his lunch period discussing Sherman tanks and B-29 raids with his pal Scooter Reid. I figured Ed's interest in history and aviation needed to be sated as well, and his reactions to the manuscript helped balance the personal and emotional parts of the story with the grit of air combat in 1942. Thank you, Ed, for all the time you gave to *Indestructible*, be it listening to me read it or dealing with me away from Independence while I wrote it. Looking forward now to a lot of drone flying around Camp Adair with you!

Jennifer, thank you for making it possible for me to travel for *Indestructible* and sequester myself away in the woods to write it. I started the project with a month-long road trip that took me from Oregon to Florida and back, stopping at archives and key points in the story along the way. Later trips took me to Virginia and the southeast. When the writing began, I hunkered down at a cabin in the Cascades for much of the spring and summer of 2015. Those long absences from Independence were tough on you kids, but you held the fort down and made all of this possible. Thank you for being such a vital part of the process.

Robin and Marici Reid provided much information for me. Both are highly experienced aviators who also happen to own a Beech 18. Their son Jonathon let me crawl around in their Beech, taking photos of the cockpit and the cabin area. They also provided a number of Beech resources to me, including several fantastic books on this remarkable aircraft.

Bill Bartsch is one of the finest and most thorough aviation historians I've ever encountered. His books on FEAF's fighter units in the Philippines and the Dutch East Indies are indispensable for anyone wanting to know about MacArthur's Air Force in the early stages of the Pacific War. He has devoted his lifetime to keeping the legacy of those doomed, but courageous aviators alive not just through his books but by graciously donating his research to the MacArthur Memorial. His collection forms one of the most valuable resources on the early days of the USAAF in WWII. His generous correspondence with me was encouraging and extremely helpful. Thank you Bill, for all the help you provided.

Jon Parshall and Jim Sawruk helped me track down details of Pappy's first combat encounter and crash in December 1941. Thank you for assisting in that process and unraveling the mystery of how A6M Zeroes were able to get as far south as Cebu that early in the Philippine campaign.

Jim Zobel is the awesome archivist at the MacArthur Memorial. He is an incredible source of knowledge regarding not just the collections in the Memorial, but also of MacArthur's life in general. I am convinced he has somehow created his own *Chuck*-inspired Intersect and has uploaded the entire archives into his own mind. I could ask him questions and I swear I could see him *flash*. Minutes later, he would emerge from the vault with boxes full of material useful to me. All that and he loves Buddy Holly and the other great '50s- and '60s-era rockers. The week I spent there was the most fun I've ever had poking through primary sources as early American rock and roll played from a stereo in the copy room.

At the United States Air Force Research Center, Maranda Gilmore provided enormous help to me when I visited in September 2014. For a week, I barraged her with questions and requests for documents, which she handled with consummate professionalism and skill. Thank you for all the hard work on my behalf, Maranda.

Jim Hornfischer has been my agent since 2006. His guidance, expertise, and friendship have proven invaluable to my growth as a writer and historian. Jim, I owe you my success and my career. The life I live has been set in a framework you played the pivotal role in constructing, and I will always be grateful for that. Looking forward to that shot of bourbon with you soon.

Thanks are also due to Jeff Pullman, whose cabin in the woods has been my writing retreat now for seven years. Allison Serventi Morgan read the proposal while she and her entire family were down with stomach flu, providing her usual superb insight before I reworked it and sent it off to Jim. Allison has been a consistent support and trusted reader for my last eleven books. Thank you, Allison; your perspective always makes the finished result better.

Grace Berry blew into our lives in 2015 and was quickly (unofficially) adopted by my family. Grace organized the thousands of pages of printed documents I acquired in my research travels. Her work made it possible for me to find what I needed with a quick review of the numerous binders she put together for me. Thank you Grace, your work made a huge difference in this process.

In 2009, Specialist Taylor Marks was killed in Iraq. Taylor was part of my volunteer OPFOR group, the 973rd Civilians on the Battlefield, which trained with the Oregon National Guard, law enforcement agencies, SWAT teams, HAZMAT units, and other organizations. Basically, we were the bad guys, role-playing everything from bank robbers to al Qaeda Iraq. Taylor was a senior in high school when he joined my group, and it changed the arc of his life from one of safety and intellectual development at the University of Oregon, where he had been awarded a scholarship, to the rough-and-tumble work of Oregon National Guard's convoy escort duties in Iraq. I gave his eulogy in September 2009 and, in the Pontiac GTO I let him borrow for his senior prom, helped escort his remains to be laid to rest. Before his family and friends, I said that I would live for two now, and that his spirit of adventure would carry me forward in the years ahead. *Indestructible* and the way I researched the story was inspired by that promise. Every day I live is one more that Taylor's spirit inspires and urges me forward. The pain of loss never goes away; we just grow around it and it becomes a part of who we are. Being able to translate his inspiration to the printed word ensures that Taylor's legacy continues to grow. He will not be forgotten.

For further details, stories, and photos of Pappy and his circle of friends and family, please visit my website at: https://theamerican warrior.com/.

Notes

62 **"The Japanese virtually destroyed MacArthur's offensive air arm ... who was responsible for the disaster."**

The disaster at Clark Field has been told and retold through the years with considerable acrimony by both participants and historians. Exactly what happened will never fully be unraveled. Legend has it that Richard K. Sutherland kept a copy of the written order directing Brereton to move all the B-17s to Mindanao, which proved MacArthur's air general deliberately disobeyed the order. Sutherland made references to MacArthur about that in personal letters between the two men in the 1950s. However, according to Jim Zobel, the archivist at the MacArthur Memorial, Sutherland's files were destroyed by his wife during their tumultuous divorce. If true, the loss to history is a significant one.

78 **"While back at Nielson after lunch, P.I. called Cavite again ... He remained a civilian, at least for the moment."**

According to Julie Gunn's written recollections, P.I. actually drove over to Cavite to try to determine his status. He was still in the inactive reserve and could have been called to active duty at any time by the U.S. Navy. The chaos in the first days of the war precluded such a move, and the Japanese destroyed Cavite on December 10.

217 **"In the meantime, Pappy Gunn went rogue...Singapore was 2,100 miles from Batchelor Field, and most of that chunk of sky was now owned by the Japanese air forces."**

What followed during this period of Pappy's life can only be glimpsed through a few surviving, credible sources. That he flew Miss EMF is beyond doubt—he was seen in her at Java, and his Distinguished Service Cross narrative describes in detail the employment of the B-17 in seven separate attacks. References can be found to Pappy during this time in the Walter Edmonds collection of interviews, Weller's "Luck to the Fighters," and a smattering of documents from the period and personal recollections written to General Kenney while he was researching his own book. One source described Pappy's physical collapse due to the number of hours he'd flown during this period. Tracking his known locations, Miss EMF's cruising speed, and his return to Brisbane came to almost exactly the number of hours flown the source gave.

246 **"They decided to fly at night to minimize detection...continue to Bataan, deliver the quinine, and pull his own family out."**

According to Frank Bostrom, the B-17 pilot who evacuated MacArthur out of the Philippines, Pappy had already arranged to rendezvous with his family by having somebody find them and bring them across Manila Bay to Bataan, where he would pick them up in the Beech.

251 **"Pappy dropped out of the cloud layer...Bullets struck home."**

Exactly why Pappy dropped out of the cloud layer is not known. It could have been just a quick orientation check, or his aircraft simply lost power and he could not maintain altitude. Either way, the Japanese aircraft spotted him immediately and shot him down.

257   **"Pappy and McFarland arrived on this scene and reported to Elsmore...A B-17 flew into Del Monte to pick them up, and Pappy hitched a ride back aboard it."**

McFarland's fate was a sad one. According to recollections found in the Edmonds interviews, he flew to Cebu City in a Bellanca civilian aircraft, which was destroyed either on landing or in an air attack. He was stranded there with his family until captured by the Japanese on May 7, 1942. In October 1944, the Japanese herded McFarland and about eighteen hundred other prisoners of war into a vessel known as the *Arisan Maru* with the intent of taking them from the Philippines to Japan, where they were to be used as slave labor.

265   **"Together, they conspired to go get the B-25s and bring them back to Charters Towers."**

Exactly what happened next has been largely obscured by decades of bar tales, exaggerations, and purposefully vague official documents. In one of the final entries of the Twenty-Seventh Bomb Group's war diary the unit historian wrote, "Numerous troubles ensued" when they went to get the B-25s from the Dutch. Davies later said in an official interview that he had been ordered to go pick the planes up. That may have been the case, as General Brett might have told his most aggressive and red tape–hating group commander to end the standoff in Brisbane and simply take the planes. No record of that order, if it was issued, was found despite extensive searches by generations of historians. The Dutch side of this stresses that the aircraft were willingly turned over to the USAAF in return for other ones due in from the States.

268 **"Fox recovered enough to ask him where he'd picked up that B-25 . . . 'Squareheads—Dutch.'"**

According to Fox's version of the meeting, Pappy went on to tell him how he walked out to the flight line at Archerfield, climbed into the B-25, looked over the controls, and left. As he regaled the tech rep with the caper, not knowing that Fox had come out to troubleshoot the Mitchells for the Dutch, Pappy joked about how dumbfounded the "Squarehead" air force types must have been when they saw their plane leave.

270 **"An argument ensued . . . Davies produced Colonel Eubanks's authorization order and said, 'Major . . . a signed order supersedes an oral one.'"**

According to one account, Pappy threatened to court-martial the major if he didn't let them go. He also added that the planes would be hitting Japanese targets in a few days.

283 **"This time, the Americans went after the docks, planting a string of bombs that damaged another Japanese ship . . . Colonel Davies sought Pappy out and furiously dressed down his friend for breaking formation."**

No other source describes this incident, and the veteran may not have actually been on the mission that day, but it does ring true.

289 **"Getting Komori and his associates off Corregidor was only part of the mission ... The other was the intelligence journal that noted all Japanese actions, reported sightings, and discoveries made of their capabilities."**

Those documents survive today at the MacArthur Memorial in Norfolk, Virginia.

345 **"There was Pappy, the only one with a shirt on ... oak leaves pinned to its front."**

Kenney recalled that Pappy and his crew were working on an A-20 when he entered the hangar, and that may have been the case. Pappy's flight records show that he was test flying both the B-25 and an A-20 at the beginning of August. The difference is subtle but important, given what followed. George Kenney was not above taking credit for other people's ideas and work, and in later years he would write that the eight-gunned B-25 was his idea, even though work on it began two months before he ever arrived at Charters Towers. *Pappy's Folly* was not officially transferred from Dutch ownership to the USAAF until September 1942, which gives some weight to Kenney's account. However, given the odd way the Dutch B-25s fell into the Third Attack Group's hands, *Pappy's Folly* quite probably might have been at Charters Towers through the spring and summer before the paperwork trail caught up with it.

347 **"Pappy flew into this chaos without any orders to be there, or to fly combat missions ... They found him bloodied and still impaled by the shrapnel, groaning, 'They got Sam. The goddamned bastards got Sam.'"**

In later retellings of Pappy's career, much has been written of his participation in this crisis. In fact, he spent three days at Port Moresby and probably flew five ground support missions against the Japanese along the Kokoda Trail in *Not in Stock*. Stories abound of Pappy making bombing runs in his B-25, or sometimes an A-20, singing as he blasted the Japanese. One 1960s article included this gem: Pappy worked the controls with his fingertips. A stub of cigar was cocked in the corner of his square face and around it he sang, "Gimme that good old Mountain Dew…"

Other sources credit Pappy with solo strafing and bombing attacks on Lae Airdrome. One of these yarns credited him with flaming ten Japanese aircraft as he jinked and strafed his way back and forth over that Japanese airdrome.

425   **"That spring, Pappy flirted with the AIB again…but that plan never came to fruition."**

It is possible Pappy made flights up to the Philippines in the spring of 1944, but those cannot be definitively proven. The airfields were overrun by the Japanese in June, and that scrubbed further missions. However, after the war Pappy's friends often came to see him in the Philippines, including John Henebry and Jim Davies. They sometimes talked about what they considered to be Pappy's craziest mission, which Nat Gunn recalled being a long-range flight to drop Mac-Arthur's "I Shall Return" propaganda, including matchbooks with the general's face on them, through much of Southeast Asia and the Philippines. If true, it is likely this happened during this time of the war.

Bibliography

Secondary Sources

Anzai, Rosemary. *For Love of Country: WWII Secret Agent Arthur Komori*. Paragon Agency, 2013.

Ball, Larry. *The Immortal Twin Beech*. Ball Publications, 1995.

Barr, James A. *Airpower Employment of the Fifth Air Force in the World War II Southwest Pacific Theater*. Pennyhill Press, 1997.

Bartsch, William H. *December 8, 1941: MacArthur's Pearl Harbor*. Texas A&M University Press, 2003.

———. *Doomed at the Start: American Pursuit Pilots in the Philippines, 1941–1942*. Texas A&M University Press, 1992.

———. *Every Day a Nightmare: American Pursuit Pilots in the Defense of Java, 1941–42*. Texas A&M University Press, 2010.

Baumgardner, Randy, ed. *Fifth Air Force*. Turner, 1994.

Berry, Evalena. *Time and the River: A History of Cleburne County*. Rose Publishing, 1982.

Birdsall, Stephen. *Flying Buccaneers: The Illustrated Story of Kenney's Fifth Air Force*. Doubleday, 1977.

Boer, P.C. *The Loss of Java*. National University of Singapore Press, 2011.

Brereton, Lewis. *The Brereton Diaries: The War in the Air in the Pacific, Middle East and Europe, 3 October 1941–8 May 1945*. Pickle Partners, 2014.

Burton, John. *Fortnight of Infamy: The Collapse of Allied Airpower West of Pearl Harbor*. Naval Institute Press, 2006.

Cannon, M. Hamlin. *Leyte: The Return to the Philippines.* Create-Space, 2015.

Casey, John W. *Warriors Without Weapons: Triumph of the Tech Reps.* Amethyst Moon, 2010.

Casey, John W., and Jon Boyd. *North American Aviation: The Rise and Fall of an Aerospace Giant.* Amethyst Moon, 2011.

Cates, Tressa R. *Infamous Santo Tomás: Authentic W.W.II Civilian Prisoner of War Camp Story.* Pacific Press, 1981.

Claringbould, Michael J. *Black Sunday: When the U.S. 5th Air Force Lost to New Guinea's Weather.* Privately printed, 1995.

Cogan, Frances B. *Captured: The Japanese Internment of American Civilians in the Philippines, 1941–1945.* University of Georgia Press, 2000.

Colley, George S. *Manila-Kuching and Return, 1941–1945.* Taylor & Taylor, 1946.

Cooper, Anthony. *Kokoda Air Strikes: Allied Air Forces in New Guinea, 1942.* NewSouth, 2014.

Cortesi, Lawrence. *The Battle of the Bismarck Sea.* Leisure Books, 1967.

———. *The Grim Reapers: History of the 3rd Bomb Group, 1918–1965.* Historical Aviation Album, 1985.

Cox, Jeffrey. *Rising Sun, Falling Skies: The Disastrous Java Sea Campaign of World War II.* Osprey, 2014.

Craven, Wesley Frank, and James Lea Cate, eds. *The Army Air Forces in World War II.* Vols. 1 and 4. University of Chicago Press, 1948, 1950.

Cummins, Joseph. *Forgotten Battlefields of World War II.* Hidden History, 2013.

Cutler, Robert S. *America's Worst Aviation Disaster in Australia.* First published as *Mackay's Flying Fortress: The Story of Australia's Worst Air Crash in World War II.* Central Queensland University Press, 2003.

Cutler, Thomas J. *The Battle of Leyte Gulf: 23–26 October 1944*. Bluejacket Books / Naval Institute Press, 2001.

Davies, R.E.G. *Airlines of Asia Since 1920*. Putnam, 1997.

Dedal, Tony. *Wings over the Philippines*. New Day Publishers, 2008.

Dull, Paul S. *A Battle History of the Imperial Japanese Navy, 1941–1945*. Naval Institute Press, 1978.

Dunn, William J. *Pacific Microphone*. Texas A&M University Press, 1988.

Dyess, William E., and Charles Leavelle. *The Dyess Story*. G.P. Putnam's Sons, 1944.

Edmonds, Walter D. *They Fought with What They Had*. Little, Brown, 1951.

Eichelberger, Robert L. *Our Jungle Road to Tokyo*. Battery Press, 1989.

Ephraim, Frank. *Escape to Manila: From Nazi Tyranny to Japanese Terror*. University of Illinois Press, 2008.

Fitzgerald, Earl A. *Voices in the Night: Messages from Prisoners of War in the South Pacific, 1942–1945*. Pioneer Printing, 1948.

Fredrickson, John, and John Roper. *Images of Aviation: Kansas City B-25 Factory*. Arcadia Publishing, 2014.

Freer, William B. *The Philippine Experiences of an American Teacher*. Scribner, 1906.

Gailey, Harry. *MacArthur Strikes Back: Decision at Buna, New Guinea, 1942–1943*. Presidio Press, 2000.

———. *MacArthur's Victory: The War in New Guinea, 1943–44*. Presidio, 2004.

Gamble, Bruce. *Fortress Rabaul: The Battle for the Southwest Pacific, January 1942–April 1943*. Zenith Press, 2010.

Gleeck, Lewis E. Jr. *The Manila Americans (1901–1964)*. Carmelo & Bauermann, 1977.

Gordon, John. *Fighting for MacArthur: The Navy and Marine Corps' Desperate Defense of the Philippines*. Naval Institute Press, 2011.

Grashio, Samuel C., and Bernard Norling. *Return to Freedom*. University Press, 1982.

Griffith, Thomas E. *MacArthur's Airman*. University Press of Kansas, 1998.

Grover, Roy Lee. *Incidents in the Life of a B-25 Pilot*. AuthorHouse, 2006.

Gunn, Nathaniel. *Pappy Gunn*. AuthorHouse, 2004.

Gunnison, Royal Arch. *So Sorry, No Peace*. Viking Press, 1944.

Henebry, John P. *The Grim Reapers at Work in the Pacific Theater*. Pictorial Histories, 2002.

Hickey, Lawrence J. *Warpath Across the Pacific*. International Research and Publishing, 1984.

Hickey, Lawrence, and Jack Fellows. *Stories from the Fifth Air Force*. International Historical Research Associates, 2015.

Hind, R. Renton. *Spirits Unbroken: Three Years a Prisoner in a Philippines Internment Camp*. CreateSpace, 2014.

Holbrook, Stewart. *None More Courageous—American War Heroes of Today*. Macmillan, 1942.

Holland, Robert B. *100 Miles to Freedom: The Epic Story of the Rescue of Santo Tomas and the Liberation of Manila: 1943–1945*. Turner, 2011.

Hornfischer, James D. *The Last Stand of the Tin Can Sailors*. Bantam, 2005.

Imparato, Edward T. *Into Darkness: A Pilot's Journey Through Headhunter Territory*. Howell Press, 1995.

Ind, Allison. *Bataan: The Judgment Seat: The Saga of the Philippine Command of the United States Army Air Force, May 1941 to May 1942*. Ind Press, 2007.

Ind, Allison, and Daniel MacArthur. *Allied Intelligence Bureau: The Secret Weapon in the War Against Japan*. Bibliopoesy Book Publishing, 2014.

Ishida, Jintaro. *The Remains of War: Apology and Forgiveness—Testimonies of the Japanese Imperial Army and Its Filipino Victims*. Lyons Press, 2002.

James, D. Clayton. *The Years of MacArthur.* Vols. 1 and 2. Houghton Mifflin, 1970, 1975.

Johnston, Mark. *Whispering Death: Australian Airmen in the Pacific War.* Allen & Unwin, 2011.

Kenney, George C. *General Kenney Reports.* United States Air Force, Office of Air Force History, 1987.

Kidston, Martin J. *From Poplar to Papua: Montana's 163rd Infantry Regiment in World War II.* Farcountry Press, 2004.

King, Dan. *The Last Zero Fighter: Firsthand Accounts from WWII Japanese Naval Pilots.* Pacific, 2012.

Lee, Clark. *They Call It Pacific: An Eye-Witness Story of Our War Against Japan from Bataan to the Solomons.* Viking Press, 1943.

Lichauco, Marcial P. *Dear Mother Putnam: Life & Death in Manila During the Japanese Occupation 1941–1945.* Privately printed, 2005.

Lorenzen, Angus. *A Lovely Little War: Life in a Japanese Prison Camp Through the Eyes of a Child.* History, 2008.

Lucas, Celia. *Living Hell: The Prisoners of Santo Tomas.* Endeavour Press, 2013.

Macauley, Doris. *Bread and Rice: An American Woman's Fight to Survive in the Jungles and Prison Camps of the WWII Philippines.* Uncommon Valor Press, 2014.

Main, Vernon, and Richard Bienvenu. *The Royce Raid: The True Story of a Secret Suicide Mission in the WWII Pacific Theatre.* Welcome One Associates, 2013.

Mantelli, Brown, Kittel, and Graf. *North American B-25 Mitchell.* Edizioni R.E.I., 2015.

Marquez, Adalia. *Blood on the Rising Sun: A Factual Story of the Japanese Invasion of the Philippines.* DeTanko Publishers, 1957.

Marshall, Cecily Mattocks. *Happy Life Blues: A Memoir of Survival.* Angus MacGregor Books, 2007.

Martin, Adrian R., and Larry W. Stephenson. *Operation Plum: The Ill-Fated 27th Bombardment Group and the Fight for the Western Pacific*. Texas A&M University Press, 2008.

McAulay, Lex. *Battle of the Bismarck Sea*. St. Martin's Press, 1991.

————. *MacArthur's Eagles: The U.S. Air War over New Guinea 1943–1944*. Naval Institute Press, 2005.

McGowan, Sam. *World War II: Sam McGowan's Articles About World War II*. Privately printed, 2012.

Merriam, Ray. *War in the Philippines, 1941–1945*. Merriam Press, 2013.

Messimer, Dwight R. *In the Hands of Fate: The Story of Patrol Wing Ten, 8 December 1941–11 May 1942*. Bluejacket Books / Naval Institute Press, 1985.

Middlebrook, Garrett. *Air Combat at 20 Feet: Selected Missions from a Strafer Pilot's Diary*. AuthorHouse, 2004.

Miller, John. *Cartwheel: The Reduction of Rabaul*. Amazon Digital Services, 2013.

Milner, Samuel. *Victory in Papua*. Amazon Digital Services, 2013.

Miner, William D., and Lewis A. Miner. *Surviving Hell; Surrender on Cebu*. Turner, 2010.

Morehead, James B. *In My Sights: The Memoir of a P-40 Ace*. Presidio, 1998.

Morrill, John. *South From Corregidor*. CreateSpace, 2013.

Morton, Louis. *The Fall of the Philippines*. Amazon Digital Services, 2013.

————. *The War in the Pacific: Strategy and Command: The First Two Years*. Amazon Digital Services, 2013.

Murphy, James T., and A.B. Feuer. *Skip Bombing: The True Story of Stealth Bombing Techniques Used in 1942*. Integrated Book Technology, no date.

Mydans, Carl. *More Than Meets the Eye*. Harper, 1959.

Null, Gary. *Weapon of Denial: Air Power and the Battle for New Guinea*. United States Air Force History and Museums, 2014.

Perret, Geoffrey. *Old Soldiers Never Die: The Life of Douglas Mac-Arthur*. Adams Media, 1996.

Phillips, Claire. *Agent High Pockets: A Woman's Fight Against the Japanese in the Philippines*. Uncommon Valor Press, 2014.

Phillips, Edward H. *The Staggerwing Story: A History of the Beechcraft Model 17*. Flying Books International, 1996.

Prefer, Nathan. *MacArthur's New Guinea Campaign*. Combined Books, 1995.

Ready, J. Lee. *The Massacre of ABDACOM: The Destruction of the United States, British, Dutch and Australian Forces by the Japanese in World War II*. Monticello, 2013.

Rees, Laurence. *Horror in the East: Japan and the Atrocities of World War II*. Da Capo Press, 2001.

Robinson, Pat. *The Fight for New Guinea*. Random House, 1943.

Rodman, Matthew K. *A War of Their Own: Bombers over the Southwest Pacific*. Air University Press, 2005.

Romulo, Carlos P. *I Saw the Fall of the Philippines*. Doubleday, Doran, 1942.

Ruffato, Luca, and Michael J. Claringbould. *Eagles of the Southern Sky: The Tainan Air Group in WWII*. Vol. 1. Tainan Research and Publishing, 2012.

Russell, Edward Frederick Langley. *The Knights of Bushido: A History of Japanese War Crimes During World War II*. Skyhorse, 2008.

Rutter, Joseph. *Wreaking Havoc: A Year in an A-20*. Texas A&M University Press, 2004.

Sakai, Saburo, with Martin Caidin and Fred Saito. *Samurai!* Bantam, 1985.

Sakaida, Henry. *Imperial Japanese Navy Aces 1937–45*. Osprey, 1998.

———. *Pacific Air Combat WWII: Voices from the Past*. Phalanx, 1993.

———. *Winged Samurai: Saburo Sakai and the Zero Fighter Pilots*. Champlin Fighter Museum Press, 1985.

Salecker, Gene Eric. *Fortress Against the Sun: The B-17 Flying Fortress in the Pacific.* Combined, 2001.

Scutts, Jerry. *B-25 Mitchell at War.* Ian Allen, 1983.

Shores, Christopher, et al. *Bloody Shambles: The First Comprehensive Account of Air Operations Over South-East Asia.* 2 vols. Grub Street, 1992, 1993.

Smith, Robert Ross. *The Approach to the Philippines.* CreateSpace, 2015.

———. *Triumph in the Philippines.* CreateSpace, 2015.

Spencer, Louise Reid. *Guerrilla Wife.* Crowell, 1945.

Stenbuck, Jack, ed. *Typewriter Battalion: Dramatic Frontline Dispatches from World War II.* Quill / William Morrow, 1995.

Stille, Mark E. *The Imperial Japanese Navy in the Pacific War.* Osprey, 2014.

Stoelb, Richard A. *Time in Hell: The Battle for Buna on the Island of New Guinea.* Sheboygan County Historical Research Center, 2012.

Straubel, James H. *Air Force Diary: 111 Stories from the Official Service Journal of the USAAF.* Simon & Schuster, 1947.

Sunderman, James F. *Air Escape and Evasion.* Franklin Watts, 1963.

Taaffe, Stephen R. *MacArthur's Jungle War.* University Press of Kansas, 1998.

Tagaya, Osamu. *Mitsubishi Type 1 Rikko "Betty" Units of World War 2.* Osprey, 2001.

Tanaka, Yuki. *Hidden Horrors: Japanese War Crimes in World War II.* Westview Press, 1996.

The Philippines Campaign of 1941–1942: The First Major Campaign in the Pacific Theater. Charles River Editors, 2014.

Tunney, Noel. *Winning from Down Under.* Boolarong Press, 2010.

Underbrink, Robert L. *Destination Corregidor.* Naval Institute Press, 1971.

United States Army. Center for Military History. *Papuan Campaign: The Buna-Sanananda Operation 16 November-23 January 1943.* Amazon Digital Services, 2012.

United States Navy. Office of Naval Intelligence. *Combat Narratives Volume 1: The Java Sea Campaign, Early Raids in the Pacific Ocean, The Battle of Midway, the Battle of Coral Sea.* Publication Branch, Office of Naval Intelligence, 1943.

Villamor, Jesus A., and Gerald S. Snyder. *They Never Surrendered: A True Story of Resistance in World War II.* Vera-Reyes, 1982.

Volckmann, R.W. *We Remained: Three Years Behind Enemy Lines in the Philippines.* W.W. Norton, 1954.

Ward, Lorraine, Katherine Erwin, and Yoshinobu Oshiro. *Reflections of Honor: The Untold Story of a Nisei Spy.* University of Hawai'i at Mānoa, 2014.

Weller, George. *Singapore Is Silent.* Harcourt, Brace, 1943.

———. *Weller's War: A Legendary Foreign Correspondent's Saga of World War II on Five Continents.* Crown, 2009.

Whitman, John W. *Bataan: Our Last Ditch: The Bataan Campaign, 1942.* Hippocrene Books, 1990.

Wilkinson, Rupert. *Surviving a Japanese Internment Camp: Life and Liberation at Santo Tomas, Manila, in World War II.* McFarland, 2013.

Williford, Glen. *Racing the Sunrise: Reinforcing America's Pacific Outposts 1941–42.* Naval Institute Press, 2010.

Willmott, H.P. *The Barrier and the Javelin.* Naval Institute Press, 2008.

———. *The Battle of Leyte Gulf: The Last Fleet Action.* Indiana University Press, 2005.

Wolf, William. *The Douglas A-20 Havoc.* Schiffer, 2015.

Womack, Tom. *The Dutch Naval Air Force Against Japan.* McFarland, 2006.

Woodward, C. Vann. *The Battle for Leyte Gulf: The Incredible Story of World War II's Largest Naval Battle.* Skyhorse, 2007.

Yenne, Bill. *The Imperial Japanese Army: The Invincible Years 1941–42.* Osprey, 2014.

Periodicals

Air Classics. Vol. 42, no. 12, December 2006.

Air Classics. Vol. 45, no. 6, June 2009.

Air Classics Review: B-25: 50th Anniversary of the North American Mitchell. 1990.

Air Classics 20th Anniversary Edition. Vol. 1, 1985.

Argosy. Vol. 363, no. 2, August 1966.

Journal of the American Aviation Historical Society. Vol. 20, nos. 1–4, 1975.

Man's Conquest. Vol. 7, no. 5, October 1962.

National Geographic. Vol. 173, no. 4, April 1988.

National Geographic. Vol. 174, no. 2, August 1988.

Philippines Journal of Science. Vol. 7, Sect. A, no. 4, August 1912.

Plane & Pilot Antique & Classic Airplane Annual. 1971.

World War II. Vol. 28, no. 1, May–June 2003.

Websites

Extensive research was conducted through Fold3.com, Ancestry .com, Newspaperarchive.com, and Newspapers.com. Also useful was Pacificwrecks.com.

Primary Source Material

Interviews Conducted by the Author

Nat Gunn, 2014–2016.

John Henebry, Third Bomb Group, 1996.

Don Good, Third Bomb Group, 1992, 2000.

Bill Runey, Forty-Ninth Fighter Group, 1992, 1996, 1998, 1999, 2015.

Wally Jordan, Forty-Ninth Fighter Group, 1992–1993.

James Morehead, Java Veteran, Forty-Ninth Fighter Group, 1997, 1998.

Archival Sources

United States Air Force Historical Research Agency

Approximately eleven thousand pages of documents were acquired via direct copying and via electronic PDF during September 2014. The files and record groups accessed related to FEAF operations from the fall of 1941 through the Leyte Campaign in 1944, Fifth Air Force operations from 1942 to 1944, the Edmonds Collection of interviews and documents, General Kenney's personal files, unit histories for the Twenty-Seventh Bomb Group, Third Bomb Group, Thirty-Eighth Bomb Group, and 345th Bomb Group, and their assigned squadrons, the records of Fifth Air Force's Air Service Command, records pertaining to Air Force Materiel Command and the establishment of modification centers throughout the United States, as well as diaries and interviews of veterans of the SWPA, including McAfee's Twenty-Seventh Bomb Group diary. Also useful was a collection of postdeployment interviews with returning veterans, conducted upon their return to the United States by USAAF personnel seeking information on which tactics worked, which did not, and what improvements needed to be made to equipment and aircraft in use in their combat theater. Additional information on the development of skip bombing was also found in unit records of B-26 squadrons employed in combat in the North African theater in 1942–1943. Also used were the 1942 United States Army Air Force intelligence digests, ATIS and ADVANTIS translations of interrogations, and captured Japanese documents and diaries. This proved particularly useful for the Japanese perspective of the Battle of Bismarck Sea. Also accessed were postwar interviews with FEAF and Fifth Air Force veterans conducted for the USAF's oral history program.

A complete listing of all record groups accessed for this book can be found on https://theamericanwarrior.com.

MacArthur Memorial Archives

Approximately fifteen hundred pages of documents, along with numerous photographs, were acquired from this remarkable collection. These included excerpts from USAFFE's G-3 operations diary, December 1941 to March 1942, extensive information gleaned from the Bartsch Collection, the Pappy Gunn Collection (donated material from Julie Gunn's personal files), communications between MacArthur and Wainwright, February to May 1942, the Marshall Collection relating to the construction of supply depots in Australia, 1942, MacArthur's personal files, FEAF's surviving documents from the fall and winter of 1941, as well as memoirs of veterans of the Twenty-Fourth Pursuit Group, Nineteenth Bomb Group, the Bamboo Fleet, and various Army Air Force units assigned to Del Monte Aerodrome and Clark Field.

A complete listing of all record groups accessed for this book can be found on https://theamericanwarrior.com.

National Archives

Extensive use of the USAF's pre-1954 photo collection found in the Still Pictures Branch at College Park was used to support research and illustration of *Indestructible*. Additional film footage, newsreels, and original radio news broadcasts were also used, including Don Bell's legendary report from the top of the NBC building during the first bombing raid on Manila in December 1941. Additional material was also acquired on Fifth Air Force operations and mission summaries.

National Personnel Records Center

Relevant material for *Indestructible* included the Form 5 reports (flight logs) for Pappy Gunn and nearly every pilot mentioned in the narrative, including Jim Davies, John Henebry, Bill Runey, Harold

Slingsby, Don Hall, etc. The need to fill out Form 5s apparently was overlooked during the chaotic period from December 1941 to March 1942. Most veterans of the Philippines and early SWPA actions have gaps in their reporting during this period.

Also accessed here were the personnel U.S. Navy files related to Paul I. Gunn, which while extensive includes significant gaps in the early 1930s. Most of Gunn's USAAF files were destroyed in the fire that swept through the facility in 1973; however, a few items survived, including a revised list of his known awards.

Searcy County, Arkansas

Legal records from the period 1900–1918 were accessed at the county courthouse.

Cleburne County, Arkansas, Archives and Historical Society

Legal records from 1898 to 1918 were accessed at the Cleburne County Courthouse in Heber Springs. The documents were covered in mold and largely destroyed because of improper storage.

The historical society and library in Heber Springs includes a special historical collection that archives the historical society's quarterly publication as well as newspapers from the 1900–1918 time frame. Unfortunately, many gaps exist in the surviving papers, including for the period when P.I. Gunn's father died. I was never able to conclusively determine his father's cause of death as a result.

Gunn Family Archives

Pappy Gunn kept a briefcase full of documents and some photographs related to his experiences in World War II. Orders, transfers, reports he wrote to General Kenney and others all survived and are in Nat Gunn's files on his father. Extensive family records Nat granted me access to included Polly's hidden diary written in Santo Tomas during early 1942, later writings and recollections by Polly, Julie, and Paul, as well as family photographs, marriage records, etc. This book would not have been able to have been written without Nat's generous help and the freedom of access he allowed me into the family's personal papers.

Index